THE EGYPTIAN LABOR CORPS

THE EGYPTIAN LABOR CORPS

Race, Space, and Place in the First World War

KYLE J. ANDERSON

UNIVERSITY OF TEXAS PRESS *Austin*

Portions of chapter 2 were previously published as "The Egyptian Labor Corps: Workers, Peasants and the State During World War I" in *The International Journal of Middle East Studies* 49 no. 1 (January 2017).

Printed in the United States of America
First edition, 2021
First paperback printing, 2025

♾ The paper used in this book meets the minimum requirements of ANSI/NISO Z39.48-1992 (R1997) (Permanence of Paper).

LIBRARY OF CONGRESS CATALOGING-IN-PUBLICATION DATA

Names: Anderson, Kyle J., author.
Title: The Egyptian Labor Corps : race, space, and place in the First World War / Kyle J. Anderson.
Description: First edition. | Austin : University of Texas Press, [2021] | Includes bibliographical references and index.
Identifiers: LCCN 2021022906
ISBN 978-1-4773-3362-4 (paper)
ISBN 978-14773-2455-4 (PDF)
ISBN 978-1-4773-2456-1 (epub)
Subjects: LCSH: Great Britain. Army. Labour Corps—Minorities—History. | Great Britain. Army. Labour Corps—Minorities—Social conditions—History. | World War, 1914–1918—Conscript labor—Social aspects—Egypt. | Egyptians—Race identity—History. | World War, 1914–1918—Campaigns—Palestine. | World War, 1914–1918—Campaigns—Egypt—Sinai. | BISAC: HISTORY / Middle East / Egypt (see also Ancient / Egypt)
Classification: LCC UA668 .A64 2021 | DDC 940.4/124108992762—dc23
LC record available at https://lccn.loc.gov/2021022906

doi:10.7560/324547

To the thousands who lost their lives working with the Egyptian Labor Corps, Camel Transport Corps, Hired Camel Transport, Horse Transport, Imperial Camel Corps, and Camel Veterinary Corps.

CONTENTS

ABBREVIATIONS

ASC	Army Service Corps
CTC	Camel Transport Corps
EEF	Egyptian Expeditionary Force
ELC	Egyptian Labor Corps
ESR	Egyptian State Railway
FGCM	Field General Court Martial
HCT	Hired Camel Transport
HMAT	His Majesty's Australian Transport
IWGC	Imperial War Graves Commission
MEF	Mediterranean Expeditionary Force
NCO	Noncommissioned Officer
OETA	Occupied Enemy Territory Administration
RAF	Royal Air Force
RAMC	Royal Army Medical Corps
RAOC	Royal Army Ordnance Corps

A NOTE ABOUT LANGUAGE

I HAVE TRANSLITERATED WORDS from Modern Standard Arabic according to a system based on the *International Journal of Middle East Studies* (IJMES). For proper nouns, including names and titles, I have omitted diacritics. For historical figures whose names have a common transliteration already circulating in English, I have included them in parentheses. Egyptian Colloquial Arabic is transliterated according to a modified version of the IJMES system; instead of jim (j) I use (g), tha (th) becomes (ṣ) or (t), and qaf (q) becomes, at times, a hamza or glottal stop (').

ACKNOWLEDGMENTS

MILES DAVIS ONCE SAID, "Man, sometimes it takes you a long time to sound like yourself." I jammed on the themes that appear in this book for many years before I started hitting what I hope are the right notes, and many people supported me along the way. First, I would like to thank my adviser and mentor, Ziad Fahmy. Ziad was the first person who told me about the Egyptian Labor Corps. His intellectual influence is clear in this work, but the most important lesson he taught me was how to be a professional academic while at the same time being a good human. Deborah Starr and Mostafa Minawi also helped me throughout my experience at Cornell. Getting this project published would not have been possible without the staff at the University of Texas Press, especially Jim Burr. The comments of the anonymous reviewers were immensely helpful and have been incorporated in different ways throughout the manuscript.

I was able to complete this research thanks to the generous support of a number of organizations. The Mario Einaudi Center at Cornell provided me with a Michele Sicca grant to visit the National Archives in London. The American Research Center in Egypt (ARCE) and the Social Science Research Council (SSRC) both contributed funding that allowed me to flesh out the story. ARCE in particular provided a supportive research environment in Cairo, with a cohort of fellows including Nefertiti Takla, Zoe Griffith, Andrew Simon, Mukharam Hhana, Jason Brownlee, and Noha Radwan. I am grateful to Khaled Fahmy, Madame Amira, and Mohamed Rabieh for helping me with my (rejected) application to the Egyptian National Archives, and I thank Latifa Salim and Ashraf Sabry for meeting with me while I was in Cairo and pointing me toward valuable primary sources. I would also like to thank the team behind *Hawa' al-Huriyya*, including Laila Soliman, Alia Mossallam, and Zainab Magdy, for meeting with me and bringing important popular culture sources to my attention. Amr Shaaban Abdallah and Nermine Hassan Sayed were more than helpful at different stages throughout this project; they gave me insight into Egyptian culture and lasting friendship.

I am indebted to many professional colleagues, friends, and acquaintances who contributed in some way. In the early days of research, Nathan Brown, the late Ellis Goldberg, Jennifer Derr, Anna Maguire, Peter Gran, and Santanu Das all provided a helpful sounding board. Ilka Eickhof organized a reading group at the Netherlands-Flemish Institute in Cairo

(NVIC), which was a lifeline for me during my research. It was regularly attended by Claire Panetta, Patricia Kubala, Ian Steele, Edna Bonhomme, Lara Ayad, Farid Y. Farid, and Yakein Abdelmagid. At SUNY Old Westbury, I benefited from the thoughtful comments and professional examples set by my colleagues, including Juan Pablo Galvis, Judy Walsh, Sylvie Kande, Jingyi Song, Xavier Marecheaux, Chelsea Shields-Mas, Robert Mevissen, and Carol Quirke. In the summer of 2019, Neil Ketchley organized a workshop on interwar revolutions in the Middle East and North Africa that provided an important forum for me to work out my thoughts on the 1919 revolution. Hussein Omar, Aaron Jakes, Aula Hariri, Daniel Neep, Elena Vezzadini, and Katharine Halls all contributed to a great discussion.

I did not set out to write a book about race in Egypt, but as I looked at my sources, I found that race was the most important analytical lens through which contemporary observers made sense of the ELC. Working at SUNY Old Westbury and drafting this book in Bed-Stuy at the height of the Black Lives Matter movement has been a great setting to learn more about issues of race and racism. I began attending Llana Barber's graduate seminar, "Movements for Social Justice in US History," and I give Dr. Barber special thanks for her helpful comments on parts of the manuscript. I would like to thank Christopher S. Rose for his important research and his multiple contributions to this book, including the map in the front matter. Drafting the abstract to present this work with Frances Hasso also helped to refine my thinking. I want to thank Eve Troutt-Powell, Cemil Aydın, Bob Vitalis, Omnia El Shakry, and Marwa Elshakry for their pioneering research on race in modern Egypt and the broader Middle East. Without their work, this book would not have been possible.

Historians usually erase themselves from the texts they write, but this book has been, to some extent, an effort to make sense of my own personal experience living and working in Egypt. In little ways, I was constantly reminded that I was coded as a white foreigner (*khawāga* or *agnabi*). This gave me access to some resources and spaces, and likely closed off others. Nevertheless, I continuously passed over references to race in the sources I was reading, thinking that they were background noise distracting from the more serious business of analyzing workers' class positions and cultural values. As I began to take these references more seriously, I turned away from an approach grounded in political economy primarily written in solidarity with the nationalist project and began to notice the deep isomorphism between concepts of race and nation at the time of the First World War. Those who disagree with this approach may see in this book another white foreigner exploiting Egypt's historical resources for personal gain. It remains to be seen whether such skeptics can still find something of value in the pages that follow.

I am eternally grateful to my parents, Janice and John, who sacrificed for my education and helped instill in me a sense of ethical responsibility and intellectual curiosity. My mother's editorial, intellectual, financial, and emotional support was crucial to starting and finishing this project. My sister, Whitney, and brother-in-law, Stephen, were always there for me during the many years it took to complete this book. Finally, I would like to thank my partner, Maggie Landon, for reigniting my love of reading, and our dog, Rosie, for bringing so much joy to my life.

THE EGYPTIAN LABOR CORPS

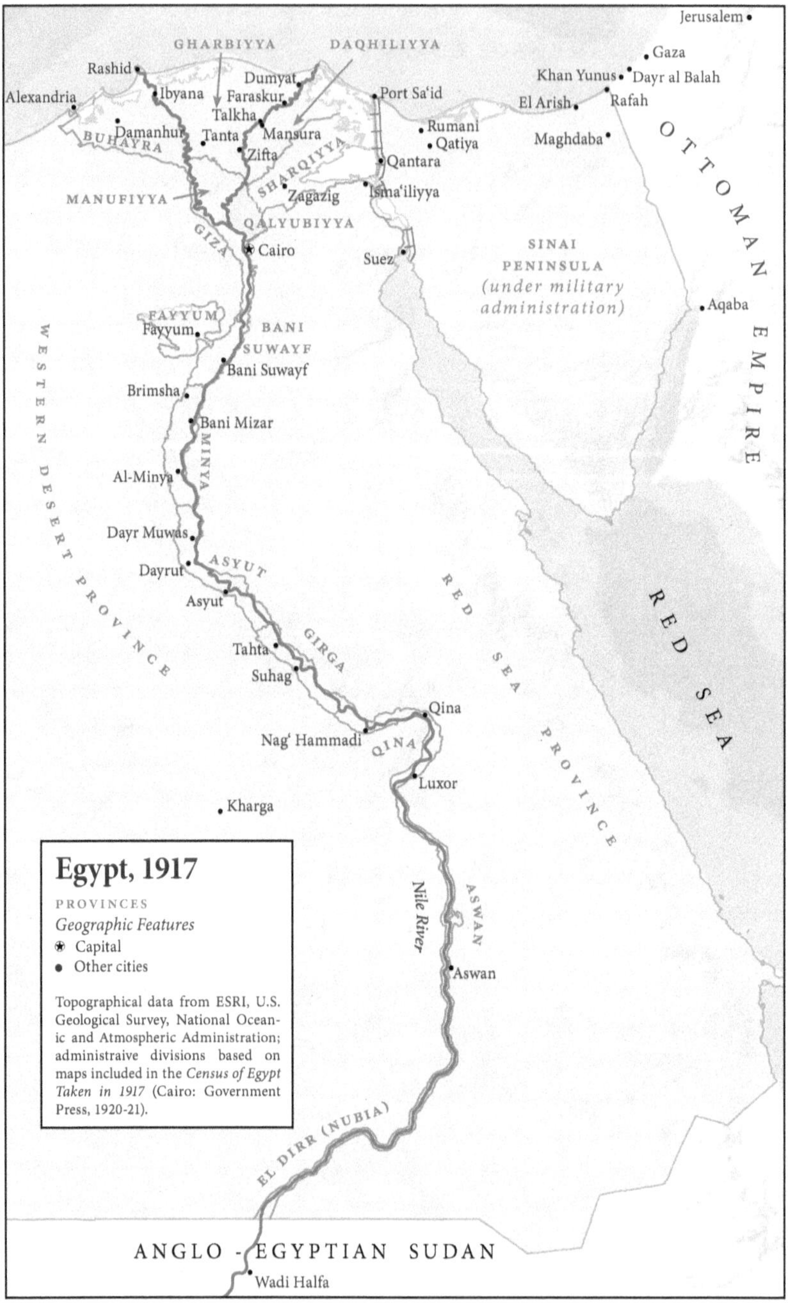

Map of Egypt by Christopher S. Rose. Used by permission.

INTRODUCTION

THE ADINKERKE MILITARY CEMETERY lies between France and Belgium, nestled in a patch of farmland that has, in recent years, seen the construction of a busy highway cutting through it. The cemetery can only be reached on foot by a fifty-meter-long grassy path, which passes through the farmland facing the highway. The cars whizzing by this small cluster of headstones obscure the fact that this was once the site of a casualty clearing station during the First World War. At this place, thousands of young men from nearby fronts were triaged and cared for. The unfortunate ones who never recovered are commemorated by headstones all made from Portland stone, a kind of smooth limestone used to build Buckingham Palace and St. Paul's Cathedral in London.

Roughly speaking, the space of the cemetery is organized the same way we organize the map of the globe today: by nationality. The entrance to the cemetery is in the southwest corner of the site. Taking an immediate left-hand turn, you can peruse long columns of headstones running north to south that commemorate the deaths of 222 men from Great Britain, the nations of the British Empire, and their allies. Further to the north of the site, you will find 142 graves of German forces and their allies, including a large subgroup of Czech soldiers, all arranged in rows running from east to west.

But if you go straight ahead instead of turning left, you may notice one solitary headstone tucked away in the southeast corner of the cemetery. Hidden under the shade of a tall tree and oriented eastward, so that you have to circle around facing toward the front entrance with your back to the highway in order to read it, is the headstone of Sabit Harun Mohamed. While the other graves in the site are adorned with crosses or national insignia, Mohamed's is decorated with finely detailed Arabic calligraphy, signifying his status as the lone Muslim buried at Adinkerke: "We are of God and to Him we shall return." Who was Sabit Harun Mo-

FIGURE 0.1. Gravestone of Sabit Harun Mohamed. Adinkerke Military Cemetery, Belgium, May 8, 2015, Wikimedia Commons, https://commons.wikimedia.org/wiki/File:Adinkerke_Military_Cemetery 04.jpg.

hamed? How did he travel from his home to the northern shores of Belgium? And why does his headstone seem so out of place in this space organized by nation?

Unfortunately, documentary evidence does not provide enough information to reconstruct Mohamed's life in great detail. He may have succumbed to injuries sustained in an air strike on the docks of nearby Dunkirk or Calais, where the German air force bombed a group of migrant laborers a few months before he died on September 6, 1917. Or he may have been working in the Fourth Army area, salvaging scrap metal and munitions behind the lines during the Third Battle of Ypres.[1] It is hard to say, because the grave registration reports—which contain many lines, if not full paragraphs, on the white soldiers buried at Adinkerke—tell us only his rank, the date of his death, and, in place of specifics, the name of the organization with which he served: the Egyptian Labor Corps (ELC).[2]

Commemoration of deceased forces attached to the British Empire in the two World Wars was the responsibility of the Imperial War Graves Commission (IWGC, renamed the Commonwealth War Graves Commission in 1960). The commission's founder, Fabian Ware, established the principles that were to guide it going forward. "In death," he wrote, "all, from General to Private, of whatever race or creed, should receive equal honour under a memorial."[3] Ware saw himself as a pioneer creating a new respect for the common soldier in a British army that had, only a century before, buried infantry troops and animals alike in open pits.[4] Thomas Laqueur calls Ware's style of remembrance "commemorative hyper-nominalism," referring to the memorials he designed at the Western Front that include long lists of the names of British and Indian soldiers.[5]

But outside of Europe, the IWGC did not attach as much importance to the names of the dead. Memorials to the men of the ELC who died in Palestine contain only tablets inscribed in English and Arabic that state the total *numbers* of casualties buried nearby. One tablet in Haifa reads: "ONE HUNDRED AND SIX MEN OF THE EGYPTIAN LABOUR CORPS ARE BURIED NEAR THIS SPOT."[6] In her research on colonial war graves in British East Africa, Michèle Barret has found that the so-called principle of equal treatment espoused in the literature on the IWGC was violated consistently in the distinction between what officials called "white graves" and those of African "natives."[7] Similarly for the ELC, more than ten thousand are estimated to have died in service to the British Empire in Palestine, but according to IWGC records, only twenty-two hundred are buried in cemeteries there today.[8] Most of the ELC men who died during the war remain unidentified, lying in unmarked graves. Sabit Harun Mohamed is, in this sense, one of the lucky ones; at least his body received a burial and commemoration. When it operated in spaces on the other side of the global color line, the IWGC, and the British Empire as whole, worked according to a different set of rules.

THE EGYPTIAN LABOR CORPS (ELC)

This book tells the forgotten story of the ELC. During the First World War, the British imposed martial law in Egypt and recruited approximately half a million young men like Sabit Harun Mohamed—mostly from the countryside, and many by force—to serve as military laborers in Europe and the Middle East. They worked as stevedores on the docks of France and Italy, dug trenches in Gallipoli, and drove camels laden with supplies in the deserts of Libya, Sudan, and the Sinai; they policed the inhabitants of occupied Baghdad, and in the advance through Palestine into Syria, which was the second-largest theater of the war, they provided the bulk of the military labor force.[9] The ELC laid hundreds of miles of railway and water pipeline connecting Egypt and Palestine, which became the infrastructural foundations of the British Empire in the Middle East for a generation thereafter.

The Egyptian Labor Corps documents the experiences of these men in the war and follows them through to the Egyptian Revolution of 1919. Most importantly, it analyzes how they influenced, and were influenced by, contemporary ideas about the racial identity of Egyptians. Race was a crucial lens through which both British and Egyptian authorities viewed the men of the ELC. For the British and their allies, the ELC was just one part of the "Coloured Labor Corps," and workers from Egypt served alongside others from places as far-flung as China, South Africa, India, Vietnam, the West Indies, and Fiji.[10] This was the clearest example for the world to see what African Americans had recognized for at least a generation as the "color line." In 1881, Frederick Douglass used the term to refer to the system of racial segregation in the American South after the failure of reconstruction.[11] It was first reformulated on a global scale by W. E. B. Du Bois in a 1900 address to the American Negro Academy in which he insisted "the color line belts the world and . . . the social problem of the twentieth century is to be the relation of the civilized world to the dark races of mankind."[12] The global problem identified by Du Bois was made acute less than two decades later by the massive movements of racialized laborers during the First World War, and as the war ground on, millions of people on the Other side of the global color line resisted this unprecedented imposition.[13]

For people living in Egypt at the time, the sight of young men being sent away from their villages to work abroad—often bound together by a thick rope—was reminiscent of nothing if not slavery. By the second half of the nineteenth century, most enslaved people in Egypt, especially if they were young men engaged in hard labor, were Black Africans (*sudāni*).[14] Even after slavery was officially abolished in 1877, it persisted surreptitiously, along with a link between Blackness, African origins, and enslavement in Egyptian popular culture.[15] So when urbane, educated Egyptians saw farmers from the countryside—whom they had come to perceive as the repository of Egyptian national authenticity[16]—in a condition akin to slavery, they understood how Egyptians had been racialized as "people of colour" during the war. I argue that the 1919 revolution should be seen partly as an attempt to articulate an alternative conception of Egyptian racial identity, which I call racial nationalism, in response.

FIGURE 0.2. Men of the Egyptian Labor Corps working on the docks of Boulogne, France, 1917. Imperial War Museum, London.

FIGURE 0.3. Two men driving an ambulance camel, al-Arish, 1917. Imperial War Museum, London.

FIGURE 0.4. Men of the Egyptian Labor Corps unloading coal in Beirut, 1918. Imperial War Museum, London.

FIGURE 0.5. A company of the Egyptian Labor Corps at Boulogne, France, 1917. Imperial War Museum, London.

TELLING THE STORY OF THE ELC

The sheer scale of the ELC recruitment effort, which enlisted approximately 4 percent of the population and indirectly affected many more, is remarkable.[17] But even more astounding is the extent to which this story has largely been forgotten today. Partly, this can be explained by the deliberate suppression of source material. Heavy British censorship during the war prevented unbiased coverage of the ELC in the Egyptian press. For the English-speaking public, most writers and readers were simply not that interested in the stories of nonwhite men working behind the front lines when their "Tommies" from back home were wrapped in glory. One reporter from the *Sydney Morning Herald* called the ELC "an army behind the army that's fighting," which gets "none of the limelight . . . none of the glory . . . and mighty little thanks for all the work they do."[18] Ignorance by contemporary observers has carried over into popular memory, and even in the outpouring of podcasts, museum exhibits, documentaries, and events celebrating the centennial anniversary of the "global First World War," the ELC has received scarcely a mention.[19]

In the past decade, historians have begun to take notice of the ELC. They have been documented in books about British military logistics and military labor.[20] Mario Ruiz wrote an article about their images being used in British propaganda efforts.[21] Alia Mossallam has also written recent articles in Arabic and English about the experiences of ELC men working abroad and in the lead-up to the 1919 revolution.[22] *The Egyptian Labor Corps* synthesizes these sources and many others in the first book-length study of the ELC from 1914 to 1919.

That the ELC is relatively unknown today also has to do with historiographic trends. Historians of modern Egypt have long seen the late nineteenth and early twentieth centuries as shaped by the competing forces of the British Empire on one hand and the emerging Egyptian nation-state on the other. Scholars focused on British imperialism have often explained Egypt's entanglement with the empire as a function of its role as a producer of raw materials like cotton.[23] Studies of global capitalism and its relationship to imperialism and nationalism have loomed large in this body of literature, and the history of working people in Egypt has often been narrated as the development of a "national working class."[24] But the important role of Egypt as a British military base, and the relationship between infrastructures of war and trade,[25] remains underappreciated. As a result, many historians of the British Empire in Egypt have bracketed the First World War as an exceptional time, implying that it cannot tell us much about the broad sweep of the occupation.[26]

Meanwhile, for Egyptian nationalist historians like ʿAbd al-Rahman al-Rafiʿi, the war served primarily as a prelude to a more significant development: the 1919 revolution. This was the moment when Egyptians acted in unison to express the "will of the people" (*faḍl al-shaʿab*).[27] According to the nationalist interpretation, the most important effect of the ELC was to help rural workers and farmers discover their "true identity" as Egyptians.[28] In this sense, the ELC is like what historian of colonial India Partha Chatterjee has called a "fragment" of the nation; their story has been told only insofar as it fits into the emergence of a homogenous national subject. According to Chatterjee, the task remains for historians to recover the singularity of such fragments, whose political imaginaries and solidarities cannot always be reduced to nationalism.[29]

While the historical establishment alternatively ignored or glossed over the participants in the ELC, popular culture, including songs, novels, and films, carried on their memories. Sayyid Darwish's anthem "Salma ya Salama" ("Safe and Sound," 1918) brought the experiences of the ELC to the masses. Stories about the men in the genre of *ḥuwādīt* (sing., *ḥadūta*) were repeated throughout the countryside and sometimes provided family members with the only news they could get about their loved ones sent off to serve.[30] As the years passed by, novels like Naguib Mahfouz's *Bayn al-Qasrayn* (*Palace Walk*, 1956) and films like Ahmad Badrakhan's *Sayyid Darwish* (1966) depicted scenes of men being conscripted to the ELC during the First World War. In the 1990s, ʿIsmat Sayf al-Dawla's *Mudhakkirat Qarya* (*Memoirs of a Village*, 1996) and Amin ʿIzz al-Din's *Al-Faylaq* (*The Corps*, 1999) kept the memory of the ELC alive for a new generation.[31] The gap between official memory and popular culture pops up again and again in this book. As chapter 6 will show, the men of the ELC filled the spaces around them with the sounds of music, theater, and chatter to help them endure the difficult circumstances of the war, and their memory has lived on through many of these same media.

The centennial anniversary of the First World War saw a sudden upsurge in public commemorations of the ELC in Egypt. From 2013 to 2017, there were a number of official events celebrating "Egypt's contributions to the First World War," most of which included some mention of the ELC.[32] Ashraf Sabry—a man from Alexandria who had fashioned himself into something of a historical researcher—often told his version of the laborers' stories on television during this period. In March 2016 he spoke over a series of pictures and film clips of the ELC on the Egyptian network ONTV:

> These were our people. . . . In just two weeks, they could not have come out as soldiers like this, unless under the skin of every one of us is a true

> Egyptian soldier (*taḥt al-gald kull wāḥid minnina maṣri gundi fiʿlan*). From the days of the Pharaohs, we have inherited this military spirit (*min ayyām al-farāʿina iḥna natawaraṣ hadhi al-gundiyya*).[33]

Sabry's attachment to a militaristic brand of Egyptian nationalism was apparent, but his characterization of the ELC as representing the "contributions of the Egyptian army to the First World War" does not line up with the historical record. The Anglo-Egyptian army of the time was only deployed in Darfur, while the ELC was a separate organization sent across Europe and the Middle East, never explicitly involved in fighting. Unlike the *tirailleurs algériens* recruited by the French, for example, Egyptians were not outfitted with weapons in the major theaters of the war.[34] It is surprising, then, to hear ELC laborers being referred to as soldiers from the Egyptian army, and historian Khaled Fahmy has already pushed back against some of Sabry's claims on Egyptian television.[35]

Sabry's take on the ELC served a clear political purpose as he spoke in March 2016. As Fahmy has argued, after a new military government came to power in the wake of the 2011–2013 uprising known popularly as the "Arab Spring," supporters of the Egyptian army became interested in crafting a narrative that decisively entwined the army with the nation.[36] In providing the ELC as proof of a military spirit that exists "under the skin of every one of us . . . since the days of the Pharaohs," Sabry established this connection by deploying an understanding of Egyptian collective identity that scholars refer to as Pharaonism.[37] Sabry drew on this long-standing conception of what makes Egyptians unique by representing the ELC as one link in a chain of military service connecting people in Egypt today with those living millennia ago.

RACIAL NATIONALISM AND THE SPATIAL TURN

Chapter 8 of this book suggests a historical relationship between the ELC and Pharaonism that goes deeper than the mere coincidence of both in Sabry's rhetoric. Pharaonism was an assertion of Egyptians' unique essence, in contrast to the other groups with which they had been linked in the late imperial imaginary. Historians Israel Gershoni and James Jankowski have analyzed how what they called Pharaonicism juxtaposed Egyptian identity with the Ottoman/Islamic World on one hand and the Arab World on the other.[38] The First World War was important in this regard, with the ultimate dissolution of the Ottoman Empire foreclosing possibilities to identify with the Caliph, and with British backing of the Arab revolt casting doubt upon Arab nationalism. As Gershoni and Jankowski see it, Pharaonism in the 1920s and 1930s was an expression of "territorial nationalism" that provided an interlude between these two more geographically diffuse identifications.[39]

However, by ignoring the ELC and the racialization of Egyptians as people of color during the war, Gershoni and Jankowski miss another important aspect of Pharaonism as an exclusionary logic: its assertion of Egyptian superiority and fitness to rule over Black Africans. Borrowing from constructivist theories of nationalism made popular by Anthony D. Smith, they argue that a group of intellectuals transformed "objective elements existing outside human consciousness" into "nationalist ideology."[40] These include "territory, *race*, language, kinship, religion, history, and the like (emphasis mine)." Such "natural factors," they write, are "only the raw material of nationalism; consciousness and will are the engines responsible for . . . transform[ing] these objective elements, giving them new meaning."[41] According to Gershoni and Jankowski, the end result of this process is that "race becomes 'nation'"—as if the two are mutually exclusive concepts, or the latter implies an "epistemological break" from the former.[42]

However, as this book will argue, the notion of a unique Egyptian race was also an ideology, and crucially, one that overlapped in many ways with nationalism in the late nineteenth and early twentieth centuries. By the time of the First World War, notions of Egyptian racial identity included a fluctuating constellation of concepts that developed in conversation with other forms of theoretically dividing humanity—including religion, class, gender, family, empire, and the nation. As chapter 8 will explore in greater detail, part of the reason why it has been difficult for historians to discern the influence of ideas about race on nationalism in Egypt has to do with the conceptually overloaded terms and the multiple synonyms used in the Arabic sources to express them. But perhaps a bigger factor involves the sociology of knowledge production in the Anglo-American world, where Toni Morrison has identified a "norm against noticing" race and its constitutive influence on the global order we inhabit today since the end of the Second World War.[43]

Egyptian nationalist writers and intellectuals in the early twentieth century worked at the intersection of global scientific idioms and a Muslim tradition that employed organic metaphors for the social "body" (*jism*). Within these theoretical confines, they carved out space for a unique Egyptian identity in opposition to the other groups with which they had been linked in the late imperial imaginary. These included Muslims, Arabs, and also, especially during the war, "people of colour." If we understand the race concept as a shifting category that assigns meaning to human physical features in order to fix individuals within social groups that reproduce biologically,[44] then it makes sense to think of Pharaonism's assertion of a biological link of descent between ancient and modern Egyptians as a type of racial nationalism.

I use the term "racial nationalism" to refer to any nationalist discourse asserting that biological concepts are necessary ingredients shaping national identity. Racial nationalists portray the nation as a living organism, imagine relations between national subgroups as symbiotic, and measure national belonging and purity in terms of descent and parentage. In central and southeastern Europe between 1900 and 1940, the peasantry was considered the pure "racial repository" of the nation, and racial nationalism was joined to the science of eugenics.[45] In colonial Tanganyika and Tanzania during the 1930s and 1940s, racial nationalism built on long-standing discourses of "civilization" (*ustaarabu*, "to become like the Arabs") and played on the semantic slippage between race and nation in the Kiswahili word *taifa* to assert an African identity valorizing patrilineal descent from the African continent.[46] Following Marwa Elshakry and Elise K. Burton, I argue that the Arabic word *umma* came to denote a similar conceptual slippage between race and nation in Egypt, blunting the secularizing force of European scientific racism and eugenics discourses and making it harder for historians today to appreciate the influence of these discourses on nationalist thought.[47]

Examples of the race concept can be traced far back in history in many contexts,[48] but the global discourse of white supremacy—which hierarchically ordered all the people of the world and put white people on top—took shape during the nineteenth century. As Ivan Hannaford has shown, disaggregation of mankind into basic groups like East and West was the first stage in the development of the idea of race in Europe.[49] In the field of Middle East Studies, the East/West distinction has been most famously critiqued by Edward Said, who attacked the attempts of academic Orientalists to create an "ontological and epistemological distinction" between Western selves and Eastern Others in their scholarship.[50] But the period from 1870 to 1914 was the "high point of the idea of race."[51] By this time, earlier, textually based attempts by Orientalists to trace the outlines of distinct "civilizations" were replaced by more scientific forms of knowledge based on the observation of bodies.[52] The popularization of Darwin's theory of evolution in the second half of the nineteenth century was a major impetus for this shift, as mankind was dislodged from its previously special place and the human race was considered another type of animal to be studied scientifically.[53]

British social sciences like anthropology and human geography developed alongside a shift toward the policy of indirect rule in the colonies. The mutiny of Bengali troops in 1857 provoked a sense of disappointment in earlier attempts to "civilize" British India, as well as hostility toward "ungrateful natives." Karuna Mantena has outlined how these two trends combined to "harden racial attitudes toward non-European people" in Victorian England.[54] After the mutiny, imperial administrators changed their approach. They tried to use empirical knowledge of the so-called native to govern in accordance with what they now called the "culture" of whatever country they happened to conquer.[55] By the late nineteenth century, British authorities in places like India and Egypt applied the latest theories from social science, which had produced knowledge about an intricate taxonomy of races that they imagined helped them rule the empire more effectively.

Meanwhile, the Ottoman soldier and statesman Mehmet (Muhammad) ʻAli laid the foundations of a distinct Egyptian identity that could come to be racialized. Born in Kavala, Greece, he was sent with a contingent of Albanians to reoccupy Egypt from Napoleon in 1801. His early rivals for power were the Mamluks, a class of white slaves from the Caucasus who had long constituted the upper echelons of government and military in Egypt. ʻAli massacred the Mamluks, but the Ottoman-Egyptian elite he developed around his royal household continued buying slaves from the Caucasus, particularly white women who served as concubines in elite harems.[56]

ʻAli went on to undertake an ambitious program of state-building. He established a modern army through a series of campaigns in Sudan, and his subsequent occupation of the country would transform it, along with the institution of slavery in Egypt. For medieval Muslim geographers, *bilād al-sūdān*—literally, "the countries of the Blacks"—referred to all African territory south of the Sahara Desert.[57] Slaves had long come from this region, but the forms of unfree labor they performed existed on a continuum alongside white slaves like the Mamluks.[58] In 1820, ʻAli looked to Sudan for a supply of docile, obedient soldiers, and began his campaign to invade and occupy the country.[59] Sudan became a center for slave trading under ʻAli's occupation, and the number of trans-Saharan slaves flowing into Egypt via Khartoum increased in fits and starts over the nineteenth century.[60] With many slaves unable to survive the perilous forty-day journey on foot from Khartoum to Asyut, ʻAli began conscripting agricultural workers from the countryside into his army. These men and their families, known as *fallāḥīn*, were by far the demographic majority in Egypt. In its final iteration, 'Ali's army included enslaved Mamluks and free Ottoman officers commanding enslaved Black Africans and conscripted Egyptian *fallāḥīn*.[61]

By 1840 this army was strong enough to constitute a real threat to the Ottoman Sultan, and 'Ali's Egyptian empire had grown to include Sudan, the Hijaz, and Syria. Concerned about the prospects of Russian incursion in the event of Ottoman collapse, the British empire intervened and launched a small expedition force against 'Ali's army. After the campaign, 'Ali accepted the terms of the Treaty of London, which reduced the size of his army and brought him back into the Ottoman fold. He was able to secure one important concession: any governor of Ottoman Egypt had to be descended from his royal lineage from that point forward. Passed down from generation to generation within 'Ali's family, the Egyptian government and its colony in Sudan grew to be distinct from the rest of the Ottoman Empire.

In the middle decades of the nineteenth century, the British continued to pursue an alliance with the Ottomans. The notion of a "pan-Islamic" coalition between the two was advanced at this time, because between them, they were understood to rule over the majority of the world's Muslims.[62] But the British approach toward the Ottomans began to change in the 1860s and 1870s. A series of high-profile acts of violence involving the Christian communities of Mount Lebanon associated Ottomans with Muslim "fanaticism" in the eyes of the British public.[63] This discourse flattened the religious diversity of the Ottoman Empire, and the long history of Europeans proclaiming the Ottomans as an example of social toleration was displaced by assertions that Ottomans, as Muslims, were uniquely intolerant.[64]

Ideas about Muslim fanaticism became increasingly articulated in the scientific idioms of nineteenth-century thought, culminating in what Cemil Aydın calls "the racialization of Muslims."[65] The concept of a Muslim race linked Egyptians with the Ottomans and other Muslims in British India, grouping them together as one of the so-called subject races in the late imperial imaginary. As imperial authorities moved away from their former alliance with the Ottomans against Russia, they looked the other way when Russians supported Balkan Christian nationalist movements in the northwest of the Ottoman Empire in 1878. At the same time, they allied with their longtime rivals, the French, to encroach on the financial prerogatives of the Ottoman government in Egypt. As chapter 1 explores in more detail, the British launched another war in Egypt and began a military occupation of the country in 1882. According to Aydın, "the idea of Muslim world unity, which initially meant Ottoman-British alliance against Russia, could turn into an anti-British [and anti-racist] argument in the aftermath of the British invasion of Egypt."[66]

Paradoxically, by simply inverting the terms of Muslim inferiority, Ottoman intellectuals adopted the premises of British social scientific thought even as they sought to reject their conclusions. As chapter 8 discusses, the idea of a unique "Islamic Civilization" was propagated by intellectuals and activists like Jamal al-Din al-Afghani and Muhammad ʿAbduh around this time. This concept accepted that Muslims as a group were essentially different from white Christians, while asserting that they were nevertheless qualified to be called "civilized" (*mutamaddun*).[67] At the same time, ʿAli's grandson, Ismaʿil, who now ruled Egypt, launched renewed military campaigns in Sudan and expanded his ambitions into Nilotic East Africa, which Eve Troutt-Powell creatively dubbed the "Islamic Civilizing Mission."[68] Veterans of the US Civil War who escaped the South during Reconstruction, including former Confederate officers Henry Hopkins Sibley and William Wing Loring, were employed by the royal family to reorganize the Egyptian army in these campaigns.[69]

Over the last two decades, historians have increasingly begun to appreciate the important influence of the race concept in Egypt around this time. As Troutt-Powell has argued, by dominating Black Africans in an empire of their own, Egyptians worked to prove their fitness for self-rule in the late imperial age.[70] Similarly, Omnia El Shakry has shown how the royal family founded the Khedivial Geographic Society of Egypt and curated collections of exoticized "oddities" gathered by the royal army during its African expeditions. The society also maintained an ethnographic collection of uniquely Egyptian artifacts to "preserve the characteristics of the [Egyptian] race."[71] In the early years of the First World War, Prince Fu'ad—who would go on to reign as King of Egypt until 1936—led an attempt to revive the society and extend its sphere of action to include more ethnographies of characteristically Egyptian groups, especially the *fallāḥīn*.[72]

Scholars influenced by the cultural turn like Troutt-Powell and El Shakry have made important strides studying the history of race and racialization in Egypt. This book builds on their efforts by focusing on the lived experience of race for the majority of people in Egypt who produced goods and services rather than texts left behind for us to read. Borrowing from the tradition of critical race theory first expounded by legal scholars in the United States, I argue that ideas about race in Egypt were most important to the extent they manifested themselves in certain *spatial* transformations, including the conveyance of people and things from one place to another, segregation, and uneven resource distribution. As critical geographer Edward Soja insists, "There is no unspatialized social reality. There are no aspatial social processes."[73] The assumption that ideas about race are important because they inform spatial change is the first part of Keith Aoki's model of how race becomes politically meaningful, which he glosses with three words: race, space, and place.[74]

Completing the triad shifts the scene from authorities who direct spatial transformations to subordinates who are forced to inhabit new spaces and make within them a sense of place.[75] As ideas about race affect spatial change, large numbers of people are forced to adjust their lives in order to adapt. They create new collective identities, which cannot help but be inscribed within the spatial limits set by the parameters of authorities. They form solidarities with others nearby, but many on the other side of the global color line only live in close proximity to one another because of a long history of segregation, violence, and the shared experience of resource deprivation. According to Aoki's framework, ideas about the existence of discrete races—which did not, in the first instance, necessarily reflect reality—came to be politically meaningful once they were picked up and reappropriated by the initial objects of racist discourse.

THE PLAN OF THE PRESENT WORK

The chapters of this book follow the historical unfolding of race, space, and place for the men of the ELC. Chapter 1 shows how the ELC was created because of the link between race and military labor that had developed over the course of the long nineteenth century. At first, British decision makers promised not to recruit Egyptians in the war because they had racialized Egyptians as Muslims, which made it difficult for them to imagine Egyptians in direct conflict with the Ottoman Empire. But as the war developed and the Caliph's call for *jihād* was ineffective, other ideas about the racial identity of Egyptians came to the fore. Over the course of the war, British authorities increasingly racialized Egyptians as a source of manpower alongside Black, Brown, East Asian, and Indigenous people across the globe. Over the long nineteenth century, British imperial administrators had developed a whole set of ideas about which races were appropriate for certain kinds of military labor through a long and geographically dispersed history of colonial wars. With the First World War presenting unprecedented logistical challenges, the Allies fell back on ready-made solutions for military logistics and decided to organize men from the nonwhite parts of the globe into what was known in French as the *force noire.* The ELC served as part of this effort in Europe, the Middle East, and North Africa, so chapter 1 ends by surveying their roles in the various theaters of the war.

After hatching the plan to form the ELC, imperial authorities in Egypt were tasked with executing it. Chapters 2 and 3 analyze the interconnected processes of recruiting and transporting workers out of Egypt. Chapter 2 focuses on recruitment, which compelled local functionaries in the Ministry of Interior to round up workers. Ideas deriving from social Darwinism and Muslim tradition circulating among the class of government officials in Egypt known as the *'ayān* meant that these men saw themselves as possessing a level of moral authority that would allow them to induce laborers to "volunteer" for the ELC. But ELC recruitment concentrated power in the hands of village authorities called *'umad* (sing., *'umda*), who ultimately used force to recruit the number of men demanded of them. This culminated in an explosion of rural violence that swept through the countryside in the summer of 1918—almost a full year before the 1919 revolution. Violence, in turn, fed back into the imperial decision-making process, as officials of the colonial state reimposed the system of *corvée* labor that the British occupation had supposedly abolished a generation before.

The system of transporting laborers from the countryside to the war also relied on preexisting infrastructures of the colonial state, and the built environments of towns and cities across Egypt were transformed to accommodate wartime mobilizations. Chapter 3 follows how recruits started off in cramped jail cells at town lockups. If they passed sanitary inspection, they were then transported by the Egyptian State Railway (ESR) system to major cities like Cairo and Alexandria, where they were trained and outfitted at new supply depots before heading out. Young men bound for Europe, the Dardanelles, and Iraq traveled by steamship across choppy seas, and were sometimes attacked by German U-Boats along the way. Some recruits were able to use their mobility to their own advantage, seizing opportunities to evade service through desertion. This chapter engages Henri Lefebvre's important concept of "producing" space, arguing that the exigencies of war, as much as global capitalism, structured this process in Egypt.

When they arrived at their final destination, the men of the ELC had only just begun their work. Chapter 4 details how they were asked to perform almost every type of logistical labor imaginable, including loading and unloading ships, driving camels, erecting storehouses and port facilities, building roads and railways, and laying water pipeline. In the Sinai/

Palestine campaign, the military advance could not have happened without the ELC, who laid over 130 miles of railroad track connecting Egypt and Palestine. The so-called Iron Track Across the Desert would become the foundation for the British attack on Ottoman Syria, as well as the infrastructure that enabled British rule in the Palestine Mandate during the interwar period. This put ELC laborers in the unique position of being both the objects and the active agents of spatial change.

Chapters 5, 6, and 7 analyze the camps where the men of the ELC lived at the intersection of race, space, and place. Chapter 5 starts by documenting how ideas about race in the late imperial age influenced representations of the ELC in the writings of British observers, but it goes on to trace how these ideas influenced the spatial configuration of the camps. ELC men were segregated and set apart from white officers and the surrounding communities nearby, provided with substandard food rations, and even denied footwear, all on the basis of their supposed racial characteristics. The racialization of the ELC was even accomplished on the space of the body, as officers and foremen enforced discipline with violence.

Chapter 6 reconstructs the soundscape of ELC camps during the war. Focusing on sound enables us to listen to the lost voices of the ELC, who did not leave behind many written accounts. Because these sounds are often embedded in the writings of British officers, they were represented as "weird," "curious," or even "pathetic." But this sense of white alienation should be taken as evidence that the men of the ELC created their own unique soundscape that dominated camp life. This makes sense, if only because of the sheer numerical imbalance between the men of the ELC and their British officers. The men used sound for a variety of reasons, including to pass the time, to convey information, to build relationships with one another and with their officers, to make work bearable, to commune with the Divine, to laugh, and to cry.

Chapter 7 documents how the men of the ELC acted to exercise their political agency in the camps. Because such actions were based on the assertion of a collective identity, they were different from the other kinds of activities the men undertook during their service. Through being segregated, transported, abused, and ultimately overcoming obstacles with one another, the men of the ELC built group solidarities and came to take pride in the work that they did. Some of these solidarities became politicized, and there were a number of protests, strikes, and mutinies against British officers undertaken by the ELC during the war. In this sense, ELC camps provide a microcosm of how race, space, and place interact to produce new, politicized collective identities.

The last two chapters shift the scene back to Egypt and ask how the ELC impacted the 1919 revolution both symbolically and practically. Chapter 8 examines representations of ELC men as having been "kidnapped" (*khaṭaf*) and treated like "Black slaves" (*zunūj*) or "African savages" (*waḥūsh ifrīqiyya*) in diaries, memoirs, official communications, and books written by nationalists during or after the 1919 revolution. I argue that the mobilizing force of such representations depended on challenging British rulers for their mischaracterization of Egyptian racial identity. In response to being oppressed by white supremacy and racialized as "people of colour" alongside Black Africans, nationalist politicians and public intellectuals centered the *fallāḥīn*—including the men of the ELC—as symbols of national essence in ways that performed what anthropologists call racial boundary work.[76] This positioned political leaders like Sa'd Zaghlul (Saad Zagloul) and Muhammad 'Abduh, along with intellectuals like Salama Musa, Muhammad Sabri (Mohammed Sabry), and Ahmad Lutfi al-Sayyid, as rural-to-urban middle strivers who were "real Egyptians," biological heirs to an ancient "civilization," superior to Black Africans, and not deserving of political subordination to white supremacy. This discourse of racial nationalism also allowed rural Egyptians to associate themselves with leaders originally from the countryside.

However, like all efforts to construct racialized mass subjects, Egyptian racial nationalism elided difference among people it labeled as "Egyptians." Chapter 9 shows how ELC laborers often defied the dictates of a revolution supposedly launched in their name, remaining loyal to their British officers, filling in for workers striking in solidarity with the nationalist cause, and even founding their own political party opposed to the mainstream nationalists. In many histories of the 1919 revolution, the attitudes of nationalist writers and politicians are made to represent or stand in for the ideas and political imaginaries of millions of diverse people—just like the "native informants" studied critically by Gayatri Spivak who were so integral to Victorian anthropology.[77] This chapter pushes back against a historiography that centers urban, educated writers and treats Egyptians like a race by adopting a theory of political action based in the conjunctural and historically contingent nature of collective identity.

SOURCES AND METHODOLOGY

The formation of the ELC provides a rare moment when a variety of observers focused in on a group of non-elite workers and peasants from the Egyptian countryside. This book is the result of a multi-sited research project collecting these observations in three languages from archives in four countries. Sources that form the backbone of the narrative are from London. With a representative of the Foreign Office in Cairo, British officials were in a unique position to observe events on the ground in Egypt. Furthermore, because there was a British adviser in each ministry, the British archives contain the internal correspondence of the Egyptian government. The breadth and depth of the British sources on Egypt makes them an important base for historians interested in this period.

But relying on the colonial archive also presents a series of problems. Focused on a narrowly defined set of interests, the colonial state did not pay much attention to the lives of ordinary people unless there was some pressing reason to do so. Because of this, historians interested in non-elites, especially people in the countryside, have often been drawn to studying violent insurgencies, since these are some of the only times imperial administrators focused on such groups. In his book *Weapons of the Weak* (1985), James Scott criticizes those who concentrate solely on acts of violent resistance like the large-scale demonstrations of the 1919 revolution. He argues that the tendency to romanticize large, violent uprisings ignores more mundane acts of resistance like work slowdowns, desertion, or what that the state classifies as "criminality."[78] In this sense, Scott's method is similar to that of Ann Stoler, who implores researchers to read the colonial archive "against the grain" by teasing out how powerful actors represent objects of discourse and resisting the impulse to take their words at face value.[79]

I found hidden transcripts of resistance in popular culture sources, such as chatter, speech, jokes in the satirical press, songs, poems, and theater. Because many of these were couched in the idiom of Egyptian Colloquial Arabic, they should be seen as records of speech acts; all Egyptians, regardless of their level of education, could understand them. Scholars like Walter Armbrust and Ziad Fahmy have drawn attention to how the differences between the Modern Standard Arabic written by educated intellectuals and the Egyptian Colloquial Arabic spoken on the street have created a "split vernacular" in expressions of Egyptian identity.[80] This split is often mapped onto the distinction between elites and everyone else, including the *fallāḥīn* of the ELC. For this reason, Anne Clément prioritizes snippets of Egyptian Colloquial Arabic in the judicial archives as fragments of the "lost voices" of Egyptian peasants.[81] The same may be said for the writings of those who observed the ELC, which often contain records of poorly transliterated Egyptian Colloquial Arabic, as well as the men's proclivities toward singing and theater. By supplementing the colonial archive with the voices of the ELC whenever we can hear them, this book attempts to reconstruct the full sensory range of their experience.

I check the validity of the British sources by comparing them to three other groups. The first is Egyptian sources, including the popular culture sources I have just mentioned, as well as contemporary press reports and memoirs from firsthand witnesses in Modern Standard Arabic. The second group is American missionary sources contained in archives of the YMCA. The YMCA was active in Egypt during the First World War, serving tea and hot cocoa to soldiers and laborers in Sinai and Palestine, and catering to troops on leave in Cairo and Alexandria. Because of their missionary activities, YMCA sources are interested in subjects that the British sources ignore, such as eating habits, sexual proclivities, and drug use among white troops and, rarely, Egyptians. The third group of sources I consulted was French state archives. These archives preserve petitions from Egyptian notables that complain of British abuses, as well as documents from French administrators responsible for organizing their own Labor Corps during the war. In many senses, they tow the same line as the British. Through this method of multi-sited triangulation, I reconstruct the story of the ELC.

CHAPTER 1

A BROKEN PROMISE

ON AUGUST 16, 1914, the Ottoman Empire violated its official neutrality in the First World War by accepting two German warships into its navy. Despite this defiance, British officials remained hesitant to supplant legal Ottoman sovereignty in Egypt. Documents in the British archives paint a picture of a colonial government concerned at the prospect of stirring what they called "Pan-Islamic" feelings by declaring war on the Ottoman Sultan. In the British imagination, Pan-Islamism connected two large hubs of their empire, India and Egypt, with the Ottomans. One British official in 1914 even attributed anticolonial nationalism in India and Egypt to the machinations of the Ottomans, writing: "as long as Turkey claims to be the secular champion of Islam . . . its every act in Moslem countries, e.g. India and Egypt, must savour of political Panislamic propaganda. Similarly, . . . Egyptian Nationalism, or Young Egypt, and Indian Nationalism in the case of Mahommedans, are cognate and sympathetic movements, tinged with, and inherently indistinguishable from, Panislamism."[1] The designation of the Ottoman Empire as the "secular champion of Islam" may seem like a contradiction in today's terms, but for British officials in 1914, there was significant overlap between concepts like empire, religion, and race.[2]

By the time of the war, British officials posited the existence of a number of so-called subject races, including the "Mohammedan Race," the "Black Race," and the "Yellow Race."[3] One letter from the British counsel-general in Egypt, Herbert Kitchener, shows how the racialization of Egyptians as Muslims informed imperial policy in the years before the war. Writing to the foreign secretary in 1912, Kitchener sought to justify his attempts to limit self-government in Egypt:

> Orientals differ so fundamentally from western races in their characteristics, principles, and in the working of their minds, that the constitutional

> institutions which have developed as the result of years of experience in western life fails to meet their requirements. We are bound to consider carefully whether . . . the endowment of a Mahommedan country with a political system copied from Europe might not do incalculable harm. . . . Although among the people of Egypt there exists a very natural aspiration towards progressive constitutional government. . . . *Party spirit is to them like strong drink to uncivilized African natives.*[4] (Emphasis mine)

Kitchener saw Egyptians and other "Mahommedan countries" as fundamentally different from "western races" in both civilizational and biological terms. At the same time, at the end of the above-quoted passage, he imagines an ambivalent relationship between Muslims and what he calls "uncivilized Africans." In his mind, there appears to exist a unique Islamic form of "civilization" that defines Muslims as somewhere above Africans yet below the "western races." At the same time, the racialization of Muslims in the eyes of men like Kitchener rendered both Egyptians-as-Muslims and Africans unfit for self-rule.

Egyptian intellectuals pushed back against the implications of this ideology by calling for political independence, but most did not reject the fundamental assumption that humans were divided into biologically distinct, hierarchically organized communities. While the Pan-Africanist Edward Blyden and the African American Frederick Douglass looked to the Mohammedan race for lessons relevant to the struggles of Black people,[5] the famous Egyptian nationalist Mustafa Kamil looked to Japan. In his 1904 treatise *Al-Shams al-Mushriqa* (*The Rising Sun*), he wrote: "some of us Oriental races (*maʿāshir al-sharqiyyīn*) said . . . that we are nations (*umam*) whose time has passed. . . . But the Japanese nation resisted this lie, showing all of the Orientals (*al-sharqiyyīn ajmaʿīn*) that there is a simple path in front of them for advancement."[6] Using a word from Classical Arabic that referred to tribal genealogy, Kamil asserted the existence of "Oriental races" (*maʿāshir al-sharqiyyīn*), which were distinct from one another, yet in a similar position vis-à-vis the West.

When the Japanese army defeated the Russians in 1905, a global pushback against the rising tide of white, Christian imperialism emanating from Europe seemed to be gaining momentum. By 1914, British officials were anxious about "the effect likely to be produced in India, Egypt etc. by the likely visit of Turkish 'dreadnoughts' flying the Caliph's flag to Alexandria, Port Said, Aden, Bombay and the Persian Gulf."[7] They imagined the Ottomans at the head of a global, politically homogenous community of Muslims. So they walked a delicate line, asserting their prerogatives in the new war, while also appealing to the states they racialized as Muslim within their empire by maintaining cordial relations with the Ottoman Caliph.

This dynamic began to shift in late October, when the Ottoman navy used its newly acquired warships in a bombardment of Russia. British administrators felt compelled to respond, and on November 2, 1914, John Maxwell, the commander of British occupation troops, announced a policy of martial law in Egypt.[8] Five days later, he announced that Great Britain was at war with the Ottoman Empire. At the same time, Maxwell issued a declaration that he would not call on Egyptians for any assistance in the war:

> In defense of Egypt's rights and freedoms, which . . . this country has continued to enjoy in the peace and prosperity that has been realized during the period of British occupation, Great Britain . . . takes upon Herself the solemn burden of the present war, without calling upon the Egyptians for aid therein.[9]

This gesture seems to have been designed to provide the political cover the British needed to fight the Ottomans. But when the Caliph declared a *jihād* against the British the following week, Egyptians did not rise up en masse to support him. This emboldened British authorities, and by the end of the year, they gave notice that Ottoman suzerainty over Egypt was officially terminated and installed the oldest living descendent of Mehmet 'Ali's royal family as the official head of state with the new title of Sultan. Egypt was henceforth a British protectorate, along with a number of states in Southeast Asia, the Persian Gulf, and Africa. The Maxwell declaration was soon violated, and by 1915, companies of the ELC were being sent to serve abroad as part of the so-called Coloured Labour Corps.

To paraphrase Ernest Hemingway, the color line in Egypt was drawn slowly and then all at once, with the First World War exposing the fundamental binary logic at the heart of colonial racism for all to see. Over the course of the nineteenth century, Egyptians had drifted away from an Ottoman-oriented "Islamic Civilization," and became associated instead in the minds of imperial administrators with a British-dominated "Mohammedan race." Total war against the Ottomans lifted the veil on the British occupation of Egypt and exposed what had appeared to be an intricate taxonomy of racial difference as a simple global color line that divided the world into white and nonwhite races.[10] The British made the promise of the Maxwell declaration because they had long racialized Egyptians as Muslims and were anxious about Pan-Islamic sympathies with the Caliph, but during the war, the racialization of Egyptians as Muslims was displaced by a simpler notion of Egyptians as "people of colour."

In making the decision to establish the ELC, British officials built on a history of colonial wars in places like India, the Americas, South Africa, and Sudan. What started as pragmatic efforts to recruit local labor in these various conflicts gradually developed into a racial understanding of who was (and who was not) appropriate for certain kinds of military labor. By creating the ELC in the First World War, cognitive associations that linked the Egyptian *fallāḥīn* as a source of manpower to other Africans, Asians, and Indigenous people across the globe ultimately enabled the British to overcome any hesitancy they may have initially felt about respecting Pan-Islamic sentiment.

The second half of this chapter surveys the various theaters of battle in the war. The decision to establish the ELC also resulted from the unique logistical challenges presented by these theaters and the labor-intensive technologies adopted to overcome them. It starts with the Western Front, where ELC companies served in military ports in France and Italy helping to supply troops fighting in the trenches. The story then shifts to the Middle East, where the British mainly struggled against the Ottoman Empire. The Ottomans began the war with a series of attempts to harass the British in Egypt from their eastern, western, and southern flanks. The British then launched their own offensives against the Ottomans in the Dardanelles, Iraq, and Greater Syria. ELC laborers were important in all these campaigns, but it was the invasion into the heart of Syria through the Sinai Desert and Palestine that ultimately came to rely on them the most.

RACE, WAR, AND MILITARY LABOR IN THE BRITISH EMPIRE

By the outbreak of the First World War, de facto British influence cloaked in de jure Ottoman sovereignty had been the norm in Egypt for generations. Popular discontent with this arrangement eventually led to the 'Urabi revolt. The British rejected the notion of Egyptian self-government on civilizational and racial terms, and they responded by dispatching the military and launching another short colonial war against the Egyptian army.[11] Between July 11 and July 13, 1882, the British navy bombarded Alexandria. A British force then landed onshore, using Alexandria as their base of operations. When they began their advance, they were first repelled at Kafr al-Duwwar in the Nile Delta. They then initiated a second advance from the Suez Canal zone toward Cairo. This proved successful at the Battle of Tal al-Kabir on September 13, 1882, when the British army slaughtered thousands of 'Urabist troops while only losing fifty-seven of their own men.[12]

A unique combination of military occupation and imperial governance followed. The British supervised the administration of Egypt through the Foreign Office (FO), which was the part of the government responsible for diplomacy with other major powers of the time, including the Ottomans. This was distinct from the rest of the British Empire, which was run through the Colonial Office, India Office, or War Office (WO). The highest-ranking British official on the ground in Egypt had the title consul-general. Between 1883 and 1907, Evelyn Baring, eventually known as Lord Cromer, held this position. He called the unique situation in Egypt "a hybrid form of government to which no name can be given and for which there is no precedent."[13] Although a member of the royal family was invested as the viceroy of the Ottoman Sultan, Baring had de facto responsibility for administering the country, and the Ottomans begrudgingly accepted the situation. Baring appointed British advisers to the different governmental ministries, and their "advice" soon became policy without technically unseating preexisting officials.[14] The advisers he appointed were all middle- and upper-class, white, Christian Englishmen from civilian or military backgrounds.[15]

The racialization of Egyptians as Muslims meant that British rule in Egypt was especially informed by the experience of British India. Baring himself started his career as the private secretary to his cousin, the Viceroy of India, from 1872 to 1876. The cross-pollination between Egypt and India continued under Baring's successors. For example, Kitchener took over as British consul-general in Egypt in 1911 after serving as commander-in-chief of the Indian army, and he would go on to serve as secretary of war when the First World War broke out in 1914.

This exchange and circulation of people and ideas between India and Egypt should be seen as one important source of inspiration for the decision to establish the ELC. Indians were the first workers from the empire to be recruited as "Pioneers," which were infantry troops with special construction skills who assisted the British Indian army by constructing field fortifications, military camps, bridges, and roads. In 1780, two Pioneer companies were raised in Chennai (Madras) and used extensively in military engagements against Indian princely states.[16] The Pioneers eventually increased to battalion size to provide labor for all units in the British Indian army.[17] When not involved in active military operations, Pioneers were encouraged to take up civilian contracts to build commercial infrastructures like roads and railroads.[18] By 1914 there were twelve Indian Pioneer regiments, fully trained and equipped for road, rail, and engineering work, as well as for infantry service.[19]

In India, the British developed an intricate taxonomy of races through their reform of the British Indian army. The army initially adopted the Mughal practice of recruiting men irrespective of their ethnic group or caste.[20] But after the 1857 mutiny, the British developed a theory of "martial races," premised on the idea that only certain groups within the subcontinent were capable of military service due to their specific biological and cultural characteristics. In part, these ideas built on theories of environmental determinism. For example, the association between cold, mountainous regions and great warriors is seen as the reason Gurkhas from Nepal were one of the favored martial races. Other proponents of martial race theory pointed to cultural factors such as discipline and religion, and so Sikhs and Punjabi Muslims were also often included.[21]

Besides British India, imperial officials could look to the Caribbean and West Africa for inspiration on how to use laborers for military logistics. The first West India Regiment was formed during the American Revolutionary War. It was made up of free Blacks and African slaves who were purchased and then manumitted. From 1795 to 1808, the British government bought an estimated 13,400 slaves for this regiment to garrison their various dominions in the Caribbean.[22] The first West Indian Labor Corps was raised during the Napoleonic Wars to support the West India Regiment in its fighting against the French.[23] Black Caribbean soldiers were considered valuable for the British in garrisoning areas where white troops were prone to disease and unable to fight in the tropical climate. From the 1840s to the 1870s, the West India Regiment was brought to Sierra Leone and the British Gold Coast for this reason, especially during the fierce Ashanti Wars.[24]

British experience in colonial South Africa provided yet another arena in which military labor became racialized in the late imperial period. The British established the colony of Natal on the South African coast through a series of small military conflicts with white Boer settlers and the indigenous Zulu state. By 1846, Theophilus Shepstone was serving as secretary of native affairs in the colony. He created his own brand of indirect rule by relocating indigenous African populations to reserves and importing Indian and Chinese laborers known as "coolies" to build burgeoning industries in sugar cane and, later, diamond and gold mining.[25] When the Second Anglo-Boer War (1899–1902) broke out, the British army relied on up to one hundred thousand Black Africans they called "Native Labourers" working behind the front lines.[26] One thousand Indians from Natal, including a young Mohandas Gandhi, also volunteered to serve in the Indian Ambulance Corps.[27] The Second Anglo-Boer War developed a racialized division of labor, with white troops doing the fighting and South African, Indian, and Chinese men doing logistical labor on the lines of supply.

British imperial wars in Egypt and Sudan in the 1880s and 1890s were underwritten by similar ideas about race and military labor. Shortly after the British defeated the 'Urabi revolt and began their occupation of Egypt, forces led by a man who called himself the *mahdi*—the eschatological redeemer from Islamic tradition—launched a massive rebellion in Sudan. A famous British General, Charles Gordon, was employed by the government at Khartoum, and as he was threatened by the *mahdi*'s forces, he became a cause célèbre in Great Britain. Finally, the British government launched the Gordon Relief Expedition, in which some eighteen thousand troops were sent to break the siege of Khartoum. They were too late, and British attempts to retake Sudan from the *mahdi* dominated military efforts in Egypt for the next fifteen years. The new Anglo-Egyptian army was built during these campaigns according to a racial hierarchy that included white officers at the top, Ottoman-descended middling officers below them, Egyptian infantry troops, and *fallāḥīn* combined with imported Indigenous Americans doing the logistical labor, all of them fighting against the Black Sudanese forces of the *mahdi*.[28] The British created a new position for Commander-in-Chief of the army, who also functioned as governor-general of Sudan after its reconquest. Known as the *sirdār*, he was a white Englishman with a special residence in Cairo.

The Anglo-Egyptian army came to depend on imported labor for military logistics in Sudan. During the Gordon Relief Expedition, 336 Canadians, including eighty-six members of First Nations tribes, were recruited to serve as "Nile Voyageurs" to aid the boats of the expedition in navigating upstream through the six cataracts of the Nile.[29] This was the first overseas expedition by Canadians in a British imperial conflict. The Egyptian *fallāḥīn* also played an important role in the expedition, with five thousand men and boys contracted by the private travel agency Thomas Cook to assist in transporting eighty thousand tons of supplies from Alexandria to the forward operating base at Wadi Halfa, 793 miles south of Cairo on the Nile.[30] As progress stalled, the expedition split into two columns and sent a force of roughly three thousand men by camel convoy on a shortcut to avoid a bend in the river. The *mahdi*'s forces overran the garrison at Khartoum, but the Anglo-Egyptian army learned valuable lessons on how to navigate desert terrain to supply their army, and Sudan was soon reconquered in 1898.

Building on these lessons, the Anglo-Egyptian army established a school to train a small camel corps. Its stated purpose was to "enable the General Officer commanding to equip a small British corps in an emergency."[31] By 1913 this school included ninety-eight personnel trained in camel driving.[32] The Anglo-Egyptian camel corps was apparently seen as state of the art, with requests from German and Italian officials to receive courses of instruction for their own men preserved in the British archives.[33]

On the eve of the outbreak of the war, the British Empire had many years of experience recruiting laborers for military logistics. At first, it seemed pragmatic to recruit locally for conflicts in faraway places like India and the Americas. But gradually, ideas about the specific racial qualities of logistical laborers contributed to the development of complex schemes to transport workers across the globe. The Second Anglo-Boer War, which saw the importation of Indian and Chinese labor along with heavy reliance on African "Native Labour," was perhaps the most obvious prefiguration of the First World War. But British military campaigns in Egypt and Sudan during the Mahdist Wars also played an important role.

EASTERNERS ON THE WESTERN FRONT

Perhaps no event in modern history has received as much attention as the outbreak of the First World War. The Guns of August followed the assassination of Austrian Archduke Franz Ferdinand, triggering a complicated system of alliances that ultimately induced Russia to begin mobilizing troops and Germany to declare war in response. Hoping to cut off France, Russia's ally, before it could scramble its troops, the Germans advanced westward. But rather than going through the heavily fortified center of the French line at Alsace-Lorraine, they attempted an outflanking maneuver to the north through Belgium. This fateful decision induced British intervention, and by the autumn of 1914 the Western Front had solidified into entrenched lines stretching from the North Sea to Switzerland that would barely move over the course of the next four years of fighting.

Less well-renowned is the important role played on the Western Front by laborers and soldiers from the colonies. When the war broke out, the British Indian army offered two cavalry and two infantry divisions to serve in France.[34] This force took part in the Battle of Ypres in November 1914, and in March 1915 an Indian infantry division led the assault in the

Battle of Neuve Chapelle.[35] To assist the Indian troops at Neuve Chapelle, the British enlisted the services of Indian laborers and organized them into the Indian Mule Corps.[36] This early experiment provided proof of concept for an idea that would be implemented on a large scale as the war dragged on. But Indian infantry troops did not last long in Europe; unaccustomed to the cold and untrained with machine guns, they were withdrawn to Egypt in October 1915, where they would ultimately be incorporated into the Egyptian Expeditionary Force (EEF).[37]

In the beginning of the war on the Western Front, the British relied on local civilian labor from France and Belgium, as prescribed in the 1909 Field Service Regulations.[38] Civilian laborers were used primarily in military ports for unloading ships and organizing their contents, which included everything from food to shelter to ammunition. The Army Service Corps (ASC) was then responsible for moving these supplies from the docks to the front. But by 1915, the British headquarters in France was worried about labor shortages caused by French civilian laborers being withdrawn by the French government to serve in the army.[39] A labor shortage could mean that ships would not be turned around quickly and supplies would be delayed to troops on the front. Furthermore, as the strength of the British army in Europe increased, the demand for labor to supply them was growing by the day.[40]

In the run-up to the Somme Offensive of 1916, the labor shortage became acute. Allied military authorities began to look to their colonies as sources for what they referred to as "coloured" or "native labour." For the French, troops from Algeria and West Africa had been serving as infantry since the autumn of 1914. In 1915, French military officer Charles Mangin announced his intention to recruit a *force noir* of five hundred thousand men from the colonies to assist in the war effort as both laborers and infantry troops.[41] As early as March 17, 1915, the French had also begun discussion with the Chinese government to provide laborers to assist with the war.[42] China, which was not officially a colony of any country but was controlled by various European powers due to the Open Door Policy, eventually sent 140,000 laborers to work on the Western Front in an act of foreign diplomacy by the Chinese government.[43] Besides Indian and Chinese labor, the British mobilized Caribbean laborers in the British West Indian Labour Corps and organized Black and mixed-race men from South Africa in the South African Native Labor Corps and the Cape Coloured Battalion, respectively.[44]

As part of this pivot to empire, British authorities began to look to Egypt as a potential source of labor for the Western Front. On March 24,

1916, the Foreign Office sent a telegram to the top British official on the ground, who was referred to as the high commissioner after the declaration of the protectorate, communicating their desire to "raise an Egyptian Labour Corps to undertake loading and unloading in French military ports." The telegram contained the further request to recruit a maximum of one thousand men on six-month indentures with the possibility of further increases.[45] This scheme was ultimately found to be impracticable because local authorities in France objected that Egyptians would take away jobs from French civilian laborers.[46]

Although the initial plans were scrapped, by January 1917 another request was sent to Cairo for one thousand Egyptians to work at Marseilles. The following month, another ten thousand were requested to work on military ports in northern France.[47] A base depot was soon established for the ELC in Marseilles, and the Directorate of Labor for the Western Front was assigned an adviser for Egyptian labor.[48] On March 24, 1917, the first ELC companies arrived in Marseilles. Throughout the spring and summer of that year, more came to work on ports at Dunkirk, Calais, Boulogne, Havre, and Rouen.[49] From spring 1917 to spring 1918, more than ten thousand ELC men were serving in France at any given time.[50] By the time most of them had reached the end of their contracts in mid-1918, the decision had been made to move them out of France.[51]

Besides working in France, the ELC also traveled to work in the Italian port city of Taranto. Italy became a minor theater of the war on October 24, 1917, when Austrian and German forces attacked the Italians at Caporetto. By the time British soldiers arrived on the Italian lines on November 4, 1917, 2,009 men of the ELC were employed there to support them.[52] The British chose Taranto as the transit point for troops and materials coming from the Dardanelles and Egypt to Italy. ELC companies arrived in July and got to work constructing docks and erecting camps for the troops.[53] By September 1917, the ELC was the primary source of labor in Taranto, with one general commenting: "the entire work at [Taranto] was carried out by Egyptians, coaling, loading and unloading of ships, trains etc., building quays, making railways, erecting huts."[54] The ELC enjoyed a good reputation, but as their contracts began to expire, they returned to Egypt from October to December 1917.[55] To replace them, the British imported companies of the West Indian Labour Corps from France.[56]

THE WAR AGAINST THE OTTOMAN EMPIRE

Although the number of ELC workers serving on the Western Front was not insignificant, the various fronts associated with British fighting against the Ottoman Empire proved to be the greatest source of demand for the ELC. Throughout the war, hundreds of thousands of ELC men would be involved in defensive and offensive struggles against Ottoman troops. The ELC played an important role in campaigns in Syria, Palestine, Iraq, North Africa, and the Dardanelles.

Efforts to defend the Suez Canal against German-Ottoman attack in January 1915 marked the first deployment of Egyptians in the war. Maxwell's line of defense was headquartered at Isma'iliyya, with sectors at Port Sa'id to the north and Suez to the south. At the time, the most effective means of transportation was a single-track railroad running along the west bank of the canal, which connected with the main railroad to Cairo at Isma'iliyya. Besides this, there were no roads in the canal zone, and the prevalence of lakes and bogs in the region made progress on foot or in wheeled transport virtually impossible.[57] In these conditions, camels became the main means of transportation for bringing up supplies for the defense. In addition to camels, Maxwell required men to drive them, and so roughly one thousand Egyptian drivers were contracted as part of the Hired Camel Transport (HCT) and distributed across the line of defense.[58] Following the Ottoman retreat and the subsequent period of inaction, most of the hired camels were returned to their owners and the strength of the HCT was reduced.[59]

Despite their lack of success, German-Ottoman commanders found a strategy they thought held some promise: exploiting the vastness of the British Empire by attacking the colonies. German officials, who also participated in the global discourse that racialized Muslims, hoped that attacks from Ottoman troops and their "Pan-Islamic" allies from all sides could foment rebellion within Egypt and distract the British from the decisive front of the Suez Canal zone.[60] To that end, an Ottoman-German delegation was sent to Libya in February 1915 to enlist the Sanusiyya (Senussi) state in western Libya in an attack on Egypt.[61] The Ottomans provided machine guns, artillery, and money delivered by German submarines to assist in the attack.[62] From their base in the oasis of Siwa, Sanusiyya forces attacked small cities along the Mediterranean coast and several oases in the southwest of the Egyptian desert. After a tactical retreat, a combined force of Australian and New Zealander (ANZAC), Indian, and Egyptian troops repelled the Sanusiyya and reoccupied the western coast in February 1916.[63] The ELC was called upon to serve in this campaign, building encampments for the troops across the western coast as well as supply depots and roads.[64] Egyptian workers also drove camels, which provided mobility in supplying multiple small engagements scattered across the oases of Egypt's western desert.[65]

The battles with the Sanusiyya called British attention to Egypt's other neighbors. On February 27, 1916, the British sent a force from the Anglo-Egyptian army into Darfur in a preemptive war against the Sultan of the Fur (Keira), 'Ali ibn Dinar.[66] Companies of the ELC were sent to Sudan to assist in transporting supplies downriver, retracing the steps of the Gordon Relief Expedition some thirty years earlier.[67] This was the only theater in which the Anglo-Egyptian army saw any significant action, with more than fifteen thousand Egyptian troops sent in to invade and occupy Darfur.[68] Perhaps not coincidentally, it was also the only theater in which Egyptians participated in a war against Black Africans, reenacting the racialized division of labor from the Mahdist Wars of the 1880s and 1890s.

ATTACKING THE OTTOMANS IN GALLIPOLI AND IRAQ

Just as Ottoman and German commanders hoped to use the vastness of the British Empire against itself, British military authorities sought to exploit an overstretched Ottoman Empire. The Ottoman Empire had long been seen as the "sick man of Europe," and the war provided the British and French with the pretext they needed for the coup de grâce. Presumably easy victories against the Ottomans not only promised increased morale but also provided an opportunity for the British and French to exit the war much stronger than they had entered, with new colonies incorporated into their empires.[69]

By the end of 1914, the Mediterranean Expeditionary Force (MEF) was formed to commence an Allied invasion at Gallipoli. A naval attack was launched on March 18, 1915, with a fleet of eighteen battleships garrisoned in the Mudros Harbor on the Greek Island of Lemnos. Alexandria was the headquarters of the MEF, and beginning in January 1915, troops arrived in Cairo and Alexandria from England, Australia, New Zealand, and India to be trained and prepared to ship out to Gallipoli. The invasion began in March 1915, but the steadfast Ottoman defenses surprised the Allies, and Ottoman forces were able to launch counterattacks that drove them back throughout April and May. By the summer, both sides had settled into a stalemate and entrenched themselves on the peninsula.

The first Egyptians employed abroad served in the Gallipoli campaign. Because Alexandria was the headquarters of the MEF, practical considerations played a role in this decision. As the fighting ground on into the summer, demand for auxiliary labor to facilitate lines of communication and transport supplies increased. By the end of the Gallipoli campaign, the British had recruited three thousand ELC workers to serve in the Dardanelles.[70] Besides working on the docks at Lemnos and Imbros, the ELC was sent to the peninsula itself in July 1915, serving in Helles and Suvla Bay.[71] The use of the ELC behind the front lines freed up the men from the ANZAC divisions to be used as soldiers in the trenches. After successive defeats by Ottoman forces, the MEF decided to evacuate Gallipoli at the end of 1915. A smaller front opened in Salonika in October, and the MEF began to pivot away from Gallipoli and toward this new front on the one hand and the Suez Canal zone in Egypt on the other. One company of the ELC made its way to Salonika in March 1916.[72] Their work consisted mainly of laying railroads and guarding logistical infrastructure.[73]

The British also saw a potential opportunity emanating from Ottoman territory in Iraq. In 1908 a British businessman discovered oil in southwest Iran and founded the Anglo-Persian Oil Company (APOC, today known as British Petroleum or BP). In 1913, a refinery was built in 'Abadan. The following year, before the outbreak of the war, the APOC obtained the contract to provide fuel for the British navy, which would be shipped through Egypt at the Suez Canal. Soon after the war began, the British landed a division from the Indian army to protect the 'Abadan refinery. When the Ottomans entered the war, they began concentrating their fourth army in the north of Iraq in Mosul and Baghdad. In November 1914, Anglo-Indian forces began a preemptive offensive to secure the refinery against this force by occupying Basra. Then they began to advance up the Tigris River. They defeated the Ottomans at the Battle of Shaiba in April 1915, and despite already having a supply line of 150 miles in a country without railways or roads, they continued to advance.[74] After marching forty miles in two weeks through bad weather conditions, the force was defeated in the Battle of Ctesiphon and retreated to the fortress of Kut, where they remained besieged by the Ottomans until April 1916.[75]

Efforts to relieve the siege highlighted the inadequate supply routes and disorganized labor of the early years of this campaign. The British attempted twice to resupply the fortress and were unsuccessful both times, suffering a total of twenty-three thousand casualties.[76] They were severely hampered by the lack of logistical infrastructure in the country. When ships arrived at Basra, they had to anchor offshore while their contents were unloaded onto small boats, which then transported their cargo to shore, where it was unloaded and stored in supply depots. There was also a shortage of depots, and almost no railways or roads north. During the embarrassing siege at Kut, the British improved the port at Basra so that ships could be unloaded faster, and they issued orders to build rest camps and supply dumps to receive men and material from the port.[77] They encountered difficulty obtaining sufficient civilian labor to undertake all this new construction; the so-called local Arabs were seen as unreliable, Iranians could only be imported in limited numbers, and the importation of more Indian labor was objected to on political grounds.[78] In March 1916, workers from Egypt arrived to supplement the labor force in Iraq.[79] In October the ELC brought in six more officers and 2,512 more men.[80]

As part of their effort to double down in Iraq after the surrender at Kut, the British sent in a new commander and authorized a new offensive on Baghdad. By March of 1917 they had succeeded in taking the city, and the Ottomans had retreated to Mosul. This second advance was slower and more methodical, with laborers laying down the infrastructure to pave every step of the way. The ELC was considered a tried-and-true source of labor based on its experience in Gallipoli and Egypt, so 5,224 more men were sent to Iraq by June 1917. All told, over 8,000 ELC men served in the campaign out of a workforce of roughly 50,000 that included men from India, Iran, and Iraq.[81] They were engaged mostly in land reclamation, the construction of wharves and slipways, and laying down a light railroad north of Basra.[82]

THE ADVANCE THROUGH SINAI/PALESTINE

While the British tested the Ottomans with attacks to their extreme northwest in the Dardanelles and their extreme southeast in Iraq, they began preparations to advance directly into the heart of the empire through a two-pronged offensive into Syria. The most famous aspect of this offensive originated from the Hijaz region of the Arabian Peninsula under the banner of the Hashemite governor of Mecca. This was led in part by T. E. Lawrence, also known as "Lawrence of Arabia," who was stationed at the British Arab Bureau in Cairo. Egyptian troops joined Lawrence in small numbers on this expedition with British officers and Bedouin camel drivers.[83] But in terms of the numbers of men and material involved, the second aspect of this offensive, which advanced into Syria from Egypt through the Sinai Peninsula and Palestine, was by far the more important one. The strategic and symbolic importance of the Sinai-Palestine campaign, along with the unique logistical challenges it presented, would ultimately make it the most important source of demand for the ELC in the war.

In 1916, as the Allies were evacuating from Gallipoli back to their headquarters in Alexandria, reports were coming in of Ottoman troops massing in Palestine and Syria. The Allies decided to transfer the bulk of the MEF to the newly formed EEF under the command of Archibald Murray in Cairo.[84] Murray began to advance out into the desert east of the Suez Canal. The Camel Transport Corps (CTC) was formally established to assist in supplying these advanced outposts. In December 1915 the order was given to raise two corps of the CTC, each consisting of 10,000 camels and their drivers. The headquarters of the CTC moved from Isma'iliyya to 'Ayn Shams outside of Cairo, and 2,020 camels were immediately hired to create the first company.[85] Orders were issued to establish ten companies in all, each one to include 2,020 camels, 20 horses, 1,168 Egyptian drivers, and 10 British officers.[86] By mid-September 1916 the CTC included thirteen companies capable of carrying loads from supply depots at the terminus of existing railroads to the new front lines east of the canal.[87] Until the railway and water pipelines were built, all water, food, shelter, equipment, and ammunition had to be carried through the Sinai Desert by the CTC. The concentration of animals led to increased demand for a veterinary corps to maintain their care, and the Camel Veterinary Corps was established and attached to the EEF.

Murray began preparations for a full-on advance through the Sinai. He began by occupying the Qatiya oasis outside Rumani and laying the groundwork for the logistics of the advance. The EEF constructed three railroad lines, the most advanced of which pushed twelve miles into the desert, and upgraded the line from Zaqaziq to Isma'iliyya from a single track to a double track railway.[88] Good roads were essential to the campaign, and the ELC laid two hundred miles of new roads in the Sinai in 1916.[89] The EEF also needed a source of drinking water out in the desert. In February 1916, construction began on a water pipeline from Qantara on the east bank of the canal to the Qatiyya oasis. A railway was also built east of Rumani, hugging the Mediterranean coast. The first branch, running sixteen miles east of Qantara to Rumani, was opened on May 19, 1916, and a second line from Rumani to Muhammadiyya on the Mediterranean coast was finished on June 9.[90]

After this infrastructure was laid out, fighting broke out in August at the battle of Rumani, which ended with the EEF defeating a combined force of approximately seventeen thousand German, Austrian, and Ottoman troops. This was the first Allied victory against the Ottoman Empire after humiliating defeats in Gallipoli and Kut, and it received significant coverage in the British press.[91] The EEF then continued their advance for seven months, beating the Ottomans at the battles of Magdhaba in December 1916 and Rafa in January 1917. After stalling for months at Gaza, the British advance into Jerusalem coincided with the Christmas holiday of 1917 and was celebrated with much fanfare.

The campaign across the Sinai into Palestine and Syria was the most significant source of demand for Egyptian laborers by far. For approxi-

Table 1.1. Schedule of men employed with the Egyptian Expeditionary Force in Sinai/Palestine, March 1916–June 1918

Date	*ELC*	*CTC*	*ICC*	*HTA*	*Remount*	*Veterinary*	Total
March 1916	8,935	10,423	16	0	0	163	*19,537*
June 1916	15,296	11,016	40	0	0	543	*26,895*
Sept. 1916	26,231	15,077	56	625	0	428	*42,417*
Dec. 1916	37,454	19,029	112	555	246	1,085	*58,481*
March 1917	49,036	20,739	170	1,275	218	1,110	*72,548*
June 1917	49,656	19,886	170	2,244	1,326	1,305	*74,587*
Sept. 1917	55,263	21,109	168	4,217	1,165	1,459	*83,381*
Dec. 1917	60,041	24,944	275	5,772	1,740	2,128	*94,900*
March 1918	62,675	23,872	219	5,949	2,025	2,838	*97,578*
June 1918	72,162	23,667	56	5,643	2,164	3,158	*106,850*

Source: British National Archives, Foreign Office 141/797/2 No. 2689/142: Wingate to Balfour (September 15, 1918).

Table 1.2. Total number enrolled in service with the British army, March 17, 1917, to June 30, 1918

Organization	*Totals*
Egyptian Labor Corps	237,407
Camel Transport Corps	62,686
Imperial Camel Corps	530
Horse Transport, ASC	14,057
Veterinary Service	7,207
Remount Service	5,312
Total	*327,199*

Source: British National Archives, Foreign Office 141/797/2 No. 2689/142: Wingate to Balfour (September 15, 1918).

mately thirty months, the number of Egyptians working in the ELC, CTC, and associated corps in Palestine stayed between 58,000 and 107,000, which accounted for more than 327,000 total enrollments of Egyptian workers attached to the EEF between March 17, 1917, and June 30, 1918. A further 179,000 enrollments were made in the second half of 1918.[92] Figures for enrollments do not necessarily translate to total numbers of

Table 1.3. Rough chronological and spatial distribution of the Egyptian Labor Corps, 1915–1918

	May 1915	*Dec. 1915*	*May 1916*	*Dec. 1916*	*May 1917*	*Dec. 1917*	*May 1918*	*Dec. 1918*
France	—	—	—	—	11,000	13,000	—	—
Italy	—	—	—	—	—	2,000	—	—
Libya/Sudan	—	—	100s	100s	100s	100s	—	—
Dardanelles	100s	3,000	500	—	—	—	—	—
Iraq	—	—	1,000	8,500	8,500	—	—	—
Palestine	1,000	1,000	27,000	58,000	75,000	94,000	107,000	179,000

Estimate by author based on official statistics.

young men who served, since many served multiple tours of duty. However, these numbers omit casual laborers employed informally by the EEF and also do not include Egyptians employed by the British military before March 1917. A report from the high commissioner noted, "Were [casual laborers] included [in the total number of enrollments by the EEF from March 17th, 1917, to June 30th, 1918], . . . that total itself would be much higher."[93] It is safe to say approximately half a million men from Egypt worked on the campaign through the Sinai Desert and into Palestine. This work made the British advance on Syria possible, and by the time the EEF captured Damascus in October 1918, it occupied most of the major centers of the Arabic-speaking Ottoman provinces.

CONCLUSION

The decision to renege on the Maxwell Declaration by enlisting Egyptians in the ELC evolved haphazardly. As new logistical solutions were implemented, possibilities for increasing the efficiency and speed of the military were realized. But most of these solutions could not be implemented without the manpower to do the dirty work of unloading supplies, building depots and railways, laying water pipelines, etc. Ottoman entry into the war opened up new theaters of battle, which further increased demand for labor. The topographical diversity of the different theaters of the war created an upward spiral of demand as each new challenge was overcome with more labor-intensive solutions.

But concerns of topography and the execution of military logistics do not fully explain why the British turned to Egyptians as a source of labor. Investigating this requires a deeper dive into the long history of the British Empire and its use of racialized labor in military campaigns during the long nineteenth century. By the time the war broke out in 1914, the British had been employing men from the colonies to provide military logistics for over 130 years in places as diverse as India, South Africa, the Caribbean, and Sudan. At the same time, concern for offending Pan-Islamic sensibilities by encroaching on subjects of the Ottoman Empire was being replaced by a racialized notion of "Mohammedans" that placed Muslims alongside other so-called subject races in the late-imperial imaginary. The war cemented this racialization, and all the intricate taxonomies that claimed to place races on an imagined scale of "civilization" were boiled down to a simple color line separating white people from everybody else. In the process, early efforts to appease Pan-Islamic feeling, which treated Egyptians differently because of their special relationship to the Ottoman Caliph, were quickly displaced by a broad mobilization of Egyptians as "people of color." The massive mobilizations of laborers in the First World War would have transformative impacts, including, as the next chapter will show, putting rural Egyptians and their communities in a position to influence the decision-making processes of the British Empire from the bottom up.

CHAPTER 2

THE NEW *CORVÉE*

THE ELC WAS PART of a long history of migrant labor in the Egyptian countryside. For hundreds of years, an institution known as the *corvée* (*al-'awna* in Classical Arabic or *al-sukhra* in Modern Standard Arabic) had been a regular, in-kind tax that each of Egypt's more than three thousand villages was obliged to pay the state in the form of working men.[1] During the Ottoman period, *corvée* labor maintained Egypt's basin irrigation system, which used canals to redirect waters from the late summer Nile flood into large reservoirs.

Mehmet 'Ali transformed the institution of the *corvée* in Egypt. He hired Louis Alexis Jumel, a Frenchmen who had been living in New York City, who introduced the cultivation of long-staple cotton on royal estates.[2] Soon, massive public works projects were undertaken with corvée labor to facilitate cotton export.[3] When the Civil War interrupted the flow of cotton from the southeastern United States in the 1860s, Egypt experienced a "cotton boom."

Cotton was a summer crop, which did not fit with the rhythms of the Nile flood. So perennial irrigation works were undertaken with corvée labor to facilitate the construction of large cotton plantations, mostly concentrated in the Nile Delta. Cotton is a labor-intensive product, requiring workers to grab the raw fibers off of each individual plant, gather it together in bales, and transport them to market. The number of African slaves brought into Egypt ballooned to as many as twenty-five or thirty thousand per year during the cotton boom, with the number of slaves reaching as high as 5 percent of the population of some Delta villages in the 1868 census.[4] In Delta plantations, Black slaves worked alongside *fallāḥīn* sharecroppers to provide the workforce harvesting cotton.

A local official, the *'umda*, took on the responsibility of organizing gangs of young men for the *corvée* in the villages.[5] Not all *'umad* were large landowners, but according to Gabriel Baer, the *'umda* was usually perceived as elevated in his village because of the stately home he lived in, the infrastructure he provided, the religious endowments he built and maintained, and even the way he dressed and the furniture he had.[6] Both *'umad* and large landowners—who were sometimes one and the same—were part of the broader class known in the countryside as *al-'ayān*. These "local notables" served as a link between their communities and the major cities of the Ottoman Empire.[7]

Evelyn Baring, the British consul-general from 1883 to 1907, often pointed to the so-called abolition of the *corvée* as one of his greatest accomplishments in Egypt. In his book *Modern Egypt* (1908), he dedicated three chapters to what he called the "three Cs": the courbash (or *kurbāj*, a thick whip used for corporal punishment), the *corvée*, and corruption. Baring considered the three Cs as a legacy of Egypt's "Mohammedan" system and saw his efforts to abolish them as a racial crusade, writing, "In the teeth of strong opposition, the Anglo-Saxon race insisted that the Egyptian labourer should be paid for his work, and that he should not be flogged if he did not work."[8] *Modern Egypt*, then, is another example of the racialization of Egyptians as Muslims in the generation before the First World War. In it, Baring made a clear distinction between the Anglo-Saxon administration and the remnants of the Ottoman-Egyptian government, which supposedly constituted "strong opposition" to the abolition of the *corvée*.

In reality, as Nathan Brown has argued, the legal ban on the *corvée* in 1892 was the result of cooperation between British imperial administrators and the Egyptian *'ayān*. It was only after the cotton boom, when large landholdings had been consolidated thanks to the perennial irrigation works made possible by *corvée* labor, that plantation owners began denouncing the *corvée*. This was because it compelled them to send workers off from their estates during the busy cotton season, and thus drove up local wages.[9] With the bedrock principle of the British occupation being the promotion of agricultural exports, the *corvée* was officially abolished in 1892 to keep the costs of production low.

After its official abolition, the *corvée* was displaced by a system of labor contracting. During the summer, contractors toured the countryside gathering young men—especially Upper Egyptians (*ṣa'āyida*; sing., *ṣa'īdi*) from the basin-irrigated south who were idle after the spring harvest—and, in exchange for a share of their earnings, brought them to worksites where manpower was scarce. Contractors provided men to work on public works projects as well as private construction and industrial projects in cities and towns.[10] Meanwhile, the *corvée* persisted on a small scale in the form of an institution known as the "Guardianship of the Nile Banks," in which local workers were compelled to monitor the river during flood season and make sure it did not overflow and drown the crops.[11]

This chapter details how the British colonial state built on the history of migrant labor in the Egyptian countryside to recruit half a million young men to serve in the ELC. Government officials began recruiting for the ELC by working through labor contractors, and they hired thousands of young men on paid contracts in this way. But over time, the colonial state came to rely almost exclusively on the *'umad* and other officials in the Ministry of Interior. Although they represented these men as the figures with the proper "moral authority" to encourage "voluntary" enrollment, they increasingly used sheer violence to compel young men to serve with the ELC.

As the war dragged on, increased demand for Egyptian labor led to a vicious cycle, culminating in violent resistance directed against recruiting officials in the summer of 1918. The British National Archives preserve reports of at least thirty-five incidents that caused twenty-three deaths, fifty-four injuries, and eighty-five arrests connected with ELC recruitment during the three-month period between May and August 1918. This wave of violent resistance has rarely been acknowledged by historians of modern Egypt, and it complicates our understanding of the period in two ways. First, violence against ELC recruiting officials compelled British administrators to reintroduce the *corvée* in an attempt to present service in the war in accordance with Egyptian custom. With this, the British reversed course on what was perhaps their signature "moral" achievement in Egypt: the abolition of forced labor. Second, as chapter 9 explores further, this wave of violence also set the stage for the Egyptian Revolution of 1919. In this sense, it constitutes an important part of the prehistory of the revolution, which included one of the largest peasant rebellions in the history of the modern Middle East.[12]

HIRED LABOR

As British demand for labor exceeded the capacity of the small Anglo-Egyptian army, the colonial state and military authorities began working to recruit civilians through labor contractors. By July 23, 1915, 1,152 workers had been recruited from Suhag, Tanta, and Bani Suwayf and hired on three-month contracts to be sent to Mudros.[13] The three-month period of the contract in this early phase of the war corresponded to the period of time migrant laborers had grown accustomed to leaving their homes for work during the summer cotton harvest.[14] We can get a further sense of how analogous these first wartime laborers were to other forms of civilian migrant labor from a memorandum produced by the army headquarters, which reports fears of men being "bribed by labor agents" on the train in Alexandria.[15] It seems the men recruited for the ELC were similar to the population that would be recruited by contractors for work in agriculture or industry.

With the war dragging on, labor contractors faced increased demand for their services in France and Iraq. Unexecuted plans to recruit Egyptian workers in the spring of 1916 reveal a great deal about the government's use of labor contractors in the early phase of the war. In response to a request, the commander of the Levant Base—a unit of the British army charged with controlling transport and coordinating supplies being sent to Allied forces in the Mediterranean and in the Suez Canal zone—worked with the British adviser to the Ministry of Public Works, Murdoch MacDonald, to send workers in "gangs of 500 at a time at fourteen days' notice for each gang" to work in France.[16] By April 1916, preliminary contracts had been drawn up between two labor contractors for this purpose.[17]

MacDonald was an important figure linking the government with labor contractors during the years of the British occupation. As a technocrat in the Ministry of Public Works, he had been responsible for organizing construction on the First High Dam at Aswan in 1902, which entailed the recruitment of six thousand workers.[18] In 1915 he was appointed director of works on the Suez Canal defenses.[19] By that time, MacDonald had more than fifteen years of experience in the Ministry of Public Works, where he would have been well situated to develop his relationships with the contractors responsible for recruiting workers to maintain Egypt's irrigation infrastructure.

Unfortunately, besides a few cryptic references to the names Alexandrini or Alessandrini and Belleni, there is not much information about the labor contractors themselves in the British documents.[20] It is possible that these characters came from the cosmopolitan population of European and Syrian Christian expatriates in Egypt who were "holding Ottoman or European citizenship but thoroughly a part of Egyptian rural society."[21] As people with a long history of moving between the city and the countryside, and with knowledge of both Arabic and European languages, these mobile, cosmopolitan figures would have been an easy choice for the British to use to secure the laborers they needed. By going through Murdoch

MacDonald and the same labor contractors that they used to gather laborers for the expansion of Egypt's irrigation infrastructure, the British built on preexisting relationships established by the colonial state to assist in prosecuting the war.

ADMINISTRATIVE PRESSURE

As the Sinai-Palestine campaign was looking like a stalemate in early 1917, discussion began in London on whether Egypt was contributing its "fair share" to the war effort. On May 21, 1917, the head of the British army sent a telegram to the commander of the EEF, writing, "It is essential that all parts of the empire should share in the strain [of the war] as far as local conditions admit. . . . As regards Egypt, I am not satisfied that this is the case."[22] The commander responded, "It has always been my opinion that . . . Egypt has not felt the strain of war at all and I have constantly studied the question as to how to utilize Egyptian resources more fully."[23] On June 2 the War Office sent a telegram to the Foreign Office inquiring the opinion of the foreign secretary, Arthur Balfour, if forced conscription could be instituted in Egypt for purposes of military labor abroad. They wanted to raise seventeen thousand more men, on a permanent basis not subject to renewals, and at the low level of pay prevailing for soldiers at the time (two piastres/day).[24]

This request was communicated to diplomatic officials on the ground, and a meeting was convened in Cairo on the subject. At the meeting, representatives of the army objected to conscription of Egyptian laborers on the grounds that they could not spare enough officers to manage such a large force. Furthermore, diplomatic officials from the Foreign Office objected because "no sense of loyalty towards the British Empire could be counted upon to secure the support of any appreciable proportion of the population."[25] In his telegram responding to the War Office, the undersecretary of state wrote, "Balfour is in agreement with . . . the conclusions reached by the committee at Cairo," effectively rebuffing their request to institute conscription through the networks of the Anglo-Egyptian army.[26]

But the impression that "Egypt is profiting by the war without endeavoring to make any adequate return" persisted among military leaders in the War Office and was continuously communicated to the new high commissioner, Reginald Wingate.[27] Wingate passed along these criticisms to Husayn Rushdi, the Egyptian prime minister, writing, "The affair has highlighted the urgent need of a telegraph here at the earliest possible moment to detail the measure that you have the intention of taking to increase recruitment."[28] Rushdi responded quickly with a proposal for a comprehensive plan, including increased pay of the laborers with the difference covered by the Egyptian government, a release from military service for every man who entered the auxiliary labor corps for at least one year, exemptions from certain taxes, and "tours of the provinces by a high functionary of the Ministry of Interior to manage the execution of these orders."[29]

At the next meeting of the Egyptian Council of Ministers, Rushdi passed along the plan to the Ministry of Interior.[30] In light of objections by the Anglo-Egyptian army, it was decided that an increase in pay was impracticable, because more wages would put ELC workers above the pay scale of officers in the army. But exemption from military service and an extra effort from provincial functionaries to round up more "volunteers"—referred to under the euphemism "administrative pressure"—could be done. So, on October 20, 1917, the Egyptian Ministry of War issued a decree modifying the draft law so that "every person liable for Military Service . . . shall be exempt from the obligation to such service if he shall enlist in and serve for a continuous period of one year with . . . any auxiliary service attached to the British troops."[31] To publicize the scheme, a decree from the new Egyptian Sultan was published in the press providing exemption from military service for anyone who volunteered for one full year of service in the "Egyptian Labor Corps (*firqat al-ʿummāl al-miṣriyya*) or the Camel Transport Corps (*firqat al-naql bi-l-jamal*) or any other branch of service attached to the armies of his Highness the King [of England]."[32]

An effort was also made to distribute the recruiting burden more evenly throughout the country. In the course of his investigations, Wingate learned that recruitment had, up until that point, "practically affected Upper Egypt alone."[33] This imbalance was explained due to the lower wages prevailing in the south, which made the terms of the labor contracts offered by military authorities more attractive to Upper Egyptians. Additionally, because the south was mostly still under basin irrigation, there existed little to no local demand for labor after the traditional harvest season in the spring.[34] The official regional breakdown of recruiting seems to contradict Wingate's assessment, with 28,986 men recruited in Upper Egypt from the beginning of the war through May 2, 1917, while 53,549 were enlisted in Lower Egypt between December 6, 1916, and the end of April 1917. But these statistics were unreliable due to the changing definition of what constituted Upper Egypt. For example, according to the report, the

Middle Egyptian provinces of Bani Suwayf and Fayyum were included as part of Upper Egypt at first, but were later changed and considered part of Lower Egypt.[35] Moreover, the bulk of the rural population lived in the fertile lands of the Nile Delta, so there was a much larger pool from which to draw in the north. But the British thought that the *fallāḥīn* from the Delta would be less willing to leave their homes for long periods of time because they were less accustomed to the practice of migrant labor. Consequently, through the summer of 1917, contracts for Lower Egyptians were fixed for three months at a time, while those for Upper Egyptians extended to six months. On November 1, 1917, this imbalance was remedied and contracts were standardized at six months for all laborers, whether from the north or the south.[36]

RACE, CLASS, AND THE *ʿAYĀN*

The Ministry of Interior served as the administrative link between the colonial government concentrated in Cairo and Alexandria on the one hand, and the countryside of Egypt on the other. At the time, the Egyptian countryside was administratively divided into fourteen provinces (*mudīriyyāt*; sing., *mudīriyya*), each directed by a *mudīr*. Provinces were further subdivided into districts (*marākiz*; sing., *markaz*), each directed by a *ma'mūr*.[37] Reforms undertaken by the British in Egypt incorporated the *ʿumad* into the Ministry of Interior.[38] Most of them were Muslims and indigenous Egyptians who could not trace their ancestry back to Ottoman Turkish fathers and their Caucasian concubines. In the course of the nineteenth century, many *ʿumad* were able to tie their official position to their family, and the responsibility was passed from brother to brother and father to son.[39] During the war, the small cadre of British officials circulating between Cairo and Alexandria leveraged this much larger network in the provinces through the Ministry of Interior.

When Rushdi issued recruitment orders to these local officials, he tried to impress upon them the need to handle the task delicately and use their "moral authority." A circular to the provinces followed the October decree, urging officials in the Ministry of Interior to "encourage the rural folk to enroll themselves in the 'Labor Corps,' and to offer their efforts to spread this idea to the public."[40] In Rushdi's communications with Wingate, he also emphasized the need to spread "propaganda in the villages by the Mamurs and the Omdehs in favor of entrance into the corps" and for "the governors . . . to support entrance into the corps with the full weight of their authority."[41] Rushdi's conception of the moral authority held by these local functionaries seemed to be that of a benign, charismatic force able to encourage the rural folk to enroll *themselves* in the ELC through propaganda rather than forcibly conscripting them against their will.

A report from the Egyptian newspaper *Al-Ahram* provides a sense of how officials in the Ministry of Interior might have conceived of their moral authority. On March 21, 1915, the *ma'mūr* of Bani Mizar in the Upper Egyptian province of Minya held a meeting in which he gathered all of the *'umad* in his district. According to the report, he addressed the assembled crowd and said:

> I have been installed by the grace of God as your partner to make security prevail. You all know that each of you is the master (*ḥākim*) of his village [with] responsibility for his work, thus he walks the straight path (*al-ṭarīq al-mustaqīm*), the conditions of his village are organized, and security prevails in it. . . . Your example is like the example of a father with his sons, for if he undertakes his works perfectly and with politeness . . . his sons will be inspired to act with morals, but if he is a bad example, his sons will follow him and forget their punishments.[42]

The *ma'mūr*'s speech invokes a mélange of traditional sources of authority to justify the administrative position of the men in front of him, as well as his own. He draws on sacred vocabulary by asserting that he was installed "by the grace of God (*bi-faḍl Allah*)," and by imploring his subordinates to walk "the straight path (*al-ṭarīq al-mustaqīm*)"—a call which echoes the oft-repeated opening chapter (*fātiḥa*) of the Qur'an. He goes on to describe the authority of the *'umad* by likening them to "fathers" setting an example for their "sons," i.e., the villagers who lived alongside them. The speech, then, constructs an elaborate hierarchy of sacred and patriarchal authority, with God's power channeled downward through the state, projected into the villages via the village headmen, and ultimately into the patriarchal kinship group, each one presumably ruled by its own authority figure who is simultaneously like the son of the local *'umda* and the master (*ḥākim*) of his own family.

Speeches like these were complemented by a series of propagandistic reports in the Egyptian press. At least seven separate articles about the ELC were published in the newspaper *Al-Muqattam* in 1917. They used a variety of terms, including *qism al-ashghāl al-miṣri* (divisions of Egyptian workers), *al-'ummāl al-mutaṭu'ayyin* (voluntary laborers), *firqat al-'ummāl al-miṣriyyin* (groups of Egyptian laborers), and *silk al-'ummāl* (corps of laborers), but they almost always portrayed the ELC in a positive light in order to buttress recruitment. One report, published on April 21, 1917, seems to openly acknowledge its function as propaganda:

> Last March, groups of Egyptian workers from the *mudiriyya* of Girga were sent to France. Their families stayed in their homes on pins and needles waiting for news to be issued about them. Therefore, *Al-Muqattam* carried signs of reassurance about their safe arrival on the 13th of this April; that they are whole and powerful and active, and this conveyed pleasantness to their communities . . . who remembered that they were well treated by the military authorities there, and their improved system of living, and good clothes, and other things. The workers benefitted from far and near because of the encampment in Suhag for recruiting the Labor Corps (*silk al-'ummāl*). If the military authorities here are looking for workers, when they realize that the door remains open for them, they take to forming into groups and heading to the encampment . . . for his excellency the leader improves their standard of living and he cares for them like a father for his children (*fa-yaḥssan gannāb al-qā'id muqābilātihim wa-yu'aṭf 'alayhim 'aṭf al-wālid 'ala awlādihi*).[43]

The report focuses on a group of ELC laborers from the Upper Egyptian province of Girga and the anxieties of their families as they awaited news about them. It states plainly that the purpose of the article was to "carry signs of reassurance" in an effort to "convey pleasantness to their communities (*ahlihim*)." But the article also provided an occasion to espouse the benefits of enrolling in the ELC. It mentions the increased "standard of living" for ELC laborers twice, including a specific reference to their "good clothes." Finally, the report uses a metaphor comparing the relationship between administrative officials in the ELC and the men they oversaw to the relationship between a "father and his sons." In this case, the father figure is identified with the leader of the recruiting encampment, but unlike the Ministry of Interior officials, who were also compared to "fathers" by the *ma'mūr* of Bani Mizar, the leaders of the recruiting encampments were white Englishmen.

It is probably no coincidence that, in addition to being a top British propagandist, the proprietor of *Al-Muqattam*, Faris al-Nimr, was also one of the most influential popularizers of scientific racism in the Arab World.[44] As Marwa Elshakry has shown, the publication of Darwin's books *On the Origin of Species, Or the Preservation of Favoured Races in the Struggle for Life* (1859) and *The Descent of Man, and Selection in Relation to Sex* (1871) had a huge influence on the Egyptian cultural and intellectual scene. Shibli Shumayyil's translation of *Descent of Man* into Arabic was widely read, and al-Nimr discussed Darwin and his interlocutors like Herbert Spencer, Gustave Le Bon, and Edmund Demolins in his other journal—which was his true passion project—the popular scientific journal *Al-Muqtataf*.[45] Thinkers like Spencer applied Darwin's theories to the social world, positing that inherited characteristics and natural selection drove the evolution of human societies. Spencer coined the phrase "survival of the fittest" in his *Principles of Biology* (1864) and his ten-volume work *Synthetic Philosophy* (1896) became popular in the United States at the height of reconstruction.[46]

Elshakry's important research highlights how translating social Darwinist thinkers into Arabic "disarmed" the secularizing thrust of debates about "the evolution of races" and transformed them into conversations over the "progress" (*taqqadum*) of "communities" (*umam*).[47] The malleability of the Arabic term *umma*—which had a long history of connoting religious community but had also developed undertones of "nation" and, as Elshakry suggests here, "race"—meant that ideas about race were not always stated as explicitly for Egyptians as they were in the writings of their European interlocutors.[48] A social Darwinist reading of the above-quoted passage throws a different light on *Al-Muqattam*'s comparisons between ELC laborers and "children"; in addition to using the metaphor of the patriarchal family unit at the heart of the Egyptian village, such representations also drew on a racist trope comparing white Europeans to caring parents and racialized Others to "minors suffering legal disability."[49]

By the time of the First World War, social Darwinist thinking had made a significant impact on a group of intellectuals in Egypt born to the families of *'umad*. Lucie Ryzova has explored how families in this group of middle-strivers often employed a variety of educational strategies for their sons that entailed sending them to Egypt's cities.[50] The word often used to translate the nineteenth-century European notion of "civilization" into Arabic at this time was *mutamaddun*, which was based on the same root as the Arabic word for city (*madīna*). To be civilized in late-nineteenth and early twentieth-century Egypt, then, was to be someone who had at least been to the city, and the *fallāḥīn* in this sense represented the obverse.

Ibrahim Zaghlul, the *'umda* of Ibyana in the Delta province of Gharbiyya, was the head of one such middle-striving family. His oldest son, Sa'd—who would go on to lead the 1919 revolution and will be discussed further in chapter 8—was sent to Al-Azhar, while his younger son, Fath Allah Sabri—who changed his name to Ahmad Fathi—studied briefly at the School of Languages before earning his *license en droit* in Paris.[51] The younger Zaghlul went on to work as a judge in Cairo and Alexandria, publishing translations of some of the most influential social Darwinist tracts of the late nineteenth century into Arabic on the side.

In 1899, Ahmad Fathi Zaghlul translated Edmund Demolins' *À Quoi Tient la Supériorité des Anglo-Saxons?* (1897) as *Sirr al-Taqqadum al-Inkliz al-Saksoniyya* (*The Secret of the Progress of the Anglo-Saxons*). Demolins had used theories from European social science to explain the global ascendency of the British Empire in terms of Anglo-Saxon racial superiority. In his introduction, Zaghlul applied these lessons to his own country and came away with an evolutionary justification for the dominant position of the *'ayān* in Egypt. He writes, "The lower classes consider the demise of the upper classes of the *umma* like the demise of the soul from the body because [the upper class] is the wellspring of morals and the reference point for maintaining customs and national character."[52] Meanwhile, his description of the *fallāḥīn*—whom he called "the possessors of humiliatingly bitter ignorance"—offered an illuminating contrast: "We still say amongst ourselves, if we want to exaggerate one's disgraceful ignorance, that they are a *'fallāḥ*.'"[53] Zaghlul's introduction shows how late nineteenth-century ideas about race could buttress notions of class in Egypt thanks to a particular reading of Darwin's theory of evolution.

Social Darwinism and the translations of Ahmad Fathi Zaghlul made an impact on another influential son of an *'umda*, Ahmad Lutfi al-Sayyid.[54] When Zaghlul published translations of Le Bon's *Les Lois Psychologiques de l'Evolution,* Lutfi al-Sayyid praised him in a 1913 article titled "Sirr Tatawwur al-Umam" ("The Secret of the Development of Nations/Races").[55] In May 1914, Lutfi wrote an homage to Fathi in his influential journal, in which he especially praised the latter's translation efforts.[56] For sons of village headmen like Ahmad Fathi Zaghlul and Ahmad Lutfi al-Sayyid, European social science had proved the existence of distinct "races" as the constituent actors in human history, and they saw contemporary political relations between them as the result of an evolutionary struggle for survival of the fittest. As Walid Kazziha put it, this led to a rather moderate and conciliatory stance toward the British on the one hand, and a sense of entitlement for certain families to rule over "low-class" Egyptians on the other.[57]

VIOLENCE AND ELC RECRUITMENT

But if officials hoped that young men in the countryside would flock to join the ELC because of the moral authority of their local *'umda*, this was wishful thinking on their part. In implementing the system of administrative pressure, local officials carried out their duties in a manner much more dependent on sheer violence than moral influence. In his report of May 1, 1916, Whittingham noted, "drivers supplied through the governors of the provinces are not all volunteers," and "forced labor . . . is practically what has been supplied up to now."[58] A description of the CTC lends credence to this conclusion: "the first recruits were volunteers, which is to say that of every three, one came to avoid the police, one was sent by the police, and one was a respectable wage-earner."[59] Violent force was also used in recruiting for the ELC, and in February 1918 the adviser to the Ministry of Interior complained, "Mamurs and Omdehs are using pure compulsion to show good recruiting figures."[60] In the summer of 1918, instructions were issued to the British inspectors against the practice of "grabbing men off roads."[61] This style of recruitment, backed up with the armed force of the local guards (*khufarā'*; sing., *khafīr*, often transliterated as ghaffir), at times amounted to snatching up unsuspecting young men and sending them off to war.

Some *'umad* also amassed fortunes for themselves by accepting bribes to exempt people from recruitment. Salama Musa recounts one story of an *'umda* "owning six acres, who gathered 5,000 LE [for himself], while the peasants went hungry because they paid these bribes out of pocket."[62] British solider and historian P. G. Elgood also notes that many local officials made personal fortunes by taking such bribes.[63] By accepting bribes and forcing those without the means to pay them into service, recruitment under the system of administrative pressure became a deeply regressive, in-kind tax on the rural inhabitants of the provinces. Many of the poorest villagers were forced into service for the military authorities.

'Umad also used their new role in recruitment to protect themselves and their property from being expropriated by the British for the war effort. They were often able to secure their own sons' exemptions from recruitment.[64] Additionally, some managed to protect their own property from confiscation by the military authorities. By the autumn of 1917, the British had moved toward forcible dispossession of camels in the provinces to meet the demands of the CTC.[65] In October of that year, the *'umda* of Asyut was involved in a trial that received press coverage after he was forced to resign for hiding his camels from the military authorities.[66] In the summer of 1917, the British recorded the activities of certain local notables who were "hindering the voluntary commitments to the ELC" around their personal agricultural estates.[67] Local officials, then, were able to take advantage of the ELC recruitment network not only through the authority accumulated in their hands, but also through

the ability to keep the state from expropriating their own family, property, and labor pool.

Representations of village headmen in wartime popular culture show how these characters became associated with violence and perfidy during the war. According to Ziad Fahmy, Najib al-Rihani was the "undisputed king of stage by the end of the war" in large part thanks to his character Kishkish Bey, a simple *'umda* from the countryside in the big city who was the butt of al-Rihani's jokes.[68] Another popular act put on by Muhammad Nagi was called *al-'umda al-'abīt*, which literally translates to "the idiot village headman."[69] One well-known play during the war reimagined, perhaps unconsciously, the journey to France undertaken by ELC laborers from the vantage point of a different class position. It was titled *Al-'Umda fi-Baris* (*The Village Headman in Paris*).[70] Egyptian vaudeville theater, then, which was increasingly popular during the war, cast the *'umda* in a light almost diametrically opposed to notions of "moral authority" that were circulating amongst officials like Rushdi and Wingate at the time.

Historian Amin 'Izz al-Din records a popular story (*ḥādūta*) in Egyptian Colloquial Arabic that also illustrates how the *'umda*'s role in ELC recruiting made him seem less trustworthy during the war. The story centers on the character of Ibrahim Abu Kuliyya from the town of Mit Ghamr in the Delta province of Daqhiliyya. Abu Kuliyya was a well-known thug (*shā'i*) who was targeted by the *'umda* for recruitment into the ELC. To trick Abu Kuliyya into service, the *'umda* announced that he was appointing him as the new chief of the local guards (*shaykh li-l-khufarā'*). So Abu Kuliyya dressed in his finest clothes and began his celebratory procession to the district capital town to receive this honor. The *'umda* gathered his posse of guards and followed behind. As Abu Kuliyya was preparing to accept his appointment at the police headquarters, suddenly the *'umda* and his men snatched him, tied him up, and sent him off to join the ELC. The incident was memorialized in a *zajal* or short song in Egyptian colloquial Arabic:

> I told you, Abu Kuliyya / Be straight! Don't be late!
> For the sake of the *'umda*, it's you he hates!
> The cops sent you to Jaffa / And you won't get your wage rates![71]

In this story, the *'umda* selected Abu Kuliyya because of personal distaste for his character. This shows how ELC recruitment became associated with the arbitrary whims of local officials during the war. Moreover, the tactics used to coerce Abu Kuliyya out of hiding involve deceit and the use of force. Through popular representations like these, ELC recruitment and the local officials charged with carrying it out became associated with exile (*rimāya*) to Palestine during the war. Furthermore, the significance of the fact that this *zajal* was couched in the everyday idiom of Egyptian Colloquial Arabic cannot be understated; it could be easily memorized, repeated, and spread throughout the countryside. This is in contrast to newspaper reports in sources like *Al-Muqattam*, which were couched in Modern Standard Arabic and geared toward the elite minority of highly educated people in Egypt.[72]

Attempts to represent the *'ayān* as possessing some kind of "moral authority" in the countryside that they could wield to convince villagers to join the ELC of their own accord ultimately rang hollow. With their actions essentially unchecked by central authorities in Cairo, local officials were able to wield considerable force in the countryside through manipulating ELC recruitment. Their growing boldness would soon lead them into conflict with the workers they were tasked with recruiting and their communities.

JOINING THE ELC

Rural Egyptians engaged with this new labor recruitment network in a number of ways. One option was to join up with the ELC. Egyptian historian Latifa Salim has found evidence in the Egyptian National Archives of men approaching the military authorities of their own initiative and asking to sign up for terms of service in the Gallipoli campaign.[73] One report from *Al-Ahram* in March 1916 announced, "Out of work laborers . . . [can] find a good opportunity (*furṣa sāniḥa*) to join in service to the Military Authorities, which gives an active wage of not less than seven piasters per day . . . and [pays the workers] salaries in advance for their travel."[74] This article—like the series of reports published in *Al-Muqattam* the following year—is tinged with British propaganda, and offers a particularly positive valence to Labor Corps recruitment by deeming it a "good opportunity." As part of this effort, it exaggerated the wages expected for a low-level laborer, which were actually five piastres per day for the ELC and six for the CTC.[75] But even at these rates, peasants could still make more than the average wage of three piastres for a day's work as a migrant laborer before the war.[76] New recruits were supposed to be given an advance on their salaries of three pounds, roughly one hundred times the daily wage of a migrant laborer.[77]

The memoir of ʿAbd al-Hamid Muhammad Husayn provides insight into the considerations at play for workers who joined up with the ELC. In the beginning of his story, he emphasizes the paramount role played by financial constraints in his village, writing, "Poverty is what governed over everything in [my] humble neighborhood . . . and poverty gives birth to certain values and laws."[78] His father divorced his mother, so he went to live with his mother's brothers and began working in his father's profession of stone masonry at the age of eleven. He treats the actual moment of his recruitment into the ELC very briefly, writing only: "I found myself joining the soldiery" (*wajadtu nafsi iltaḥaq bi-l-ʿaskariyya*).[79] He enrolled in the ELC multiple times. After his first tour of duty in Gallipoli in 1915, he returned to Egypt and joined up again for multiple tours in Sudan. Finally, in 1917 Husayn re-entered the ELC for a final tour supporting the EEF in the Sinai-Palestine campaign.[80] Because he was relatively well-educated, Husayn rose quickly through the ELC hierarchy. He attained the rank of *awmbāshi*, which gave him administrative responsibility over the storehouse for his ELC encampment in Palestine.

Poverty and financial constraints would have played an important role in decision making for many families at the time. After the outbreak of the First World War in the summer of 1914, general uncertainty led British industry to reign in expenses. With demand decreasing in the Lancashire cotton mills, it soon became clear that the cotton harvest of summer 1914 would be "left unpicked, rotting in the ground."[81] Buying and selling cotton ground to a halt when the market at Alexandria simply shut down in August and September. Soon afterward, banks and moneylenders became fearful of debtor insolvency, and began to make a more concerted effort to collect outstanding loans from farmers.[82] Workers in Egypt's major cities also suffered from economic hardship at the beginning of the war. Unemployment skyrocketed as major businesses tried to cut back on expenses and the business interests of enemy nationals were closed. Many of the workers in cities were originally migrants from the countryside, so in light of public security concerns, steps were taken to remove migrant laborers back to their villages of origin. In September 1914, three thousand Upper Egyptians were relocated from the Mediterranean ports of Alexandria and Port Saʿid, and an additional nineteen hundred were sent back home from the Delta town of Damanhur.[83]

For this large population of cash-strapped peasants and laborers, the ELC could provide opportunities for financial relief. If laborers got themselves classified as skilled, they could receive bounties of fifty to one hundred piastres (i.e., ten to twenty times the daily wage for an "unskilled" laborer in the ELC) for each additional time they reenrolled.[84] British military authorities established schools that provided courses for laborers to attain skills as mechanical transport drivers, clerks, or officers' attendants (*suffrāgis*).[85] Others would take a premium for waiting until a man was condemned to service and then offer to take his spot in the ELC. One British adviser wrote of "thousands" of recruits "ready to volunteer" who "stand out for something extra before joining." According to this report, men could make from one to seven pounds extra by doing this (i.e., 2,000 to 14,000 percent of the daily wage for a low-level unskilled laborer in the ELC). The report also contains secondhand information about eighty men in Damanhur "waiting outside [of the district building] . . . who were willing, for a consideration, to take [the recruits'] places."[86] Although British characterizations of their own policies in Egypt should certainly be taken with a grain of salt, it seems that there is some evidence that workers approached the recruitment effort as a financial opportunity and sought to join up with the military authorities.

Another reason some may have gone into service with the ELC is because they were told to do so by their parents. Many of the men who served in the ELC were not the primary breadwinners of their families, but instead were collecting wages to help support the household. One officer in Palestine writes of a sixteen-year-old boy who served in his company.[87] In a circular sent to provincial officials on May 26, 1918, Rushdi defined the pool of potential ELC laborers as young men between the ages of eighteen and forty-five, but "heads of families" were to be exempt if "nobody can provide for the needs of his family in his place."[88] This seems to indicate that, according to the letter of the law, subordinate males within someone else's household were the ideal candidates for the ELC. Additionally, no more than three men per family were to be subject to recruitment, indicating that recruiting officials endeavored to take family interests in mind.[89]

A letter to the editor published in *Al-Muqattam* in early 1915 purports to be from a man who sent his sons off to work with British forces fighting to repel the Ottoman advance on the Suez Canal. The author identifies himself as Hasan Mustafa Salim, a graduate of Al-Azhar University from the *'izba* of Awlad Musa, Sharqiyya Province. He describes how he felt a duty to answer the government's call for laborers:

> It is a religious duty for all of the classes of the *umma*, the smallest and the biggest, the richest and the poorest, the educated and the ignorant, to send their money and their sons under the protection of the Egyptian government—may God help it and grant it victory![90]

The letter from Salim corroborates the notion that ideas about the sacred intersected with ideas about class and nation to produce a discourse of duty and obligation for men in the countryside. The author brandishes his credentials as a graduate of Al-Azhar, Egypt's most prestigious center of Islamic higher education, to declare enrolling in the ELC a "religious duty" (*wājib shar'an*). But he also identifies himself as a *fallāḥ* and calls on all "classes of the nation" (*ṭabaqāt al-umma*) to send what they can to support the war effort. According to his letter, Salim joined with another family in sending two camels to the military authorities. He also wrote, "In my family there are sons in the army and others prepared to answer the request of the government . . . it is the duty of everyone living in the Nile Valley to go along with this."[91] While the propagandistic nature of reports in *Al-Muqqatam* means that we should view this letter critically, if the story of Hasan Mustafa Salim is true, then at least two families in a small Delta village willingly sent their sons and their animals to participate in one of the first campaigns of the war.

There is significant evidence in both Arabic and English, then, to show that some people joined up with the labor effort, not because they were compelled to do so by violent force, but because other aspects of their personal circumstances dictated it was a prudent choice. The financial strain at the start of the war put many small farmers in a precarious position, and the ELC offered competitive wages with opportunities for long-term employment and potential advancement. Others may have been compelled to enlist because of their position as subordinate men in the family. As the letter to the editor of *Al-Muqattam* illustrates, fathers could have sent their sons off to war to score political points with the British or local officials, or to make a statement about duties to the *umma*. ELC laborers were complex individuals from a variety of circumstances, and their reasons for joining to serve in the war were numerous.

PETITIONING AND VIOLENT RESISTANCE

While some joined up with the ELC, there were also large numbers clearly recruited against their will. This is evident by the efforts they devoted to escaping service. Young men across the country resorted to a variety of means to negotiate with, subvert, or resist recruiting officials. One was petitioning the government. According to one report, the Ministry of Interior received 4,919 petitions and granted exemptions in 596 cases, approximately 12 percent of the total, from May 1918 to March 1919.[92] The ministry received petitions "from recruits or their parents," indicating something about the age of those targeted for forcible recruitment and showing that kinship networks were often mobilized in the course of drafting petitions.[93] ELC officers also continuously forwarded petitions from the ELC to the recruiting department from workers during their terms of service.[94] Petitioning was a common method employed by villagers seeking a redress of their grievances with the state.[95] In a study of petitions sent to the Egyptian Khedive in the late nineteenth century, John Chalcraft argues that they should be seen as a distinct mode of rural politics that evokes "not passivity, silent subversion, or revolution, but sophisticated engagement and negotiations with state practice and discourse."[96]

Besides petitioning, men and women in the countryside used violence to resist incorporation into the ELC. The Foreign Office files in the British National Archives contain thirty-five reports of violent resistance to recruitment from May 19, 1918, to August 27, 1918, which have seldom, if ever, been acknowledged by historians of modern Egypt.[97] All told, the records show that battles between villagers and local officials over the subject of ELC recruitment in the summer of 1918 led to the deaths of three local guards, two village headmen, and eighteen villagers. A further thirty-five local guards and twenty-two villagers were wounded, and at least seventy-nine villagers were arrested.

The most common type of violent resistance was for individuals to physically fight back against officials as they grabbed them off the street or from their homes. Eighteen of the thirty-five cases (51 percent) can be categorized as this type of individual resistance involving only one person. These acts of resistance were generally unsuccessful, as local officials ultimately apprehended the perpetrators. Although firearms constituted the largest category of weapons used in such attacks, the records show almost as many cases of stabbing, along with a significant number in which recruiting officers were seemingly beaten with any implement that was ready at hand for the villagers, including sticks, stones, kitchen knives, and axes.[98]

Eleven out of thirty-five cases—31 percent—include families getting involved in resistance. From the reports, it seems that the *'umad* at times used ELC recruitment as a way to settle personal disputes, and families who felt that they were targeted unfairly for personal reasons often lashed out violently. One telegram from the Upper Egyptian district of Dayrut mentions that locals accused their *'umda* of selecting a recruit "to revenge his cousin, who had been convicted of having intimate relations with the sister of a certain Abdel-Mutaleb."[99]

Another report from the *mudīr* of Bani Suwayf describes a conflict between the inhabitants of an *'izba* belonging to a certain Mahmud Salim Bey on the one hand and the local *'umda* on the other. Apparently, after a man from the *'izba* had reported the *'umda* to the provincial authorities for "an irregularity in connection with the collection of barley, etc.," the *'umda* detained him and decided to send him off to serve with the ELC in Palestine. But as the man was being transported to the front, he managed to escape. Before news of his escape had reached the plantation, the *'umda* returned with a force of local guards to secure the man's brother in order to enlist him instead, and this led the people of the *'izba* to believe that the *'umda*'s intention was to "collect all the recruits required from only their Ezba."[100] The villagers then descended on the *'umda* and beat him and his local guards with long sticks known as *nabābīt* (sing., *nabbūt*), which were often used by *fallāḥīn* in a popular combat game. One person in the melée fired a shot at the *'umda*, and he was killed instantly.

It is easy to imagine wives, mothers, and sisters getting swept up into violent acts of resistance as men in their families were sent off to the ELC. The cries of devasted women form a common soundtrack to the departure of a levy of laborers in the Egyptian press sources.[101] Egyptian social historian Amin 'Izz al-Din also recorded the "screams of the children and the wails of the women that happened when the men were gathered."[102] One report from Nag' Hammadi in the Upper Egyptian province of Qina speaks briefly of relatives who "interfered" with the recruiting process. Upon seeing this interference, the guards fired at the offenders, "wounding a man and a woman."[103] That women took part in violent acts is not surprising. Zeinab Abul-Magd's research has uncovered several women in the province of Qina had joined the world of organized banditry dating back to the 1880s.[104]

Wives were also called to testify against their husbands after they had been apprehended for resisting recruitment. One report from Kafr al-Sarim in the Delta province of Gharbiyya tells the story of a man named 'Abd al-Salam Farag, who was approached by the *'umda* and compelled to join the ELC. Suddenly, his relatives who lived in a neighboring house came to his assistance, using sticks and an axe to beat the guards who had come to apprehend him. The district *ma'mūr* proceeded to the scene and arrested five of the men in the family, but seven others managed to escape. An investigation followed that saw authorities in the local Parquet depose a number of people, including the wives of the accused. Apparently, the *'umda* attempted to tamper with the witnesses.[105] The British archives preserve other accusations of witness tampering in investigations of village headmen charged with recruiting abuse, including one case in which a witness was "forced to sign a statement by physical force."[106] Having women testify in public investigations of violent resistance to recruitment, then, provides us with evidence that they not only participated in such incidents but that it put them in danger from their local *'umda*.

Besides resistance on an individual or family level, mass uprisings also took place encompassing larger groups, up to and including entire villages. At least seven examples of such mass resistance are preserved in the Foreign Office records. The largest comes from the Delta province of Daqhiliyya, which tells the story of a police lieutenant posted at the "Biala Outpost" who was preparing to leave for the Talkha district center with recruits in tow when "about two hundred villagers gathered and interfered with him, persistently asking for the release of Mohamed el Sayed."[107]

Another example shows how disputes over Labor Corps recruitment could become subsumed into local village politics. On May 25, 1918, a force of guards from the village of Brimsha in the Maghagha district, Minya province, had taken a levy of recruits to the local military outpost at Shaykh Mas'ud, and upon their return the inhabitants of the neighboring village of Manshiyyat Halfa fired shots at them. Investigators discovered that Manshiyyat Halfa was attached to Brimsha for administrative purposes, but had recently petitioned to become independent. Their request was denied, and a special *'umda* was appointed for them instead. The villagers of Manshiyyat Halfa alleged that the *'umda* of Brimsha had a personal vendetta against them because of this, and so when three men from Manshiyyat Halfa were seized by the guards from Brimsha, the villagers took it as an affront to their community as a whole and responded collectively.[108] This fascinating story shows how ELC recruitment could interact with local disputes and fuel distrust of local officials among the villagers. Recruitment became a new factor in local politics, which was itself becoming increasingly confrontational and violent after the outlawing of local elections by the British during the occupation.[109]

ELC recruitment transformed the terrain of village life, not only for those recruited, but also for their families and communities left behind. Rural Egyptians responded to recruitment in ways that engaged with the state, such as sending in petitions, as well as in ways that rejected it with violence directed at government officials. The situation came to a head in the summer of 1918 when at least thirty-five separate incidents of violent resistance took place in a three-month period. These incidents have rarely been acknowledged in the historiography of modern Egypt, and they should be linked together as part of a broad wave of discontent with ELC recruitment in the countryside during the First World War.

REINSTITUTING THE *CORVÉE*

As early as February 1918, British officials were aware of the problems with the system of administrative pressure. In a report that month, the adviser to the Ministry of Interior, John Haines, complained, "Mamurs and Omdehs are using pure compulsion to show good recruiting figures. This gives recruiting a bad name and it is against the wish of the army."[110] On May 6, 1918, a meeting was convened of British advisers and military authorities to find a solution to problems with recruitment. At the meeting, Haines suggested that "Labor should be requisitioned from the villages on a sort of corvée system."[111] This would be based on the vestiges of the old *corvée* known as the Nile Defense Works.[112] Preparations for the Nile Defense Works had included lists of sixteen thousand men eligible to work for 150 days before the Nile flood.[113] These Nile Defense Works were the last remaining relic of the old *corvée* system, but they received a new lease on life during the First World War to provide cover for ELC recruitment in the countryside.

The British attempted to portray the reintroduction of the *corvée* as a measure to reduce the abuses of the *'umda*. When the Sultan of Egypt complained about ELC recruiting in July 1918, Wingate pointed to the reintroduction of the *corvée* scheme as a solution.[114] The preface to the Ministry of Interior announcement of the scheme stated that the reasons behind its promulgation were, "the numerous complaints received by the Ministry, some of which presume an exercise of abuse, by the Omdehs and public employees, of their powers, for reasons of a purely personal nature."[115] The British accused the *'umad* of neglect when they saw that the proportion of recruits to total population was much smaller in some districts as compared to others.[116] It was hoped that the use of *corvée* lists could centralize and systematize recruiting. By having a list, the British attempted to take some of the discretionary power away from the local functionaries, thereby reducing complaints of abuse and corruption from the population.[117]

But if the theoretical goal of reintroducing the *corvée* lists was to limit the exposure of recruits to the arbitrary whims of the *'umda*, the practical implementation of the system actually left much up to their discretion. The Nile Defense Works lists prepared by the Ministry of Public Works could not be imported to the task of military recruitment without some modifications. In a circular to the provinces, the Ministry of Interior instructed none other than the local *'umad* to draw up the new lists "on the basis of lists prepared over the past year for the men charged with guardianship of the Nile Banks." The final lists were supposed to exempt anyone less than eighteen years or more than forty-five years of age, along with military recruits who had already passed a medical exam, heads of families, and employees of "societies and administrations occupied with technical employment."[118] According to the British, the *'umda* was the only figure with enough "local intelligence" about the villages in which they lived to be able to make judgments about such detailed classes of exemption.[119]

Complaints persisted about the *'umad* into the summer of 1918. According to the Ministry of Interior report, the recruiting reforms succeeded in that the *'umda* "has no choice about whom he sends." "But," the report continued, "the trickery is in the lists themselves."[120] By giving the *'umda* the ability to write the list, the British had essentially institutionalized their arbitrary power in the villages. The Ministry of Interior soon came up with a further reform proposal. It was suggested that the *'umda* should recruit double the number of men required for his district, after which the local *ma'mūr* would "make enquiries and release half of those produced." It was hoped that this would "give greater contentment" to the workers and peasants subjected to recruitment by giving them a chance to appeal to an authority above the village headmen—even if the total number recruited remained the same.[121] In August 1918 the adviser to the Ministry of Interior reported back on the status of the reform: "I was in Mansura Markaz a day or two ago when the Mamur was going through [the recruits] and everything was going smoothly."[122]

CONCLUSION

The idea to round up hundreds of thousands of young men from the Egyptian countryside to work in the First World War ran into problems when it was actually implemented. Military authorities received pushback from diplomats in London and Cairo, officials in the Egyptian government, and officers in the Anglo-Egyptian army. These administrators, far from instituting their negotiated solutions from on high, came to rely on local intermediaries who had the knowledge, experience, and ability to gather recruits. In turn, local officials acted less like subordinates to the central state, and more like leaders of their own private fiefdoms. Within the villages, the *'umda* were now able to consolidate wealth into their hands and simply exile any of their personal rivals into service with the ELC.

The complex picture of the British colonial state that takes shape in this story is of a set of institutions enmeshed in the global machinations of the First World War, yet fundamentally dependent on local intermediaries who were, at times, able to refashion imperial efforts of the state to suit their own ends. The decision to reimplement the *corvée* in 1918 is perhaps the best example of the limits of colonial state power, as British authorities were forced to reverse course on a policy that had been a cornerstone in the rhetorical defense of their empire in Egypt from the times of Evelyn Baring. While some scholars advance a totalizing picture of colonial state power that systematically imposed its will on the Egyptian population,[123] the picture of the colonial state that emerges from this close study of ELC recruitment is more open to top-down influences from global developments and bottom-up pressure from local communities.

Neither can workers and peasants in the rural countryside be seen as separate, self-contained actors, thinking only in terms of their economic interests or always in conflict with the state. It is true that a great many rejected the recruitment effort and worked to free themselves from service to the ELC. In enacting their displeasure with recruitment—through both peaceful means, such as petitioning, and the use of violence—men and women who were on the receiving end of state power also managed to influence state policy. But efforts to reduce all ELC recruitment to "forced conscription" miss crucial parts of the story. Cash-strapped workers chose to join the ELC, and some found ways to make extra money by offering to take the place of the forcibly conscripted or by getting themselves classified as skilled. Even in the bloody summer of 1918, men like ʻAbd al-Hamid Muhammad Husayn were volunteering to re-enter the ELC on multiple tours of duty.

Ideas about race, class, and religion informed a sense of collective consciousness among rural elites known as the *ʻayān* and made them seem like the logical choice to represent the *fallāḥīn* in the countryside. This was why they had been incorporated into the Ministry of Interior by British reform efforts in the generation before the war. When the war broke out, the resources of the colonial state were rearticulated to facilitate the movement of young men out of the Egyptian countryside. Military authorities relied on the networks of the Anglo-Egyptian army, the Ministry of Public Works, and the Ministry of Interior to identify and detain hundreds of thousands of potential ELC recruits. But because Ministry of Interior officials had to answer not only to the state, but also to their local communities, the process had transformative effects in villages across the country. The next chapter will examine what came after recruitment: the process of sorting through potential workers and transporting those fit for service to the theaters of battle in Europe and the Middle East. This process followed the same basic pattern of reworking the existing resources of the colonial state to fit the exigencies of the war, but it entailed major spatial change in Egypt's cities and in logistical infrastructures across the country.

CHAPTER 3

FROM HOME TO THE FRONT

THROUGHOUT THE SPRING OF 1917, Egyptians arrived in France to work loading and unloading ships on French docks. Their first stop was Marseille, a southern port city on the Mediterranean that had welcomed travelers from Egypt for hundreds of years. But unlike the merchants who traditionally made the trip, the *fallāḥīn* of the ELC were organized as military laborers. A correspondent for *Al-Muqattam* describes the scene upon the arrival of a company of Egyptians in spring 1917:

> The men were full of power and activity, and were pleased by the new scenery that they saw around them. A big party welcomed them when they disembarked, and eyes turned to look at them as they passed by in the streets. Their good organization and their khaki clothes showed that these were men prepared for work. Their health was very fine.[1]

As the previous chapter has shown, *Al-Muqattam* was notorious for pro-British propaganda during the war, so this characterization of the men as "pleased" at the prospect of working in France should certainly be viewed skeptically. However, if we read "against the grain," the report contains a number of important references to the journey undertaken by Egyptian laborers as they traveled from their home villages to theaters of battle.[2] References to the men's "good organization" likely referred to the various subdivisions and hierarchies established within companies, which broke them into discrete units that could be more easily managed. The "khaki clothes" they wore would have been a drastic departure from the traditional long blue or white cotton robes (*galālīb*; sing., *galabiyya*) that were the preferred style for many back in their villages. The reporter also noted the "fine health" of these newly outfitted laborers, which was ensured through medical examinations and a rigorous sanitation regimen.

ELC laborers disembarking at Marseille did not arrive in this condition naturally. Their journey would have seen them travel from their home villages to the closest town, then on to the big cities of Cairo and Alexandria, and finally across the Mediterranean by steamship. For many of these men, it was the first time they crossed the sea. This chapter reconstructs their journey, along with the journeys of hundreds of thousands of other young men who made their way to the Dardanelles, Iraq, and Palestine in the First World War.

As the men of the ELC moved through space, they transformed the map of Egypt. The notion of "producing space" may perhaps seem counterintuitive at first. Today, we generally think of space as something that exists prior to human activity; we can fill it up, modify it, and move around within it, but it remains in some sense an empty container for our actions. French philosopher Henri Lefebvre introduced the idea of "the production of space" to argue against this a priori conceptualization, insisting instead that space is a social product of relations between people, ideas, and the natural environment. Interactions between these three elements produce unique conceptions of space. For Lefebvre, today's hegemonic notion of space as an empty container is itself the product of the capitalist mode of production, which corresponds historically with the widespread consumption of maps and the development of geography as a social science.

Maps and spatial diagrams are what Lefebvre calls "representations of space," which are produced by "scientists, planners, urbanists, technocratic subdividers, and social engineers."[3] Human beings understand and move through their environment in an infinite variety of ways, but representations of space identify some spatial practices with "knowledge" (*savoir*), while erasing others. Lines on the map naturalize the existence of political borders or normative pathways from one place to another, making them seem as if they were simply part of the landscape. Analyzing the production of space as Lefebvre understands it forces us to explore the tensions between representations of space on the one hand, and the myriad ways in which the built environment is occupied and inhabited by subjects working to decipher their surroundings on the other.

A committed Marxist, Lefebvre's focus on the capitalist mode of production as the engine behind the production of space led him to concentrate a great deal of his research on the development of cities as deposits of surplus capital.[4] But instead of focusing on capitalist economic development and its tendency toward urbanization as the engine behind the production of urban space, this chapter illustrates how efforts to prosecute wars end up producing their own kinds of "logistics spaces."[5]

In a criticism of Lefebvre, Paul Virilio laments how so many have forgotten that the city is "but a stopover, a point on the synoptic path of a trajectory."[6] According to Virilio, "the invention of the city as such lies in logistical preparation for war."[7] While the connection between the production of space and war may have been easy to ignore for French philosophers writing in the 1960s and 1970s, for Egyptians, it is much closer to the surface. The Egyptian Colloquial Arabic term for Cairo—and Egypt as a whole—is *maṣr*, which derives from the name for the military encampment built after the Arab-Muslim conquest of Egypt. According to Lane, the classical Arabic root *m-ṣ-r* signifies "a thing intervening between two things . . . hence, a great town," and the second Caliph, ʿUmar ibn al-Khattab, who sent a general to conquer Egypt, was referred to as *maṣṣr al-amṣār*, or "the one who built the [garrison] cities."[8] The semantic associations underwriting *maṣr* in Egyptian Arabic echo Virilio's conception of the city as "the ancient military glacis, ridge road, frontier or riverbank, where the spectator's glance and the vehicle's speed of displacement were instrumentally linked."[9]

This chapter follows ELC laborers as they made their way through towns and cities across Egypt, documenting the infrastructural changes necessary to convey them along their journey to war. Each section includes a representation of space used by the authorities charged with shepherding ELC laborers along their way, but the smooth lines of these maps and diagrams never quite captured the ways ELC recruits actually behaved. Along their journey, the men worked to protest, escape, and evade colonial authorities. Each new node in the network added new opportunities, and as the recruits' itinerary became more complex, colonial authorities struggled harder to impose some order on the sprawling space they had knit together.

INTERNMENT AND INSPECTION IN PROVINCIAL TOWNS

As a British provincial inspector in the Egyptian Ministry of Interior, Thomas Russell's primary job consisted of making tours around the countryside and issuing reports on Egypt's villages. Maps were an important tool for Russell and other inspectors in planning their tours to ensure that they hit all the major towns and villages in their respective provincial jurisdictions. Since the days of Mehmet ʿAli, most of the villages in the surrounding countryside had been attached to a district for administrative purposes, and districts, in turn, were attached to a province. These district and provincial capital towns were the most immediate points of contact between the administration of the state and the surrounding villages, and as such usually constituted the first stop for the men of the ELC.

For British inspectors like Russell, the built environment of district towns made life there "unattractive." He described three-week periods traveling through the districts as "living in discomfort in a small town with no social amenities, no cinemas and clubs, with no intercourse of families and nothing to do except work and intrigue."[10] At each stop on his tour, he would stay in "rest-houses" built of "primitive mud brick" which "hardly lived up to the idea of repose that their name would suggest."[11] Other Englishmen accustomed to touring the provinces during the war also fixated on the mud brick construction materials used for most buildings, as well as their "extremely primitive" interiors.[12] When Russell stopped in provincial capitals like Asyut, Tanta, or Zaqazig, he could stay in the more stately homes of English judges and other officials.[13]

ELC laborers began their journey from home to the front by walking on foot to the nearest district or provincial capital town—sometimes bound together by a thick rope around the trunk to prevent escape. There they were kept in holding cells until a sanitary inspector could examine them on their regular tours.[14] District capital towns each had small "lockups," which were administered by the Ministry of Interior and supplied by the prisons department.[15] During their internment in these cells, ELC recruits would likely sleep the same way prisoners had for years—on a mat on the asphalt floor.[16] Lockups were notoriously overcrowded before the recruitment effort, and the establishment of the ELC only exacerbated the problem. For instance, in his testimony to the Milner Mission in 1920, a British political officer in the Delta province of Manufiyya reported that the *ma'mūr* of the district of Manuf "often kept seventy or eighty men locked up in a room for several weeks waiting to be sent to the Labour Corps."[17] Authorities in Cairo were aware of this practice, as a circular from August 1918 notes that "some Mamurs of markazes detain the men recruited a very long time before they are examined."[18]

British officials made efforts to address these long wait times. One circular proposed to decrease internment times by allowing districts that were not seen by inspectors in a timely fashion to send their recruits to districts that were more accessible.[19] An attempt was made to fix a standard date for medical examination of recruits in all of the provinces, but it failed due to "differences of opinions of Mudirs caused by local reasons."[20] It was not uncommon for a district to receive the sanitary inspection team on a tour just once a month, and an attempt to increase this pace to once every two weeks failed in December 1918.[21] The number of recruits was allowed to pile up in jail cells while the men waited for sanitary inspectors to come see them.

Military authorities ordered that each recruit must undergo a medical exam at the district before they could enroll in the ELC. Many recruits were rejected at this stage and sent home. For example, from the six-month period from November 1916 to April 1917, the RAMC claimed that 130,000 Egyptians presented themselves to doctors for examination at the recruiting stations. Of this number, 30,000, or 23 percent, were denied entry.[22] Recruits were rejected for various reasons, with one RAMC source emphasizing the especially high prevalence of eye disease.[23]

Although the march to the district capital town and the long internment therein was doubtless a grueling experience for the recruits, some were able to turn the concentration of men in the holding cells to their advantage. During the spate of draft riots in the summer of 1918, protesters in the Faraskur district undertook a unique demonstration, with twenty-six men staging a sit-in by locking the holding cell door from the inside.[24] When the police tried to force their way into the room, a crowd of onlookers from the town gathered outside the building and began throwing stones at them. Eventually, the crowd attempted to break into the lockup and release the interned men, but the armed force of local guards resisted them, firing a few shots at the assembled crowd in the process. The district authorities resorted to telephoning the *mudīr* of Daqhiliyya, and he took a police force and proceeded there by train.[25] A different force was also sent from the port city of Dumyat (Damietta) on the Mediterranean coast, and the combined strength of these two groups was ultimately able to subdue the crowd. The demonstrating laborers were removed from the district prison and sent on to the nearby town of Mansura by rail to continue their journey to the front.[26] Although their protest was ultimately unsuccessful, this report shows how the spatial concentration of recruits in the holding cells of capital towns could work against the military authorities.

For those who were unable to evade enrollment, the next step would be to sign a contract. While this ritual was hardly indicative of a recruit's actual desire to join the ELC, it was nevertheless a crucial piece of theater for the British to maintain the illusion that the ELC was "recruited entirely on voluntary lines."[27] The contract presented all the stipulations that were supposed to govern ELC labor, including a six-month term of service beginning at the date of the recruit's arrival in the field and a daily salary, which usually ranged between five and six piastres a day.[28]

Of course, there are a number of problems with taking these contracts

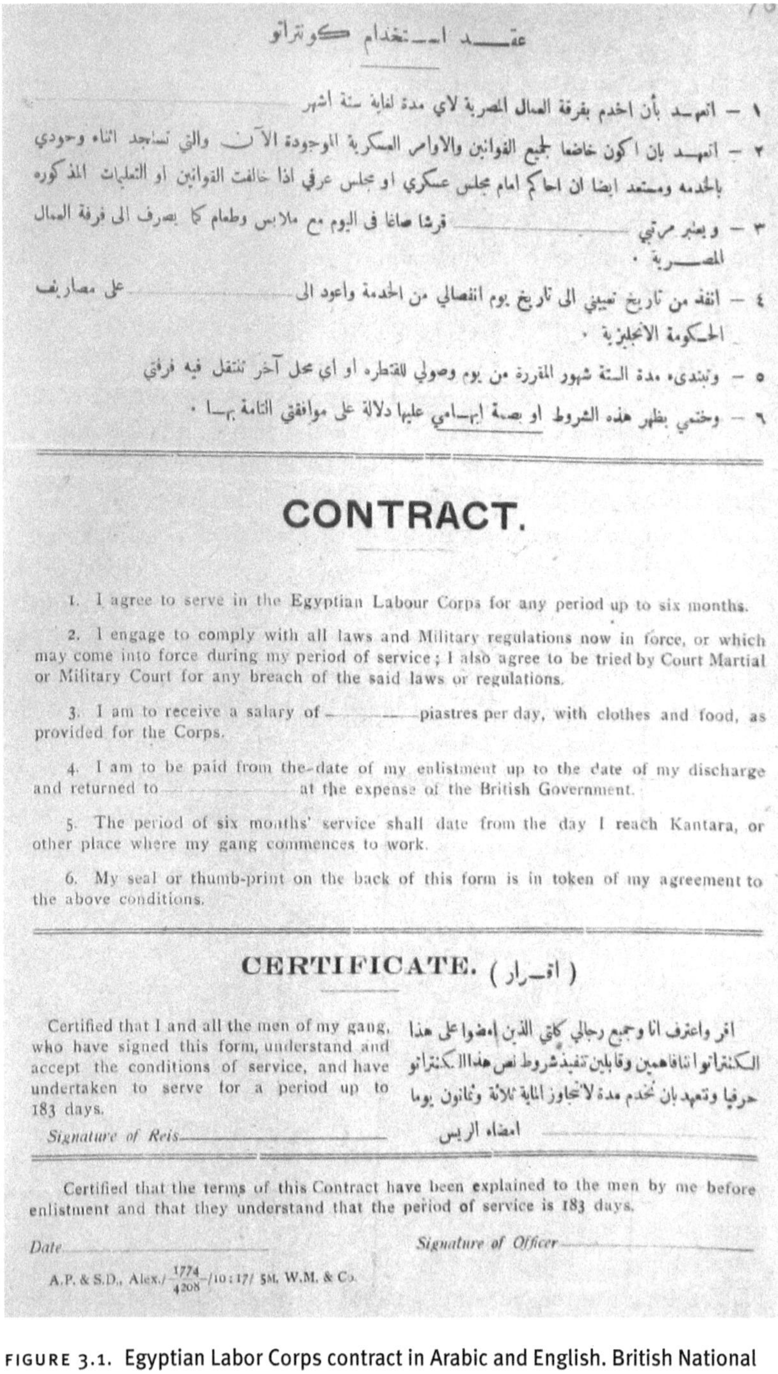

عقـــد اســتخدام كونتراتو

١ – اتعهـد بأن اخدم بفرقة العمال المصرية لاي مدة لغاية ستة اشهر

٢ – اتعهـد بان اكون خاضعا لجميع القوانين والاوامر العسكرية الموجودة الآن والتي تستجد اثناء وجودي بالخدمه ومستعد ايضا ان احاكم امام مجلس عسكري او مجلس عرفي اذا خالفت القوانين او التعليمات المذكوره

٣ – ويعتبر مرتبي ________ قرشا صاغا في اليوم مع ملابس وطعام كما يصرف الى فرقة العمال المصرية .

٤ – انقد من تاريخ تعييني الى تاريخ يوم انفصالي من الخدمة واعود الى ________ على مصاريف الحكومة الانجليزية .

٥ – وتبتدىء مدة الستة شهور المقررة من يوم وصولي للقنطره او اي محل آخر تنتقل فيه فرقتي

٦ – وختمي بظهر هذه الشروط او بصمة ابهامي عليها دلالة على موافقتي التامة بهـا .

CONTRACT.

1. I agree to serve in the Egyptian Labour Corps for any period up to six months.

2. I engage to comply with all laws and Military regulations now in force, or which may come into force during my period of service; I also agree to be tried by Court Martial or Military Court for any breach of the said laws or regulations.

3. I am to receive a salary of ________ piastres per day, with clothes and food, as provided for the Corps.

4. I am to be paid from the date of my enlistment up to the date of my discharge and returned to ________ at the expense of the British Government.

5. The period of six months' service shall date from the day I reach Kantara, or other place where my gang commences to work.

6. My seal or thumb-print on the back of this form is in token of my agreement to the above conditions.

CERTIFICATE. (اقـرار)

Certified that I and all the men of my gang, who have signed this form, understand and accept the conditions of service, and have undertaken to serve for a period up to 183 days.

اقر واعترف انا وجميع رجالي كالذين امضوا على هذا الكنتراتو انا فاهمين وقابلين تنفيذ شروط نص هذا الكنتراتو حرفيا وتعهد بان نخدم مدة لا تتجاوز المائة ثلاثة وثمانون يوما

Signature of Reis ________ امضاء الريس ________

Certified that the terms of this Contract have been explained to the men by me before enlistment and that they understand that the period of service is 183 days.

Date ________ *Signature of Officer* ________

A.P. & S.D., Alex./$\frac{1774}{4208}$/10:17/ 5M. W.M. & Co.

FIGURE 3.1. Egyptian Labor Corps contract in Arabic and English. British National Archives, Foreign Office 141/797/2.

as indicative of any kind of informed consent on the part of the workers. For one thing, most recruits were unable to read. The British had translated the contracts into Arabic, but it was Modern Standard Arabic—a higher, literary register of the language, which would have been awkward for most laborers to comprehend, even if recited aloud. Those recruits who could not read and write were unable to sign the contracts, but the British worked around this by including a seal or thumb print on the back, which was taken as a token of the recruit's agreement.[29] According to historian Latifa Salim, in some districts, seal-makers popped up in close proximity to the town jail cells to make seals for the recruits who did not already have their own, and those who refused to sign or put their seal on the contracts were beaten until they complied.[30]

As they had been for generations, then, district and provincial capital towns were the most immediate points of contact between the men of the ELC and the state. The provincial prison and lockup system was rearticulated as a site of internment and inspection for the ELC, where time operated on the schedule of sanitary inspection tours and recruits sometimes waited for weeks in cramped conditions. But the length of internment and the consequent overcrowding of local prisons also created opportunities for communities to resist. These towns were the portals to the migrant labor network of the ELC, where hundreds of thousands of young men from the villages of Egypt began their long journey from home to the front.

LOGISTICS CITIES

The next stop on the journey to the front was usually a city. Cities like Cairo and Alexandria, along with large provincial capitals like Asyut, Suhag, and Mansura, served as the major nodes in the supply network for the war effort. Deborah Cowen calls cities like these "logistics cities," characterized by the concentration and commingling of military barracks, supply depots, distribution camps, and railroads and roads within them.[31] During the war, infrastructures concentrated within these cities facilitated the movement of material and people to the various fronts of battle. They became sites for the organization, supply, and distribution of ELC laborers.

The urban plan of logistics cities in wartime Egypt can be seen in historical maps of Cairo and Alexandria during the war. Military buildings in Cairo were positioned for their proximity to logistical infrastructures. The main barracks for British troops were located on the Nile at the Qasr al-Nil bridge, the barracks of the military mounted police were adjacent to the Cairo railway station, and the workshops of the Egyptian State

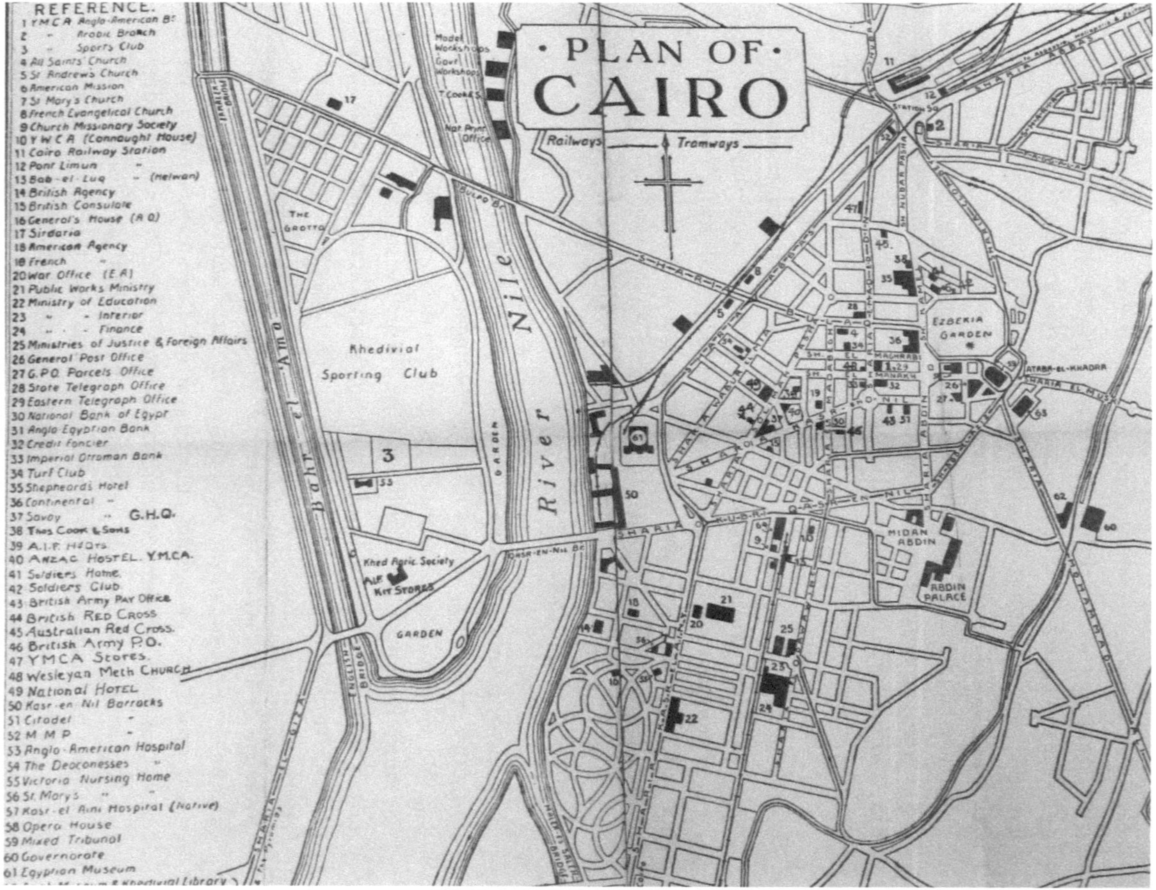

FIGURE 3.2.
Cairo during the First World War. University of Minnesota, Kautz Family YMCA Archives Y.USA.9-2-22 Box 7.

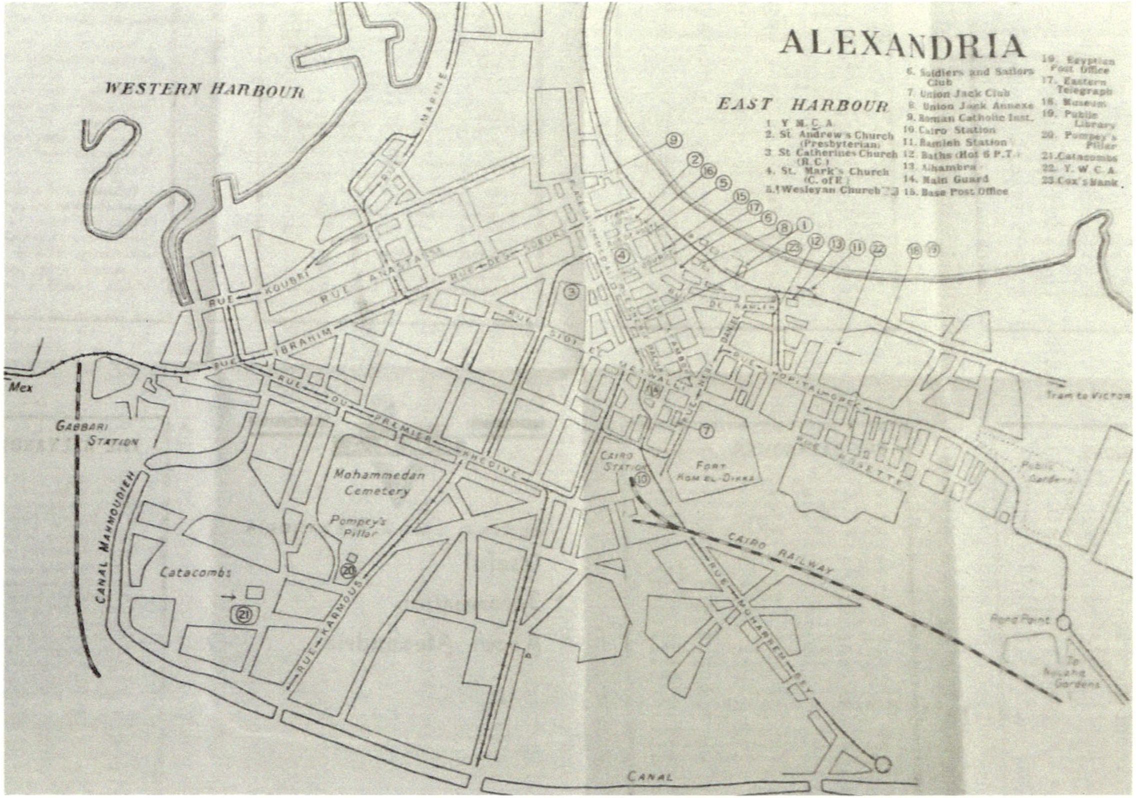

FIGURE 3.3.
Alexandria during the First World War. University of Minnesota, Kautz Family YMCA Archives Y.USA.9-2-22 Box 8.

Railway (ESR) were located on the Nile north of Bulaq. In Egypt's second city, Alexandria, the main guard garrison was located next to the railway station, and the military post office, Egyptian Post Office, and eastern telegraph station were all across the street from the eastern harbor that opened onto the Mediterranean Sea. The main tramline serving the city terminated at the same port. Logistical infrastructures, then, were colocated within these cities, facilitating the circulation of people and things through them and on to other locations.

By 1914, Egypt had a dense railway network, with the highest ratio of track length to inhabited area in the world.[32] The core of this railway network was managed by the ESR. During the war, George Macaulay, the head of the ESR, was heavily involved with military authorities in discussing how to offer more assistance to the war effort.[33] In May of 1917, Archibald Murray, the commander of the EEF, wrote that Macaulay had "given . . . assistance in every possible way and has invariably complied with every request I have made."[34] This included providing rails and rolling stock to military railroads instead of using them for civilian purposes, and conveying agricultural resources and ELC men on state-owned railroads.

The railways of the ESR conveyed ELC recruits from the town lockups in district and provincial capitals to the supply depots and distribution camps in the cities. The first supply depot for Egyptian laborers serving in the war was established at 'Ayn Shams outside of Cairo in December 1915. This catered to the men of the CTC bound for the Sinai-Palestine front. Charles Whittingham, who had previously served as the inspector-general of the prisons department in the colonial government, was tapped to run the CTC. He sent British inspectors to gather camels from the Egyptian countryside and formed purchasing commissions to acquire the remainder from Sudan, India, Somalia, and Algeria.[35]

Supply depots and distribution camps were the major hubs for outfitting the ELC. The Levant Base in Alexandria served as the initial supply depot for the first companies of the ELC heading to Gallipoli in 1915.[36] But in July 1916, after disbanding the Levant Base and forming the EEF, a supply depot specifically for ELC recruits was formed at Hadra in the eastern suburbs of Alexandria.[37] Soon thereafter, a second large supply depot was formed on Ruda Island south of Cairo.[38] Most ELC recruits passed through one of these two camps before they made their way to the front. As demand for the ELC increased, distribution camps were also opened throughout the country. During May and June of 1916, four camps were established at Kharga, Samalut, Shusha, and Fayyum.[39] A large distribution camp was opened in Asyut in October 1916, with a second one opening in Suhag, ninety miles south along the Nile, soon thereafter.[40] According to Murray, both camps proved of great value as recruits could be collected in them and "dispatched to the coast by special trains in drafts of 2,000."[41] The presence of railway, telegraph, and maritime infrastructures in these towns and cities made them ideal sites for supply depots and distribution camps.

In their brief time passing through the logistics cities, recruits were transformed from ordinary workers and peasants into military laborers. First, at the distribution camps in provincial towns, the recruits were issued two blankets and an overcoat. Then they traveled by train to the supply depots in Cairo and Alexandria, where they were disinfected, clothed, and equipped.[42] At the Hadra depot, for example, new arrivals would first enter the recruits' compound, which consisted of "a walled-in enclosure, fitted with latrines, ablution benches, shower baths, cooking places and living tents reserved entirely for new recruits."[43] Here, medical officers cut each recruit's hair with clippers and shaved their body and pubic hair. Recruits then proceeded to the disinfection station close by, carrying their blankets and personal effects with them. On arrival at the steam disinfector, the recruits removed their clothing, wrapped it together with their belongings in one of the blankets, and left the entire bundle to be disinfected by RAMC staff. The recruits' second blankets served as robes during their passage to the "bath-house," where they proceeded two at a time into a large bath of fluids including cresol, soft soap, paraffin, and sulfur.[44]

Recruits then moved on to the equipment store a few yards away, where they received their new uniform, including brown linen slacks, a khaki tunic with "E.L.C." emblazoned on the front, and an overcoat. Finally, the men recovered their belongings from the main disinfector and marched to the store, where the rest of their equipment—boots, cap, etc.—was provided to them. According to one medical officer, "the whole process . . . occupies an average time of three-fourths of an hour, in which period the new recruit is changed into a fully equipped member of the Egyptian Labour Corps, and is ready for service in any part of the war area, be it Palestine, Salonika, or France."[45]

After disinfection and outfitting, the next step was to instill a modicum of military discipline by organizing the men on a hierarchical basis. Recruits were issued identification numbers printed on "discs to be worn . . . with a string around the neck."[46] Individuals were grouped into squads of fifty, often including men who had been recruited together from the same village or district.[47] Their numbers were tallied on a list written

ten out to accompany the gangs wherever they moved. Recruiting inspectors chose a *ra'īs* as the head of each squad. According to British authorities, such figures were "accustomed to control [the recruits] when working for ordinary contractors."[48] Squads were organized into companies that were supposed to be about five hundred to six hundred men, each under a commanding officer assisted by two junior noncommissioned officers (NCOs).[49]

One of the major difficulties faced by the ELC was finding and training officers. The first companies were assigned officers on leave from the colonial government, or other white men who had experience working in Egypt. Although they lacked military training, they had the advantage of familiarity with Egyptian Colloquial Arabic and the cultural life of the country.[50] Most CTC officers came from this group, and by the end of the war, 92 out of 170 CTC officers were Englishmen recruited from the Anglo-Egyptian government.[51] But as demand for Egyptian laborers increased, it became impossible to staff every company with an officer who had experience working in Egypt. British authorities began accepting junior officers with any army experience, granting them a rank of second lieutenant and giving them command of a company with two NCOs below them.[52] One veteran of the CTC looked on this new wave of officers disdainfully, writing, "With one exception, every senior officer who has been brought in has, owing to his lack of knowledge of local conditions, been unsuccessful."[53]

The problems with the new officers were systemic. The ELC was the ad hoc product of the unique circumstances of the First World War, and there was no official history or organizational traditions that allowed for new officers to be initiated. When Ernest Venables first enrolled in the ELC as an officer in 1917, he enquired for its "'standing orders' or 'regulations,' but was informed that none existed." "It's organization, it's history," he explained, "is still being formed from day to day."[54] The shortage of qualified officers meant that they were sometimes assigned companies larger than those ideally envisioned by military authorities. By the end of his own period of service, Venables would oversee companies with as many as a thousand laborers—double the official standard of five hundred.

At the logistics cities, officers and ELC men came together for the first time and struggled to understand each other. Courses of instruction in Egyptian Colloquial Arabic were held at distribution camps to help the new officers, and all NCOs desiring to transfer to the ELC or CTC were required to serve a probationary period of one month at the supply depots, taking language courses and drilling new recruits, before being posted to the corps.[55] But mastering Egyptian Arabic in a few weeks proved impossible. The end product was a style of communication summed up by Venables as "an almost incredible instance of colloquial mixtures." "Our conversation," he wrote, "had imperceptibly become a blend of Army slang, soldiers' Hindustani, and Arabic."[56]

The men of the CTC had the added difficulty of becoming acquainted with their camels. According to one British officer, "Life at Ain-el-Shams was rendered exciting and even perilous by the savage disposition of many of the camels. Nearly every day one or more men went to the Hospital with camel bite, and frequently when a camel got loose at night and excited the others, the camp was kept awake practically all night."[57]

Some recruits were able to turn all this confusion to their advantage and escape from the ELC once they reached the logistics cities. For example, in 1915 a trainload of two hundred recruits from the province of Bani Suwayf deserted while their train was stopped at the Alexandria station.[58] In 1917 another trainload deserted before reaching Cairo.[59] Desertion was a problem at the distribution camps as well. One report from May 1917 mentions that recruiting authorities at the Asyut distribution camps had "found it necessary to surround the camp with barbed wire."[60] Yet the large distribution camp at Suhag seems to have been relatively free from attempts by workers to escape.[61]

As the nodes of the labor mobilization network multiplied and the supply depots and distribution camps proliferated in logistics cities, the constant flux that resulted from the circulation of migrant laborers, officers, soldiers, and animals provided opportunities for recruits to escape. In this sense, laborers were able to use the vast spatial reach of the migration network against the intentions of planners. Instances of desertion in turn inscribed themselves on the space of the network, as when military authorities were forced to build barbed wire fences around the distribution camps in Asyut and Suhag.

SEA AND SAND

After moving from their villages to local district and provincial capital towns and on through to the major logistics cities, the men of the ELC had to cross vast expanses of sea and sand before arriving at their eventual worksites. When Murray began to plan his advance eastward across the Sinai Desert and into Palestine, he looked to the migratory patterns of the nomadic people who had been making the trek for generations. Of the three Bedouin caravan routes over the Sinai, Murray chose the northernmost one to follow, which runs in parallel to the Mediterranean through Rafah and al-ʻArish and intersects the Suez Canal at Qantara.[62] This is where he set out to build the railways and water pipelines that would convey troops and laborers from Egypt to Palestine.

One of Murray's first initiatives was to undertake a large-scale survey of the Suez Canal zone east of the British lines. This was carried out by the Topographical Section of the Intelligence Branch of the Anglo-Egyptian government in cooperation with the Royal Flying Corps.[63] The result was the standardization, printing, and issue of tactical maps of the Sinai Peninsula to the whole British army on the Sinai/Palestine front.[64] Murray described the process as "the attainment of the highest topographical accuracy in the survey of almost featureless desert."[65]

In the spring of 1916 the ESR began construction on the most advanced rail line, pushing twelve miles east of Qantara toward the Qatiya oasis.[66] The railheads on the east bank of the canal were connected to the ESR line on the west bank by swing bridges.[67] One hundred and fifty kilometers of standard-gauge track belonging to the ESR, which was initially supposed to be earmarked for renewals of ESR track in Egypt, was rerouted for this purpose.[68] The railway across the Sinai reached Rumani by May 15, 1916, but construction soon slowed as the summer heat made work unbearable.

Significant progress was also made in the construction of an intricate water supply that could reach the troops in advanced positions in the Sinai. Up to late 1915, the small garrisons and posts stationed on the east bank of the canal had been supplied with water by barges sent from Port Saʻid and Ismaʻiliyya.[69] These cities had access to the so-called "Sweetwater Canal," an aqueduct that had been built from 1859 to 1869 to convey fresh water from a nearby lake to the arid zone on the west bank of the canal. Beginning in 1916, the ELC constructed six filtering points near the Sweetwater Canal, where water could be purified and then carried by syphon-pipes across the bed of the Suez into concrete reservoirs on the east bank.[70] At Qantara, plans were made for an additional filter plant capable of pumping 500,000 gallons per day, two 250,000-gallon reservoirs, and two sets of 66-horsepower pumping engines to drive fresh water to Rumani.[71] By November of 1916, fresh water was flowing through the new pipeline into the reservoirs at Rumani.

ELC workers laid standard-gauge rail lines a distance of 215 kilometers (133 miles) from Qantara on the Suez Canal to Khan Yunus in Gaza. By autumn of 1917 the line was carrying 22,890 tons of supplies a week.[72] Moreover, because no known sources of fresh water existed in the area, the ELC laid 157 kilometers (97.5 miles) of water pipeline and constructed pumping infrastructure capable of moving 500,000 gallons a day.[73] Prior to the war, the overland route from Isma'iliyya to Jerusalem via Gaza by camel caravan took at least three weeks, and was not only highly expensive, but dangerous.[74] The railway that the ELC constructed linked to the old Ottoman line in Palestine and could take passengers from Qantara to Jerusalem in less than thirty-six hours.[75] This transformed the possibilities for the movement of people and supplies between Egypt and Palestine.

With the completion of this new supply line across the Sinai Peninsula, British officers serving with the ELC developed a new symbolic vocabulary through which to imagine the new space. Frequently, British officers referred to the trek from Egypt across the Sinai and into Palestine as going "up the line."[76] Furthermore, illustrating the conceptual similarity of sea and sand, the persistent metaphor of a "bridge" was used to describe Murray's line of supply. A British medical officer attached to the EEF wrote that the British army "crossed the Sinai Desert literally on a bridge of water and steel."[77] In the foreword to his published dispatches, Murray was praised for "bridging . . . the desert between Egypt and Palestine."[78] One article in the *ELC News* referred to the "Iron Track Across the Desert" and predicted that "the enormity of the task of laying a permanent line of communication across the inhospitable wastes of the Sinai . . . will become more and more recognized . . . as civilians and tourists of the future travel in comfort from Cairo to Jerusalem."[79] The article referred to the ELC as the "pioneers who made this journey possible."[80] The railroad and water pipeline transformed how people in the region conceptualized space and time, bringing Cairo and Jerusalem closer together.

This change found its corollary in the production of new representations of space. British military authorities under Murray made maps and logistical diagrams illustrating the lines of supply and communication across the Sinai and into Palestine. Figure 3.4 shows a diagram of the water supply in November 1916, sketched out by the Ordnance Survey and taken from the official history of the Sinai-Palestine campaign. Egyptian laborers are distributed at regular intervals, responsible for maintaining the lines of supply that enabled troops to continue their advance. These were places where Egyptians were *supposed* to be, and routes they were *supposed* to travel, and as such, this representation was meant to act as a guide for officers in leading their men. But the simple lines of these diagrams obliterated the actual daily routines of the laborers and soldiers, providing an illusion of smooth simplicity in the functioning of military logistics that did not correspond to reality.

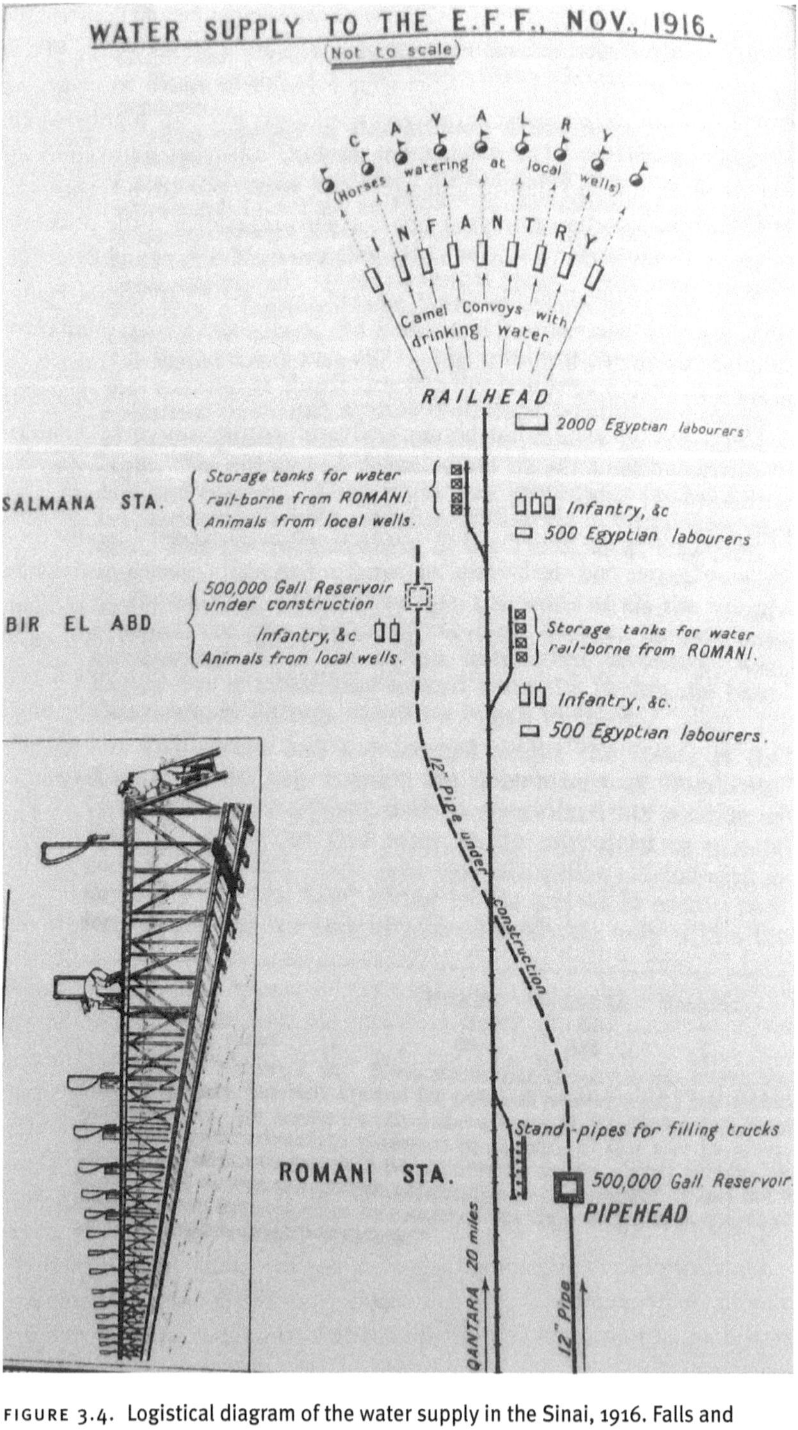

FIGURE 3.4. Logistical diagram of the water supply in the Sinai, 1916. Falls and Becke, *Military Operations, Part 1*, 271.

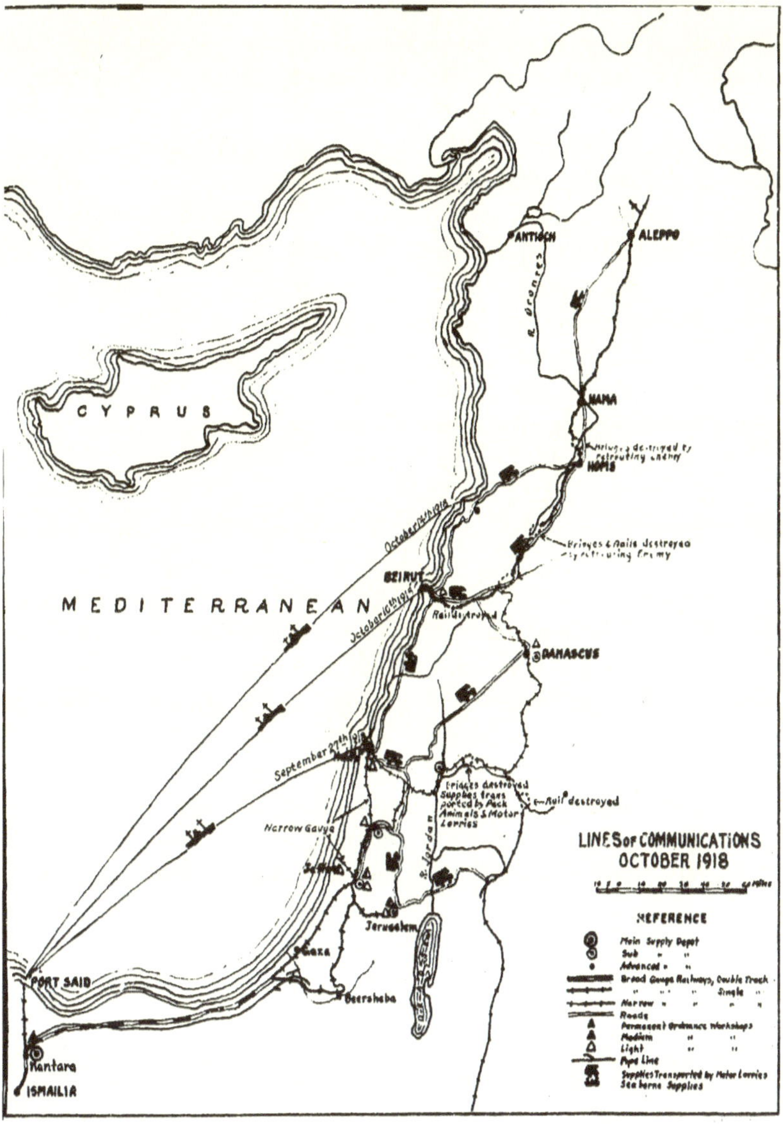

FIGURE 3.5. Lines of communications in Palestine and Syria, October 1918. Nicholas, "British Supply Operations."

As the size and complexity of the logistical network increased, the movement of supplies and materials within it became more difficult to control. Venables relates a story when he was sent up the line with eight hundred Egyptians under his command without any equipment "such as cooking utensils, water tanks, etc." He was told that it would be there waiting for them when they arrived, but upon arrival, it was nowhere to be found. So he stole equipment earmarked for another company at the supply dump and continued on his way past the railhead.[81] Accounts such as these provide evidence of the chaos inherent in the production of logistical space during the war. Equipment got ruined, but whatever was still serviceable could be reused, so officers had to inspect every single article before it was handed over to the new men. According to Venables, Egyptians could steal equipment during this process as well (see chapter 7).

Instead of crossing a "bridge of steel and water" over the Sinai Desert, ELC men heading to the Dardanelles, France, Italy, or Iraq would pile into steamships and make the journey by sea. The first companies to travel by boat arrived in Gallipoli in 1915. At the island of Mudros they constructed quays, docks, and landing stages for loading and unloading ships. They also erected buildings and made roads suitable for the passage of troops and heavy guns between the camps.[82] The ELC not only utilized the docks at Mudros but also constructed them, with the first laborers responsible for building the same port facilities that would accept later arrivals.

A fleet of steamships connected these developing port cities. Immediately after the outbreak of the war in 1914, the British issued a call to procure the ships they needed to move men and materials between the various theaters of the war. The colonial government worked with the Royal Admiralty and the Egyptian Board of Trade to requisition merchant ships for military purposes.[83] For example, the RAMC used Nile steamers borrowed from the Thomas Cook tourism company as hospital ships in Egypt.[84] Most ELC laborers heading to Europe traveled on His Majesty's Australian Transport (HMAT) ships, which the government of Australia had requisitioned from private merchants and refitted for military transport.[85] In 1917, British authorities suggested that twenty-seven hundred Egyptian laborers could be conveyed to Basra on HMAT *Aeneas* or *Shropshire*.[86]

For many of the workers and peasants of the ELC, the journey by steamer would have been their first trip across the sea, and one that likely produced a lot of anxiety. One British source wrote: "To cross the sea is a big undertaking for the Saidi," and reported that the British inspector of the Girga province had accompanied the first squad sent across the Mediterranean to Mudros in 1915.[87] Another article from *Al-Muqattam* relates a story of fifty-three laborers who went by boat to the Dardanelles: "all of them were from the interior of Egypt (i.e., the rural provinces) and had never ridden a boat before."[88] ʻAbd al-Hamid Muhammad Husayn recalls how one of his compatriots died during the return journey from the Dardanelles while on a steamship (*bārja*).[89]

The German U-Boat attacks against Allied shipping in the Mediterranean made the journey perilous. There were as many as twelve U-boats employed on merchant warfare per day at the height of the German campaign in 1917.[90] An article from *Al-Muqattam* claims that a German U-Boat sank one ship carrying fifty-three laborers, but the men were picked up by a Greek merchant ship and returned to Port Saʻid.[91] In addition to the threat of German U-Boats, British steamers were also at risk of other accidents on the high seas, including crashing into other ships.[92] In the event of such a disaster, Egyptian migrant laborers were expected to calmly evacuate into lifeboats and paddle to the nearest ship. Victims of shipwrecks who were not able to find their way onto a lifeboat were forced to swim for their lives or else drown in the ocean. While the *ELC News* records one story of an ELC man who survived a shipwreck by swimming "three-quarters of a mile in a very choppy sea," others were surely not so lucky.

CONCLUSION

ELC recruits began their journey from home to the front by marching to district or provincial capital towns. They slept on the floor in cramped jail cells until British medical inspectors could get around to seeing them. After waiting for weeks, those who passed inspection were sent by train to the nearest supply depot or distribution camp, usually located in one of the big cities like Cairo or Alexandria. There they were transformed into military laborers, outfitted, and organized into companies with officers, NCOs, and foremen in a hierarchy over them. They continued by train to major ports of embarkation: Alexandria for laborers traveling to Europe or the Dardanelles, Port Saʻid for those heading to Iraq or Syria, and Qantara for those who would make the trek up the line to Palestine.

These journeys were diagrammed by officials whose work is preserved in official histories, published memoirs, and public archives. Maps and logistical diagrams codified and guided British policy, yet the ways that the men of the ELC inhabited the spaces along their journey did not correspond simply to their representation. The construction of infrastructure never went exactly according to plan, coming up against the physical limits of people and the environment. Ships sank, sanitary inspectors were delayed, and supplies ran out as the distance the network had to cover grew larger and larger. Attempts to close the gap between spatial practice and representations of space structured the production of a logistical space that could move the men of the ELC from their home villages to the front. Henri Lefebvre's theory calls attention to these gaps, but rather than focusing on the production of *urban* space driven by the capitalist mode of production, ELC laborers traveling from the countryside of Egypt to theaters of battle in Europe and the Middle East traced the outlines of a *logistics space* designed to help prosecute the First World War.

Studying logistics spaces provides a promising direction for future research on the history of modern Egypt. First, it deconstructs the usual distinction between civilian and military spheres of activity that so often holds up in the literature. The railroads, docks, and steamships built up by the British to transport cotton to Lancashire textile mills were easily transformed into vehicles for moving bodies during the war, but these only existed in the first place because of a series of colonial wars in the nineteenth century. The rearticulation of infrastructures that had been built up over a generation of British occupation to transport the men of the ELC to war substantiates Deborah Cowen's claim that "the networked infrastructure and architecture of the supply chain animates both war and trade."[93]

Second, analyzing logistics spaces breaks down the conceptual division between city and countryside, showing the interpenetration and mutual dependence of these two supposedly separate spheres. Cities like Cairo and Alexandria are recast within the context of logistics spaces as stop-off points for travelers and materials headed to faraway lands. While scholars can and should produce critical geographies of Egyptian cities, excessive focus on the production of *urban* space ignores the fact that the demographic majority in Egypt lived in the countryside. Following the passage of ELC laborers traveling from home to the front brings this transitional, migratory aspect of city life to the foreground.

Finally, laborers made their own contributions to the production of logistics space. They appropriated the networked spaces along their journey for their own ends in efforts to subvert, resist, and escape the ELC. Spatial concentration could work in the laborers' favor, as when recruits staged their sit-in at the district lockup in Faraskur in the summer of 1918, or when others found ways to deliberately fail their medical examination by injecting a concoction into their bladder to fool the medical examiner. At other times, the logistical network provided opportunities for desertion and stealing supplies. ELC men participated in the production of this space just as much as the elites who drew up maps and diagrams. While authorities in the colonial government shepherded hundreds of thousands of young men on their journeys, these young men also worked to turn the unique circumstances of the war to their own advantage, and military authorities could never quite impose their will on the unwieldy migrant labor network. The next chapter traces the production of space outside of Egypt, in the theaters of battle where ELC laborers did their work. Just as in their journey to the front, Egyptians played an important role in constructing infrastructures during the war, and their work contributed significantly to the British occupation of Palestine.

CHAPTER 4

"IF THIS IS THE HOLY LAND, WHAT MUST HELL BE LIKE?"

WHEN ALLENBY CONQUERED JERUSALEM on December 11, 1917, he was faced with the problem of governing over a large civilian population. He declared martial law in the territory occupied by the EEF and established an administrative body staffed mainly by former employees of the Anglo-Egyptian government.[1] Ronald Storrs, who worked in the Ministry of Finance from 1904 to 1909, became, as he put it, "the first military governor of Jerusalem since Pontius Pilate."[2] The new administration combined political and military functions into a single body, making it answerable to both the Foreign Office and the War Office in London. In April 1918 it was reorganized into the Occupied Enemy Territory Administration (OETA).

No official map was produced along with Allenby's declaration of the OETA, but figure 4.1 shows a reconstruction of its borders as understood by the British government in their official history of the war. According to Suzanne Lalonde, the borders of OETA South, which consisted of Jerusalem and the neighboring Ottoman *sanjaks* of Nablus and Acre, relied on a 1918 map of Palestine published by the Survey Department of the Anglo-Egyptian Ministry of Public Works.[3] This fixed the southern boundary at a line between Rafah and Aqaba, and the eastern border at the river Jordan. With the San Remo Conference transferring sovereignty to the civilian authorities known as Mandates in April 1920, the OETA was a short-lived experiment. But OETA South was especially significant because it established Egypt's eastern border that still exists today.[4]

Conceptualizing a space that could come to be referred to as OETA could not have happened without a profound reworking of the circulation of people and things between Egypt and Palestine during the war. As this chapter will show, networks of roads, railroads, telegraphs, and camel convoys were established by the ELC as they made their way across the

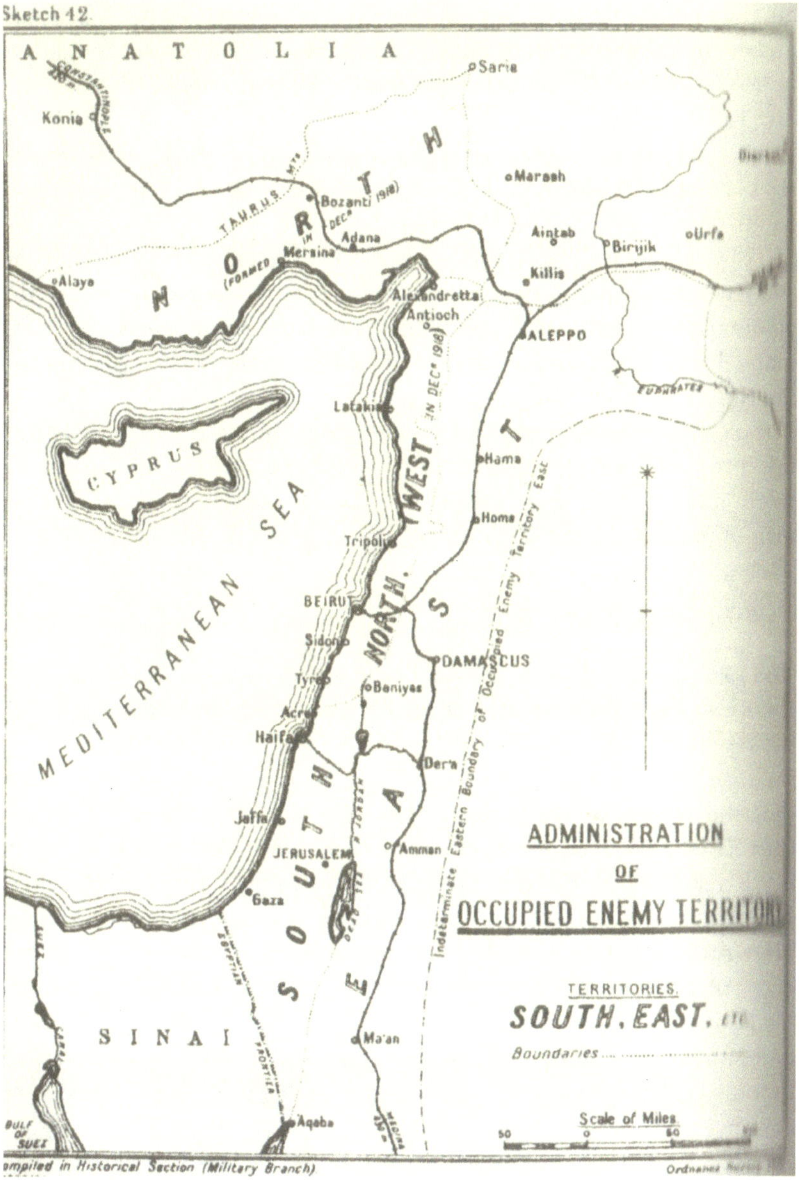

FIGURE 4.1. Occupied Enemy Territory Administration (OETA), 1917–1920. Falls and Becke, *Military Operations, Part 1*.

Sinai and into Palestine. Additionally, there were seaborne lines of supply and communication from Port Sa'id on the Suez Canal to Levantine ports at Dayr al-Balah (Deir el-Belah), Haifa, Beirut, and Tripoli. Coastal Syria and Palestine were, for a short time, integrated into an informal Middle Eastern empire ruled from Cairo for Great Britain, which reconstructed the contours of Mehmet 'Ali's Egyptian empire in the first half of the nineteenth century.[5]

However, as chapter 3 just demonstrated, maps are only part of the story when it comes to the production of space. While technocrats in the colonial government drew the smooth lines and graphic icons on these maps, hundreds of thousands of young men did the actual work of laying railroads and building the infrastructures that made OETA possible. It took years of day-in, day-out labor to transform the land of Palestine into proper terrain for the logistics of the British military. It was difficult work, and the many emergency situations that popped up meant that the men of the ELC were called upon to serve in a number of roles.

WORKING IN THE WAR

The ELC undertook virtually every type of labor imaginable for military logistics. They loaded and unloaded ships, transported supplies across the desert by camel, built roads, railroads, and water pipelines, and did innumerable other odd jobs. The most important and significant job they did was to lay the railroad across the Sinai Desert and into Palestine. They built it according to a task system that ideally meant a squad was given a single task to complete each day. In the letters of ELC officer Ernest Venables, it is clear that he envisioned this system in racial terms. He writes that the majority of his men were "drawn from the 'peasant class' of Egypt. . . . When, however, they become accustomed to receiving food every night without having to pay for it, and to being clothed and accommodated without any worry to their pay, they are naturally apt to become lazy, if not properly managed."[6] Working from these premises, he continued:

> The task system is an ideal one with Egyptians. . . . It sometimes happens that a new gang will think that the officer does not mean what he says when he apportions the work . . . as the sun sinks in the west and they see the other squads going away one by one, they are made to realize that they will not leave their work till it is finished. 7 o'clock, 8; the sun has set and the moon is up, and still the relentless British officer stands there, deaf to

> the beseechings of the Rais to "excuse them this time." The natives are working "like [n———]" now that their work is being made all the harder by the dim light.[7] (Epithet deleted)

While acknowledging the hard work that ELC men performed on their fields at home, Venables draws on the trope of the "lazy native" to assert that, under the regime of the ELC, these men could not be trusted. This, of course, ignored the difficult circumstances of being removed to a foreign land and, in many cases, forcibly conscripted, which would have disinclined the men to hard work. The task system was designed as a way to compel work, and Venables describes it here as an encounter between the white British officer and the racialized native. The officer based his own identity as a white British man on his ability to impose a system upon his men "relentlessly," and the laborers were referred to as "Egyptians" who were forced to work "like [n———]" (epithet deleted). Venables places this racial epithet in quotation marks, seemingly indicating that he had heard this term used to describe the ELC, or possibly used it himself. Chapter 5 will discuss these epithets and other racialized depictions of the ELC men in more depth.

For the ELC men working on the railroad between the Suez Canal and Gaza, there were two basic types of tasks: the preparation of a level track along the route that had been marked out by the military authorities, and the laying of rail lines themselves. Forward squads preparing the level formation stayed a considerable distance ahead of the rail-layers because the latter continued steadily as rails were supplied. Leveling the track sometimes required the construction of huge banks, with large mounds of dirt brought in from the surrounding area. Other times, workers would have to remove any obstacles that disrupted the way. In the morning, the *ra'īs* of each squad was given a task, with a fixed cubic capacity of the cut or fill necessary to level the track. This was supposedly calculated based on the number of cubic meters each laborer had to account for, with consideration given to the hardness of the soil, the distance it had to be carried, and the number of men in each squad.[8]

Most of the technology employed on the railroad was relatively simple. According to Venables, the chief instrument was referred to as a "fass," which was a kind of garden hoe that Egyptians were accustomed to using in agricultural work. Soil was loosened by the fass and scraped into large, round baskets, each holding about twenty kilograms (forty-four pounds).[9] These were lifted on the shoulders of carriers, who walked them over to a designated area and emptied them before returning once again. While the forward squads prepared a level formation, a smaller number of men worked in the rear carrying rails, cars, and tools, and laying the line as fast as it could be received from the supply depot. These rear squads were able to ride out on the train in the morning and return the same way each evening, while forward squads walked from the camps to their worksites and back.[10]

The distance from the main supply depot to the worksite increased as the railroad progressed, so companies had to periodically move their makeshift camps a few kilometers further up the line. According to Venables, a camp was merely "that spot on the sand where the tired Gyppies roll themselves up in their blankets and sleep," while "further up the sand hills, their officer does the same."[11] The default form of shelter was the bivouac or "bivvy," which consisted of "a hole excavated in the sand long and broad enough to accommodate two men lying side by side, a stick thrust into the ground at each end, with a piece of string tightly stretched between, and a blanket flung across the string in hip-roof fashion . . . a ground-sheet for a floor, and another blanket for bedding."[12] Whereas the ELC camps in France were fixed in the port cities on lines of supply that ran toward the relatively static trenches on the Western Front, ELC camps in Sinai-Palestine were "scattered in large and small parties, over hundreds of miles of desert . . . continually shifting their positions as the various works progressed or the troops advanced."[13]

With Ottoman forces now closer than ever, the urgency of the work increased, and the façade of order envisioned in the task system began to break down. Venables describes this in one of his letters home: "At first . . . we were able to work on a routine basis, but conditions have often demanded that routine must be discarded, and repeated effort made to meet the unending emergencies. It has often happened that we have been unable to assign a certain task to squad for the day, but have had to ensure that as much as possible was done in the working hours."[14] As certain "emergencies" arose, then, the basic premise of the one-task-per-day system was violated. According to Venables, emergencies had gotten so commonplace that they constituted the normal state of affairs. He responded by abandoning the task system and forcing the men under his command to work long hours.

Examples of such emergencies abound in the sources. During the Second Battle of Gaza in April 1917, Venables' men were "given the privilege of being called in as stretcher-bearers," carrying the wounded on stretchers to the nearest hospital.[15] In another incident, a train was running in the middle of the day and two trucks ran off the line, both of which had to be pushed back by "a big squad of Gyppies, with Johnny Turk watching from his grand stand."[16] According to the official history of the Sinai/Palestine campaign, British military authorities even used the ELC to create a diversion during the Third Battle of Gaza. On November 1, 1917, the day before the actual attack on the Ottoman troops began, ELC companies were marched down to the beach at Dayr al-Balah in full view of the Ottoman force to make the enemy officers believe a landing was taking place behind their right flank.[17] This put ELC laborers at risk of attack, but it would expose the Ottoman position in the process, which would give British forces an advantage. Egyptians were called on to perform all kinds of emergency tasks like this, which often put them at risk of injury or death.

Many men of the ELC were employed on docks, which presented their own unique dangers. Venables described the port at Qantara as "tangles of ropes, gangs, brooms, and wires, swaying derricks and swinging blocks." "The disconcerting habit these latter fiendish inventions had of swooping silently through the air, to the dire peril of a newcomer's skull," he wrote, "made me wish to be far away, even in the Wadi, where shells did not display this silent uncanny stealth."[18] Despite these conditions, ELC stevedores in Qantara were able to discharge an average weight of over thirty-one tons per hour, with the best day's work being 628 tons discharged over eighteen boats.[19] Meanwhile, ELC men in France were working on the lines of supply, well behind the Western Front, but they were nevertheless subject to enemy attack. At Dunkirk, the Seventy-Second, Seventy-Fifth, and Seventy-Sixth companies were badly bombed by a German air raid, with "several" Egyptians killed and wounded.[20] According to the official report, these laborers were "in a state of panic," so they were moved in early June 1917, with two companies going to Rouen and the third to Havre.[21]

For the hundreds of thousands who worked in forward positions laying railroads and water pipeline in the Sinai Desert and Palestine, their work necessarily put them close to the front lines and in danger of enemy fire. Venables describes how his men first came in sight of enemy troops at Gaza on October 2, 1917. In the morning, a German biplane flew overhead, and the Egyptians "sat gaping skyward."[22] Nothing immediately happened, and so work resumed, but soon after the men heard the sound of artillery shells exploding in the distance, saw a cloud of smoke and dust, and watched as two scared mules galloped past them eastward. As the shelling grew closer and more frequent, Venables walked the line, steadying his men and signaling for them to lay down in the holes they had been digging. At first, the men stayed low, but when one shell landed and exploded in the midst of a squad, they jumped up and ran away. Soon the whole company followed their example, running "rearward, helter-skelter, anywhere away from that whining and banging."[23]

In this particular incident, only a few men were wounded by shrapnel, and they were "at once bandaged by the Royal Engineers' men with their emergency field dressings and taken to the nearest first-aid post."[24] Meanwhile, Venables busied himself with the task of rounding up "fugitives."[25] Riding his horse in a wide semicircle, he spent most of his day cutting off laborers as they made their way southward. One hundred and fifty-three men made it the full seven miles back to the base depot at Dayr al-Balah, where they were arrested and sent back to their company at the front.[26] Although his company suffered no casualties in this incident, Venables grimly recalls his efforts to "count the prostrate figures of other ELC companies' men who had been killed as they waited squatting by the railway track on the main camp, literally and dreadfully without knowing what had hit them, still enfolded in the blanket which had become their shroud."[27]

Unlike the relatively flat desert of the northern Sinai where the railroad was built, the roads constructed by the ELC in Palestine wound their way through hilly terrain. Venables was employed on a section of the road connecting Jaffa and Jerusalem and had responsibility for nearby quarrying where he supervised the locating, choice, boring, blasting, and dispatch of thousands of tons of stone. The irregular nature of the ground made it particularly difficult to transport the stones from quarry to worksite. Venables described the precarious way they were moved:

> The sight as a whole is an interesting one, the hillside being dotted with khaki figures, loosening with pick and bat large and small boulders, which they carry, or roll, down the road construction. At first a newcomer might be scared for the safety of their life and limb on this work. With a cry of 'Hoa!' they will send a rock weighing several tons hurtling down the hill side. A man standing in its track gazes up at it, and just as one expects to see him crushed to pulp, he calmly steps out the way without hurrying himself.[28]

Roadwork put ELC laborers at considerable risk. Falling boulders could cause serious injury as they were rolling down the hillside. Although Venables assures his reader that the men were adept at keeping themselves safe, he recognizes the possibility that one of them could easily be "crushed to a pulp" working in this fashion.

Once the stones made their way to the worksite, the first task was to pull up the old Ottoman roads and lay down the heavy understones to make a firm foundation for the new roads. Other squads were responsible for breaking up stones into gravel for surfacing. This was then sprinkled atop the foundation and smoothed over by a fifteen-ton steamroller, which was driven by one of the ELC men. The work had to happen without interrupting traffic, and according to Venables, this aspect also made it dangerous:

> The improved road was used as a speed track for lighter cars, which often came tearing along regardless of any warning sign post of the presence of repairing squads on the road. One of these swept two of my Gyppies off the map one day, landing one under the steamroller. His comrades at once howled a funeral dirge, but I managed to disappoint them by dragging him clear before the slow relentless wheel reached him . . . neither was seriously hurt.[29]

Although constructing roads could put the men at risk from falling boulders, vehicle traffic, and the heavy machinery they used, Venables seems to mock the dangers, sarcastically noting that he "managed to disappoint" the men by saving one of their comrades' lives. But his comment should be taken as evidence of the justified anxiety felt by many under his command. For a brief moment, they feared one of their own had been crushed to death by the steamroller.

BATTLING THE CLIMATE AND SICKNESS

While they were facing down Ottoman artillery shells, another major difficulty the men encountered was the weather and the sickness it brought with it. While working in the Sinai, they had to contend with the insufferable climate of the desert. One medical officer summed it up: "Heat, dust, vermin, blinding suffocating sandstorms, the terrible 'khamasin'—which is a red-hot hurricane seemingly straight from the throttle of Hades—want of water and everything else needed to support life, the miles of daily march over an eternal sameness of shifting sand."[30] The *khamāsīn* sandstorms, a climatic phenomenon familiar to anyone who has ever spent considerable time in Egypt, "drive against our faces like a blast from a furnace-throttle . . . volleying over the hills with a tough as of razor-edged icicles [that] hid the far end of the camp in their solid murk and filled our eyes and throats, our meat and drink, with grinding grit."[31]

While propaganda outlets like *Al-Muqattam* wrote that the men in

France "wear clothing that is appropriate to the countries in which they work,"[32] according to Venables, this was not the case in Palestine. In the Sinai Desert, ELC laborers had grown accustomed to dressing in "sun-helmets, shirts, and thin drill shorts."[33] After a long day's work, many of them simply rolled out their blankets and slept under the stars. When winter hit in Palestine, Venables' company was surprised by a "rain of a torrential heaviness not imagined at home."[34] The men awoke to find their blankets and the ground beneath them soaked through. They were "pretty well drenched, in which state they worked all next day, hoping hour by hour that the rain would cease and the welcome sun would shine." But winter in Palestine consisted of a series of torrential rainstorms, lasting without cessation for two, three, or even four days.[35]

According to Venables, at the first outset of rain, the list of those claiming sickness became huge, with as many as one out of every five men falling out to see the doctor. He sent them all to what he called the "details camp" nearby. An Egyptian medical officer visited this camp every morning in a motorized ambulance from the Egyptian hospital. According to Venables, "On wet mornings, this gentleman did not arrive, so that the sick men had to walk in the rain and mud, to the Egyptian Hospital itself, two kilometers away, and return, if not detained." Later on, after his company had moved four kilometers up the road, Venables wrote that he "applied in vain for medical visit, and our sick had to go eight or twelve kilometers in double the journey."[36]

Winter rains made work impossible. Floods of water would wash away the earthen banks the men had constructed, carrying rails and bridges with them. The dirt roads used by motor transport in dry weather became impassable. Usually, lorries carried supplies and ammunition across these roads, but in the rain they would get stuck, and, according to Venables, "everybody, including Egyptians, would have to work to get them back on the road."[37] The difficulty of marching to and from the work sites while carrying the day's supplies was also compounded by the rain. In a letter home, Venables described how "slowly the company struggled on, through wadis that were now racing floods, along a track which was nothing more than a mass of churned mud."[38]

Long marches in the rain hit the men in Palestine the hardest. In one letter home, Venables tells the story of a company of six hundred men who arrived fresh from Egypt at the old Palestinian village of Dayr Sunayd with orders to march up the road to Latrun. The men started their trek carrying their packs with them, but soon the rain caught them, and they tried to ditch their equipment—including the tents and blankets that were supposed to serve as their shelter when they arrived. The road around them had become a quagmire, and their heavy packs were burdens weighing them down. "As they became wet through," Venables wrote, "they gave in at once, and wanted to lie down by the road and die." Stragglers were beaten by their officers, who were, according to Venables, "using force that could not . . . be characterized as brutal, for it was to save the men against themselves." "Some men dropped out," he wrote, "and lay by the side of the road—'Amut ya effendum, Amut' (I am dying, sir, I am dying)."[39]

Such scenes were witnessed more than once. Venables describes his own men after getting caught in their first storm as "crouching in the mud, moaning helplessly, 'Ahsan Amut' (it is better to die.)"[40] On January 13, 1918, the winter weather took the life of one of the men under Venables' command. That night, after work, two laborers were discovered lying by the side of the road after a long march through a rainstorm. Venables and one of the NCOs in his company took the men on their shoulders and carried them back to camp. When they arrived, they were "given stimulants . . . and wrapped in blankets and placed by the fire." One of the men recovered, but the second passed away from exposure. He had straggled on the march back from the worksite and was left to die on the side of the road.[41]

Venables characterizes incidents like this as "Oriental fatalism," shifting the blame to the men themselves and their supposed racial or cultural characteristics, rather than the British commanders who put them there in the first place. But he did admit that the men had been poorly supplied, writing, "By Christmas, Capt. H's efforts had been successful, and we received tents." Proper shelter, it seems, was not initially forthcoming. Confronted by floods and mudslides that would be unimaginable in the dry climate of Egypt, worked to exhaustion, and whipped by overseers shouting orders in an incomprehensible language, a few of the men may have found some small solace in surrendering to the elements. And if, stranded on a muddy road in Palestine, these desperate individuals chose to fall back on their belief that their immortal soul would live on after they were gone and simply let themselves die, this should not be impossible for us to understand.[42]

As winter in Palestine wore on, the men gradually adapted to deal with the rain. They dug deep drainage ditches around the outside of their tents to prevent flooding of the ground underneath. At first, some took blankets and spare clothing out with them during the day, but they soon learned to keep them inside the tent where it was dry. They also learned not to adjust the ropes during a storm, and how to position the tent's doors so that they did not face the prevailing winds. The stone enclosures and abandoned homes that dotted the landscape were used as shelter for cookhouses, stables, and drying sheds. The rain got so bad that Venables soon decided, "flatly against official regulation," to order his foremen to collect firewood and make fires in their tents so they could get warm and dry. "If any tents are burned down," he wrote, "I shall have to spin some fearful fairytales. Men's health, however, is more important than regulations, and luck has been on my side."[43] One evening, "scarcely an hour after the men had come in, wringing wet," Venables saw a squad that was relaxing, still dressed in their work clothes from earlier. He immediately began chiding the *ra'īs* of the squad for neglecting his men's health, when the man replied, "'Kull wahid nashif y'effendum' . . . (Everyone is dry, Sir)." It was true, too, though Venables could never figure out how the men managed to dry themselves without changing their clothes.[44]

The weather was a challenge in other theaters of battle as well. On November 26, 1915, there was a severe storm in Gallipoli, followed by a blizzard that left three inches of ice on the ground.[45] According to the official Australian history of the campaign, "The Egyptians could not work in the cold."[46] One officer working in the Dardanelles put it more poetically, writing, "the wild, bitter climate of the Aegean Isles proved too much for the sun-nurtured Egyptians, and a large amount of sickness prevailed in their ranks."[47] Likewise, in Iraq, Egyptians "declined to work at all in wet weather."[48] The British War Office came to a similar conclusion regarding Egyptian laborers in France: "There is no doubt that Egyptians are not able to stand the cold climate of North France, and should not remain after the end of October. They are quite useless in very cold weather."[49]

ELC laborers were exposed to the war, the weather, and the consequent sickness and death of their colleagues. Nevertheless, they persisted on a daily basis and continued with their work. Perhaps the most difficult thing for many to face was the deaths of their colleagues going unaccounted for and unacknowledged. Because of the poor record-keeping practices of the British Empire with respect to the men of the ELC, it is hard to say just how many men died in these dangerous conditions. Official statistics were only kept for deaths that occurred in hospital, and medical officials estimated that "casualties which occur after discharge from Hospital must be considerable, considering that they are discharged from Hospital unfit, to convalescence in their villages."[50] Ultimately, it is unclear if such convalescence even took place, as arranging travel back home would have been an arduous task for an injured or sick man. What is clear is that thousands of Egyptians died as a result of their service, and thousands more were injured in the war. The grave circumstances of the Palestine front were aptly summed up by one British officer who passed by Venables "wringing wet" during the rainy winter months and sardonically enquired, "If this is the Holy Land, what must Hell be like?"[51]

PRAISE AND PAY

The EEF was largely dependent on the progress of railway and water pipeline to advance across the Sinai Desert—so much so that the official history of the campaign concluded, "the speed of the advance had been and was to remain dependent on that of the railway and, to a lesser degree, the pipeline."[52] But although this passage acknowledges the importance of the infrastructure, it neglects to mention the men who did the actual work of building it.

Though largely forgotten in the official history, the men of the ELC won the praises of their contemporaries. In his dispatches to London, Murray wrote, "Egyptian Labour Corps men are . . . working by day and night. The work is well organized. It is interesting to watch a train steam into a depot, to see the men spring on the trucks, and in the shortest possible time the empty train steams out again."[53] He made particular note of Egyptians' willingness to work in dangerous conditions, writing, "The past six months have been very trying, but their behavior under fire in all cases has been exemplary. Several instances have occurred of natives showing particular devotion to duty."[54] He even compared the performance of Egyptians favorably to the British, writing, "Although they were considerably bombed, the work proceeded without delay. Taking into consideration the climate of Romani in July, it is doubtful if British troops could have done the work as well in the time required."[55] When Murray was replaced by Allenby in late 1917 and the EEF conquered Jerusalem, the new commander recognized the ELC in his "Special Order of the Day." He wrote that the ELC's work has been "of the greatest value in contributing to the rapid advance of the troops and in overcoming difficulties of communications."[56] Likewise, in the pages of the *ELC News*, one officer wrote, "It is beyond contradiction that the Palestine campaign could not have achieved its glorious consummation without the ELC."[57]

ELC men were also praised on the docks of Europe. According to the official War Office report, the ELC "has been most satisfactory, and at places like Boulogne and Marseilles, high praise has been freely bestowed on them for their work."[58] Malcolm Coutts, official adviser for Egyptian labor in France, wrote of the ELC, "At rough dock work these men are hard to beat, and at handling certain classes of goods, such as case goods and heavy bales, hay, straw, etc. In my opinion, they are far superior to any other class of native or other labor. Given proper supervision and task work, I would back the ELC against any native labour in the world."[59] At Marseilles in particular, all coaling work was done by the ELC. Their speed in carrying out this work was "proverbial," and they "gave the greatest satisfaction to all the Naval Authorities concerned."[60] "At unloading a ship of barge and loading trains," Coutts wrote, "they have few rivals. There is no doubt that these men have more than justified their being brought to this country."[61] Likewise in Taranto, Italy, almost all work at the port was done by the ELC, including "coaling, loading and unloading of ships, trains, etc., building quays, making railways, and erecting huts. Skilled as well as unskilled work was carried out by them, and all reports speak most highly of the work performed by the ELC."[62]

The press in Egypt, under heavy British censorship, hoped that tales of the men's valor and adventures abroad could serve as an antidote to widespread anxiety over their fate. Once again, the newspaper *Al-Muqattam* was most active in propagating these messages. One article about the CTC reported a number of tales of heroism from Egyptian laborers, including the *ra'īs* Nur al-Din Sayyid, who carried ammunition 150 yards to soldiers in the trenches under fire in Palestine, and the camel driver Ahmed Yunis, who continued his work under fire despite a serious headwound that would ultimately require the medical removal of one of his eyes.[63] Another article about the ELC mentioned a report of an unnamed Egyptian laborer who saved the life of a British soldier who had gone out for a swim and was caught in a current that pulled him far from shore.[64] In the popular daily newspaper *Al-Ahram*, as well, a report was issued about ELC laborers in France, noting that they were welcomed with a "party," and that all who attended were surprised at their "greatness."[65]

The Egyptian press was especially focused on the awards that some Egyptians received for their service. Two articles in *Al-Muqattam* published on consecutive days in October 1917 list the names of five men who the Sultan of Egypt had granted the "silver order of merit," and twenty-six who had been granted the "bronze order of merit."[66] All the men listed in these articles worked for the CTC except for three ELC laborers who had worked as stretcher-bearers in Dayr al-Balah, Palestine. *Al-Watan* published a similar article listing the men in the Egyptian army who had received awards from "the British government" based on their service in the Suez Canal zone and Sudan.[67] Murray's dispatches seem to corroborate that at least some Egyptian laborers were recognized for awards. He writes, "Several instances have occurred of natives showing particular devotion to duty, and these have been rewarded under G.R.O. no. 2491, dated 23 May 1917."[68]

Venables describes a situation where he was asked to send a report to the Headquarters of the EEF recommending eight men who were deemed worthy to receive official recognition. In doing so, he wrote, "My chief difficulty is to choose the eight who have been most useful, and who have shown most coolness under fire . . . there are scores who should wear a medal for what they have done."[69] In their work on the roads of Palestine, even the oft-critical Venables found much to admire. He wrote, "Gyppies had to be taught the gentle art of laying these stones so that they would remain as a firm and even foundation. In time they became quite expert at the work, and took a keen interest in it . . . and were therefore reserved for this more or less skilled work."[70] Venables refers to their work here as "art" and calls the laborers "quite expert." Later on, he referred to the man who was charged with driving the steamroller over these roads as "marvelous," and wrote, "He was a really capable man who had a good idea of using a roller, and of keeping his machine in order."[71] Venables also praised the ELC when they worked as stretcher-bearers, writing that it was "a duty which they carried out with remarkable skill and sympathy: at once learning the correct step, carrying the wounded most carefully and showing concern for their safety and comfort."[72]

Thomas Brookes Minshall also found much to praise about the work of the ELC. He wrote, "I've watched long lines of these 'elsies' (as the Australians have nicknamed them) hurrying to and fro with baskets or dirt on their shoulders for the foundation of the line, and it is marvelous the speed they build the line."[73] He wrote of their courage under fire: "During the attacks you will see [the Egyptians] moving forward with all many of loads for the line, and, I fully believe they realize the more energy they put into their work the better chance the men in the trenches have of securing victory."[74] Of the CTC drivers who carried the wounded in battle, he wrote that they did "valuable work." "Regardless of the danger they carried the wounded many times through heavy shell fire to the dressing stations in the rear, and carried on their work of mercy the whole day long and right through the following night."[75] As we will see in chapter 5, white officers in Palestine like Venables and Minshall discriminated against Egyptians as a group, but they often could not help but praise the work of the individuals they saw in action.

The men of the ELC did not just want kind words and fancy awards from the British authorities—they expected to be paid. From the beginning of the war, Egyptians were recruited on temporary contracts and paid a base rate of five piastres per day for ELC laborers and six piastres per day for CTC drivers. In France, the six-month period of the contract dated from a company's arrival in country,[76] while in the Sinai/Palestine theater, the period of service began "from assumption of duty with [one's] unit."[77] The pay may have increased at one point in France, because by November 1919, Coutts listed the daily pay rate for an "unskilled laborer" at eight piastres per day.[78] But in the Sinai/Palestine campaign, which employed more Egyptians and was closer to home, basic pay rates did not climb this high because, according to British officials, "it would not be right to pay [ELC laborers] on a scale similar to that of men in the British Army—which would be the case if their pay were raised to eight or nine piastres."[79] Why it would not be right is left unsaid, but Egyptians working alongside mostly white troops of the EEF were paid less for their labor in the same field of battle.

It was much easier to sign a contract than to actually deliver money to laborers. Egyptians working for the EEF in the Sinai-Palestine campaign were supposed to be given an advance on their salaries.[80] When they made their way up the line, the men could draw further advances at scheduled times. According to Venables, the process involved requesting an advance from the officer, who would prepare a list of the names and identification numbers of those looking for an advance, and then travel to the base in Ramallah to get the money and bring it back. Some of the men declined these advances, living off the spartan rations they were provided and then drawing the whole of the six-hundred-piastre balance due to them upon their return to Qantara. But according to Venables, most of the men in his company took their advances, and "the bulk of the money . . . soon falls into the hands of certain crafty individuals, usually the Raises who, by loans and other transactions, get a grip on the more ignorant, and extort every possible piastre out of them."[81]

According to Coutts, in France "no arrangements were made in Egypt to enable the men to allot pay to their families."[82] French authorities refused to allow the ELC to use the *Mandat Internationale*, and it was only the men from Port Sa'id or Alexandria who could make use of post orders to the French postal officers in their hometowns. As time went on, Coutts noted that "the men were enabled to make certain remittances which proved a great help to them."[83] However, as chapter 8 documents in greater detail, it seems that at least some of the families of the men who died while serving never received the compensation which was due to them by law. According to Coutts, there was a sliding scale of compensation for the families of the men who died in France, and all cases were to be dealt with by the branch headquarters in Rouen.[84] But due to poor record keeping, it must have been difficult for some families to get their just due.

CONCLUSION

The men of the ELC transformed the built environment of Palestine during the war, enabling the conceptualization of a new space known as OETA. Working according to the task system, squads of men were given a set amount of daily work, and once their task was completed, they were supposed to be finished. In this way, labor could theoretically be planned down to the smallest detail. However, as the railroads and water pipeline being laid by the ELC stretched farther and farther into the Sinai Desert and Palestine, aspects of this task system began to break down. Companies approached enemy fire and soon found themselves overwhelmed with emergencies that required the suspension of the task system and a whole new set of duties they had to undertake. These emergencies became so commonplace that they constituted the normal state of affairs as the men crossed the Sinai into Palestine in late 1917. The ELC was even used to create a diversion during the Third Battle of Gaza, exposing themselves to enemy fire, but giving the EEF a tactical advantage in the process. They rescued cars from the mud, pushed artillery guns back on track, and carried the wounded to the nearest hospital in the midst of the battle.

Working in these conditions put the men in danger, and many sacrificed their bodies and their lives. They were at risk from enemy artillery, accidents caused by munitions, and the difficult weather they had to endure. Many suffered debilitating injury or got sick. British authorities not only exposed them to grave danger, but also had poor record-keeping practices that made it hard to track the men who suffered death and injury. Families waiting at home were kept in the dark about the fates of their loved ones, and some never received the compensation envisioned for them by law.

At the most basic level, this chapter is about acknowledging the contributions and sacrifices that the men of the ELC made as part of the war effort. They worked as stevedores on the docks in Europe, camel drivers in the desert, and policemen in Baghdad. Perhaps their most significant contribution was building an "Iron Track across the Desert," which consisted of more than 130 miles (215 kilometers) of railroad and water pipeline that enabled the transportation of people and supplies between Egypt and Palestine across the Sinai Desert. They did all this in a little over a year, setting the foundations for the British invasion of Palestine during the war, as well as for British occupation of Palestine during the Mandate period.

CHAPTER 5

RACE AND SPACE IN ELC CAMPS

ʻABD AL-HAMID MUHAMMAD HUSAYN worked as part of the war effort from the outbreak of hostilities in Egypt until the end of the war. Born in 1893 in Giza, he learned to read and write Arabic at a one-room schoolhouse called a *kuttāb*. His father divorced his mother when he was a young boy, and poverty forced him to begin working as a manual laborer at the age of eleven. About a decade later, when the British army started recruiting Egyptians for the invasion of Gallipoli, Husayn "found himself joining soldiery" in the ELC.[1] He served tours of duty in the Dardanelles and Sudan, and went on to Palestine in 1917, where he reenlisted multiple times.

Like Husayn, Ernest Kendrick Venables served in the war from the time it first broke out in his country. Venables was the son of a government clerk, born in 1890 in the town of Birkenhead, Cheshire County. He worked as a schoolmaster but enrolled in the British army in 1914. He had a penchant for writing down his observations in diaries and frequent letters home. First assigned to a field ambulance unit of the RAMC, he served for one year in Alexandria before being granted reassignment to work with the ELC. In April 1917 he moved to the supply depot at Ruda Island outside of Cairo for training, and then up the line to Palestine.[2]

By the end of 1917, both Venables and Husayn were serving in the Palestine theater. It is hard to know if their paths ever crossed, but during the war, Palestine was full of hundreds of British officers like Venables and hundreds of thousands of Egyptian laborers like Husayn, all working together in relationships governed by unequal power dynamics and living side by side in military encampments.

A cursory glance at the writings of Venables and Husayn—who have left behind some of the best firsthand accounts of ELC life in English and

FIGURE 5.1. Artist's rendering of 'Abd al-Hamid Muhammad Husayn, 1968. "Safahat min Mudhakkirat Shaykh Majhul," *Ruz al-Yusuf*, March 1968.

Arabic, respectively—provides a sense of the imbalance between the two groups they represented. Venables' writings consist of hundreds of pages preserved in the archives of the Imperial War Museum in London. Husayn's account, meanwhile, is a mere three-and-a-half pages, published fifty years after the war in the popular Egyptian magazine *Ruz al-Yusuf*. Yet this paltry source, refracted through the prism of the 1967 war be-

FIGURE 5.2. Egyptian Labor Corps officer Ernest Kendrick Venables, 1917. British National Archives, War Office 339/108423.

tween Egypt and Israel, constitutes the only firsthand account written by a man of the ELC that I have been able to find. The majority of ELC men did not write their memoirs. The lack of public education and widespread literacy in Egypt at the time was surely one reason for this. Historians of British imperialism have shown the lack of writings by ELC workers can at least partially be attributed to the policies of the occupation, which slashed funding for public education while prioritizing balanced budgets.[3]

British imperialism, then, paradoxically brought people like Venables and Husayn together while also inventing a variety of techniques to keep them apart. Examining this paradox, this chapter focuses on ELC camps during the war and traces the relationship between British officers and the men of the ELC at the intersection of race and space.[4] Racist ideology influenced representations of ELC men in the writings of British journalists and officers who lived at the camps. However, one of the major arguments of this book is that studying such representations alone is insufficient to understand how ideas about race structured everyday life. It is not the ideology of colonial racism, but rather how such ideas were manifested in a variety of spatial practices that makes race viscerally real for racialized Others. Ideas about race served to homogenize the experiences of groups of people, a process that was mediated by their influence on the production of space. Over time, contingent identities began to appear as natural or primordial, and, as we will see in chapters 7 and 9, collective identities centered on the ELC ultimately became the basis for political action during the war.

This chapter documents the first part of this process as it unfolded in ELC camps in Europe and the Middle East. It starts by examining how colonial racism influenced representations of ELC laborers in the writings of English-speaking soldiers, officers, and journalists. These representations functioned like a palimpsest that overlaid a veneer of popular science and derogatory, dehumanizing epithets on top of older traditions, including the racialization of Muslims, Orientalism, and the infantilization of Indigenous people. While studying these representations is in itself illuminating, this chapter goes on to discuss how ideas about the racial identity of Egyptians were inscribed in the space of the camps. British officers segregated the men of the ELC, gave them substandard equipment, and were quick to punish them with physical violence. All of these policies were influenced by British ideas about the "peculiar racial characteristics" of Egyptians, and they worked together to create a common experience among the men who served in the war.

RACE AND PERCEPTIONS OF THE ELC

From the beginning, ideas about race underwrote British efforts to recruit the ELC. In mid-1916, as the British army in France ramped up for the Somme Offensive, men like the prime minister, H. H. Asquith, and the foreign secretary, Arthur Balfour, began discussing whether to import "coloured labour" to meet the shortfall in demand for manpower.[5] Not all British politicians were entirely in agreement on how these workers should be treated, and the memory of "Balfour's Blunder"—a scandal that involved the importation of nearly fifty thousand Chinese laborers to work in South African mines in 1903–1904—was kept alive by liberal politicians who demanded respect, fair play, and justice in dealing with the "Black and Yellow subject races."[6] But even this liberal rhetoric showed an unwillingness to critique the logic of colonial racism. Among the classes of professional civil servants, this attitude was, as Nicholas Griffin put it, "primarily a socially inherited one, molded by a tradition of leadership and cultural superiority inculcated at the public-school level, and confirmed in the cloisters of Oxford and Cambridge."[7]

The attitude at the highest levels of the British Empire was shared by petty officers, soldiers, and journalists living alongside the men of the ELC. Depictions of admired superiors show that some middling officers understood proper authority to be associated with whiteness. Venables expressed an admiration for a certain Captain H.:

> Slacking and other offenses meet with no mercy from him. At the same time, he is exceedingly careful of Gyppies well-being and will go to any lengths to ensure the best for his men...this fact has made him an idol with the Gyppies, among whom he is known as the 'Big Mudir' . . . *he is a "white man" all through.*[8] (Emphasis mine)

Venables' admiration for Captain H. shows how, in British officers' conceptions of white identity, violence and intimidation—referred to obliquely here by Venables as "no mercy"—were linked to paternalistic attitudes that posited British officers "knew what was best" for the Egyptians under their command.

Paternalistic notions of white identity were constructed alongside and in conversation with the racialization of Egyptians. To some extent, representations of the racial identity of ELC men built on the long-established tropes about "Orientals" and the racialization of Muslims that were discussed in chapter 1. In his first letter home, Venables noted that the men under his command were "Mohammedans, and therefore ignorant fanatics, fatalistic in the extreme."[9] At other times, he lamented the "Oriental inclinations" of the laborers under his command.[10] When the men seemed resigned to death, he chalked up their approach to "Oriental fatalism," writing, "The silly wretches would creep away, to a wadi or other secluded spot, and lie there."[11] The charge of Oriental fatalism allowed him to displace the blame for the deaths he witnessed away from the British authorities who put the men in such difficult circumstances. Instead, any difficulties were chalked up to the essential and ahistorical differences between "Orientals" and white Englishmen.

Other British officers drew on Orientalism in their representations of the ELC. For example, in an article in the *ELC News*, the author writes, "The gangs that laid yesterday's kilo of railway track are the lineal descendants of the gangs that raised the pyramids. The rais whom we disrated at morning orderly room was a blood brother, centuries removed, to Pharaoh's rais whom Moses felled to earth."[12] Similarly, an article from the *Times* of London begins, "Five thousand six hundred and fifty years ago an urgent call went out through Egypt for labour . . . to-day the lineal descendants of these half-slaves abandon their homes of their own free will and go labour in a better cause."[13] Despite having different authors, both of these reports make almost identical comparisons between the men of the ELC and workers in the Pharaonic age. As Ron Fuchs has suggested, the unique setting of the "Holy Land" may have contributed to the dissemination of biblical metaphors like references to the Pharaohs in the minds of the men of the EEF in Palestine.[14]

Representations of ELC laborers as "lineal descendants" of ancient Egyptians shows how Pharaonism was an aspect of the racialization of Egyptians in the late imperial imaginary. As Omnia El Shakry has documented, this can be seen in the experiments of Onofrio Abbate, an Italian physician who worked in the service of the Egyptian royal court from 1845 to 1915. Building on conceptual links between ancient Egyptians and the *fallāḥīn* in particular, Abbate compared the remains of skeletons from the ancient necropolis of Kawamil and modern cadavers at the Qasr al-'Ayni hospital in Cairo.[15] El Shakry calls these experiments "a unique glimpse into the transition from a textually based Orientalism concerned with collection and commentary to an experimental and clinical science of native difference."[16] Late imperial culture, then, worked to provide a veneer of scientific legitimacy to centuries-old claims about the static and unchanging nature of "Orientals" by finding an empirical way to make the same point.

At times, Venables posited a whole series of racial distinctions between the men under his command. In his unpublished manuscript, he writes:

> The best of them were from the Sa-eed, in the far south. . . . At first there were Nubians and Berberins from still further south, but these disappeared, although they were preferred as individual servants, as in the civilian life of Cairo and elsewhere. . . . The few Sudanese here and there were hefty, dependable fellows, worthy of the saying: "the blacker the better," but they did not always get on well with Egyptian comrades, whom they privately looked down on as inferiors . . . our peasant johnnies were good workers if well supervised, though endowed with a large share of that hu-

> man propensity expressed by the Italian proverb "It's nice to do nothing"—with its apocryphal corollary: "then have a rest."[17]

This passage is remarkable for the intricate racial mosaic it constructs. Among Egyptians, Venables seemingly distinguishes between the majority group of *fallāḥīn*, presumably from the populous northern Delta regions, and Upper Egyptians from the "Sa-eed" (*ṣa'īd*). But both of these groups together are juxtaposed to other Black Africans, including Nubians, "Berberins," and Sudanese. Despite the fact that slavery had officially been abolished for forty years by the time he was writing, Venables recognized that Egyptians "in civilian life of Cairo and elsewhere" were accustomed to employing Africans as slaves. But he inverts the terms of Egypt's supposed "Islamic Civilizing Mission" by saying that it was the Sudanese who privately looked down on Egyptians as "inferiors."[18] He sums up this inversion by repeating a saying with which he apparently agrees—when it comes to workers—"the blacker the better." He distinguishes between Egyptians and Africans, but only to rate the former lower on what he elsewhere refers to as the "scale of civilization."

Egyptian reporters covering the ELC also seemed to make distinctions between Sudanese and Egyptian men in the organization. An article from the newspaper *Al-Ahali* covering the recruitment of the army reserve in winter 1916 noted that the force included "sixteen Egyptian-Sudanese blocs (*faṣīla miṣriyya sūdāniyya*)."[19] Another article published by *Al-Muqattam* contains a strikingly condescending reference to the Sudanese men of the CTC:

> It was heard that a great number of the Sudanese drivers scoff at the notion of fighting when they are far from those who actually do it (*yuhaza'u bi-l-qitāl 'ala ib'ād shāmikha al-qātilīn*), why don't they just settle the conflicts between themselves with daggers, like they do in Sudan?[20]

The reporter in this notoriously pro-British paper portrays the Sudanese as both scared of violence and uniquely inclined to engage in it instead of legal arbitration. The comment paints the Sudanese as "uncivilized" compared to their Egyptian colleagues, and plays on the long-standing racial distinctions between Sudanese and *fallāḥīn* in the Egyptian press discussed in the introduction and chapter 2.

But while Egyptians were set apart from their Sudanese colleagues at times, Venables also grouped Egyptians alongside Black Africans based on their physical appearance. As a schoolteacher, he kept up with the scientific ideas of his day, including theories about biological race.[21] In his unpublished manuscript, he turns the eye of an amateur scientist toward the physiology of the Egyptians under his command. He describes them as "stickily built, dark-skinned, heavy-jowled, and round skulled, some of the dolichocephalic type, but more approximating the negroid."[22] Here, Venables shows familiarity with anthropometry, which attempted to classify human diversity by comparing physical measurements of the body. By the beginning of the twentieth century, the cephalic index—which was obtained by dividing the maximum width of the skull by its maximum length—was the dominant measurement used to classify "racial stocks."[23] According to Elise K. Burton, "certain ranges of cephalic index measurements, labeled at one extreme 'dolichocephalic' (longheaded) and at the other 'brachycephalic' (broad-headed) were assigned to racial subtypes, which in turn became strongly associated with specific regions and nationalities."[24]

A British medical officer writing under the pseudonym "Serjeant-Major, RAMC" published an account of the Sinai-Palestine campaign that also grouped ELC men alongside Black Africans. Serving at the largest of the so-called native hospitals, he would have interacted with ELC men regularly. The way in which he recounted these experiences shows how contemporary ideas of racial identity could overlap with notions of empire and nation:

> The Medical Officer in command of the Kantara establishment possesses all the dominant racial traits which have made British rule over Eastern people such a success wherever our flag flies . . . his government of the hospital evidence another quality, much rare though also essentially British—that of *being able to tell one black man from another*, to realize the fundamental divergences of character and temperament between *the various coloured races*, and to adopt his methods accordingly. The writer has no experience of the Oriental peoples under our sway East of Suez, "where the best is like the worst," but from a fairly extended acquaintance with the lower-class Egyptian—the typical ELC or CTC [Camel Transport Corps] man—he is convinced that upon a true estimation of his peculiar racial qualities depends all our success in governing him both in the present time of war and hereafter.[25] (Emphasis mine)

By representing Egyptian laborers as "Orientals," the medical officer drew on a long-established distinction between Western selves and Eastern Others in the Western European cultural tradition.[26] But his contrast between the *racial* traits of the (white, British) commanding officer and the "peculiar racial characteristics" of the ELC shows how the older, binary logic of Orientalism's East/West distinction could be reformulated according to the racial idioms of the early twentieth century. A scientific approach to racial taxonomy—which the medical officer refers to here as the "essentially British" ability to "realize the fundamental divergences of character and temperament between the various coloured races"—was easily boiled down to a simpler formulation of "being able to tell one black man from another." The men of the ELC, then, are referred to alternatively as Black men and part of the "various coloured races." The global color line employed by men like this British medical officer adopted the empirical veneer of science, but—in the same way that Edward Said famously characterized Orientalism—it was still fundamentally about self-definition through Otherization.

The men of the ELC were also racialized alongside Black Africans in the epithets white officers used to refer to them. In his diaries, ANZAC soldier Fred Garrett calls Egyptians in Gallipoli "dusky sambos" and "[n——-]." His typically terse entry for September 8, 1915, reads: "500 civilian Egyptian labourers arrived. Dirty scum."[27] Venables was also given to using racial epithets, including, as we have already seen multiple times, the term "gyppies."[28] Chapter 4 documented his writings about a squad that failed to complete its task by the end of the day, so that "The natives are working 'like [n———]' now."[29]

The other time this word appeared in Venables' letters was also in connection to the task system. When describing how high authorities would question his practice of allowing men to return to camp early when they had finished their allotted task for the day, Venables writes:

> The general, colonel, or whatever he may be cannot even understand that. "Oh hand it, they are only a lot of [n———], give them some more to do" and it takes some tact to explain that, even if they are only "[n———]," it is impossible to break faith with them, and that even from the material point of view, it will be more profitable in the end to treat them fairly.[30]

The question of what to do with laborers who either finished their work early, or did not finish early enough, seems to elicit this particular word. Seeing this word used to describe Egyptians serving in the ELC is a clear example of how complex racial hierarchies—such as those that divided Egyptians-as-Muslims from Africans—could be boiled down to a simple color line in the mind of the British officer corps.

Analyzing representations of ELC laborers in the writings of British journalists and officers shows how these midlevel authorities racialized Egyptians during the war. In some senses, this was similar to how laborers from all over the world were perceived by the British and French authorities during the First World War.[31] Egyptians were part of the "Coloured Labour Corps," classified as "negroid," and called derogatory racial epithets. But the racialization of Egyptians also built on traditions of Orientalism and the racialization of Muslims. Egyptian race had a complex set of connotations in the minds of British officers like Venables and others like him. This set of ideas would affect policy toward the men in the camps.

SEGREGATION IN FRANCE

The racist perceptions of officers impacted life in the camps when they inscribed themselves in physical space. On the Western Front, as across the globe, the endeavor of imperial war necessitated the circulation of people and materials at ever-increasing speeds. But the logic of colonial racism worked to separate, enclose, and subordinate racialized Others. Labor Corps camps in France are a microcosm of how ideas about race impacted spatial change during the war.

In France, the so-called Coloured Labour Corps were kept racially segregated. Both French and British authorities resolved to ensure that they were separated from one another, from the French population, and from white troops and prisoners of war.[32] A map in the French national archives shows how this segregation was conceived through the design and construction of a camp for the Chinese Labor Corps at the French port city of Cherbourg. French authorities envisioned logistical infrastructures as barriers to enforce segregation, with a road between the Chinese camp and the local French inhabitants on the one hand, and a canal between the Chinese and the white troops and prisoners of war on the other.[33] The infrastructures of logistical space could, at times, serve the paradoxical function of speeding up circulation of goods and materials, while simultaneously enclosing racial Others and maintaining segregation. In this respect, the production of space in wartime Cherbourg resembled a pattern seen in cities throughout the United States in the twentieth century, where, as Ronald Bayor has shown, "highways and roads were used as barriers and boundaries to hold the black community in certain areas."[34]

The racial segregation of Egyptian laborers in France can best be illustrated by comparison to the situation of white migrant laborers. As demand for labor in France increased consistently from 1916 to 1918, military authorities worked to rationalize and standardize labor supplies by imposing greater controls on foreign migrant labor. Although in theory these policies did not distinguish between whites and nonwhites, in practice Spaniards, Belgians, Greeks, and other white foreigners often successfully evaded such attempts at regulation.[35] Spaniards, for example—who made up roughly 70 percent of all European migrant workers in France during the war—mostly entered the country surreptitiously and, once there, evaded regulations that were designed to prevent migrant laborers from changing jobs in search of higher wages.[36]

The Coloured Labour Corps, by contrast, was closely regimented and grouped by nationality, with military authorities making all arrangements for their transportation, housing, and food.[37] The ELC was no exception. The ELC in France was organized under a separate division, and each individual was classified by nation, race, and local affiliation.[38] Recruits were grouped together with others from the same or surrounding villages. These groups would go on to travel and serve together. The official British War Office report on Egyptian labor in France justified this policy on quasi-racial lines, stating, "Anyone who knows the native will readily understand how much this meant to these men, especially those who were inclined to become 'homesick.'"[39] It was this supposed knowledge of "the native"—derived from burgeoning "scientific" disciplines like the experiments of Onofrio Abbate—that guided the military's decision to keep Egyptians from the same villages and districts together.

In France, white British officers and Egyptian laborers were kept strictly segregated. Egyptian laborers slept together in a large tent, with each man given a wooden board on the ground and three wool blankets for bedding. While British troops slept in similar accommodations, they kept separate camps. For example, the diaries of William St. Leger include a secondhand story of a man who spent a night in an ELC camp in Boulogne with twenty British soldiers, sleeping in a separate tent from the many Egyptians in the company.[40] British camps in France also featured an officer's mess—a space reserved for white officers and equipped with special rations. These segregated spaces were usually explained in "separate but equal" terminology, but in reality they worked to reproduce racial hierarchies.[41]

ELC laborers in France had their movements closely controlled and were only given limited opportunities to leave the camp outside of work. Official regulations called for a barbwire fence to surround every camp of Egyptians in France to keep them enclosed and prevent the possibility of desertion.[42] Egyptians were to be confined to camp when not at work, and special passes to leave camp and visit the city were granted "locally when considered desirable by local authorities."[43] Parties on leave were not to exceed eight laborers at a time, and all parties were to be accompanied by a "reliable NCO." Egyptians were also to be restricted to the main thoroughfares in the cities, and British regulations stated, "Shops and other places must not be entered by Egyptians unless in the charge of a European."[44] Segregation thus manifested itself not only in the camps, but also in the regimentation of rest time, especially as compared to white migrant laborers. Even on the rare instances when Egyptian workers were allowed to leave their camps and visit the adjoining cities, French society adopted a system reminiscent of Jim Crow–era segregation in the United States, keeping Egyptians and other nonwhite laborers out of white spaces.

There was also a racial element to the geographical distribution of logistical labor within France. "Coloured labour" and prisoners of war worked on the lines of supply and communication in the back areas, Chinese laborers were further forward, and white ASC personnel were on the front lines.[45] Egyptians served in the back alongside laborers from South Africa who were divided according to skin color, with Blacks in the South African Native Labor Corps and light-skinned workers in the Cape Coloured Battalion. The War Office stressed the necessity of keeping Black South Africans separate from white labor "of low physical category" for fear that, due to the relatively faster pace and higher output of Black labor, "the native working alongside has his ideas of the position of the white man disturbed."[46] Military authorities thus recognized that their endeavor had the potential to upend the entire system of empire. By relying on racialized workers to win the war, authorities demonstrated the hollowness of white supremacy and made it clear that it was the people in the colonies who were propping up the metropole, and not the other way around. To prevent this realization, strict segregation had to be maintained.

SEGREGATION IN THE MIDDLE EAST

The mobility and shifting geography of the Sinai-Palestine campaign meant that segregation like that at the fixed French campsites was impossible. Moreover, ideas about the common racial characteristics of Egyptians and the local population around them meant that ELC laborers had much more interaction with their surrounding communities in Palestine and Iraq. In one of his letters from Palestine, Venables wrote, "Our Egyptians have no difficulty in making themselves at home in this newly opened country, where the natives are more or less of the same race and language."[47]

Nevertheless, British military authorities constructed segregated spaces behind the front lines. A caste system was established at the base depot at Qantara, with separate hospitals and prisons for Egyptians, Indians, and white troops.[48] The base depot had an officers' mess that excluded Egyptian laborers and had special rations for white officers. Qantara also had a large YMCA facility that mainly catered to white officers and a concert hall surrounded by fields of bivouacs and temporary shelters. At the sporting fields of the Qantara YMCA, white officers of the ELC competed against one another in an association football league, which was regularly reported on in the pages of the *ELC News*. For Egyptians, however, sporting events in the Suez Canal zone were more of a sideshow. On New Year's Day 1919, the EEF celebrated the armistice with a large gathering of visitors, including naval officers and civilians, and a prearranged program of boxing and sports. One event was a "blindfold boxing match between pairs of nafars, armed with a glove on the right hand, and provided with a rattle in the left to indicate their whereabouts." According to the *ELC News*, "It was very amusing to see well-intentioned swipes being delivered at the wing. Occasionally one reached something more solid, causing great astonishment to the recipient when it came from the rear."[49] The segregated nature of sporting events set the white officers apart from the Egyptians in their command; while white athletics were reported on seriously, competitions featuring Egyptians were reduced to a spectacle.

THE BODY OF THE LABORER

Ideas about race also manifested themselves on the smaller scale of the body. Through a variety of practices including the uneven distribution of resources, the hierarchical ordering of bodies in space, and the use of corporal punishment, late imperial notions of race became viscerally real for the young men in ELC camps. For example, proper footwear was consistently withheld from ELC men, especially those working in the Sinai/Palestine theater. Figure 5.3 shows a picture of a gang working in Palestine in their bare feet. This photo was taken as part of the British propaganda campaign, meant to illustrate the happy subjects of the empire who had "volunteered" to assist the British.[50] But it betrays the substandard provision of footwear to the laborers. Documentary evidence shows that this was explained on account of the supposed racial characteristics of Egyptians. Venables noted that many of his men did not wear shoes, but he explained that this was their preference, because "long use had made their soles as tough as leather."[51] Another British officer overseeing Egyptian la-

FIGURE 5.3. Egyptian Labor Corps men making a road at Romani, some without shoes. Imperial War Museum, London.

borers in Basra wrote, "It is impossible to get British boots to fit natives who have never worn boots, their feet being very broad and short."[52] Ideas about the biological characteristics of "native" feet thus seemed to influence the provision of shoes and boots to ELC laborers in multiple theaters of the war, despite the fact that many carried out their work on difficult terrain like the hot sands of the Sinai Desert or the rocky hills of Palestine.

The provision of food was also informed by the racialization of Egyptians, including their supposed status as "Mohammedeans" or "Arabs." Refusing to countenance breaks or slowdowns to accommodate fasting Muslims, British authorities worked to minimize fasting during Ramadan by receiving a special legal dispensation (*fatwa*) from the Grand Mufti of Egypt authorizing Egyptian laborers not to observe the fast while they were serving in the war.[53] On the Muslim holiday of *'id al-fiṭr* (celebrating the end of Ramadan), Coutts issued each company in France live sheep to slaughter, writing, "Any little attempt of this kind to remind them that we were trying to enable them to keep up their home customs was, I am glad to say, much appreciated."[54] He tried to free the men up to celebrate Muslim holidays through an interchange of Egyptian and Chinese labor.[55] But Coutts never applied such logic to the Christians among the laborers, who were forced to work on their own holidays. He justified his policy by writing, "Egyptians are Mohammedeans as a nation, but have a few Copts (Christians) among them."[56] Efforts to secure rations for Muslim holidays, then, stemmed from the racialization of Egyptians as Muslims, erasing the diversity of Egyptian religious identity and marginalizing the minority of Christians who worked with the ELC.

It seems some officers also conceived of funeral rituals as Muslim ceremonies.[57] In France, Coutts found it necessary to make separate arrangements for the Christians among the ELC to be "buried in Christian burial ground . . . modified from the burial service (Church of England) being used at the discretion of the Chaplain."[58] It is unclear when he made this change, but it could have been prompted by improper consecrations in the early phases of the war. At least initially, the ELC was officially defined as a "Muslim" organization. This is evident in the official provision of holidays, the arrangement of live sheep for ritual slaughter, and the consecration of the dead. This can be seen as a carryover from the prewar racialization of Egyptians as Muslims.

Another important practice that manipulated Egyptian bodies and was informed by contemporary ideas about race was known as the *ṭābūr*, meaning "line" or "column" in Egyptian Colloquial Arabic. Twice a day, once in the morning and again in the evening, laborers would assemble in formation while their officer walked up and down the long columns to subject them to inspection. The ritual occurred with such regularity that in the pages of the *ELC News*, one officer used it metonymically to stand in for a day in the life of the ELC: "From tabour to tabour, the world forces its objective crises upon our notice."[59] Likewise, Venables wrote, "In any company, from Egypt to the furthest point in Palestine, a 'Taboor' (parade) is a familiar sight."[60]

There was a spatial hierarchy of bodies in a *ṭābūr*, with the men of the company divided into squads, and squads led by a *ra'īs* who was appointed among them. This hierarchy was meant to instill a certain type of military discipline in the men. Venables describes how this was ideally envisioned:

> My policy has been to choose an Egyptian from the company, those who show ability in control, to train them and invest them with the necessary measure of authority. Being men of stronger personality than the average [Egyptian], they are useful in assisting control. . . . This state of things was not reached without much difficulty, however, as the Egyptian has ordinarily no idea of obeying an order, and requires some time to realize an

> authority ~~not backed up by immediate and visible force~~ whose force is invisible. Excessive coercion on the part of the Raises, too, was gradually abolished, though their authority was rigidly maintained.[61]

Venables hoped that a hierarchy would create a more impersonal, "invisible" type of power and control, but he struggled to describe the form of power he was working to create. He even crossed out his first attempt in the letter. Ann Stoler reminds us that it is precisely in these moments of stumbling and rewriting that important concepts are working themselves out.[62]

The philosopher Michel Foucault studied techniques like the *ṭābūr* and others sketched out by British imperial officials, including Jeremy Bentham's infamous panopticon. He argued that they belonged to a form of power that "seems all the less 'corporal' in that it is more subtly 'physical.'"[63] The *ṭābūr* is one example of such a subtly exercised power. Foucault called the force exerted by these techniques "disciplinary power." Rather than being compelled with violence, disciplinary power organized bodies, constructed spaces, and classified behaviors to create a new type of modern subjectification. In his influential book *Discipline and Punish* (1977), Foucault argued that techniques like the *ṭābūr* are meant to produce disciplined subjects who can police themselves and do not need to be threatened with violence to comply with the social order.

There are some aspects of the *ṭābūr* that resemble the disciplinary techniques studied by Foucault. For example, it gave ELC officers an opportunity to verify the number of men in each squad and to appraise the *ra'īs* for the day's work. Venables devoted considerable attention to "training the men to wear their uniforms properly, and look after them," and he used the *ṭābūr* as a time to inspect uniforms, which he saw as a "useful criterion of orderliness."[64] When taking stock of the men, if any of the clothing they had been issued as part of the uniform was damaged or lost, Venables would fine them, "some to the extent of a pound or two, for their carelessness."[65] Venables thus used the *ṭābūr* as a time to examine the men up close and impose some sense of what he called "orderliness."

However, according to Venables, the spatial hierarchy envisioned in the abstract notion of the *ṭābūr* could rarely be implemented in practice. He described an attempt at the formation in one of his letters:

> The squads or "khallat" as they are called, squat on the ground (the usual native position when not actually working) four by four, though *the spaces supposed to be preserved between each two khallat are often oblit-*

> *erated, and the tabour becomes a crowded mass of crouching Gyppies.* In my company, I have each khallat standing, in two ranks, as white troops do, giving them thereby the appearance of men (and some of them are of very fine muscular build) instead of crouching monkeys. By this means, too, I can pass down between the ranks, see each man individually, note any deficiencies or damage to clothing, detect men who are sick, and often, by the expression on their faces, guess what mischief they have been up to.[66] (Emphasis mine)

The actual execution of the *ṭābūr* in ELC camps, then, seems to have failed to produce disciplined subjecthood. The idea was for each squad to arrange itself "four by four," but the spaces that were supposed to exist between the men were often "obliterated." All that was left, according to Venables, was a "crowded mass of crouching Gyppies." Although it is a throwaway line, the racial epithet "Gyppies" he uses here is significant because it shows how the supposed racial characteristics of Egyptians were called upon to explain the gap between the abstract plan for the *ṭābūr* and its concrete implementation in space.

The associations go much deeper, and Venables evinces a completely racialized understanding of the *ṭābūr* as a practice. For example, he speaks of his need to adjust it in his company so that his men are standing. As figure 5.4 illustrates, it seems Egyptian laborers did often assemble while crouching in a deep squat with their weight on the backs of their heels, a stance which Venables refers to here as "the usual native position." The use of the appellation "native" to describe this position shows the cognitive associations of this style of bodily comportment in the Anglo-British imagination. John Wood, the late nineteenth-century English writer and scientific popularizer, wrote often of such a crouched position in his book, *The Natural History of Man; Being an Account of the Manners and Customs of the Uncivilized Races of Men* (1870). In his description of indigenous Australians, Wood writes of the "crouching or squatting position, such as is employed by the natives when sitting, the knees being drawn up to the chin, the legs close to the body, and the hands clasped over the legs."[67] Averse to this type of bodily expression, Venables required his men to stand up straight, "as white troops do, giving them thereby the appearance of men . . . instead of crouching monkeys." Despite his efforts to treat Egyptians more like "white troops," he still expected the worst of them when he says he uses the *ṭābūr* for guessing "what mischief they have been up to." In the end, when practices like the *ṭābūr* failed to produce disciplined subjects, it was explained not by the unique and stressful

FIGURE 5.4. Egyptian Labor Corps men squat in front of a YMCA Employee in Qantara. University of Minnesota, Kautz Family YMCA Archives Y.USA.4-5, Armed Services: Audio/Visual Materials, Box #46 A.

circumstances of the war, the mutually incomprehensible languages of officers, NCOs, and men, or the completely foreign circumstances in which Egyptian laborers found themselves, but rather by drawing on ideas about the supposed racial characteristics of Egyptians.

Once failures in discipline could be blamed on Egyptians' supposed racial inferiority, it was not long before officers abandoned their efforts to produce disciplined subjects through the subtle means studied by Foucault and resorted to violence. Venables describes how, when the "invisible" type of power meant to be instilled by the *ṭābūr* broke down, he used corporal punishment to maintain the façade of order:

> These men are no doubt far below us in the scale of civilization, they are often lazy and rascally, but, at the same time, I like to give them some understanding of their position as useful workers. As on parade, so when proceeding to and from work, squads are required to preserve an orderly formation and not straggle all over the road . . . the punishment I meted out to one squad whom I caught straggling was such that they never forgot. *It is only the fear of being suddenly spotted by the "mudir"* [i.e., the

> officer] *that causes them to proceed in two orderly files on the right-hand side of the road.*[68] (Emphasis mine)

Venables chalks up the indiscipline in his men to his belief that they were "no doubt far below us in the scale of civilization." With this in mind, he quickly jumps to his supposed need to depend on "fear" to maintain order. He discusses his use of corporal punishment in other letters, too, including once when two laborers were "laid across the ration bags and received twenty-five lashes."[69] Most of the time, Venables referred to the violence that underwrote his command more obliquely, like when he wrote, "'slacking' received short shrift at our hands."[70]

Ideas about race played a part in the corporal punishment meted out to ELC laborers in France as well. Referencing what he had heard of the Egyptians working in French ports, William St. Leger, who was posted at Cambrai, France, in late 1917, wrote, "Force is often, if not always the only authority that a native will recognize. [An ELC Officer that St. Leger spoke with] says that when natives refuse to work with him, he gives them a jolly good hiding and after that they give him no trouble."[71] Like Venables, then, St. Leger justified the use of violence when dealing with ELC laborers. This was not appropriate in all cases, but for St. Leger, force was the *only* authority that would work on Egyptians due to their status as "natives." Producing disciplined subjects through more "invisible" types of power seems to have been abandoned once officers in France found themselves dealing with people on the Other side of the global color line.

William Knott, a conscientious objector from the army who was assigned to the RAMC in Palestine, wrote in his diaries about corporal punishment from a more sympathetic viewpoint. He described the "brutish way natives are treated," observing that "long leather whips are used by Englishmen and overseers, taking off the skin, and great gashes exposing the raw flesh are made."[72] Knott could not help but see this violent treatment in racial terms, writing, "The treatment of these Egyptians is a scandal. They talk about modern civilization and abolishing slavery, yet these men have taskmasters paid by the British government to whip them like dogs with long leather whips. Even the British and Australians kick and bully them unmercifully."[73] For Knott, the corporal punishment received by the ELC was reminiscent of the whips of slave overseers. He recognized the hypocrisy of the British government, which prided itself on abolishing the slave trade, yet produced a system that resembled slavery during the war.

When Egyptians died, the ways that their bodies were consecrated were also informed by ideas about race. Knott describes one instance in which a sick Egyptian laborer was "roughly handled and told to 'ephot' [*iskut*] (shut up)." After being "neglected all night," the man was found dead by his officers. "No service or respect was shown," Knott wrote, "but his body flung on a stretcher and thrown in a grave like a dog."[74] This was in contrast to the numerous, spontaneous efforts by army units to commemorate their fallen white comrades, including the wooden cross set up on the battlefield by the 161st Infantry Brigade for its fallen in the first battle of Gaza, the three columns erected by the 155th Brigade of the Lowland Fifty-Second Division to commemorate their crossing of the river Auja, and the numerous attempts to establish monuments to the fallen soldiers of the EEF in occupied Jerusalem.[75] The dehumanization of Egyptians, then, continued even with respect to their bodies after they had passed away.

The body of the laborer was one of the smallest scales on which British military authorities produced a space that could simultaneously fuel British military logistics and maintain the racial hierarchies of the late imperial age. Military authorities conceptualized Egyptians in ways that built on their racialization as Muslims, but they also treated them just as they would any of the other so-called subject races and easily resorted to corporal punishment to enforce deference to orders. This recourse to violence distinguishes modern techniques for producing disciplined subjects—like those studied by Michel Foucault—when they are applied on the Other side of the global color line. Violence, rather than disciplinary power, ultimately underwrote the order of the camps. This is why it is always important to trace the actual implementation of techniques for producing disciplined subjects in space and lived reality. It is not insignificant, for example, that Bentham's panopticon was rarely put into actual practice.[76]

CONCLUSION

This chapter has tried to show how British ideas about race made their effects felt in the everyday lives of the men of the ELC. British perceptions of these men were influenced by empire-wide discourses about "subject races," the racialization of Muslims, and Orientalism. In one sense, Egyptians were grouped together with other "subject races" in the "Coloured Labour Corps." They faced the same segregation, racial epithets, and corporal punishment as laborers from across the globe. Petty officers and journalists looked upon these laborers assembled from all corners of the world with a patronizing attitude at best, and outright disdain at worst. But Egyptians were also uniquely marked as Muslims through special dietary provisions, holiday observances, and funeral rites. This erased the diverse religious practices of the men of the ELC, who included a number of Christians among them.

One key argument of this chapter is that merely studying the attitudes and representations of British officers stops short of capturing the lived reality of race. For the men of the ELC to feel the force of British ideas about race, those ideas had to be manifested in physical space. Therefore, I have paid careful attention to the built environment of the ELC camps in France, Gallipoli, Iraq, and Sinai/Palestine. Egyptians in France were segregated, cut off from contact with white civilians, white troops, and, at times, their white officers. When they were allowed to leave their walled-in encampments, they ventured out into newly segregated cities, always under the watchful eye of an officer. In the Middle Eastern theaters of battle, the situation was different, as the mobile fronts made strict regimentation difficult, and ideas about the similar racial characteristics of Egyptians and Palestinians or Iraqis meant their officers gave them more latitude for free intercourse. But Egyptians were nevertheless subject to segregation behind the lines in the base depots of the Suez Canal zone, and in the "native" hospital and detention systems.

At the smallest scale, ideas about race inscribed themselves on the bodies of the men. What were considered the normal dietary habits of "Muslims" and "Arabs" structured the rations provided in the camps, and, because Egyptian *fallāḥīn* were accustomed to walking around barefoot, British authorities thought it no problem to deny them footwear—despite clear regulations that called for the provision of proper footwear and the fact that the scorching sand of the Sinai gave way to the rocky hills of Palestine beneath their feet. In what is perhaps the largest scandal of the whole enterprise, Egyptian laborers were whipped mercilessly. This recourse to corporal punishment was informed by contemporary ideas about race, and the scars left behind by the officers' whips were a physical reminder of the racialized order for all to see.

CHAPTER 6

LISTENING IN ON THE ELC

WHEN THE OFFICER'S WHISTLE signaled the end of a day's work, the men of the ELC hiked from their work sites back to camp, unloaded their packs, debriefed at *ṭābūr*, and then got their night's rations. When they were done, sometimes only for a few short hours of darkness, their time was their own. As Venables put it, "some nights were distinctly lively."[1] Small groups gathered outside of their bivvies, chatting about farming, girls, and the war. A few might sing rounds of their favorite songs, improvising call-and-response lyrics over familiar melodies. "Usually in the evening," Venables wrote, "we see and hear groups chanting their curious native songs, a leader singing a line or a stanza, and the group joining in the refrain, swaying their bodies to and fro, and slapping their hands in rhythm."[2] From the perspective of the officers, these were "curious native songs," but the men of the ELC heard the revitalizing sounds of a space that had been reclaimed and made their own, if only for a short time.

Many sources agree on one point about the ELC: you had to hear it to believe it. It is hard for historians trained in their own unique disciplinary formation to see things from the perspective of ELC laborers; the men left few records of their experiences, and the majority of the sources we do have are descriptions by undiscerning white observers couched in terms of what Graham White and Shane White call "white alienation."[3] But occasionally, we can glean some insight into the men's reactions to their new circumstances if we turn an ear to the snippets of Egyptian Colloquial Arabic that preserve the "lost voices" of the *fallāḥīn* within these sources.[4]

This chapter attempts to "reconstitute the auditory environment" of the young men who served in the ELC by focusing on the sounds that sustained them during their service in the war.[5] Egyptian Colloquial Arabic—which is meant to be spoken and heard—is scattered in bits and pieces throughout the accounts of officers and journalists who lived in

ELC camps during the war. ELC men sang songs and put on theatrical productions, and analyzing these forms of popular culture at the camps can tell us a great deal about how the men made these spaces their own. We can even hear the ephemeral aspects of the sounds, which largely exist beyond the representative capacity of language, by listening to the recording of one song popular with the laborers: "Ya 'Aziz 'Ayni" ("Oh, Apple of my Eye," 1915), by Na'ima al-Misriyya.

While highly visual sources like the maps and diagrams analyzed in chapter 3 illustrate plans of the authorities who structured space, focusing on the oral/aural traces left behind by the ELC allows us to reconstruct the sense of place they tried to forge in their new environment. This chapter builds on understandings of the so-called great divide between visual cultures of the eye and oral/aural cultures of the ear studied by Walter Ong and other sensory historians.[6] While the watchful officers were represented in work songs by the "eye" (*'ayn*), the men of the ELC relied on their ears and their voices to make it through the day. The sounds they made served many functions: they helped to overlay a level of creativity onto their otherwise monotonous jobs, they built rapport between the men, and they conveyed information about the war. If a work song, Sufi ritual, or theatrical performance was just right, the men might forget about their difficult situation and drift off into a place of spiritual transcendence.

CHATTER AND SPEECH

ELC men loved to chat with one another and with the officers around them. According to Venables, "an ELC camp could be recognized on approach by the vocal din." In his unpublished manuscript, he writes, "Squads have their own ways of relaxation, sheer chatter being by far the most common . . . a call for silence preceded any roll-call or other assemblage."[7] Similarly, in his letters home, Venables describes a journey from Judaea to Qantara during which he passed by several ELC camps and was "impressed" by how "one becomes aware of a camp of Egyptians . . . by the babel of voices from afar, after which one may see the lights at closer range."[8] He described one of the cooks in his company as "a blackface whom, from his chattering propensities, we had Christened 'Abu Kallam'—Chatterbox."[9] This appellation, which literally translates to "the father of speech," is a common way of referring to someone in Egyptian Colloquial Arabic, and Venables likely adopted this idiom from the men in his company. Moreover, his description of the chatty cook as a "black-face" shows how the racial characteristics of ELC men could be easily linked to the sounds they made.

Other sources refer to the verbose proclivities of the ELC. The Australian official history of the Sinai-Palestine campaign mentions the "hard-working, singing Egyptians of the Labour Corps."[10] An article in the *Times* of London reports, "chanties . . . seem to be a necessary part of their existence—as necessary as breathing."[11] According to a medic stationed in Qantara, "With native in hospital almost the entire day is spent in talking. Interminable animated discussions go on between them as they sit in conclave. . . . When they are not wrangling together in this inimitable, gentle, bantering way, they are telling each other long tales of enchantment after the style of the 'Arabian Nights.'"[12] It is unclear whether the men actually re-created the stories of Shahrazad or whether the medical officer was merely recounting the only piece of Arabic literature with which he was familiar. Nevertheless, the frequency and volume at which the men conversed—whether working, eating, relaxing, or convalescing—is mentioned again and again in the sources.

Descriptions of the men's conversation as "sheer chatter" or a "babel of voices" indicates that the speech was essentially trivial or pointless. But when Venables—who seems to have understood Arabic better than most—listened closely, he found there was a deeper meaning to the sounds he heard. He writes of an "interesting conversation" after the final whistle, "when all was supposed to be quiet and still." One squad was "talking politics, and expressed the Egyptian opinion that the Turks were thieves, and the British were out for their own ends, too." The night watchmen, seeing Venables standing nearby, gave the men the hint to be quiet. According to the letter, "from within their bivouacs they murmured 'all right Abdul, we know you have to do what the Mudir [lit. "director," i.e., officer] tells you.'" But Venables continues: "They received a shock when I remarked, 'Lakin yumkin gennaboh el mudir maogood' (but perhaps the mudir himself is here)." Rather than charge the men with sedition after hearing their disparaging remarks—a move which he felt was within his rights—Venables let it slide because, as he wrote, "these men are some of the best workers I have."[13] The men of the ELC spoke on all matter of subjects, and some could use the one source of leverage they had over their officers—the importance of their work—to seize as much leeway as they could. They discussed not only the war, but also the British occupation of Egypt, all while evincing a familiarity with what Venables calls "the Egyptian opinion." This indicates that the men of the ELC were following political events back at home and may even have discussed the nationalist movement.

The observations of a medical officer with the RAMC corroborate that men's conversations could steer toward politics and the war. Having observed a number of ELC men waiting in convalescence, the officer wrote that among their favorite topics of conversation were "the latest exploits of the dreaded Turk."[14] Chatting, then, could potentially serve an important purpose for the men. It allowed them to exchange information about the war, debate the merits of the enterprise in which they were participating, and express criticism of the British and Ottoman Empires. Far from trivial and pointless, the men spoke to inform one another and to develop their opinions about their own circumstances and those of Egypt as a whole.

The men not only chatted with one another but also bantered with their officers. Venables recalls a story from another company that was engaged in a difficult march during a horrific rainstorm. He records a laborer saying, "'Amut ya effendum, Amut' (I am dying sir, I am dying)," to which the officer replied, "'Temut Khalis?' (Are you going to die completely?)" The laborer, in on the joke, came back at him, "'La ya effendum, shawaiya bas' (No, sir, only a little)."[15] A similarly humorous story from the *ELC News* recounts a disciplinary trial after a fight between two ELC laborers that had left one man with a swollen lip and a bruised forehead. The defendant recited his story, "which," the author tells us, "needless to say, was totally different from the injured party's." Soon the injured man exclaimed, "Huwa keddab (He is a liar!)" "'Esscot' (Shut up!)," the officer in charge of the proceeding replied. After a short pause, "'Huwa Keddab' (He is a liar)" was repeated again by the claimant. "'Effil hanakak' (Shut your mouth!)," the officer shouted. There was another pause while the defendant proceeded with his tale, and again the claimant exclaimed, "'Huwa keddab' (He is a liar) more determined than ever." The officer sternly reproved him, "'Mush awez kallam zay dee *Abadan*!' (I don't wanna hear anything like this *ever again*!)" "Erstfallen," the claimant responded resignedly, "'Tayib hadir' (OK, fine)," and after a long pause, he interjected under his breath, "'lakin huwa keddab' (but he is a liar)."[16] Stories like these show that, even when faced with difficult conditions like a march through a rainstorm or a disciplinary hearing, the men of the ELC kept their sense of humor. Chatting and joking gave them an ability to build a rapport with the officers and with each other, even if such opportunities were fleeting. The fact that these snippets of conversation are preserved in Egyptian Colloquial Arabic—even if they are transliterated awkwardly by the officers recording them—lends a sense of authenticity to the sources.

WORK SONGS

In addition to conveying information and building rapport among the men, sounds also sustained them while they worked. According to Venables, the men "cannot work in silence, and if they are not chanting some of their picturesque 'songs,' they are keeping up an endless chatter and noise which sounds like quarrelling, but is really nothing else but their necessary accompaniment to work."[17] Fred Garrett, an Australian soldier in Gallipoli, described the songs and chants that were bellowed out while the men of the ELC built roads around him:

> Two rows of them stand facing the leader, who stands facing them. "Halyar heyli," says the leader, and swinging the rammers across in front of the other foot, they drop them with a "Unmen dahlah" all together and so on chant and chorus. They don't put any weight behind the hammers but merely let them drop with their "unmendahla."[18]

According to Garrett, who was entirely ignorant of Arabic, the lyrics to an ELC song were almost incidental. They were most important as a rhythmic refrain to keep the men on time for a particular task. In a call-and-response format, the leader could start with a line, and then the men assembled around him would respond in kind. With the response from the men forming a steady backbone to the song, the song leader was free to improvise with words and melody.

Singing and chanting seems to be one way that ELC laborers overlaid the monotonous tasks they were compelled to undertake with a layer of creativity. By making and listening to sounds, the men could transport themselves, if only in their minds, to some other place. Like religious mystics, they became simultaneously present in the moment and absent from the harsh conditions surrounding them. The spiritual connotation of some of these chants, which Fred Garrett heard as "unmendahla," but which likely contained an exhortation to God (*Allah*), reinforce this mystical aspect of sound.

Venables's letters contain stories that illustrate the transformative impact songs could have for the men as they worked. In the lead-up to the Third Battle of Gaza, his company found themselves confronted with one of the dreaded "emergency tasks" that were popping up more and more frequently. After working a twelve-hour shift from four in the morning until four in the afternoon, Venables was called in and told that a huge bank across a steep valley needed to be filled so that a road could be constructed over top. He instructed the *ra'īs* of each squad to simply get as much done as possible in one shift to prepare for fast-advancing troops and artillery. After a few minutes' rest and a drink of water, the whole company went back to work just as they had all day. Within a few hours, one *ra'īs*, "a fine southern Egyptian who managed his men perfectly with no fuss," led his squad in a round of singing and began running back and forth, up and down the line. The spirit was "infectious," and in a few minutes, "all the men of the company were singing at the top of their voices . . . and at the same time digging as if possessed, or running with full baskets to add to the growing bank."[19] After this spurt of activity, the majority of the work had been finished, and the men were allowed to return to camp, having just completed a seventeen-hour shift of hard labor.

Such scenes were not uncommon, and Venables' final letter recounts a similar story from another company at Al-Lubban. As the men began climbing a steep hill, "Squad No. 7, who had been with us all summer and who had been helping to keep the men going by their chattering remarks, started singing, which was taken up along the columns."[20] According to Venables, the men happened to be passing the spot where his own company was bivouacked, and the enthusiastic noise woke up two of the guards he had placed on the road ahead. Work songs, then, were not simply the monotonous dirges described by Fred Garrett; they could contain an infectious spirit that steeled the men against the difficult work they were compelled to endure.

White spectators struggled to make sense of the aberrant acoustics emanating from the men. Some took their singing and conversation as evidence of the men's happiness. The *Times* of London opined, "When evening falls and they return to their camp they bellow a lusty stave at the top of their voices to a handclapping accompaniment, pleased with the prospect of supper and repose."[21] Another reporter at the *Sydney Morning Herald* wrote of the ELC, "they are undoubtedly cheerful—always laughing and singing at their work."[22] Likewise, Venables insisted in one of his letters that "the best time to judge the well-being and happiness of the men is in the evening at camp after a day's work. . . . Here, they squat in little groups, amusing themselves in their various simple ways. They will talk and smoke for hours, drifting from one topic to another."[23] He also wrote of how squads "return to camp . . . simple, happy-going souls, singing, to impress the others with their prowess."[24]

This tendency to interpret the sounds of the ELC as evidence of their happiness also pops up in the pro-British press in Egypt. An article in *Al-Muqattam* emphasized that the men's hours of work "have been limited in order to facilitate their enjoyment of necessary rest and the joys of life that are a natural right of everyone." "We deduced from what we heard this evening," the article continued, "that these workers, whether in Egypt or anywhere else, are laughing, and their happy voices and pleasantness shows the promise of their life and that they . . . are well-treated."[25] In another report, *Al-Muqattam*'s correspondent in France wrote of the ELC laborers at the Western Front, "They executed the orders that were presented to them with happiness, which they showed on their faces as they walked to the ports, [the sounds of] their music preceding them."[26] Observers writing in Arabic and English whose interactions with ELC laborers began with the preconceived notion that the men were "volunteers" tended to interpret the sounds of music at the camps as evidence that the recruits were content with their service.

The truth, at least for most white officers and journalists, was that they had little idea of what the men were actually saying. According to an RAMC officer, "A thorough knowledge of the quaint variety of Arabic spoken in rural Egypt [i.e., Egyptian Colloquial Arabic] is almost a *sine qua non* with the officer."[27] But a joke in the *ELC News* shows how officers struggled to understand the language: "Of course, I speak Arabic perfectly. At least, I can understand what Egyptians say. Well, perhaps not always, but anyway I can make them understand me, that is, if the Egyptian is a fairly intelligent fellow. Of course, I may have to wave my arms about a bit and all that, but—well, you understand, don't you?"[28] The officer begins the joke with a confident assertion of his linguistic abilities, but gradually hedges until it is clear that most of what counts for "communication" between himself and the Egyptians in his command is "waving his arms about a bit and all." From reading the officers' newspaper, one gets the sense that British officers traded on these kinds of false representations of their linguistic skill. For example, another joke goes, "With the natives, yes, I'm *tout à fait* (though I'd like to know what the hell they say!) / Arabic, sir? I'm quite schooled (Again the brass hats' legs are pulled!)"[29] Despite their representations to the "brass hats," then, most ELC officers seem to have struggled to understand the spoken Arabic of the men around them.

The officers' struggle to understand the ELC is encapsulated in one exchange that saw them debating the meaning of a popular work song. A letter to the editor in the *Palestine News* refuted an article from the previous issue that claimed the song in question had a refrain of "'Yemar dinak ya Mackensen.'" This, the author had alleged, was "Hun propaganda" meaning "'God bless your cause Mackensen'" (a presumed reference to the famous German commander, August Von Mackensen). But the letter to the editor—signed H. J. Higgs, Lt. Col.—offered a conflicting interpretation of the song: "I am afraid . . . the actual words are 'Amar dinak, ya Mahassin,' Strengthen (or God Bless) your cause, Oh Generous One." According to Higgs, this was "sung by the fellaheen before Hun propaganda was thought about or Mackensen was born." The editor of the *ELC News* had a third interpretation. In an article titled "The Truth at Last!—The ELC News Clears Matters Up," he insisted that the song was "intended by its singers to refer to a certain officer 'Makenzie,' through whose hands most of the Egyptian personnel of the Corps passes." "The Egyptians are always aware of the names of their officers and do their best to pronounce their names correctly," he wrote, "but sometimes are a little wide of the mark."[30] With such diverging views, and absent any other source attesting to the words of the song, it is hard to say what the men were actually singing. But the exchange seems most significant to me as an index of how anxious white officers were about the sounds made by men under their command; the possibility that the men were spreading anti-British propaganda always lurked beneath every unknown utterance.

Unfamiliarity with Arabic and with the feeling of being a minority meant that white officers and observers of the ELC often felt alienated, out of place, and lonely. "I am the only Englishman in camp," Venables wrote in an early letter home. "Arabic, Arabic, hour after hour, none of my own language, there is no one with whom to speak it."[31] Later on, he wrote that the whites-only officers' mess in Qantara was "a change after our loneliness."[32] When he heard the men under his command singing, he found it "rough and hoarse," and wrote, "They have no idea of tune and harmony in the western sense."[33] Venables wrote that a funeral ceremony for one of the fallen men took place "to the sound of their pathetically mournful dirges."[34] Likewise, a medical officer for the RAMC described the men having just been discharged as "clapping their hands rhythmically, chanting *weird* folk-songs, and waving improvised flags (emphasis mine)."[35] The *Times* of London reported on one of the men's work songs with a characteristic sense of white alienation:

> Before they settle down to a job . . . one of them will intone, as it were, any remark that may occur to him as suitable for the occasion. If, for instance, the work consists of pushing railway trucks about the docks, he

> may consider that "Allah! Al-Allah!" meets the case, and the gang, adopting it as their refrain for that particular task, chant it briskly in unison, using the minor key. To this chorus the soloist contributes an antistrophe of stimulating cries, facetious asides, or any nonsense that comes into his head, and thus encouraged, the gang work [*sic*] with a will.[36]

For this observer, the lyrics of work songs were simply "nonsense," and the song-leader would pick any phrase that "occurs to him as suitable for the occasion." The song itself was interpreted as a necessary accompaniment to work, more important for its rhythmic utility than for any information or affect it expressed. When white observers called ELC work songs "weird" and "pathetic dirges," we should see these statements as evidence of white alienation in the midst of a soundscape that ELC laborers had come to dominate with their chatter and song. It makes sense that the camps would be filled with the sounds of ELC men; they constituted, by far, the numerical majority.

Paradoxically, while Venables wrote that his men "have no idea of tune and harmony in the western sense," the reporter for the *Times* noted that they were "using the minor key." Here, white observers were struggling to describe the complex system of *maqāmāt* (sing., *maqām*) used in the Arabic musical tradition. The word *maqām*—which literally means "place" or "location" in Arabic—refers to the arrangement of tones in a scale. Similar to modes in Western music, *maqāmat* combine major, minor, and neutral steps into a prearranged set that all artists stick to in a given tune. Unlike the limited number of keys in Western music (one major and one relative minor key for each of the twelve tones of the chromatic scale), there are at least seventy-two *maqāmāt*. Ethnomusicologist Habib Hasan Tumah describes the *maqām* as a "technique of improvisation." The lead melody develops within the prescribed set of tones but is manipulated in new and different ways by the performer as cycles of the song repeat themselves. According to Tumah, the *maqāmat* tradition maintains a rigid, "tonal-spatial factor," while the "rhythmic-temporal component . . . is subjected to no definite organization."[37] This means that unlike Western songs, which are built with a limited number of sections, Arabic music is more open. Performances can last for hours, sustained by the play of improvisation within the strict rules of the *maqām* rather than the preset organization of the song. By fixing themselves firmly within the "place" of the *maqām*, performers in the tradition of Arabic music aim to transcend space and time. This sense of acoustic ecstasy that allows for both performer and audience to lose themselves in the moment is known in Arabic as *ṭarab*.[38]

The songs described by Venables show how the sense of improvisation encapsulated in the *maqāmat* tradition informed the aesthetic sensibilities of the men. One of the popular work songs was known as "Kam Layla, Kam Yawm?" ("How Many Nights, How Many Days?"). The song is structured as a call-and-response between a *mughanni* (singer) and the *maradd* (chorus). As in the work songs of migrant laborers on the archaeological dig sites of Upper Egypt studied by Anne Clément, the *maradd* generally repeated a single verse throughout the song, but it could also be involved in an active dialogue with the *mughanni*.[39] With his words being repeated back at him, every other line gave the *mughanni* a chance to improvise something new to demonstrate his verbal and melodic prowess. For example, after a particularly difficult stretch covering emergency shifts, the beginning of the question "how many days, how many nights" might be completed with "have I not seen sleep?" (*kam layla, kam yawm / mabashūftish nawm*). The open, improvisational nature of the songs gave the *mughanni* opportunities to show his skill with wordplay, but, in this example, the raw materials he worked with were the experiences of suffering he was forced to endure in the ELC. With each new verse, the *mughanni* simultaneously displayed his creativity and recounted his helplessness. "Kam Layla, Kam Yawm" seems to have functioned primarily as a vehicle for the men to publicly lament the number of days they had been serving or, as the end of their contract came due, joyously announce the number of days they had left until they returned home. If we listen closely to work songs like this one, then, rather than conveying contentment, we actually hear a deep sense of melancholy.

When white officers like Venables were there to listen and record, performing work songs provided an opportunity for the men to interact with these authority figures in camp. Venables writes that his presence overlooking a squad was often signaled by inserting the line, "the man is up there" (*kam layla kam yawm / huwa al-rāgil fuw'*), to which the chorus always responded with the line, "save us from his eye!" (*min 'aynuh salāmt*). This was a warning to the men to look busy if they wanted to avoid the whip. While the officer was represented by his watchful eye, the men could outsmart him if they kept their ears tuned to the work songs. The line recalls the common belief in the "evil eye" (*'ayn al-ḥasūd*) among speakers of Egyptian Colloquial Arabic. According to Mustafa Mughazy, the evil eye is usually invoked when others express admiration toward valuable possessions or family members in a way that indicates envy.[40] Although the context is radically different here, the notion of associating the seeing "eye" (*'ayn*) with an evil that can be warded off by conjuring up an oral formula could be seen as an example of a preexisting cultural norm being reworked at the camps.

When they heard the signal of the officer's approach, some men seized the opportunity to appeal to him through song. According to Venables, "An officer's presence within hearing distance gave a chance to weave in the common grumbles: too much work, not enough rest, pay, or cigarettes, hints usually given and taken good-humouredly."[41] This demonstrates the workers' adaptation to the system of military labor. In the hierarchical environment of the ELC, laborers' ability to establish a link with the officer could prove useful to them. In bypassing the authority of the *ra'īs* who was their direct supervisor at work, a relationship with the officer could allow the laborers to timidly put forward modest requests regarding their working conditions.[42]

This is significant because it shows a conscious awareness of the inequalities of the system the British had created. While colonial authorities in Egypt claimed the men of the ELC were volunteers who were incorporated into the organization according to the dictates of law, the laborers knew that their situation ultimately depended on the capricious whims of the white officers who oversaw them. They thus took a utilitarian approach to building a rapport with these officers. This point casts a different light on the frequent displays of obsequiousness and praise that ELC rank and file bestowed on the officers. When white officers heard themselves addressed with terms like "y'effendum" (i.e., *ya affandi*, which translates to "sir") and "gennaboh al-mudir" (i.e., *ganābuh al-mudīr*, which translates to "his excellency, the director"), they took it as a sign of respect. But ELC laborers could just as easily have been employing these terms ironically in an effort to manipulate the officers with their speech.

Like "Kam Layla, Kam Yawm," a desire to return home was expressed in another popular song, titled "Ya 'Aziz 'Ayni" ("Oh Apple of My Eye"). Multiple sources attest that the men of the ELC sang this tune a lot. An article in the *ELC News*, entitled "The Love Letters of a Nafar to his Bint," satirically depicts the love letters an ELC laborer might write to his wife or girlfriend back at home. It includes the line, "If you could but hear how hastily I join in the 'bida ruah baladi' chorus, it would indeed gladden your heart."[43] According to Venables, one of the favorite songs of his men "has a refrain 'Y'Aziz y'aini ana abidd aruh bil beladi' ('My beloved, life of my eyes, I long for the day of my return to my home')."[44] Outside observers like Venables could only give imperfect representations of this song. Even for those few verses of the many that could have been improvised by the singers that they did manage to capture, they recorded only the words. But like the African American slave songs studied by Graham White and Shane White, the voices of the ELC could transform words into richly detailed patterns of sound; sweeping slides between different tones, extended melismas (one syllable carried over several tones), and portamenti (continuous gliding from one pitch to another) could fill simple words with complex feelings of joy or sadness.[45]

Luckily, there is a contemporary recording of "Ya 'Aziz 'Ayni." It was adapted from a popular folk song by Yunis al-Qadi (lyrics) and Sayyid Darwish (music), and recorded by the rising star Na'ima al-Misriyya in 1915.[46] The lyrics are as follows:

> Oh, Apple of my eye / I want to go to my home (*balad*)
> My home, Oh, my home / And the authorities (*al-sulṭa*) took away my son
> Oh, Apple of my eye / I want to go home to my home
> Doctor, doctor! / come examine my son!
> I called the doctor / to come and examine my heart
> But the doctor said to me / "I've got no medicine for you"
> He said, "Take ten bottles of rose [water?] / all wrapped up in velvet"
> They will distract me from my beloved / and suffice in lieu of his beauty.[47]

The song is told from the alternating points of view of a laborer who has been taken away by "the authorities" (*al-sulṭa*) on the one hand, and his family, which awaits anxiously for news of his travails, on the other. The singer expresses a desire to return to their *balad*, which is an ambiguous word in Egyptian Colloquial Arabic that can mean either "village" or "country," and which I have translated here as "home." The desire to return home causes a sense of pain incurable by a doctor's medicine.

While this song likely began as an old tune sung by laborers compelled to join in the *corvée* during the Ottoman period, its recording by al-Misriyya in 1915 put a standardized version into circulation in Egypt. When the men picked up this song and made it their own, they transformed it into a lamentation on the difficulties of working in the war. The melody of each verse is one long portamento, gliding in waves from high to low pitches in a way that would have worked nicely in time with the swinging *fass*.[48] The gradual decline in tonal frequency may have been intended to mimic the sinking spirits of the men, as day after day was filled with back-breaking labor. The song being told from alternating perspectives of the worker and his family at home puts both the *mughanni* and the *maradd* in the position of imagining themselves back in the villages of Egypt with their families. Songs like "Ya 'Aziz 'Ayni" could transport the men out of the difficult place they found themselves in and help them to escape their circumstances, if only in their minds.

POPULAR RELIGION

The mystical abilities of sound were also harnessed in the men's popular religious practices, which many of them maintained during their service in the war. Muslim prayers—which happen five times a day and begin with a call to prayer followed by a vocal series said aloud by a prayer leader (*imām*)—were a common feature of camp life. According to Venables, "At ordinary times a space would be left alongside the camp, where men could say their prayers, and of course no one would even pass in front of a kneeling worshipper."[49]

Prayers were also invoked in extraordinary times, including funerals. After one of the men in his company died, Venables gave the men the next day off to bury the deceased. He watched the consecration, "winding up the hillside, now pleasantly green under a smiling sunny sky." The ceremony was done in a unique hybrid of traditional Muslim and British military style. First, "with scrupulous care they laid him in the grave, surmounting the mound with a stone above his head, chanting meanwhile the requisite passages from the Koran, and the prayers for the dead." Then the officers and men were given the order in a dialect typical of the mishmash of speech that had developed in the camps: "Salam, alt!" Finally, all those assembled gave a military salute.[50] This ceremony, which improvised a combination of Egyptian Muslim and British military styles, recalls the men's improvisational approach to songs like "Kam Layla Kam Yawm." Mixing elements from familiar traditions back home and the military environment of the war, the men of the ELC created new forms of consecration just as they made the soundscape of the camps their own.

Another popular spiritual practice utilizing sound was the Sufi *dhikr*. Venables described such a scene: "Two lines of devotees stood facing each other, while the leader at one end intoned passages from the Qoran, the performers swaying sideways as they turned their heads over one shoulder and then the other, uttering the sacred name: 'Allah! Allah!' the rhythm quickening until sometimes participants fell to the ground, from vertigo or exhaustion."[51] The mystical *dhikr* ritual is a way of chanting the name of God paired with movement and dancing to incite a sacred sense of *ṭarab*. Practiced in different ways by Muslims, it has roots supposedly dating back to the Prophet himself. Reported on the authority of Abu Hurayra, the Prophet said, "The world is damned, and so is everything in it, except for remembering God (*al-dunya mal'unatun mal'unun mā fīhā illa dhikr Allah*)."[52] The Qur'an uses the word *dhikr* and its derivatives to speak both of the prophetic call to "remind" people of God's existence, as well as the "remembrance" that such calls inspire. As William C. Chittick puts it, "The use of one word for a movement with two directions—from the Divine to the human and from the human to Divine—is typical of the Qur'an's unitary perspective."[53] Professing God's unity (*tawḥīd*) is one of the first spiritual principles for Muslims, and Sufi mystics have interpreted this injunction by incorporating a number of practices like the *dhikr* into repertoires allowing the spiritual explorer to pass through various stages—also known as *maqāmat*—that culminate in unity between the self and the divine.[54] This final stage of Sufi practice is referred to as "knowledge" (*ma'rifa*), and at different places and times, various Sufi masters have emerged creating unique sets of practices to attain such knowledge. Over time, these practices were institutionalized in Sufi brotherhoods known as *ṭuruq* (sing., *ṭarīqa*; lit. "path").

The enjoyment of *dhikr* ceremonies by the ELC is significant because it illustrates the continued influence of Sufi *ṭuruq* among the communities from which men were recruited. In the late nineteenth century, the Grand Mufti of Egypt, Muhammad 'Abduh, had become critical of Sufism organized by the *ṭuruq*.[55] Rashid Rida, a Muslim scholar and close associate of 'Abduh, described his own experience witnessing a Sufi *dhikr* in the 1930s:

> I sat in the spectators' space. . . . Mawlawi dervishes appeared in their meeting-place in front of us, with their shaikh in the seat of honour. There were handsome beardless youths among them . . . dancing to the moving sounds of the reed-pipe, turning swiftly and skillfully so that their robes flew out and formed circles. . . . I asked, "What's this?" and they told me, "This is the ritual prayer of the order founded by our Lord Jalal al-Din al-Rumi." . . . I could not control myself, and stood up in the centre of the hall and shouted something like this: "O people, or can I call you Muslims! These are forbidden acts. . . . To those who commit them God's word applies, 'they have made their religion a joke and a plaything.'"[56]

Rida rejected the *dhikr* of the Mawlawiya. According to Albert Hourani, he thought of such rituals as "practices through which the beauty of the visible world might distract the believer, the line between sacred and profane love be blurred, and purely human inventions replace the forms of worship which the Qur'an and Hadith stated to be pleasing to God."[57] As religious scholars who studied "the way" (*shar'īa*) of obedience to written law, men like Rida and 'Abduh had a complicated relationship with "the paths" (*ṭuruq*) to sensual knowledge of the Divine (*ma'rifa*) followed by Sufi mystics.[58]

Egyptian religious scholars like Rida and 'Abduh were joined by British officers of the ELC in their antipathy toward Sufi *dhikr* ceremonies. In a letter home, Venables writes of the ritual: "I have often been told that it is dangerous for an infidel white man to be near on such occasions, but I was never objected to."[59] In expressing fear for his own safety, and by imagining that the men under his command saw him first and foremost as an "infidel white man," Venables participates in the popular discourse that racialized Muslims. According to Venables, other officers participated in this discourse more stringently than himself, and he writes, "In our own companies this rite [i.e., the *dhikr*] was not frowned upon, our 'nafars' being allowed to spend their spare time as they pleased, with the proviso of being on the mark the next morning."[60] It seems that at least some British officers joined Egyptian religious notables in stamping out the *dhikr*. Nevertheless, the men of the ELC and others from their communities back home continued seeking spiritual transcendence in this oral/aural practice.

The spiritual practice that was perhaps most at odds with the logic of wartime exigency was fasting. British military authorities refused to countenance breaks or slowdowns to accommodate Ramadan, so they worked with the Grand Mufti of Egypt—at that time Muhammad Bakhit Al-Muti'i—to procure a special legal dispensation (*fatwa*) authorizing ELC laborers not to observe the fast while they were serving in the war.[61] Venables writes of how, "During the fast of Ramadan, which at that time came during the hottest season, a pronouncement from their own Imam was read to the 'taboor' at intervals, dispensing them from observance."[62] However, according to Venables, despite hearing this injunction, "some men attempted to go the whole day without eating or even drinking, which resulted in some cases of illness."[63] Like those who resisted recruitment into the ELC in the first place, some men found themselves once again pitted against an alliance between British military authorities and Egyptian officials.

When Ramadan was over, the men celebrated a holiday known as *'id al-fiṭr* ("the feast of the breaking of the fast"). In France, Coutts gave his men the day off by organizing an interchange with the Chinese Labor Corps.[64] In Palestine, Venables celebrated with a special mutton ration, an afternoon off, and extra pay, which was divided between the squads according to the results of unique competitions. For example, the first squad to make it to the morning *ṭābūr* when the whistle blew received some boxes of cigarettes. Venables described the scene in a letter home: "The signal, then a mighty yell, a cloud of dust, a few seconds' fierce scramble, and squad no. 4 had the verdict."[65] There was also a "Raises' race," which "gave the nafars a chance to see their solemn squad leaders sprinting like hares, and to yell for their own particular Rais, the winner being Rais no. 2."[66]

Imagining the men of the ELC laughing at the exploits of their "solemn leaders sprinting like hares" brings to mind Mikhail Bakhtin's conception of the carnival. Bakhtin sees the depiction of the carnival in European literature as a "temporary suspension of all hierarchic distinctions and barriers."[67] During carnival, the laws and norms that determine the structure of ordinary life are waived for a short time. In his work *Problems of Dostoevsky's Poetics*, Bahktin describes the carnival, which he calls "life turned inside out," in terms of a spatial transformation:

> All *distance* between people is suspended, and a special carnival category goes into effect . . . people who in life are separated by impenetrable hierarchical barriers enter into free and familiar contact on the carnival square.[68] (Emphasis in original)

The ordinary condition of separation between people, which Bakhtin describes here with the spatial metaphor "distance," is temporarily revealed by the carnival to be a socially constructed phenomenon. As in segregated ELC camps, the people in ordinary life are, for Bakhtin, living side by side, but prevented from "free and familiar contact" with one another due to the "impenetrable hierarchical barriers" that surround them. The carnival releases pressure that has built up as a result of this inequality by allowing marginalized voices to be heard in transformed spaces Bakhtin calls "carnival squares." However, a crucial feature of the carnival is that it is only a temporary release valve; when the holiday is over, familiar hierarchies resume and inequality persists.

THEATER

The men of the ELC constructed other carnivalesque spaces by putting on theatrical performances for themselves and the officers. The roots of professional theater in Egyptian Colloquial Arabic were laid by pioneers like Ya'qub Sannu' (1839–1912), Muhammad 'Uthman Jalal (1829–1898), and Muhammad Taymur (1892–1921). In the years leading up to the First World War, Egyptian theater was revolutionized by the theater troupes of Najib al-Rihani and 'Ali al-Kassar. According to Ziad Fahmy, by 1914, "colloquial Egyptian theatrical productions began playing regularly in Cairene and Alexandrian theaters, and they forced out of business many of the Fusha [i.e., Modern Standard Arabic] troupes, which struggled to attract a regular audience."[69] Additionally, "a number of semiprofessional traveling troupes crisscrossed the country, visiting Egyptian provincial towns 'from Aswan to Bani Suwayf to the Delta and the coastal towns.'"[70] The rural Egyptians who made up the bulk of the ELC, then, would likely have been familiar with these performances by the time they began their service.

The most common form of theatrical performance put on by the men was known as a "fantazeeah" (*fāntāziyya*, or "fantasy"). This was described by Venables as "a generic form of entertainment; actually, an invitation to Officers to be present, with consequent prizes of cigarettes for the best show to put on."[71] Like certain lines in the work songs, theatrical performances were explicitly meant to take place in the presence of officers. Venables describes the setting of one such performance:

> Under the starlit sky, on the broadest space the hillside camp could produce, all the nafars squatted or stood in a wide circle. At one side was the part meant for the stage, and opposite were the Officer's boxes (literally boxes, biscuit and others). The footlights consisted of a row of candles placed in biscuit tins; the orchestra squatted near the stage, keeping up a weird noise with whistles and tins used as drums.[72]

The *fāntāziyya* was an event that required a repurposing of the space of the camp. Old ration boxes provided by the British could be used by ELC laborers in unanticipated ways, providing seats for the assembled audience, serving as props in the production, and even as instruments. In their makeshift orchestra, "with whistles and tins used as drums," the men of the ELC used whatever implements were ready at hand to make music as an accompaniment to the performances.

Events like the *fāntāziyya* provided opportunities to subvert the established norms of camp life in the presence of officers and fellow laborers. One of the shows that was regularly performed by the men on these occasions involves three characters: a husband, his wife played by a man in drag, and a character known as the *'ifrīt*, which is a mischievous spirit in Islamic tradition.[73] Venables describes the play in a letter home:

> The husband, Mohamed, has to go out that evening, and tells his wife, another "actor," suitably disguised, not to let anyone else in on any account, warning that there might be a visit from an "afreet." Mohamed does a false alarm ghost noise, which causes his wife to exclaim, "ya Moham-

> med afreet!" And he upbraids his wife for timidity. Then, the smallest nafar gets in a sack and rolls head over heels to the lady, and she shouts, "Ya Mohammed, Afreet!" Taken up in chorus by the whole crowd.[74]

The plot is remarkable for the ways it upset the established norms of camp life. While a disciplined work schedule and plenty of opportunities for competition encouraged a culture of aggressive masculinity within the ELC, which we will explore further in the next chapter, the character of Mohamed's wife gave one laborer the opportunity to dress in drag. Wearing women's clothing and exclaiming in a high falsetto voice would likely be the last thing expected of a man normally seen pushing a shovel or hauling dirt, but the whole point of the *fāntāziyya* was that it was *not* normal, functioning as a brief respite from the harsh realities of wartime work. Other plays were "topical hits" that featured "many sly digs . . . at those in authority."[75] For a brief moment, at least, the *fāntāziyya* allowed space for ELC laborers to air their grievances, practice creativity, and transcend the difficult circumstances they found themselves in.

Nighttime entertainment provided by songs and theater could be accompanied by the consumption of intoxicating substances. While there is no mention in the sources of ELC laborers drinking alcohol, there are numerous references to smoking cigarettes and, occasionally, hashish. Venables saw cigarette consumption as a necessary aspect of keeping up the *esprit de corps* in his company. In one of his letters, he writes, "After the necessities of life and health, the [Egyptian's] first request is for cigarettes. In fact, I have heard them say among themselves that they would give up a part of their ration for cigarettes!"[76] Venables also detected "hashish addiction" through "hazy and wavering stance," but he assured his reader that such cases were "exceptional."[77] The use of hashish by ELC laborers was also attested to by journalist Cecil Sommers, who wrote in his book *Temporary Crusaders*, "Today I took part in a court-martial. . . . A wretched member of the Egyptian Labour Corps was charged with having in his possession several ounces of hashish, a deadly crime."[78]

Another episode preserved in the British archives notes the theatrical proclivities of Egyptian laborers. In a report back to the colonial state, an ELC recruiting officer wrote that he witnessed an impromptu theatrical production put together by the recruits at the district center to entertain themselves one night as they waited to go off to serve in the war. According to the officer, ELC laborers:

> procured an empty biscuit box and installed one of their number to represent my clerk, on either side of him were two gentlemen . . . representing

> the Mamoor Markaz and the doctor, and in front of the box, strutting up and down, was a particularly dirty ruffian representing my unworthy self. The remainder sat down in rows of four some little distance away. One of the men would then be brought up with a great show of reluctance whereupon an official would shout out in a tremendous voice "Iktem!" [*iktab*] (Sign!) He would then be forced to sign and pushed over to the other side amidst howls of delight from the others.[79]

The record of this bit of theater—including the poorly transliterated traces of Egyptian Colloquial Arabic—shows ELC men satirically portraying British recruiting officers in front of them. It also shows that the ELC recruits assembled to watch the performance did not perceive their contracts as consensual, or, at least, they recognized that many of their colleagues felt this way. The "howls of delight" from the crowd indicate that this story of forced conscription resonated. The men of the ELC were conscious of the violence that underwrote the incorporation of many of them into the organization, even if British propaganda attempted to portray them all as "volunteers." They used their theater as a way to express this consciousness to one another, and to the officers who recorded the event.

CONCLUSION

This chapter has reconstructed the sounds that the men of the ELC made at camp in the hopes of listening in on their lives at war. Unlike the white officers and journalists who observed them, the men of the ELC left behind few written sources for historians to read today. What we do have is a number of traces of their speech, music, and theater. These were recorded imperfectly by observers who largely felt alienated by the fact that the ELC had come to dominate the soundscapes of the camps. But if we read against the grain, we can come away from this exercise with a number of insights about the men's lives and their service.

The soundscape of the camp helped the men adapt to the difficult circumstances of war. Songs and chants made work bearable, allowing them to practice some degree of creativity even while engaged in monotonous tasks. The sounds they heard and made could transport the men to another place, if only in their minds. The mystical capabilities of sound meant that it was often linked to spiritual practice, whether the men were working to chants of God's name, praying, or participating in Sufi *dhikr* rituals. The popularity of the *dhikr* inspired anxiety in British officers and Egyptian religious reformers alike, but that did not stop the men of the

ELC from doing it. Such rituals not only provided some familiarity in a strange new land, but also helped the men to transcend the spaces they had been forced to occupy and transported them to another place, if only in their mind.

Sounds also provided the basis for new relationships to form among the men. They chatted with one another about subjects ranging from the mundane to the politically charged. They worked together to put on theatrical performances and sang songs in improvisational, call-and-response format. Leaders could emerge from among the men on the basis of their vocal talents. Songs like "Kam Layla, Kam Yawm" depended on the *mughanni* to provide creative melodies and wordplay to keep them interesting. Sacred ceremonies like prayers, funerals, and Sufi *dhikr* rituals also required leaders who were talented vocalists. Future research could investigate whether these individuals were the same person, and what other kinds of power and authority such figures had at camp. In this sense, the study of sound can help to deconstruct the binary distinction between the religious and the secular.[80]

In addition to building new relationships with one another, the men of the ELC also used sound to engage with their officers. White officers felt alienation at the camps, which had come to be dominated by the men of the ELC. But, at times, their attitudes shifted. ELC men joked to establish a rapport with their officers, which was maintained through the performance of songs and theatrical productions with an audience of officers specifically in mind. For the rank and file, making a direct link with the officers was a shrewd move in the context of a military hierarchy that had placed *ru'asā'* as an intermediary between them. Such a relationship could become useful when the men wanted to appeal the decisions of their *ra'īs* or request small improvements in their working conditions, which they did explicitly in the common song "Kam Layla, Kam Yawm"? This casts the frequent vocal displays of obsequiousness toward the officers in an ironic light; rather than indicating respect, the men ironically could have been performing a level of deference to the officers in the hopes that they might grant them what they desired. What the men of the ELC had come to understand, perhaps better than the British officers themselves, was that their situation at camp depended on the capricious whims of individuals. While the British Empire represented itself as operating according to the rule of law and mutual contract, the laborers understood that violence and *noblesse oblige* were the true forces structuring their day-to-day lives.

CHAPTER 7

THE MEN OF THE ELC TAKE ACTION

AS THEY SERVED TOGETHER in the war, the men of the ELC began to feel a sense of affinity with one another. Their conversations turned to politics and their songs became confrontational. They mostly acted to take out their frustrations in small ways, but sometimes they organized massive protests, strikes, and mutinies. In France, Egyptians were some of the unruliest workers imported for the war. They mutinied against their officers so many times that military officials found it prudent to relocate them by the end of 1917. This kind of politicization could be found to some degree in any theater of the war, whether the docks of Lemnos, Imbros, and Taranto, the scorching deserts of the Sinai and Siwa, the rocky hills of Palestine, or the swampy wetlands north of Basra.

This chapter examines the emergence of a collective identity among the men of the ELC. Such a process, which cuts across the boundaries between individuals and forms a new conception of the political subject, was the necessary precondition for organized action. Any collective needs to determine how it defines itself before an appropriate course of action can be evaluated and undertaken. This sense of identity is different from the togetherness that permeates a gang of laborers working side by side. What Hannah Arendt calls the "somatic experience of laboring together"—which may be encapsulated in the mystical sense of *ṭarab* achieved in the course of singing a work song—functions to "ease labor's toil and trouble in much the same way as marching together eases the effort of walking for each soldier."[1] But this is distinct from the kind of identity necessary for political action, which consists not of an association of "specimens which are fundamentally all alike because they are what they are as mere living organisms"[2]—as in a race—but between a plurality of human beings "who are all different and unequal."[3] Collective identity, then, is the process through which different individuals come together and decide to transcend their differences in order to take action.

COLLECTIVE IDENTITY

Most of the men of the ELC had rarely traveled far beyond their villages—let alone outside of Egypt—before they enrolled. As such, their strongest antebellum identification was most often with their local community at home. For example, the laborer ʿAbd al-Hamid Muhammad Husayn introduces himself in his published memoirs as "the son of al-Kharta al-Jadida, in the neighborhood of al-Imam al-Shafiʿi."[4] This filial metaphor may have been a common way to refer to one's hometown, but it is significant because it indicates a particular attachment to a neighborhood. The place itself is located within a constellation of sacred geography, important for its proximity to the tomb of the renowned Muslim jurist al-Shafiʿi, the eponymous founder of one of the four major schools of Sunni jurisprudence.

Laborers like Husayn who identified primarily with their home villages would have had these identifications initially reinforced by British military policy. This required that "men who had enlisted together from the same village under their own headmen were kept together in the same companies."[5] This is corroborated by Venables, who writes that Egyptians "enlist in squads of 50, usually from the same 'belad' (village), each squad having a 'rais' (leader) who is usually a man of some importance in the village at home."[6] From the moment they were first recruited into the ELC, then, men from the same province or village were kept together in groups numbering in the dozens or hundreds. They traveled together on trains to the supply depots, and, for those serving in the Western Front, Italy, or the Dardanelles, they took the same boat.[7] The average company of five hundred to one thousand men would have contained a number of discrete groups or "squads" from different parts of Egypt who were recruited, outfitted, and traveled together.

As these men worked together, their local identities became displaced by identification with the company or squad, each of which was assigned its own unique number. According to Venables, the Thirty-Ninth Company, which he joined in late 1918, became "a unit with an awareness of identity."[8] Venables even used the Egyptian Colloquial Arabic terminology to show how the men under his command spoke of these new identifications, writing, "'tissa-wa talateen' (thirty-nine) had a distinctive ring," and "Squad No. 8 was known as the 'osta' (captains)."[9] As we saw in chapter 6, snippets of Egyptian Colloquial Arabic like these help to lend credibility to Venables' claims.[10] Certainly, a sense of solidarity had developed among the British officers of the ELC, as is evident in the pages of the regular newspaper that circulated among them, the *ELC News*. One article from the second issue states this plainly: "The ELC has spread its tentacles over a goodly portion of the map, and we hope that this little paper may promote the feeling of unity, homogeneity of interests, and esprit de corps."[11]

The many opportunities for competition during the average workday reinforced the formation of group and subgroup identities. Venables wrote about these small competitions in his letters home: "Usually we find that a number of men work together, and these little groups compete against each other. There is also great rivalry among the squads as to who shall finish first."[12] As the men moved into Palestine, their work consisted of boring large holes in the earth to affix roads on rocky terrain for wheeled transport. In the course of this work, Venables recounted "one or two boring competitions" that "produced some exciting contests, as not only is the prize of cigarettes a strong incentive, but there is considerable rivalry in the claim to be champion pair of the company."[13] Competition turned work into action, as the relative energy of each strike of the hammer into the rocky hillside and each load of dirt transported atop a man's shoulders carried a message intended for those around him about the relative importance he placed in the group and his decision to conform to the standards set by the officers.

The competitive spirit that held groups of workers together was maintained outside of the workspace. According to Venables, when a squad finished a day's work:

> They were allowed to return to camp, singing lustily to signalize their prowess, not without some opprobrious comments on squads of townies, described . . . by more derogatory epithets, and who, where possible, were transferred to work more suited to their weakly physique and lack of perseverance.[14]

ELC men were expected to work hard and complete their task, and the squads that finished early used their singing and speech to signal pride in their accomplishment and set themselves apart from others in the group. Speech, in this instance, also became action, signaling membership in a collective that excluded others from joining. Those who finished late were characterized by their "weakly physique and lack of perseverance," and, at times, they could even be transferred to other kinds of work.

Back in the Suez Canal zone, the competitive energy of the squads was kept alive in programs of organized sports. According to an article in the *ELC News*, a large crowd of spectators, including naval officers and civilians, gathered in Port Sa'id on New Year's Day 1919 to watch a program of boxing at the nearby ELC camp. The article notes, "Several interesting fights were put up between nafars of the ELC, who showed much determination and courage and often no small amount of skill."[15] At the same event, "a number of tugs-of-war between various gangs were highly amusing, the nafars looking on getting vociferously excited, and being sometimes restrained with difficulty from lending a hand to their losing champions."[16] Organized sports like these provided opportunities for inter- and intra-group competition, which contributed to the consolidation of collective identities among the men of the ELC. In acting together or in competition with one another, the men began to feel a sense of sameness among themselves.

With competitions at work and at rest, and with the losers taunted for their "weakly physique," the outlines of a distinctly masculine culture celebrating bodily strength, stamina, and working prowess arose among the men of the ELC. This is not so different than the culture of competitive masculinity that emerged in Egypt among the upwardly mobile middle classes after the war.[17] An article from *Al-Muqattam* meant to celebrate the achievements of the brave men serving in the war provides one anecdote that makes these cultural norms explicit. It tells the story of a group of camel drivers for the CTC in Palestine who "hid themselves and ran away" in an effort to escape the dangers of battle. According to the article, the group was shamed for their lack of masculinity: "Their colleagues and others said they were 'girls' (*banāt*) who were not worthy to be called 'men' (*rajāla*)."[18] As we have already seen, while the reports of *Al-Muqattam* were largely designed as propaganda to support the British in the war, this story, if true, illustrates the importance of masculinity as one aspect of the emerging collective identity that developed among the men of the ELC.

The men of the ELC also differentiated themselves in nuanced ways from the so-called local Arabs while serving in Iraq, the Sinai Peninsula, and Palestine. To get a sense of how the local population was perceived in the Middle East, we can look to the writings of a British medical officer, who described the roughly four thousand people of al-'Arish as "a thoroughly cowed, disheartened, poverty-stricken crew."[19] When the EEF entered the town, they immediately undertook a sanitation campaign; a house-to-house tour was organized with an Egyptian doctor acting as an interpreter, and each house was "thoroughly cleansed, sprayed with germicide, its compound scavenged, and all garbage and rubbish consigned to the nearest incinerator."[20] ELC laborers were used on sanitary routines and sent out scavenging on details like this in al-ʿArish and other villages occupied by the EEF as it advanced through the Sinai and into Palestine.[21]

In addition to sanitary work, ELC laborers were organized and trained into a police force, which, at its peak, included a thousand men guarding the camps on the lines of supply and communication in the villages of southern Palestine.[22] In Iraq, Egyptians were employed as a police force to "preserve order and public security" in Baghdad.[23] The relationship between ELC laborers and the local population, then, was governed by a different set of power dynamics in the Middle Eastern theaters. Compared to their compatriots in France, ELC laborers in the Middle East had greater freedom of movement and did not occupy the lowest or most marginalized position in the space of the camp—a position that was reserved for "local Arabs." This was reinforced in the daily interactions between Egyptian sanitary crews, scavenging details, and police guards.

While their status as members of the EEF set them apart from the local population, the men of the ELC also seemed to integrate with people in the Sinai and Palestine in nuanced ways. According to Venables, the men under his command were "fond of prowling about this new land, which, if not as fertile and as well-cultivated as their own mud flats of Egypt, is at least preferable to the desert."[24] After receiving their pay, the laborers would visit local markets to purchase supplies and food, giving them further opportunities to interact with Palestinians in their villages. The camps where the ELC men lived and worked also provided opportunities for Egyptians and Palestinians to interact. According to Venables, locals who "came down from the hills" were a constant presence in the ELC camps, often bringing fruit with them and reselling it to British troops at a profit.[25] Sports gave the two groups an additional chance to mingle. For example, one report in the *ELC News* recalls a competitive two-mile race in Qantara. The winner was so fast that the commanding officer sent for him and asked him to be the company messenger, but the man replied that he was a Palestinian from a village close by and was therefore ineligible for the task.[26] Moreover, the British soon took to recruiting "casual laborers" from among the local populations to assist in the logistical work required for the army. In the official statistics on laborers working in Palestine, the British High Commissioner of Egypt noted, "were [casual laborers] included [in the total number of enrollments by the EEF], it would represent a very much larger proportion of the total than was the case last year, and that total itself would be much higher."[27] The British army may not have kept statistics on the casual laborers they recruited from Palestine, but they acknowledged that the number grew as the war dragged on.

One of the major ways that the men of the ELC interacted with the local population around them in the Middle Eastern theaters of the war was through their speech. Officers like Venables could tell the difference between the Egyptian Arabic of the ELC men and the Levantine Arabic of the Palestinians, and while the British modified the small amount of Arabic they knew to fit the Levantine dialect, the men of the ELC were, according to Venables, "simply blurting out their guttural Egyptian dialect."[28] However, this did not keep them from "apparently understanding quite readily the replies given by the Palestinians in their softer, more undulating tongue."[29] When the men were camped in Egypt, getting ready to move out or helping to construct fortifications for the base depot of the MEF at Alexandria, they also spoke to the people around them. Venables recounts one incident at the Hadra supply depot outside of Alexandria in which the propensity of his men to strike up conversations with the locals got them in trouble with the police:

> Our Soudanese gateman had a nearby lady friend, with whom he was chatting one evening, when a mounted constable from the police station opposite came over to contest his claim with our janitor, who riposted lustily, calling out in his own tongue, which at once brought a rush of his fellow countrymen, who dragged the interfering Iskanderani from his horse and proceeded to give a pretty good rendering of a large-sized rugby scrimmage. The Egyptian police lieutenant came dashing into the reed hut used as our officers dining room, exclaiming hysterically that his constable was being murdered. My barked request for order attained instant quiet, and the number of Soudanese in the crowd told its own tale.[30]

The men of the ELC, then, could use their speech to flirt with local women. But mere chatter could spin out of control and go horribly wrong. In this story, a laborer chatted up a woman who had caught the eye of a local policeman, and the latter used it as an excuse to come and "contest his claim." Perhaps confident because of the official monopoly over the use of force theoretically enjoyed by the police, what the officer did not realize is that the true power in the situation was on the side of the men of the ELC, who had strength in numbers. They "dragged him from his horse and proceeded to give him a pretty good rendering of a large-sized rugby scrimmage." The police lieutenant, apparently unable to stop the assembled crowd of laborers on his own, called in the ELC officers for help. Venables came to his rescue with another speech act, a "barked request," which resulted in "instant quiet." As the story continues, Venables explains that he ultimately cooperated with the police, and "all participants were arrested and sent to Area Headquarters."[31]

This incident provides insight into the process of collective identity formation at ELC camps. Venables described the man who started it as "Soudanese," focusing on his racial characteristics. Moreover, those who came to his aid were also of Sudanese origin, perhaps lending credence to the notion that ties to local place of birth before the war remained important for the men during their service. But the very fact that the presence of the contesting policeman produced such a display of solidarity from the other men shows how interaction with the local population could serve to reinforce both preexisting identities and the new sense of identity that was beginning to emerge at the squad and company level because of shared experiences in the war. One can only imagine the interesting conversations that took place among the men as they were locked up in the area headquarters while recovering from the scrum. Finally, this story illustrates the contingency of political action. When individuals act politically, they attempt to invent or reinforce collective identity, but in the spatial world inhabited by plural individuals, actors can never be assured of how others will react and interpret their actions. In this example, a simple speech act sets off a whole chain of events, leading to a physical confrontation between a gang of ELC workers and the police, and the subsequent arrest and imprisonment of a group of men.

By the end of their service, the men of the ELC had likely come to think of themselves as part of the same group. One editor of the *ELC News* described how this process took place:

> It is not long before the nafar finds that he is a member of a gang. Songs and jokes become public rather than a private concern. A communal interest in concerts and sports develops. Gang strives to emulate gang, and one company to better the efforts of another. See their flags prepared with much care and no little skill against the happy return to their Village, Hear their boasts! They are new men.[32]

Despite its paternalistic undertones, this report provides a plausible account for how group and subgroup identity developed among the men of the ELC. Living together with their squad for days on end and given countless opportunities to compete against one another in work and in sport, the men of the ELC could come to see themselves as part of the same collective. Through their interaction with the population around them, these men differentiated themselves in nuanced and complex ways from the "local Arabs." In the Middle Eastern theater of the war, the men of the ELC were simultaneously Arabs and not-Arabs. They had forged a unique identity, sometimes differentiated according to squad or company, but all in a similar situation.

WEAPONS OF THE WEAK: STEALING, SLOWDOWNS, AND DESERTION

When they became aware of their collective grievances, the men of the ELC often acted in concert to change their situation. One approach they employed, likely the most widespread, involved techniques that James Scott has famously called "weapons of the weak." Scott criticizes the tendency of scholars to focus on large-scale rebellions and revolutions in their studies of worker and peasant politics, noting that most forms of this struggle between the peasantry and those who seek to extract labor, food, taxes, rents, and interest from them "stop well short of outright collective defiance."[33] Instead, Scott calls attention to the "ordinary weapons of relatively powerless groups," including foot dragging, dissimulation, desertion, false compliance, pilfering, feigned ignorance, slander, arson, and sabotage.[34] By employing techniques like these, relatively powerless groups like the men of the ELC were able to turn the circumstances of their subordination to their own advantage, carving out space to live a little more comfortably.

One technique that Egyptians employed was work slowdowns. British officers often referred to this as "laziness" or "slacking." Venables detailed the long hours that the men under his command would spend at home laboring in their fields, but he quickly followed this up with a lamentation on how, "when . . . they become accustomed to receiving food every night without having to pay for it, and to being clothed and accommodated without any worry on their part, they are naturally apt to become lazy, if not properly managed."[35] British officers designed the task system with these ideas about the inherent laziness of "the natives" in mind. But as we saw in chapter 4, the task system was abandoned in the face of emergencies.[36] With this overwork in mind, we should see slowdowns as a tactic to manage workload creep. So-called "slackers" were singled out and punished, at times through the formal methods of military discipline, and at times with violence.[37] This could serve as an example to the others, but Venables' unceasing complaints about "slacking" indicate that the technique continued to hold some promise for the men.

Many who were overworked and freezing in the wintry conditions of Palestine sought relief from the medical officer. When the first winter rains hit in Gaza, as many as one-fifth of the men in Venables' company did not join the morning *ṭābūr*, opting instead for the so-called sick parade.[38] As he saw it, "many were not actually sick, but merely wet and cold, and were seeking this means to escape, even if only for a few hours, from working with the company."[39] This was not a onetime occurrence, and Venables noted that many had used the sick parade to avoid work.[40] He was also critical of the Egyptian medical officer. Rumors circulated about the practice of *baqshīsh*, or the giving of bribes by ELC men to the medical officers so that they could be admitted to the hospital, but Venables found no evidence of this in his own company.[41] Nevertheless, mass "sick-outs" could be a successful strategy that allowed the men to escape from the harsh weather and overwork they were forced to endure in Palestine.

In addition to being overworked, the men were underfed, and to remedy this situation, they organized efforts to smuggle extra rations out of military stores. When Venables arrived at the camp under his command in Gaza, he noticed that "instead of there being, for example, fifty loaves in each sack there were forty-five, forty, and even as low as thirty-three."[42] Eventually, he discovered that the supplies, which had to be transported by camel convoy from the terminus of the advancing railway to the ELC camps at their forward positions, had been "systematically stolen" by camel drivers.[43] By skimming the rations that they were assigned to transport, some men were able to work around the limitations imposed on them by the rationing system of the British army and turn the complexities of the military logistics system to their own advantage. But Venables worked to close this loophole by abolishing the camel convoys and appointing new men to manage the stores. One can only imagine what kind of schemes the officers failed to uncover.

For those unable to bear being overworked and underfed, one appealing option was desertion. In his work on weapons of the weak, Scott surveys the secondary literature from Southeast Asia to postrevolutionary France and concludes, "Desertion and evasion of conscription . . . have undoubtedly limited the imperial ambitions of many a monarch."[44] So too amongst the Egyptian laborers in Palestine, who were clearly prone to desertion and escape from their companies. Venables reports coming across one deserter from another company lying ill and starving in a Palestinian village.[45] This prompted him to reflect on his experiences with wandering Egyptians during his time in Palestine:

> Throughout the winter, one had met Egyptians on the road from the hills, men belonging to the Labor, the Camels, Donkey Transport, or other Corps. Some are no doubt deserters, many are men discharged from the hospital, trying to find their units, and wandering on and on, not knowing where they will eventually arrive. At the risk of encouraging these vagrants, we have insisted on their staying in our camps overnight, rather than leave them to be caught in a storm on the road, and, where possible, have put them on a more direct track to their destination.[46]

According to Venables, the sight of lone Egyptians, detached from their companies and wandering about the wilderness of Palestine, was a relatively common occurrence. This allowed for deserters to blend in with men who had legitimate claims to be separated from their company, such as those recently discharged from the hospital. Desertion among Egyptian laborers in Palestine is also attested to in the pages of the *ELC News*, which includes one story of an Egyptian who deserted and was eventually taken as a prisoner of war by the Ottomans.[47] It seems that some Egyptian laborers were able to successfully escape from their companies, but when they did so, they faced a dangerous prospect of surviving in harsh terrain with a high risk of starvation or capture by the enemy.

All these techniques were open secrets to British officers, who joked about them in the pages of the *ELC News*. One satirical article showed how desertion and faking sickness were widely acknowledged as common techniques employed by Egyptian laborers: "Of my original comrades there remain but few. Fifteen deserted in the first week and fourteen have been discharged medically unfit, so there remain but a few of us faithful to the cause. My particular Abdel Mougood is now, I regret to say 'mush mougood' (not here)."[48] In the final line, the author uses the code-switching common to the ELC officer corps to make a play on the Arabic name "Abdel Mougood" and the Egyptian Colloquial usage of the Arabic word *mawgūd* (someone/thing that is present), providing an inside joke that built solidarity among the corps by acknowledging shared experiences in a shared language. Although the article is exaggerated for effect, it seems as though desertion and sick-outs were regular occurrences.

PROTESTS, STRIKES, AND MUTINIES

While the men of the ELC could employ "weapons of the weak," on some occasions they opted for more direct action. Most commonly, their grievances were expressed in the form of complaints that they had overstayed their temporary contracts and were being kept in service for longer than the agreed-upon amount of time. However, this relatively procedural issue masked the deep structural inequalities and systemic racism that the men were fighting against. Group solidarities, which had built up within the companies and squads of the ELC through months of segregation and cohabitation, soon became the basis for efforts to redistribute power relations within the camp. Laborers made demands of their officers, negotiated with them, and, at times, violently attacked them.

The first recorded strikes of ELC laborers seem to have taken place during the Gallipoli campaign. ʿAbd al-Hamid Muhammad Husayn was part of this early campaign and was assigned to work at the Mudros harbor on the island of Lemnos. In his published memoir, Husayn writes, "We encamped [at Mudros] for three months, then we were oppressed and denied our breaks (*thumma taẓulmna bisabab al-ijāzāt*) . . . the English fired bullets at us to get us to break the strike."[49] The verb for "oppression" (*ẓulm*) is expressed here in the passive form, shifting the object of oppression—the first-person plural—to the collective subject of the sentence ("we were oppressed") in a move reminiscent of how organized labor action attempts to transform workers into the subjects of their own history. In the following sentence, Husayn names "The English" (*al-inglīz*) as the perpetrators of this oppression, and describes how they fired shots at the laborers, injuring seventeen and killing one.[50]

Fred Garrett's war diaries also include the story of an incident among ELC laborers in Gallipoli. On August 23, 1915, Garrett writes:

> At daybreak this morning we were all called back to quell a disturbance among the Egyptians. They were refusing to work on account of one of their members sentenced to a flogging. . . . They were very threatening and commenced to come at us with sticks and stones. . . . First a volley of two rounds were fired overhead, then two rounds at their feet, then the Officers gave the order to let them have it. Five were killed and 9 or 10 wounded. This settled them. . . . It was an awful sight, and the effect of the sight of blood on the Egyptians was instantaneous. Even our officers turned their heads.[51]

In this account, the primary grievance of the men is not about the length of their contract, but a reaction to the "flogging" of one of their compatriots. Garrett writes that the men were "very threatening" and armed with "sticks and stones." But the personal antipathy of white officers toward the men could not stop them from recognizing their humanity in that one bloody instant. Garrett writes, "Even our officers turned their heads," when they saw the ensuing slaughter of the men. The decision to respond with live fire seems consistent with Husayn's story recounted above. Any use of force on the part of the men, then, was likely to be outmatched by the British.

These early incidents were harbingers of things to come in Europe, as the ELC turned out to be one of the most rebellious groups of workers on the French docks. The first signs of protest in France came on May 26, 1917, when ELC laborers at Dunkirk deserted en masse and fled into the surrounding villages.[52] Although the sources are silent as to the cause of this incident, it may be related to the German aerial bombardment at Dunkirk around that time that struck and killed a number of men.[53] Troubles apparently continued with this company, and on June 4, 1917, men of the ELC were reported to have threatened their officers there.[54]

Beginning in September 1917, a series of disturbances broke out among ELC workers in France. The largest incident occurred in Boulogne, where the Seventy-Third and Seventy-Eighth Companies mutinied and refused to work. According to the official British report on labor in France, "[The Egyptians] would not listen to reason. Force had to be used and several men were killed and wounded before the rising was quelled."[55] An ELC officer recounted the mutiny at Boulogne to William Brett St. Leger, which he recorded in his diary. According to this source, the Boulogne mutiny included fourteen hundred Egyptian laborers who were "raving with fury" and looking to kill their British officers. The Egyptians used improvised weapons including poles, buckets, and "anything and everything within reach," and "began wrecking everything." The British troops responded by firing on the men "from three sides of a square, and . . . the Egyptians simply melted away."[56] Twenty-three Egyptians were killed, with an additional twenty-four wounded in the incident.[57]

Another large incident took place on September 10, 1917, in Calais when the Seventy-Fourth Company refused to work. British officers opened fire, killing four and wounding fifteen.[58] The incidents among ELC workers in France continued on a somewhat smaller scale throughout the autumn of 1917. On September 16 there was a mutiny at the ELC Base Depot in Marseilles, and throughout October, ELC laborers in

France continued to strike and agitate. The British began to adopt a more conciliatory tone. By October 25, 1917, the Seventy-Fourth Company at Calais, the Seventy-Fifth Company at Havre, and the Seventy-Sixth Company at Rouen were all on strike.[59] The British responded by negotiating with the laborers and ultimately moved them all to a rest camp in Marseilles. By the end of 1917, ELC laborers were moved out of France, and although they were considered as a potential pool of laborers there as late as 1918, they would not return again.[60]

The records of the British War Office include the Field General Court Martial (FGCM) proceedings from the Marseilles mutiny on September 16, 1917, which provides the most in-depth look at any of these cases. According to the records, a laborer named Mahmud Muhammad Ahmad was tried and found guilty of "conduct to the prejudice of good order and military discipline" for striking a white officer, Second Lieutenant A. G. Turley, on the head with a stick.[61] Ahmad was accused of leading a group of fifty to one hundred men in a refusal to work during the morning *ṭābūr*, then arming the men with sticks, hitting the officer, and ultimately "ordering the men to break down the fences and cut the barbed wire" with a rifle and bayonet in his hands.[62] He was tried by the FGCM on September 26, 1917, and found guilty of two charges: using violence to his superior officer at camp, and "civil offense of wounding with intent to murder."[63] He was sentenced to death and executed by firing squad on October 10, 1917.

The FGCM records preserve a version of Ahmad's narrative of events translated into English. Called as the sole witness for his own defense, Ahmad argued that his original agreement had been violated, saying, "When I was enlisted, the Pasha said my agreement would last for seven months, including both journeys to and from Egypt." Interestingly, when Ahmad is recorded as blaming the misunderstanding on "the Pasha," his comment indicts not the British, but Egyptian officials in the government. Whether this was an instance of projection on the part of the British official who transcribed the testimony is unclear. Nevertheless, according to Ahmad, the laborers had enlisted their foremen on September 15 to "represent to the commandants that [the men] had completed their agreement."

So far, the issue has been presented mainly as a procedural misunderstanding; Ahmad's primary complaint is that the men have overstayed their contracts, and the role of "the Pasha" in mediating this contract gives the British officer, who transcribed this testimony and left it for future historians to read, plausible deniability that any systemic problems with the ELC are to blame. However, according to the testimony, the incident turned violent when Ahmad's complaint was received with the reply: "You sons of dogs will be kept here by force."[64] The officer transcribes Ahmad's account of what followed:

> When we found this was how we were being treated, we all made for our tents and got some sticks. When we had armed ourselves with sticks, [the British Officer] came up with a rifle and bayonet, saying he had orders to shoot [insert: and] use his bayonet if ~~they~~ [insert: we] didn't work. I protected myself with my forearm on being threatened by him. I then took the bayonet and rifle from the sergeant and remained perfectly quiet till the Base Commandant arrived. . . . I gave up the rifle and bayonet to the Base Commandant. When we were ordered to give up our sticks, we all complied. Then [the foremen] came and put us under guard. The commandant was not aware who was the ringleader. I was arrested on the word of the NCOs.[65]

The hand of the British interpreter is easily seen through a slippage in the use of pronouns, when the scribe crossed out "they" and wrote "we" to make it seem like it was Ahmad himself who was saying these things. It is just as likely that the interpreter framed the narrative in a way that would facilitate a conviction. Even with this caveat in mind, it seems Ahmad argued that he acted in self-defense. He did not deny the fact that a small, lightly armed insurrection had occurred, but he believed that he had been wrongly singled out for punishment.

According to his recorded and translated testimony, the primary cause of the disturbance was that the ELC laborers believed they had already completed their contract, which he understood to be "seven months, including both journeys to and from Egypt." From the perspective of the British War Office, these contracts were for six months, not including travel time. In point of fact, the official report on British labor in France notes that "not one single officer of the ELC who came to France was aware of the nature of the contract signed by their men. They had merely hazy notions about it."[66]

The so-called haziness surrounding the contract was one important cause of the disagreement, but it seems to have been exacerbated by the poor treatment of ELC laborers. Ahmad expressed this in his accusation that the British officers had told him, "You sons of dogs will be kept here by force." It is the dehumanizing epithet "sons of dogs" that sets the chain of events in motion. The hazardous consequences of speech acts, which have the potential to become political, could spark violence that elevated the stakes of the situation. Violence cut across the physical and conceptual boundaries of camp life, as when Ahmed "broke down the fences and cut the barbed wire," or struck a white officer. Such acts had the potential to steer the collective identities already present at camp in a new political dimension.

Finally, it is significant that Ahmad had been disciplined on two previous occasions: once for insubordination on April 12, 1917, and once for "causing a riot in camp" on May 31, 1917. In this figure, the British found an easy target: a "rebellious agitator" on whom to pin the blame for the incident at Marseilles. Ahmad was not the only repeat offender in France, and the official report for British labor notes that "about fifty of the worst characters were sent to prison for various terms."[67] The British responded to individuals who were inclined to take action against the ELC hierarchy by spatially isolating them and thus depriving them of the capacity to act in any way that might influence others.

The month of September 1917 also saw uprisings of ELC laborers in Taranto, Italy. According to the records of the British Foreign Office, "trouble on the 26th of September was caused by the eighty-first company, who were given to understand by the eighty-second company that they (the latter) were moving off to Egypt in two days' time."[68] When the men of the Eighty-First Company thought that their fellow workers were returning home while they themselves were being forced to stay longer, they refused to work. The men were called out to a *ṭābūr*, and "the matter was fully explained to them," but they refused to move back into the camp at the end of the *ṭābūr* and instead "began rioting." The document describes the British response:

> [The rioting] was checked by their officers and an armed guard which was called out. Beyond making a demonstration in force, the guard was not used. The company was then closed in by a barbed wire fence and left where they were for the night. The next morning, the 27th, they gave in and said they would resume work. . . . Since that date they have given no trouble.[69]

The British responded with force, though it is hard to say the number of casualties that were inflicted. The source is quick to assert that "the guard was not used," but as we have seen, this restraint was not the norm in dealing with strikes in other European theaters of the war. Authorities built a "barbed wire fence" around the workers' encampment to prevent future uprisings, illustrating how the built environment could also be constructed to politically neutralize communities that constituted a threat.

The men of the ELC undertook a variety of political actions in different theaters of the war, including strikes, mutinies, and protests. The most contentious theaters were in Europe, where Egyptians in Gallipoli, France, and Italy mutinied against their officers. These demonstrations were most often couched as being a response to violations of the contract. But these violations took place in a context of systemic abuse and maltreatment, and served more as a spark than the root cause of the problem.

CONCLUSION

The men of the ELC undertook many different types of political action at the camps. They could employ what James Scott calls "weapons of the weak" and try to influence their situation through subtle and nonconfrontational means. When they found they had unsuitable rations, for example, they organized a group with the men from the camel convoy to steal the food they needed. Mass sick-outs at the rate of one out of every five men were recorded by Venables, and desertion seems to have been widespread. It would be a mistake, then, to assume that every political act at the camps was violent and spectacular.

But sometimes, the men decided that more direct, confrontational action was needed. Protests, strikes, and mutinies broke out. These were especially concentrated in the European theaters of battle, including France, Italy, and the Dardanelles. It was here that men experienced the most stringent segregation, and here that they responded with the most brutal force. Egyptians in Europe rose up en masse, with as many as fourteen hundred men joining one demonstration in Boulogne.

When they broke through the barbwire fences that segregated them, seized the weapons of their white officers, and used them to fight back, ELC laborers were acting in ways that cut across physical and conceptual barriers. These actions must have appeared miraculous; the men were able to upend the dominant hierarchy of white supremacy that ruled in the camps—if only for a moment. But they ultimately proved disastrous when the British responded with overwhelming force and massacred laborers in France, Taranto, and Gallipoli. On the Palestine front, protests, strikes, and mutinies seem to have been comparatively few, but there is one case that stands out: War Office records show sentences of execution passed down to two laborers, Husayn Muhammad al-'Urabi and Muhammad 'Abdallah Hassan, who were found guilty of beating their *ra'īs* to death in Qantara.[70]

Collective identity was the basis for political action and undergoing change at the camps. The men used their speech, their work, and their participation in organized sports to act in concert with one another. The norms that developed through such action prioritized masculine laboring prowess and the willingness to expose oneself to bodily harm. While these norms assisted British military authorities in their efforts to use the men of the ELC as cannon fodder in the war, they could easily be translated to more confrontational, violent, and political actions vis-à-vis their superiors at camp. When the men used their own bodily strength to strike down their officers and foremen, they broke through the barriers that kept the hierarchy of the ELC in place and created the possibility of a new kind of order that was quickly snuffed out by overwhelming British force. The next chapter shifts the focus to people back in Egypt, who were also beginning to develop a politicized sense of collective identity that was outraged by the treatment of the ELC. It was this emerging collective that would act—not always in unison—in the 1919 revolution.

CHAPTER 8

"I WILL NOT ACCEPT SLAVERY!"

AS THE WAR ENDED, nationalist politicians in Egypt struggled to organize a *wafd* ("delegation") to participate in the Paris Peace Conference. The *wafd* would go on to become the most popular political party in interwar Egypt. Their leader was Sa'd Zaghlul (Saad Zagloul), the older brother of Ahmad Fathi Zaghlul, whose side job popularizing social Darwinist thought was discussed in chapter 2. The oldest son of the *'umda* of a village in the Nile Delta, the elder Zaghlul moved to Cairo at the age of fourteen to attend al-Azhar University, where he studied under luminaries of Islamic modernism like Jamal al-Din al-Afghani and Muhammad 'Abduh.[1]

Zaghlul soon traded in his Azhari robes for the suit of a modern gentleman. In 1893, while he was working as a lawyer and vacationing in Istanbul, he met two influential young journalists who were speaking out against the British occupation, Ahmad Lutfi al-Sayyid and Isma'il Sidqi.[2] In 1906, Zaghlul was named minister of education, where he famously clashed with his British adviser by insisting on Arabic as the language of instruction in government schools.[3] When the British colonial government launched an experiment in Egyptian representative democracy in 1913, Zaghlul won a seat on the legislative assembly, but it was suspended the following year upon the outbreak of the war and the institution of martial law.

On March 8, 1919, Zaghlul and the leaders of the *wafd* were arrested and exiled to Malta. Protests soon broke out in Cairo. A strike coordinated by a network of middle-class professionals, including lawyers, government ministers, students, and religious notables from al-Azhar spread across the country. At the same time, one of the largest rural rebellions in the history of the modern Middle East took place, with masses of people in villages and towns attacking the infrastructures of the colonial state.[4]

FIGURE 8.1.
Sa'd Zaghlul, 1926.
W. Hanselman.
Wikimedia Commons.

Authorities relaxed their pressure on the *wafd*, allowing them to travel to Paris and negotiating with them in a process that would eventually lead to a unilateral, highly conditional drawdown of British troops in Egypt. In the meantime, the EEF was mobilized to crush the rebellion in the countryside, killing approximately three thousand people along the way.[5] This episode is known in Egyptian historiography as the 1919 revolution, and popular memory in Egypt has enshrined it as the founding moment of the modern Egyptian nation-state.[6]

The ELC played an important symbolic role for nationalist activists and intellectuals during the revolution. In their rhetoric, the men of the *wafd* lambasted the hypocrisy of what the British called "voluntary" recruitment, insisting that what was happening with the ELC was closer to "slavery" (*ifrīqiyya*). Representations comparing ELC workers to "Black slaves" (*zunūj*), "men of color" (*hommes de couleur*), and "African savages" (*waḥūsh ifrīqiyya*) drew their mobilizing force from popular conceptions of national identity that posited Egyptian racial difference from, and superiority to, Black Africans. At the same time, the good works of the ELC and their contributions to British victory in the war were taken to undermine claims of white political supremacy. In response to the racialization of Egyptians as people of color, nationalist politicians and public intellectuals centered *fallāḥīn*, like the men of the ELC, as the true symbols of Egyptian national and racial authenticity. The dominant discursive mode of nationalism that emerged in the decade or so after the revolution—which posited a biological and cultural link between modern Egyptians, especially the *fallāḥīn*, and the ancient Pharaohs—was an Egyptian version of racial nationalism. This discourse worked to differentiate political leaders like Zaghlul, who were rural-to-urban middle-class strivers, as heirs to an ancient "civilization" and not deserving of imperial subordination.

Many scholars have already pointed out the historical relationship between ideas of race and the emergence of the modern nation-state.[7] Philosopher David Theo Goldberg traces the transformation of the race concept in Europe from its original sense of aristocratic lineage and breeding to a modern notion that understands racial distinctions as inherited within population groups. A key moment in Goldberg's schematic history takes place with the shift from biblical monogenism, which traced all human beings back to Adam and Eve and ascribed racial difference to environmental factors, to polygenism, which posited different origins for different races of humans and explained hierarchy in terms of biological difference between groups instead of pedigree within them.

The story culminates with Goldberg asserting that "race and nation signify intersecting discourses of modernist anonymity."[8] According to Goldberg, as our social relationships become denser, the race concept provides a grid of intelligibility through which we make sense of who we can identify with and who we can exclude, oppress, exploit, and annihilate. In Goldberg's telling, the modern race concept is similar to Benedict Anderson's "imagined community" of the nation, but it pushes the logic of national identification to its extreme by inserting a sense of biological determinism into definitions of the collective.[9] Goldberg's contingent history of the race concept reminds us that there is no single meaning for race across space and time. The task remains to uncover the varied semantics of the terms through which the race concept has been expressed in historically specific contexts.[10]

However, the stress Goldberg places on secularization in the history of race in Europe does not translate completely to modern Egypt. As this chapter will show, ideas about race in Egypt existed at the intersection of the global discourse of scientific racism on one hand, and notions of identity and community drawn from the Islamic discursive tradition on the other. As the locus of the dominant political community (*umma*) in Egypt shifted from Muslim believers to "indigenous Egyptians," the stress on the metaphysical as opposed to strictly physical aspects of communal belonging remained. Like racial nationalists in interwar Romania and Yugoslavia, nationalist intellectuals in Egypt came to perceive peasants as the cornerstone of ethnic identity.[11] In this way, the abuse that the British had heaped upon the *fallāḥīn* of the ELC became a metaphor for abuse of the national essence, and politicians and intellectuals of rural extraction found themselves positioned to lead a mass movement.

THE ROOTS OF RACIAL NATIONALISM IN EGYPT

While the words race and nation emerged into wide circulation in English during the late sixteenth century, the Arabic language has long contained a number of words that can be used to fix individuals within homogenous social groups that reproduce biologically. In her recent historical study of race science in the Middle East, Elise K. Burton offers a helpful framework for thinking about these different Arabic words. Some are associated with typology or logically abstracting similarities from diverse individual cases, including *ṣanf* (pl. *aṣnāf*) and *nau'* (pl. *anwā'*). By the time that intellectuals writing in Arabic were becoming familiar with European race science, the word *jins* (pl. *ajnās*)—which is etymologically derived from the same Greek word that gives us "genus"—was most often used to translate the modern concept of "race."[12] Recognizing this can be confusing for scholars and Arabic speakers, because the word *jins*—which literally means "type"—is regularly applied to gender and nationality today. Likewise, the word most often used to signify the concept of race in contemporary Arabic is *'unṣur*. This comes from a second category of terms that refer to ancestral root or lineage, including *'irq*, *sulāla*, and *nasab*. As Rachel Schine has shown, these are attested in Arabic since before the time of the prophet and continued to be used in the Classical literary language.[13]

In the late nineteenth century, a third group of words traditionally related to religious communities—including *umma* and *milla* (*millet* in Turkish)—came to take on the added connotations of nation and race.[14] According to Louis Massignon, the word *umma* in the Qur'an "denotes the group of people to whom God sends a prophet and more especially those who, having listened to his preaching, believe in him."[15] In this sense, the Qur'anic *umma* of Muslims "transcended but did not efface prior social differences" based on familial ties and kinship and represented in the Qur'an by words like *qawm*, *sha'b*, and *qabīla* ("people" or "tribe").[16]

When Islamic modernists wrote about the *umma* in the late nineteenth century, they did so at a time when, as discussed in chapter 1, the British Empire was racializing Muslims in Egypt, India, and the Ottoman Empire as "Mohammedans."[17] Jamal al-Din al-Afghani, an itinerant Muslim scholar from Iran who lived in Egypt from 1871 to 1879, was the most prominent voice speaking out against the oppression of Muslims at this time. One of his recurring themes was the rejection of what he called "blind imitation" (*taqlīd*). He applied this attitude to Islamic tradition and modern European science equally, arguing that Muslims should look to both with an attitude of reasoned skepticism. This careful sifting of different traditions—rejecting and preserving only certain elements of each—allowed al-Afghani to combine traditional Islamic notions of community and identity with European modernist discourses, and left behind a hybridized legacy for intellectuals in Egypt to appropriate.

Al-Afghani was clearly influenced by European notions of social Darwinism. This is ironic because his only surviving book is known as a critique of Darwinism. According to Marwa Elshakry, it was initially published in Persian during al-Afghani's brief stay in India from 1879 to 1882, and was translated into Arabic as *A Refutation of the Materialists* (*Al-Radd 'ala al-Dahriyin*) in 1886, when Shibli Shumayyil's translations of Darwin were at the height of their popularity.[18] Al-Afghani rejected Darwin's ideas primarily on the basis of their claim to novelty, placing them in conversation with earlier theories like Greek atomism and materialism, and brushing them off like the classical Arabic scholars who had refuted Greek science with Muslim theology.

But in the essays he dictated to his protégé Muhammad 'Abduh in *Al-'Urwa al-Wuthqa* (1884), Al-Afghani lays out a vision of history and sociology that is clearly inspired by the terms of the Darwinist school he sought to refute in his earlier work. One illuminating essay is titled "al-Jinsiyya fi-l-Diyana al-Islamiyya" ("Racism in the Islamic Religion"). It asserts that Muslims, "despite their differing countries [of origin] oppose taking race or nationality (*al-jinsiyyāt*) into account" and refuse "any type of group solidarity (*ay nau' min anwā' al-'aṣabiyyat*) except for Islamic solidarity."[19] Nevertheless, al-Afghani recognizes the important influence of what we might translate as "racial chauvinism" (*al-ta'aṣṣub li-l-jins*) defining it as an evolutionary characteristic arising from the struggle for survival. He writes that humans were "forced, after a long period of struggle, to join up on the basis of descent in varying degrees until they formed races (*ajnās*) and dispersed themselves into nations (*umam*), such as the Indian, the English, the Russian, and the Turkoman and so forth, so that each group of them (*kull al-qabīl minhum*), through the conjoined power of its individual members, could protect its own interest from the attacks of other groups."[20] Here we see the *umma* compared not to other religious communities like Christians and Jews, but to racial or national types (*ajnās*) like the Indians or the English.

In other essays, al-Afghani compared the religious community of Muslims to "a great body (*al-milla ka-jism 'aẓīm*)."[21] Such notions of the social body (*jism*) were present in classical Arabic literature exemplified by Ibn Khaldun, who posited solidarity (*'aṣabiyya*) as the force that compelled dynasties to ascend to power and then fall from grace in cycles throughout history.[22] But they also resonated with the organicist sociology of Herbert Spencer, who coined the term "survival of the fittest" in his influential *Principles of Biology* (1864).[23] Conceived in biological terms, the *umma* could evolve naturally, and, by locating the cause of European "civilization" (*tamaddun*) within the Protestant reformation, al-Afghani saw in European history the evolutionary course that Muslims must follow.[24] By imagining history as a process of evolution (*ḥarika*) through different stages that each distinct civilization must undergo, al-Afghani adopted a progressivist teleology that is closer to Spencer than Ibn Khaldun.

Through 'Abduh, the Islamic modernist ideas associated with al-Afghani impacted a rising generation in Egypt, but their locus of effort would shift from the *umma* of Muslims to an *umma* of Egyptians. This was especially true for the group of men gathered around Ahmad Lutfi al-Sayyid after he became editor-in-chief of the newspaper *Al-Jarida* and head spokesman of the party whose program it proclaimed: the *umma* party (*ḥizb al-umma*).[25] The party was founded in 1907, and its membership initially included about five hundred people split between wealthy members of the *'ayān*, Ottoman-Egyptian aristocrats, and intellectuals.[26] The men of the *wafd* who would go on to lead the 1919 revolution—including Sa'd Zaghlul, 'Ali Sha'rawi, and 'Abd al-'Aziz Fahmi—were all drawn from its ranks.

In his varied writings and speeches, Lutfi al-Sayyid rejected the idea that the *umma* of Muslims championed by al-Afghani was a viable political entity. He agreed with the British Orientalist Edward G. Browne, writing, "'Pan-Islamism' (*al-bānyislāmizm*) is a myth that was created in the minds of the writers at the [London] *Times* in Vienna."[27] In a 1912 artiticle published in *Al-Jarida*, Lutfi al-Sayyid expounded on the fallacy of Pan-Islamism:

> There are those who say that Egypt is not a homeland (*waṭan*) for Egyptians only, but for all Muslims that come to her land, whether they are Ottomans or non-Ottomans, French or English, Chinese or Japanese, thereby leaving Egyptian national or Egyptian racial identity (*al-qawmiyya al-miṣriyya aw al-jinsiyya al-miṣriyya*) destroyed.[28]

Unlike the deterritorialized *umma* of Muslims, the *umma* of Egyptians is attached to a specific homeland (*waṭan*). However, it is not reducible to this land, and also encompasses a group of people that is analogous to other groups in their own lands across the world. For Lutfi al-Sayyid, the homeland left its imprint on all people born within it, whether Muslim or non-Muslim. This notion resonated with theories of environmental determinism that can be found both in Ibn Khaldun and modern European race science.

The similarities between the bonds of Egyptian nationality (*al-qawmiyya al-miṣriyya*) and Egyptian race (*al-jinsiyya al-miṣriyya*) are illustrated by their use as synonyms in Lutfi al-Sayyid's writing above. In one particularly illustrative article, "Tadaminna" ("Our Solidarity"), he expounded on the crucial role that he believed notions of race played in bonding the *umma* of Egyptians together:

> No one among us has any doubt what it means [when we say] that we constitute an *umma* distinguished from any other by our special characteristics (*al-mushakhṣiyyāt khāṣa bi-nā*), and which no other in the community of nations (*jamī'a al-umam*) shares with us. We have our own particular [skin] color, our own inclinations, and a single, comprehensive language. And we have a majority religion, and ways of performing our activities, and a blood which is nearly one blood flowing through our veins.[29]

Here, Lutfi al-Sayyid describes Egyptian identity in ways clearly influenced by modern race science. While some of the elements of membership in the *umma* could be acquired, like language and religion, they existed alongside biologically determined qualities like skin color (*lawn*) and blood (*dam*). In the writings of Lutfi al-Sayyid, both acquired and natural bonds combined to create an Egyptian *umma* with distinct characteristics (*mushakhṣiyyāt khāṣa*).

Operating from a presumed link between the environment and cultural formation, Lutfi al-Sayyid pointed to his own origins in the Egyptian countryside to establish his *bona fides* in speaking on behalf of Egyptians. Like both 'Abduh and Zaghlul, Lutfi al-Sayyid was born the son of an *'umda* in a Nile Delta village. He begins his autobiography with a clear statement of the importance of this line of descent:

> I was born in a real Egyptian family (*usra miṣriyya ṣamīma*) that did not know any homeland except Egypt, boasted of nothing except its Egyptianness (*miṣriyyatiha*), and belongs nowhere except Egypt—that good country that established civilization (*al-tamaddun*) in the most ancient of ages, and that has natural wealth and ancient honor that grants it refinement and glory.[30]

Here, Lutfi al-Sayyid touts his rural origin to define himself and his family as "real Egyptians" (*miṣriyya ṣamīma*). He links his village and the *fallāḥīn* who live there with the ancient Egyptians who established "civilization" (*al-tamaddun*) millenia ago. The notion of *tamaddun* is here detached from its etymological association with the city and its concomitant reference to people who travel there for education (see chapter 2). Instead, it becomes associated with the birthright of a particular people. Lutfi al-Sayyid was not alone among his contemporaries in making this link between rural Egyptians and an essential identity of "Egyptianness" (*miṣriyya*) that could be traced back to the pharaohs.[31] According to Charles Wendell, Mustafa Kamil of *Al-Liwa'* "often boasted of his *fallāḥ* blood, and insisted . . . the greater part of the Muslims of Egypt [like the Christians] are of antique Pharaonic stock."[32]

To be sure, "real Egyptians" coexisted with other "foreign" elements in colonial Egypt, and Lutfi al-Sayyid's conception of membership in the *umma* vacillated between versions of ethnic and civic nationalism. This tension is evident in a 1909 article published in *al-Jarida*, "al-Jam'iyya al-Misriyya" ("The Egyptian Community"): "The Egyptian community consists of ethnic Egyptians (*al-miṣriyyīn al-aṣliyyīn*) and other new races (*'anāṣir*) of foreigners who have moved to Egypt and established residence there and made it an important place for their activities, so that it had quickly become the source of their wealth and the citizenship of their lives (*muwaṭan ḥiyātihim*) in the present and the future."[33] Here Lutfi al-Sayyid distinguishes between ethnic Egyptians (*al-miṣriyyīn al-aṣliyyīn*) and the other foreign races (*'anāṣir akhira jadīda min al-ajānib*) in Egypt, but he provides a pathway to citizenship for the latter, who have settled permanently in Egypt and made it their home. Reflecting on this passage, Wendell tries to chart a course between Lutfi al-Sayyid's civic and ethnic nationalism, but he steps knee-deep into the semantic muck surrounding ideas of race in Arabic:

> His exhortation stressed no mystique of "blood and soil," which has at times fostered the elimination of minority groups within a given population. . . . Not that such a mystique was entirely lacking from his conception of Egyptian nationhood, but that it leaned toward the gentler Romantic tradition of nationalism, rather than the violently chauvinistic extreme into which it is capable of degenerating.[34]

Ethnic nationalism, then, was both present and not present in the writings of Lutfi al-Sayyid, and although Wendell acknowledged the tendencies of such thought toward "degeneration," he ascribed the influential journalist to a "gentler" tradition.

Rather than dwelling on the physical distinctiveness of the *umma*, Lutfi al-Sayyid often stressed its composition as an almost metaphysical creation. But unlike God's *umma*, which is created when He deems to reveal His sacred message through prophecy, the *umma* imagined by Lutfi al-Sayyid was endowed by Nature. In a speech delivered on the occasion of the restoration of the Ottoman constitution in 1908, he said:

> It is scientifically accepted (*min al-musallim 'ilman*) that every political association, or every *umma*, is a product of nature (*'amal min 'umāl al-ṭibī'a*), that is to say, a natural entity (*kā'in*) which lives out its life according to the natural laws governing movements of all creatures. The laws of nature . . . give each individual his just share of freedom. For God has created no man a slave, but if a man weakens, he falls into slavery. . . . In the same way, the *umma* has received her freedom from nature, and if she becomes weak, will fall into slavery; i.e., she will be ruled by an absolute government not of her own choosing, which will reduce the individuals comprising the *umma* to slavery.[35]

Like al-Afghani before him, Lutfi al-Sayyid here envisions an *umma* that is subject to natural laws. But instead of taking this in the direction of Darwinian evolution and Spencer's "survival of the fittest," the natural law that concerns Lutfi al-Sayyid is expressed in terms of the natural right to freedom: once an *umma* arises to consciousness of itself, it cannot tolerate being ruled over by another. By occupying Egypt and restructuring the Egyptian state, the British had reduced the *umma* to the collective condition of slavery.

As historian Aaron Jakes has documented, the use of slavery as a metaphor to describe the relationship between the British and Egyptians was not isolated to Lutfi al-Sayyid. In 1907, journalist Ahmad Hilmi published an article in *Al-Liwa'* in which he asked, "how can you free a slave (*āmah*) and enslave a nation (*ummah*)?" According to Hilmi, while the British were "breaking the shackles of slavery from the hands of negro individuals (*afrād al-zunūj*)," they espoused another "contradictory principle" that called for "enslaving nations and depriving whole peoples of their freedom in the name of spreading colonialism (*al-isti'mār*)."[36] In his recent book and an earlier review essay published with Ahmad Shokr, Jakes emphasizes slavery's commodification of enslaved people and interprets representations of slavery in nationalist discourse as a metaphor for Egypt's increasing economic entanglement with the British occupation.[37]

But, as we have already seen, slavery in Egypt was not just a metaphor. When the institution was officially abolished during the childhood of Lutfi al-Sayyid's generation, the majority of enslaved people in Egypt were Black Africans. Even after the official abolition of slavery in 1877, the trade continued surreptitiously, along with a link between Blackness, African origins, and enslavement in Egyptian popular culture. Representations of Egyptians as "slaves" to the British, then, entailed a rejection of the global color line, and juxtapositions of "enslaved" Egyptians to free "Negroes" (*zunūj*) drew their mobilizing force in part on popular antipathy to Black people.

In the writings of Lutfi al-Sayyid, the Black Sudanese to Egypt's south did not seem to rise to the level of an *umma* governed by the natural laws of independence and self-rule. At times, he effaces the difference between Sudanese and Egyptians by using the trope of "The Unity of the Nile Valley," which Eve Troutt-Powell has characterized as a turn of phrase popular among the Egyptian "colonized colonizer."[38] In one article from October 1910, Lutfi al-Sayyid asks:

> Who are the sons of the Nile? They are those who are [to be found] between its source and its mouth. They are those who live in that [distant] torrid region and whose color is black; and those who live in the temperate zone, and whose is color is, as you see, somewhere between black and white. . . . It would be senseless were skin color to cut off blood relationship (*qāṭi'an al-riḥm*) between two brothers.[39]

Here he acknowledges the difference in skin color between the Sudanese and the Egyptians, but this does not keep him from asserting a "blood relationship" (*al-riḥm*) between the two. The reference to blood here does not denote a serological relationship as in European scientific racism, but a more mystical link grounded in common rearing by the Nile River. Such representations are consistent with Lutfi al-Sayyid's stress on the metaphysical as opposed to the physical bonds of the *umma*.

However, at other times, Lutfi al-Sayyid asserted that it was violent conquest that brought Sudan into the Egyptian fold. In an article from July 1910, he wrote, "Sudan belongs to Egypt by right of conquest . . . the colonization of Sudan is the exclusive right of the Egyptians (*istiʿmaru al-sūdāni min ḥaqqi al-miṣriyyīn dūna siwāhum*)."[40] The assertion of "brotherhood" with the Sudanese allows Lutfi al-Sayyid to brush off the revolt of the *mahdi* as something akin to a family disagreement: "What happened was that some Sudanese (*baʿḍ al-Sūdāniyyīn*) rose against the Egyptian community (*al-jāmiʿa al-Miṣriyya*). So the rebels were chastised and the rebellion ended (*fa uddiba 'l-thā'irūna wa 'ntahati 'l-fitna*)."[41] Here he blames the rebellious Sudanese for causing "chaos" (*fitna*), thus justifying their reconquest by a combined Anglo-Egyptian force in 1898.

While *Al-ʿUrwa al-Wuthqa* celebrated the Sudanese uprisings and blamed Egyptians for "shedding the blood of their brothers in religion at the mere order of it by those who are different from them in race and belief,"[42] for Lutfi al-Sayyid and his contemporaries, Egyptians were blameworthy, not for attacking the Sudan, but because they lacked vigor in doing so. Mustafa Kamil made the point clearly in 1896: "If you really listened carefully [within yourselves] you would hear your consciences telling you that you are the humblest of all nations today. The Negroes (al-Zunūj) whom you used to put to work as your slaves (*alladhīna kuntum tastakhdimūnahum 'abīdan ariqqā'a*) have become more vigorous than you in preserving the rights of their homelands!"[43] Perhaps this commentary from the most prominent writer at *Al-Liwa'* sheds light on the contrast between Egyptians and "Negroes" (*al-zunūj*) in the later writings of Ahmad Hilmi in the same journal.

Zunūj was the Classical Arabic word for slaves taken from the highlands of Tanzaniyya and Kenya, and its usage illustrates the association between Blackness and slavery in the intellectual culture of Egyptian nationalists.[44] When Mustafa Kamil referred to the forces of the *mahdi* as *zunūj*, he effaced the particularity of the Sudanese uprising and grouped all sub-Saharan Africans together under one general heading as Black descendants of slaves. The paradoxical position occupied by Lutfi al-Sayyid—who asserted that every *umma* was free by natural law but nevertheless insisted on Egypt's absolute right to colonize the Sudan—can be explained with reference to this sense of superiority to Black people among Egyptian nationalist intellectuals at the time.

VOLUNTEERING OR KIDNAPPING?

When Egyptians who had been enculturated into this intellectual tradition saw *fallāḥīn* from the countryside bound together by thick ropes and sent off to join the ELC, it provided a new impetus for representations of "slavery" at the hands of the British empire. No longer was the *umma* a metaphysical entity in a figurative state of slavery, which could not be seen but only interpreted by learned men. Now, young men from the countryside, whose rural roots were taken to be the very essence of Egyptianness, were virtually enslaved in public spaces for everyone to see.

In writings and speeches, Zaghlul and others highlighted how violent resistance to ELC recruitment in the countryside exposed the hypocrisy of the British by undermining the colonial state's claim that the ELC consisted of "volunteers." Zaghlul wrote often in his diary-style memoirs of trips to check on his rural estates, which gave him ample opportunity to interact with the communities that were subject to ELC recruitment. On May 28, 1918, Zaghlul mentioned incidents he had personally witnessed:

> People have been making an uproar over the methods used by the men of the government to gather and force young men into "volunteering" for service with the British army. They kidnap people from the markets, streets, mosques, and courthouses, and they call on them to sign something saying that they request to volunteer! And those who refuse to sign get beat until they sign! Many violent incidents have happened between the citizens (*al-ahālī*) and the government (*al-ḥukkām*) because of this kidnapping (*khaṭaf*), [with] many deaths and casualties.[45]

Zaghlul refers to "volunteering" ironically here, and later calls it "kidnapping" (*khaṭaf*). Historian Latifa Salim quotes a similar reflection in an unpublished section of Zaghlul's diaries from November 1918, when he wrote, "The men of the government boast that they oppose forced conscription, even prohibit it, but the authorities in all the corners of the country, for several days, have taken to kidnapping (*yatakhaṭṭafūn*) people from the markets and the roads, and from their homes in the villages."[46] In the same vein, the prominent lawyer and statesman Ahmad Shafiq pointed out the hypocrisy of ELC recruitment in his memoirs, recounting the story of one man who "violently resisted 'volunteering,' which, of course, was not really based on his wishes, and, ultimately, the poor fellow was killed."[47] Like Zaghlul, Shafiq uses the word for "volunteering" (*al-ṭatū'*) ironically to describe the men of the ELC.

As nationalist statesmen and intellectuals traveled through the countryside during the war, they were shocked and appalled when they saw levies of ELC recruits bound together in handcuffs and chains, marching to the closest town lockup. In one speech, Zaghlul recounted the image of a British soldier "driving Egyptians handcuffed in iron shackles."[48] Similarly, in an unpublished section of his diaries from November 1918, he told a story of ELC recruits from the village of Asta in the province of Minya who tried to resist recruitment, but were beaten back by a group of soldiers and policemen and marched away toward the district lockup, "handcuffed in iron shackles."[49] 'Abd al-Rahman al-Rafi'i, who was a witness to the First World War, also wrote that ELC recruits were "tied by ropes and driven away like cattle."[50] Salama Musa describes the scene at a recruiting levy he witnessed as a young man:

> I traveled to the countryside . . . and I saw how the English governed over us [using] Egyptian employees—overseers, governors, police commanders and policemen—to kidnap (*khaṭaf*) our resources. . . . A man would be tied by a thick rope around his torso, and he would be behind another just like him, and they would march in this state until they reached the district. There, they were put into a jail cell, and then sent to Palestine.[51]

The image that stood out in Musa's mind the most was of Egyptians snatched up off their fields, bound together by a thick rope, and led away to join the ELC.

This image continued to resonate with audiences in Egypt long after the war was over. A 1969 article about the ELC in the popular magazine *Al-Musawwir* included stylized drawings of recruits tied together by a rope across their torso. The author, Egyptian historian Amin 'Izz Al-Din, characterizes the early years of ELC recruiting as "voluntary contracting" (*ta'āqud ikhtiyari*), but later on he refers to it as "kidnapping."[52] When Latifa Salim, an Egyptian historian from a younger generation, summed up the evidence she had documented about the ELC, she wrote, "From this we can see that supplying the British army [with workers] became a forced tax that widened in scope as the war went on, and *processions of slaves* bound in iron shackles went by to fight the battle for freedom, as

FIGURE 8.2. "Al-Shughul fi-l-Sulta" (Working for the Government), 1969. 'Izz al-Din, "Awwal Dirasa," *Al-Mussawir*, March 1969.

the allies called it (emphasis mine)."[53] Ellis Goldberg describes a similar type of chronological development, whereby the "British . . . offered wage employment to peasants in the Labor Corps and forcibly conscripted them when too few volunteered."[54] Scholars of the ELC, writing in both Arabic and English, thus recast the dichotomy opposing freedom and slavery as a historical evolution from "volunteering" to "kidnapping."

"BLACK SLAVES" (*ZUNŪJ*) AND RACIAL NATIONALISM

Salama Musa's reflections are a reminder that Egyptians from a variety of backgrounds were deeply affected by scenes of ELC recruitment. Born in Zaqaziq to a relatively prosperous Christian family, Musa graduated from the Khedivial College in 1907. His father passed away and left him with an inheritance, which he used to fund multiple trips to Paris and London between 1907 and 1913. In his memoirs, Musa recounts the impact these trips had on his life. He joined the Fabian Society and stayed up to date on the latest currents in social Darwinist thought, which he believed held the key to progress for nations that had been downtrodden by colonialism.[55] While in Europe, he followed debates over eugenics and sent articles to Faris al-Nimr's science journal *Al-Muqtataf* when the Eugenics Laboratory and the Eugenics Education Society were founded in London in 1907 and 1911, respectively.[56]

He returned home to Egypt periodically during these years and had a number of formative experiences there that would also impact his views. Paris was in the grips of "Egyptomania," and Musa was struck by the many questions he received about ancient Egypt during his stay. He found it appalling that Europeans were the top experts on ancient Egypt, while his fellow countrymen either knew nothing of the Pharaohs or saw them as condemnable infidels. The first thing Musa did when he came home in 1909 was to book a ticket with the Thomas Cook tourism company and travel down to Luxor.[57] He spent two months touring Upper Egypt and studying Pharaonic antiquities before returning to Europe again. When he finally settled down in Egypt for good in 1914, he began working with Shibli Shumayyil—the famed translator of Darwin's works into Arabic—on a journal known as *Al-Mustaqbal* (*The Future*). The journal published articles on many forward-looking themes, including science, reformist socialism, and the progress of the age. However, with the heavy-handed policies of British censorship during the war, the journal was shut down. Dejected, Musa returned to his family's sizable landholdings near Zaqazig and immersed himself in writing and study.

It was at this time, when his career ambitions had been thwarted by the colonial government and his writing began to chart a new future for Egyptians by looking toward the Pharaonic past, that Musa witnessed the recruiting levies for the ELC. In his memoirs, he wrote that the scene looked like "a village of Black slaves (*ka-innahum fi qarya zanjiyya*)," and that the English were "like slavers who kidnapped men from their homes to sell them in the slave market."[58] The idea of Egyptians being treated like "Black slaves" (*zunūj*) must have especially offended Musa because of his noted antipathy toward Black Africans. As Marwa Elshakry has shown, Musa disagreed with the editors of *Al-Muqtataf* while filing reports as a foreign correspondent on eugenics research, insisting that "science had proved that blacks' brains were closer to those of apes."[59] Seemingly horrified by the idea that Egyptians were being grouped with Black Africans in the so-called Coloured Labour Corps during the war, Musa would begin to assert Egyptian racial distinctiveness and civilizational superiority in his writing.

In *Misr Asl al-Hadara* (*Egypt, the Origin of Civilization*, 1935), Musa developed a full-fledged theory of Egyptian racial nationalism. The title itself shows just how much conceptions of communal belonging had changed by the interwar period. Whereas an earlier generation translated the concept of civilization as *tamaddun*, which signified the process of traveling to the city that theoretically anyone could undertake throughout their lifetime, Musa uses the word *ḥaḍāra* to denote a changed understanding of civilizations as distinct population groups into which all the peoples of the world can be sorted. For all Muslims and Christians living in Egypt—and especially for the rural *fallāḥīn*—Musa argued, "running in our veins is the blood that was flowing in our forefathers five thousand years ago."[60]

Building on the comparative anatomy of Australian-British scientist Elliot Smith, Musa pointed to scientific expeditions in the countryside that observed similarities between the *fallāḥīn* and ancient Egyptians in terms of bone structure and "physical appearance" (*saḥna*).[61] He argued that human beings were separated into six distinct "human stocks" (*sulālāt al-bashariyya*), and arranged these groups chronologically according to their "level" of civilization; first came Aboriginal Australians, second were Black Africans (*al-zunūj*), third were the Mediterraneans, fourth was the Alpine race, fifth was the Nordic race, and the final group was the Mongol race.[62] Egyptians, he argued, belonged to the third category. These human stocks had an organic existence similar to human individuals, each developing a "personality" (*shakhsiyya*) that depended on both biological and environmental considerations. Over time, each human stock sorted itself into distinct "communities" (*umum*; sing., *umma*) with their own particularities.[63] Building on the social Darwinist ideas that inspired him in his youth as well as the conceptual fuzziness surrounding the overdetermined Arabic word *umma*, Musa developed a notion of "Egyptian national personality" (*al-shakhṣiyya al-miṣriyya*) that, as Omnia El Shakry has put it, was "strikingly similar" to ideas about race at the time.[64]

While Musa was witnessing the levies of men sent off to work for the ELC, Muhammad Sabri (Mohammed Sabry) was in Paris studying history. Born the son of an agricultural inspector in the Nile Delta, Sabri began his education in a village *kuttāb* before moving to Cairo to complete his schooling. He enrolled in the Sorbonne in 1913 and continued to study there throughout the war. Upon completion of his *license* in 1919, he served as the personal secretary of the *wafd* during the Paris Peace Conference.[65] In 1919 he published the first of a two-volume history of the 1919 revolution, modeled on the histories of the French Revolution written by his mentor Alphonse Aulard.

The book begins with an extended meditation on two policies instituted by the British that dramatically changed the complicated nature of the British occupation and placed the status of Egypt on more clearly intelligible grounds: the declaration of the British protectorate and the recruitment of workers for the ELC. For five pages, Sabri quoted liberal critics of the imperial government in Egypt, but unlike British liberals who treated wartime policy as an aberration, Sabri insisted that the British had acted as a "malevolent foreign government" (*un gouvernement étranger et malveillant*) since the days of Mehmet 'Ali.[66] The ELC was important not because of its novelty as a technique of oppression, but because "the oppression of which the peasant (*paysan*) was victim, especially during the war, awakened or rather strengthened in him the feeling of his rights." This was why "suddenly, the *fallāḥ* (*fellah*), oppressed for a long time, showed himself capable of fighting for what he considers to be his political rights."[67] For Sabri, the oppression of the ELC had allowed the *fallāḥīn* to become conscious of their essential identity as Egyptians.

Sabri also expounded a picture of the Egyptian nation that was heavily influenced by the racial nationalism of Lutfi al-Sayyid. He compared the nation to a family, and different groups of Egyptians to members in this organic unit: "there is not a single family which does not enfold one or more members in its bosom (*son sein*)."[68] Here, Sabri uses the French term *sein*, which can also be translated as "womb," to describe the common ground shared by different groups within the nation. He criticized British policies, which sought to "sow division and discord between the classes of a nation, which is the same family."[69] For Sabri, Egyptians formed a "homogenous nation." "Egypt is not a geographical expression," he wrote, "it is a true nation which is only waiting for the recovery of its sovereignty to play, as in the past, its civilizing role."[70] Here, Sabri draws a connection between ancient Egypt as a "civilization" and the nation-state formed out of the 1919 revolution.

The declaration of a protectorate and the recruitment of the ELC led Sabri to recognize how the war had left Egyptians on the wrong side of the global color line. He wrote:

> Egypt suffered at seeing herself treated with disdain and cruelty, like "damn [n——]" and gypsies by the innumerable and ignorant functionaries, filled with arrogance, that England had been sending to Egypt since the declaration of the protectorate, and by the Tommies who believed that "Egypt was English and that the natives were men of colour imported to the country."[71] (Epithet deleted)

Sabri both carefully studied and personally witnessed the revolution, and he understood that the racialization of Egyptians as "men of colour" was one of the most important aspects of British policy that motivated people to act. He noted the racial epithets that were hurled at Egyptians, even putting them in quotation marks to signal that they were speech acts from soldiers and officers stationed throughout the country.

When Sabri decried the "Tommies," who acted like "the natives [of Egypt] were men of colour imported to the country," he may have been relating the scenes he saw in Egypt to similar ones he must have witnessed in France during the war. Chapter 5 has already documented how the "Coloured Labour Corps" in France was subjected to strict segregation and Jim Crow laws when they went to the surrounding towns and cities. But to some extent, ELC laborers were treated the same way in Egypt: they were segregated in the so-called native hospital system, set aside in jail cells, and led away from their villages bound together by thick ropes. In creating the ELC, the English had imposed a system of racial segregation in Egypt. In Sabri's telling, Egyptians launched the 1919 revolution in response to this, rejecting their association with "men of colour" (*hommes de couleur*).

A petition in the archives of the French Foreign Ministry preserves the sense of Egyptian superiority to Black Africans that could be entailed in this rejection. On March 20, 1919, in the wake of the horrific massacre and gang rape at Nazlat Al-Shubak,[72] a lawyer who referred to himself as "Abu Shadi" sent a telegram to the French embassy in Cairo. He protested, "Whereas England wants to treat Egyptians like African savages (*li-'nn kānit ankiltara turīd an taftaraḍ al-miṣriyyīn waḥūsh ifrīqiyya*) and insult the fortunes of our women, just as they have oppressed the fortunes of our men, shame on you! . . . We protest to your Excellency over what has happened so far."[73] Abu Shadi, an anonymous lawyer who does not

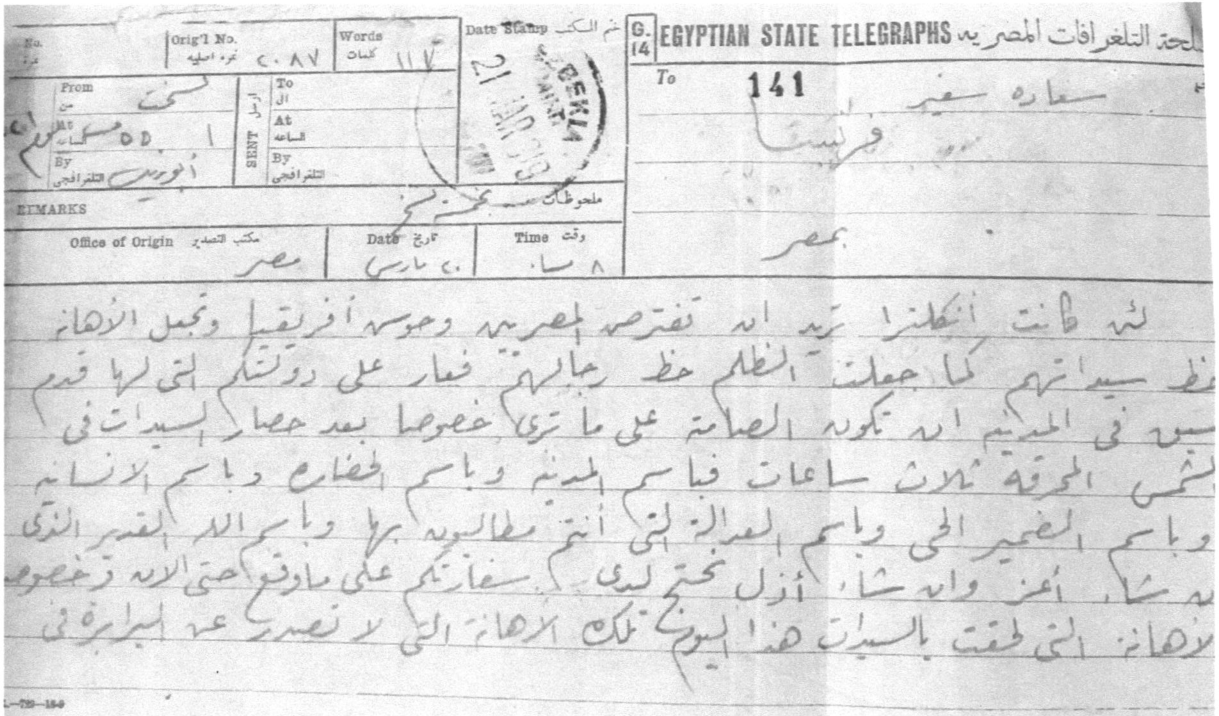

FIGURE 8.3. Petition from Abu Shadi to the French Embassy during the 1919 revolution. Archives Diplomatiques, Ministère des Affairs Étrangères, La Courneuve K/56/1/12.

FIGURE 8.4. Mausoleum of Sa'd Zaghlul. Wikimedia Commons by Ashashyou—Own work, CC BY-SA 3.0.

resurface again in the archives, was shocked and appalled not only at the rape of women that took place in Nazlat al-Shubak, but also by attempts to treat Egyptians like "African savages" (*waḥūsh ifrīqiyya*). Although the reference is not specific, he is likely referring to ELC recruitment. This petition, then, corroborates the notion that racializing of Egyptians alongside Black Africans—embodied most clearly in the creation of the ELC—animated popular protest during the revolution.

Building on notions of Egyptian racial nationalism espoused by intellectuals like Musa and Sabri, the leaders of the *wafd* would go on to adopt Pharaonic themes in their nationalist discourse during the interwar period.[74] According to Gershoni and Jankowski, before the revolution, there were only a few scattered references within Zaghlul's speeches to Egyptians as "the sons of Pharaonic civilization and of Arabic civilization."[75] But Pharaonism became most influential in the period immediately after the revolution. The aesthetics and politics of Pharaonism are both evident in the construction of Zaghlul's tomb. As Ralph Coury has shown, the first suggestion floated in the press for commemorating Zaghlul after his death in 1927 was a "mosque-like Arab/Islamic structure," in which prayer might be possible.[76] But these suggestions were countered by the idea that "the tomb should be national and not religious, inasmuch as Saad was a national and not a religious leader."[77] For the *wafd*, national meant Pharaonic, and Zaghlul's mausoleum was completed in Pharaonic style in the 1930s. Pharaonism, then, asserted a common identity between Christians and Muslims that linked contemporary Egyptians with the ancient past. In the debate over the construction of Zaghlul's tomb, Pharaonic themes provided a counter to the link between Egyptians and Muslims, which was so commonly articulated in racial terms during the years of British military occupation (see chapter 1).

"I WILL NOT ACCEPT SLAVERY"

In addition to inspiring a search for Egyptian racial distinctiveness, the association between ELC recruitment and slavery may also have influenced the rhetoric of the *wafd* during the revolution. In a storied meeting with British high commissioner Reginald Wingate on November 13, 1918, Zaghlul's colleague 'Ali Sha'rawi is reported to have interjected, "I will not accept slavery, and I will not be satisfied living under its yoke!"[78] According to the memoirs of 'Abd al-Rahman Fahmi, who was also present at the meeting, Sha'rawi's steadfast refusal was an oft-repeated refrain as news of the meeting spread throughout Egypt.[79] Ironically, Sha'rawi himself came from a social milieu of Ottoman-Egyptian households that depended on slavery for its reproduction even after the official abolition of slavery in Egypt in 1877.[80] In refusing a relationship with the British like that of "slaves to their owner," Sha'rawi's rhetoric appealed to contemporary ideas about the racial superiority of Egyptians to Black Africans, even as it mobilized support for antiracist action against white supremacy.[81]

Zaghlul also drew on contemporary ideas about Egyptian racial identity in his communications with foreign dignitaries. Conceptual slippage between the concepts of "race" and "nation" permeated his letters, which were collected and translated in *The White Book*. For example, in one communication on January 11, 1919, he refers to the "bitterness and hatred stored up in the hearts of the small races against the domination, by brutal force, of the Great Powers," and then, on the following page, he writes of the need for "the emancipation of small nations" in response to this predicament.[82] The similarity between race and nation in Zaghlul's mind is mirrored here by the use of the same adjective before both words, occurring only a short distance apart in the text.

Playing on the quasi-racial sense of unity underwriting conceptions of the nation at the time, Zaghlul posited the existence of a unitary "Egyptian" identity in an effort to induce the British to repay the sacrifices of the ELC by granting the *wafd* a seat at the Paris Peace Conference. In a letter to British prime minister David Lloyd George dated January 12, 1919, Zaghlul pointed out that "the enormous sacrifices that we have made during the war, in blood and treasure, for the triumph of your cause, were indispensable to you, and, moreover, you have recognized many times that these sacrifices were one of the principal factors of the victory."[83] By using the first-person plural pronoun "we" here, Zaghlul identified the *wafd* with the ELC. Recognizing the praise that British military authorities had bestowed upon ELC labor, which this book documented in chapter 4, the contributions of the ELC in the war became an important weapon in Zaghlul's rhetorical arsenal.[84] For example, in another letter to the members of the British House of Commons dated July 14, 1919, Zaghlul noted, "General Sir Edmund Allenby—the most competent man in the world to make the statement—declared publicly that the aid of Egypt was the most important factor of success in the decisive British campaign against the Turks."[85]

The good works of the ELC opened conceptual space for the men of the *wafd* to begin to identify *themselves* with the *fallāḥīn* who formed the bulk of its labor force. Less than two decades before, Zaghlul's younger brother had called the *fallāḥīn* "the possessors of humiliatingly bitter ignorance."[86] For many urban intellectuals in Egypt, the primary attitude toward rural farmers was patronizing and didactic.[87] But in the wake of the First World War, urban intellectuals had renewed impetus to identify themselves with the workers and farmers who made up the majority of the ELC.

Most importantly for Zaghlul, the decisive role that Egyptians and other nonwhite laborers played in the war effort had upended the global order of white supremacy by illustrating the extent to which the metropole relied on the colonies, rather than the other way around. In a letter to the British House of Commons, Zaghlul wrote:

> In appealing to her dominions, her colonies, and the non-European races over whom she was ruling, for aid in blood and treasure, the British made it perfectly clear that in their opinion the world was no longer big enough to contain two moralities, one for Europe and another for Asia and Africa.[88]

The global circulation of migrant laborers and soldiers in the war perforated the conceptual and spatial barriers that had previously separated "Europe" from "Asia and Africa," creating a networked space that was incongruent with the racialized logics of the past generation. The creation of this new spatial imaginary, marked out by the paths of millions of migrant laborers traveling from all corners of the globe to participate in the First World War, entailed shared experiences of sacrifice that could become the basis for a global shift away from white supremacy and toward sovereignty for every *umma*.

PASSING AS EGYPTIAN

Zaghlul's effectiveness as a carrier of this message depended on how well he passed as an Egyptian. In the early twentieth century, African Americans like Charles W. Chesnutt, Jessie Fauset, James Weldon Johnson, and Nella Larsen wrote about racial passing to explore the performative aspects of race, and the multiplicity of racial identity over and above mere physical appearance.[89] In the context of the United States, where race is defined in terms of the black vs. white dichotomy, racial passing is usually understood to occur when a person who is a member of one racial group (often a light-skinned Black person) is able to "pass" themselves off as a member of a group to which they don't truly belong. But this is not how I intend to use the term here. Instead, I follow the lead of scholars who have studied stories of racial passing as an entry point into interrogations of the socially constructed nature of identity categories like race and gender.[90] The phenomenon of racial passing suggests that race operates through visible markers of identity like skin color, but in novels like Nella Larsen's *Passing*, we are repeatedly reminded that skin color is not the only—or even the most important—way to define one's race.

In the African American tradition, it is the ambiguous appearance of multiracial individuals that allows for them to "pass" in different contexts.[91] In Egypt, as we have seen, the notion of an Egyptian race was already ambiguous and in flux. This allowed for individuals with broad phenotypical variation to claim "Egyptianness" (*al-miṣriyya*). Egyptian intellectuals like Ahmad Lutfi al-Sayyid tried to chart a path for Egyptian racial identity that existed somewhere between black and white, and emphasized the Egyptian *fallāḥ* as the ideal of Egyptian racial purity between these two poles. This allowed for Sa'd Zaghlul—the son of an *'umda* who looked and spoke like the people of the countryside—to come to embody the hopes of the *umma* for self-determination. It was rural origin and parental descent, over and above mere skin color, that allowed for someone to truly "pass" as Egyptian.

A comment from 'Abbas Mahmud al-'Aqqad, an Upper Egyptian journalist born in the city of Aswan who lived through the revolution, illustrates how Zaghlul's status as a *fallāḥ* meant that he was perceived as uniquely Egyptian:

> The religious scholars have said to us that the greatest miracle of any of the Prophets was that they were created according to the exact specifications of the community (*umma*) to which they were sent by God. Thus . . . Muhammad was sent with the Qur'an to a community of eloquence and speech. . . . In the same way, I believe we are seeing what the scholars foretold in our own times. . . . Sa'd was the best leader for Egypt, because he was a *fallāḥ* in a community (*umma*) of *fallāḥīn* . . . there is no sign more clear than this of the truth of the Sa'dist renaissance and its accord with the natural order of things (*wa-laysat āyya afṣaḥ min hadhi al-āyya 'ala ṣidq al-nahḍa al-sa'diyya wa jaryaniha ma' ṭabā'a' al-amūr*).[92]

Al-'Aqqad, then, relates Zaghlul to a prophet, and, like all prophets of the Abrahamic tradition, argues he has been chosen by God because his characteristics are a perfect embodiment of the community (*umma*) with which God intends to communicate. For a message sent to Egyptians, God could choose none other than a *fallāḥ*. It was Zaghlul's rural roots, in this case, that gave him the credentials he needed to be considered Egyptian in race.

The movement attracted to Zaghlul is referred to by al-'Aqqad as "the Sa'dist renaissance" (*al-nahḍa al-sa'diyya*), illustrating the personal link between Zaghlul and the revolution in the popular imaginary. Muhammad Sabri echoed this sentiment when he referred to Zaghlul as the "father of the revolution" (*pere de la revolution*).[93] With the nation understood as a family, Zaghlul could come to play the role of patriarch. Because he had been born and raised in the countryside and then traveled to Cairo to receive an education, Zaghlul embodied the "civilized" (*mutamaddun*) Egyptian who could inhabit multiple worlds. For mobile intellectuals with rural roots like Sabri and al-'Aqqad, Zaghlul became a figure who could lead Egyptians "in accordance with the natural order of things."

People who stayed in the countryside, too, seem to have been attracted to Zaghlul because of his presumed *fallāḥ* identity. We can get a sense of this in the unique book *Mudhakkirat Qarya* (*Memoirs of a Village*, 1996) by 'Ismat Sayf al-Dawla. Born in 1923 in the village of Hamamiyya in

Asyut, Sayf al-Dawla was asked to write the "biography of his village" because he was a "son of the village that drank up her stories through his pores."[94] It was not necessarily the events that Sayf al-Dawla witnessed himself, then, so much as the stories (*ḥikayāt*) he heard throughout his life that qualified him as an authority on the people of Hamamiyya. The oral/aural origins of Sayf al-Dawla's source material are clear through his extensive use of Egyptian Colloquial Arabic in the voices of certain characters throughout the text, as well as the dialogic nature of the story.

The coming of the revolution to Hamamiyya unfolds through a dialogue between the narrator and the character Fikri 'Abd al-Nabi. In the heat of the revolution, he is approached by a man who asks him to join and brandishes his credentials as an associate of Sa'd Zaghlul (*rajal 'aẓīm min rijāl Sa'd Basha*).[95] The man gives Fikri weapons, and the latter agrees to join up, saying, "I heard in Asyut that the government of the *bāshūwāt* that Rushdi Bey leads has fallen. Tomorrow the revolution will achieve victory and we can start a government of the *fallāḥīn* (*wa-ghadan tantaṣar al-thawra wa-taqūm ḥakūmat al-fallaḥīn*)." It was Sa'd Zaghlul's personal credentials, then—and most especially his status as one of the *fallāḥīn*—that helped convince Fikri to join in the revolution in Sayf Al-Dawla's story. Meanwhile, the government of the prime minister Husayn Rushdi—who was born to a Turkish family and married to a white French woman[96]—is denigrated as "the government of the *bāshūwāt*," using the word for Ottoman aristocrats mostly born to white mothers who had comprised the upper crust of Egyptian society for centuries.

Racial nationalism, then, worked in both directions. In communicating to a global audience, political leaders like Zaghlul could claim a stake in the works of the ELC, and frame political sovereignty for himself and the *wafd* as a way for the Allies to repay their debt and show their appreciation for assistance in victory. At the same time, communities across Egypt that were ready to rid themselves of the oppressive English and corrupt Ottoman Turks could think of men like Zaghlul as *fallāḥīn* just like themselves, and began to look to him as the "father of the revolution."

CONCLUSION

This chapter has focused on the symbolic role of the ELC in the 1919 revolution. In the letters written by Sa'd Zaghlul and published in *The White Book*, representations of the racial unity of all Egyptians—Muslims and Christians, urban elites and rural peasants—meant that the praiseworthy service of ELC laborers in the war had given the *wafd* the right to sit at the Paris Peace Conference. The community of Egyptians (*al-umma al-miṣriyya)* was seen as an almost metaphysical entity, analogous to a family or a biological organism, and the service and suffering of some of its members extended out to all. Allied reliance on racialized laborers from across the world had undermined the white supremacist global order that hypocritically "contain[ed] two moralities, one for Europe and another for Asia and Africa." Rather than Egyptians in the colonies relying on the British to help them become "civilized," it was the British who were exposed as dependent on the labor of Egyptians to win the war.

While the 1919 revolution was an antiracist act in this sense, representations of ELC laborers as "Black slaves" (*zunūj*) and "African savages" (*waḥūsh ifrīqiyya*) elicited strong affective responses because they offended conceptions of Egyptian racial identity. The recruitment of *fallāḥīn* for the ELC made it clear that the British had racialized Egyptians alongside "people of color." In response, intellectuals like Salama Musa and the leaders of the interwar *wafd* party advanced a Pharaonic conception of national identity that asserted Egyptian racial distinctiveness and a historical right to rule over Black Africans to the south.

Egyptian nationalists centered *fallāḥīn* as the essence of "Egyptianness" in ways that performed racial boundary work to chart a course between the two sides of the global color line. Many of the political and intellectual leaders we have been introduced to in this chapter, including Muhammad 'Abduh, Ahmad Lutfi al-Sayyid, Muhammad Sabri, Salama Musa, and Sa'd Zaghlul, shared similar origins; they were born and raised in the countryside and later sent to the cities to pursue education. They were *fallāḥīn* who had become "civilized" (*mutamaddun*), and because of their rural roots, they could "pass" as Egyptian. The phenomenon of racial passing calls attention to aspects of racial identity beyond mere skin color, and in the Egyptian context, this included where you were from, how you spoke, and who your parents were. The *fallāḥīn* became the racial repository of the nation, and the role they played in the 1919 revolution would prove to be a major factor in how future generations interpreted it through a nationalist lens.

CHAPTER 9

THE ELC AND THE 1919 REVOLUTION

NATIONALIST IDEOLOGY AND political rhetoric posited the *umma* as a unified subject that deserved to represent itself on the global stage. Taking these statements at face value, historians have interpreted the protest actions that emerged across the country after the arrest and exile of Zaghlul and the *wafd* as different manifestations of the will of this collective subject. For example, al-Rafi'i writes, "The revolution broke out in March 1919 . . . and spread throughout the breadth of [Egypt's] villages . . . incorporating each of them surprisingly quickly. This was a manifestation of its greatness and magnificence, and through this act, the will of the people (*faḍl al-sha'b*) was clear."[1] Similarly, Nadav Safran writes, "the revolution of 1919 broke out. The whole nation, fellah and pasha, illiterate and educated . . . stood behind Saad Zaghlul, fighting with great courage and heavy sacrifice in apparent support of the Liberal Nationalist ideals he represented."[2] Gershoni and Jankowski echo this approach when they write of the revolution, "beginning in [November] 1918 with peaceful maneuvers by Egyptian politicians . . . in 1919 it escalated into widespread protest and violence directed against the British presence in Egypt."[3]

The problem with this narrative, as we have already seen in chapter 2, is that a wave of violent resistance swept through the countryside in the summer of 1918, almost a year *before* the arrest and exile of Sa'd Zaghlul and the *wafd*. Zaghlul was aware of these protests as early as May 1918.[4] Throughout the summer of 1918, the men of the ELC and their home communities had undertaken political action, which did not consist of writing articles and giving speeches, but of putting their bodies on the line to resist ELC recruitment. As a witness to this action, Zaghlul picked up their cause and acted himself.

Ellis Goldberg and Reinhard Schülze have analyzed protests in the countryside on a granular scale and found that, over and above any identification with the *wafd*, the revolution was spurred on by grievances over the broad set of policies that moved animals, agricultural products, and working men out of the countryside for the war.[5] While Goldberg is right to note that "it would be a mistake to regard the large number of acts of sabotage carried out by individuals or very small groups as necessarily implying a widespread network of collective action,"[6] his mechanistic model of individual rational choice ignores the multiple solidarities running counter to individual interests that emerged at this critical juncture. This includes solidarity with ELC laborers, who continued to be sent to Palestine by the hundreds of thousands throughout the revolution. Schülze, meanwhile, analyzed the various types of political activity that spread through the countryside as a function of the extent to which British colonialism had "penetrated" into a given village or locale and "re-structured" the rural economy. This did much to recover the all-important global context, but Schülze's attempt to map popular protest onto the colonial economy reduces the former to mere epiphenomena.

This chapter analyzes popular culture and protest action from 1918 and 1919 in an attempt to provide a more nuanced picture of the political subjectivity—or subjectivities—that actually animated the 1919 revolution. Contrary to notions of Egyptians as a collective subject that acted in unison, it finds that protesters in different parts of the country often acted for a variety of reasons, and sometimes at cross-purposes with one another. Identification with the *wafd* could function as a secondary goal of action aimed at more localized circumstances. At other times, and especially in the two northernmost provinces of Egypt's culturally distinct southern region known as Upper Egypt or the *ṣaʿīd*, protesters seem to have been uniquely aggrieved by ELC recruitment.

ELC RECRUITMENT AND (DE-)MOBILIZATION

From the time when labor recruitment picked up speed in 1917, Egyptians everywhere took notice. A writer for *Al-Muqattam* attempted to assuage social anxiety over the departed men, stating, "Last March, groups of Egyptian workers from the *mudīriyya* of Girga were sent to France. Their families stayed in their homes on pins and needles waiting for news to be issued about them. Therefore, *Al-Muqattam* carried signs of reassurance about their safe arrival on the 13th of this April."[7]

But reports like these were transparently propagandistic, and stories about the poor conditions facing the ELC circulated throughout the country in the form of rumors and pop culture references. Historian Amin 'Izz al-Din suggests that stories of the abuse suffered by workers and the high death toll among them traveled home with those returning from the war, which in turn discouraged people from accepting work with the British military and contributed to recruiting shortfalls. One rumor in particular—that the government was primed to gather unmarried women and girls—reportedly incited widespread consternation and a spike in marriage rates in the countryside.[8] By May of 1918, horrifying rumors that hundreds of ELC men had been killed when the Germans broke through the Fifth Army in France reached the Sultan of Egypt, who brought them up in a meeting at the British Residency.[9] Scattered reports of rumors like these should be seen as the tip of an iceberg of social anxiety about the ELC.

Widespread press censorship displaced any critique of wartime policies onto a variety of popular media in Egyptian Colloquial Arabic, including theater, poetry, and songs. Sayyid Darwish, who was "the single most important figure in early twentieth-century Egyptian musical production,"[10] was particularly critical of the war in his songs. Born in Alexandria in 1892, Darwish began his career playing in coffee shops and was first hired by the Egyptian-based Mechian Record Company in 1914.

While most of his tunes were fun and light in their subject matter, a few from this early phase lamented the wartime mobilization policies of the colonial state. For example, "Ista'gibu ya Afandiyya" ("Isn't It Shocking, Gentlemen?," 1914) describes the kerosene and gas shortages taking place in Egypt as the British army hoarded fuel at the outbreak of the war.[11] The title of the song is posed as a question to the *afandiyya*, or upper-middle-class "gentlemen" like Sa'd Zaghlul and the intellectuals discussed in chapter 8.[12] In framing his song as a "shocking" question to them, Darwish highlights the important difference that social and economic class made in how Egyptians experienced wartime hardships; while the poor suffered as they always had, the *afandiyya* were "shocked" at what was going on. Another song from this period, ironically titled "Al-Kutra" ("Abundance," 1919), was also phrased as a message to out-of-touch elites.[13] These songs from Darwish's wartime repertoire can be read as an index of the different ways that various social groups in Egypt experienced British military mobilizations during the war.

In what would become one of his most popular tunes, "Salma ya Salama" ("Safe and Sound," 1918), Darwish composed the music to accompany a *zajal* by Badi' Khayri that celebrated the safe return of an ELC worker from service in the war. "Salma ya Salama" quickly turned into a national hit. According to Ziad Fahmy, the song is "universally known" in Egypt today, and the chorus is typically sung by children returning from school trips.[14] The lyrics are as follows:

> Safe and sound / Oh, safe and sound
> Sound your horn, steamer, and drop anchor / I'll disembark right here
> Never mind America or Europe! / Nothing is better than my country!
> The ship bringing us home / Is so much sweeter than the one that took us away
> Captain, I say!
> Safe and sound / Oh, safe and sound
> At least we have something to show for it all / We saved up our pay and are coming home
> We've seen guns and we've seen war / And we've seen dynamite with our eyes
> There's only one Lord, and we only live once / We went and we made it back
> And we're no worse off.[15]

Unlike the representations of ELC workers as "slaves" found in the writings of the *afandiyya*, this song portrays the men as proud and thrifty, approaching wartime work as an opportunity to save money and experience adventure. Nevertheless, the difficulties and danger of the experience are acknowledged. The lyrics also convey nationalistic themes in the singer's desire to return to his *balad*. The song imposes a nationalistic reading of this term by making parallels between the *balad* and other countries, proclaiming, "Forget America! Forget Europe! There is nothing better than my country (*mafīsh aḥsan min baladi*)!" In the lead-up to the revolution, then, representations of the ELC in this popular tune contributed to the dissemination of patriotic themes, reaffirming Egypt's greatness in comparison to colonial powers.

Another popular song about the ELC that also played on the slippage between "village" and "country" in the Egyptian Colloquial Arabic word *balad* was "Ya 'Aziz 'Ayni." As we saw in chapter 6, multiple British sources corroborate that Egyptian laborers sang this song during the war.[16] According to a document in the British archives, a nationalistic version of the tune centered on the experiences and recruitment of the ELC became popular in Egypt in the summer of 1918:

Oh, my love: I wish to go back home / Oh you who have fallen victims to your desire, go to the Military Authorities.
They will take off your clothes and give you a uniform / they take you to the mountain, while your father's and mother's hearts are full of grief.
My home, my home: The Military Authorities have taken my son / my home, my home: The Military Authorities have ruined my home.
Oh, my dear, I wish to go back home / when they wrote down my name, it was against my will.
They took me by surprise (or by force) as I was in the fields / the train has shrieked the signal to start.
It cried, saying, "where are you going?" / "is it one year or two that you are to be away?"[17]

It seems that "Ya 'Aziz 'Ayni" had been changed from the old folk song about the *corvée*, recorded by Na'ima al-Misriyya in 1915, to a full-fledged protest song against ELC recruitment. As chapter 6 has shown, changing songs by improvising new lyrics was a common practice for ELC laborers. The lines added in this translation indicate clear anti-British themes based on the experiences of the men. They even complain of the so-called haziness surrounding ELC contracts, asking the rhetorical question, "is it one year or two that you are to be away?" ELC laborers themselves may have improvised some of these changes in France or Palestine and brought them back when they returned to Egypt. In the lead-up to the 1919 revolution, a new, politically charged version had made its way to the streets of Cairo as part of a protest against ELC recruitment.

It is likely no coincidence that this modified version of "Ya 'Aziz 'Ayni" was reported in Cairo in August of 1918, the same time at which resistance to ELC recruitment had reached a fever pitch in the Egyptian countryside. Chapter 2 documented the thirty-five Ministry of Interior reports on these incidents.[18] Seven of them were mass riots incorporating groups larger than a single kinship unit, including the riot in Talkha recounted in chapter 2, as well as the sit-in that saw dozens arrested in Faraskur recounted in chapter 3. This violence made a major impact on the colonial state, which reversed decades of official policy and reinstituted the *corvée* in an effort to stave it off. Initially, this seems to have been successful, as there are no reports of violent incidents from the autumn of 1918 preserved in the archives today.

As the war wound down and news of the armistice spread through Egypt in November, the gap between expectations of demobilization and the reality of continued recruitment led to a renewal of violence. News of the Ottoman defeat reached Egyptians in early November.[19] But ELC recruitment continued apace, and according to one report, over 179,000 men were brought in between May 10 and December 31 of 1918.[20] On November 9, Prime Minister Rushdi complained to the British residency of the "disturbance that the [continued] conscription of ELC laborers has produced in the agricultural situation of the country."[21] But there remained a significant demand for workers, which had to be met through continued recruitment. Allenby explained the sources of this demand in his reply:

> There are many services, such as railroad construction, maintenance of roads for motor transport, shipping and supply work and base ports, and at advanced bases, which the cessation of hostilities does not affect as regards reduction in labour requirements; there are other services such as salvage, transportation of ordnance and stores to the base and disposal of surplus animals and material which necessitate increased demands for labour.[22]

Because twenty thousand to twenty-five thousand ELC men were released from service each month after the armistice, military authorities needed to make up for their absence. For the men of the ELC, the harsh imposition of wartime was seemingly unchanged by the fact that the war had ended.

Even for those men who had completed their term of service, demobilization was not a simple task. A British medical officer described how, when the contracts of ELC men expired and they were allowed to return home, they "immediately go into paroxysms of joy at their deliverance. Hastily gathering their belongings together, they make for the railway station in a delighted, vociferous crew . . . generally, in their excitement, they run all the way to the station."[23] But the trains did not take the men straight home, because they had to wait in quarantine.

By the summer of 1918, Palestine was ravaged by a cholera epidemic.[24] A committee was formed in the Public Health Department of the Anglo-Egyptian government and tasked with investigating the question of what to do with the men of the ELC set to return to Egypt from Palestinian districts that were experiencing the outbreak. At first, they recommended that "ELC should not be allowed to return from Palestine to Egypt until danger has passed." But this idea was rejected because it would involve "a breach of contracts concluded, and might effect recruiting and discipline in Palestine."[25] Officials in the colonial government looked to find a compromise between the politically expedient answer and the recommendations of public health officials. Ultimately, they imposed a five-day quarantine for all ELC men returning from Palestine. By the end of January 1918, approximately five thousand ELC men were passing through quarantine camps in Qantara each week on their way home from the war.

Public health officials were likely concerned because the ELC had previously been a vector for the transmission of infectious diseases to Egypt. Christopher Rose's research has shown how an epidemic of relapsing fever was linked to ELC laborers returning from the Gallipoli campaign in 1915–1916. At the same time, more than thirty thousand cases of typhus, another louse-borne bacterium, were reported in Egypt, especially concentrated in the Nile Delta and along the Suez Canal.[26] According to one official, "the increase of typhus fever and relapsing fever is the result partly of the depletion of the staff for war work and partly of the movement of native labourers employed on military works."[27] By 1918, the "Spanish" influenza pandemic (H1N1) had hit Egypt, with one estimate putting the final number of deaths throughout the country at 170,000.[28] The quarantine seemed prudent from a public health perspective, but for the men of the ELC and their families, it likely added to their anxiety.

In the midst of this, extraction of animal and agricultural resources from the countryside continued. The Supplies Control Board, which had been established in March 1918 to set maximum prices on key agricultural commodities necessary for the war effort, maintained its price ceilings through the first half of 1919.[29] At the same time, a combination of increased food exports, declines in directly imported foodstuffs, and increased competition for agricultural inputs like nitrate fertilizers due to the war had depleted reserves and led to the beginnings of serious food shortages throughout Egypt.[30] When peasant cultivators realized they could get higher prices on the local black market than the fixed prices offered by the Supplies Control Board, they began withholding their produce. In response, officials in the Ministry of Interior began requisitioning grain from the countryside by force in a pattern that mimicked the recruitment of men for the ELC.[31] By the end of 1918, aggregate food consumption in Egypt was reduced an estimated 3 to 10 percent by these requisitions, depending on the crop.[32]

The trail of violent resistance to ELC recruitment picks back up in the archives after the armistice. The Ministry of Interior reports two separate incidents, one from December 1918 and one from January 1919.[33] Another report from January tells of "scores of cases . . . where ghaffirs have suffered injuries bringing recruits in for service in the Egyptian Labour Corps."[34] Detailed reports on these "scores of cases" have unfortunately been lost, but this cryptic reference seems to indicate that widespread violent resistance to ELC recruitment began anew around this time.

The idea to form the *wafd*, then, did not take shape in a vacuum. The people of the countryside experienced food shortages, had their livestock requisitioned, and suffered from pandemic disease. In addition, hundreds of thousands of young men continued to be sent away, even though news of the war's end was widespread. As discussed in chapter 8, nationalist leaders, politicians, and public intellectuals in Egypt were aware of this popular anger and shared many of the same anxieties.

THE ELC, RURAL PROTEST, AND RAILWAY SABOTAGE

Anger directed against wartime policies structured protest actions throughout the country during the revolution. Songs and chants made this point clear enough. One song, passed on to Wingate during the climax of the revolution, was described as "the song which the little boys in the street in Cairo and the ladies in the harems have been singing lately."[35] A translation of it is preserved in the British archives, titled, "Bardun Ya Wingate" ("Excuse Us, Oh Wingate!"):

> Excuse us, Oh Wingate! / Our country has been conquered.
> You have taken away our barley, our camels and donkeys / But corn is still plentiful, so leave us alone.
> They asked us for our help / Good lord! Let them go to the Mudir.
> They can get plenty of our wealth out of him / Money beyond estimate, so pity us.
> Our laborers were sent out, as well as our soldiers / They left their land and went to the battlefields.
> They served in the trenches / Even to the mountains of Lebanon.
> They lay blame on us! / Behold us, and the calamities they have caused us.
> Had it not been for our laborers / They with their rifles could have done nothing in the midst of the sandy deserts.
> You, who are in authority / Why did you not go yourselves to the Dardanelles?
> You, Oh Maxwell, you saw no hardships / Drink the cup of sorrow now.[36]

Addressed to the high commissioner himself, the song lists a series of grievances based on the war. References to barley, corn, donkeys, and camels refer to the natural and animal resources that had been requisitioned by the Supplies Control Board and other authorities of the colonial state. The lyrics discuss ELC recruitment in particular, taking pride in the contributions of laborers to the Allied victory in the war and using their service as leverage against the continuation of British influence in Egypt. Reports of songs like these led the British to form an early interpretation of the revolution that blamed rural unrest on "methods adopted to provide Egyptian labor corps for Palestine and [the] manner in which supplies were collected for the British Army."[37] We should be careful not to simply adopt the opinions of the colonial archive, but songs like "Bardun Ya Wingate" indicate that these issues were on people's minds.

The widespread practice of destroying infrastructure should also be understood as a reaction to the wartime mobilizations, because railways in particular had become associated with efforts by the military authorities to transport food, animals, and working men out of the countryside. In his unpublished manuscript, Venables describes the scene at a train station as he witnessed it: "The departure of a levy was an occasion of despondent disarray: the recruited men walking along together escorted by native police, who were hard pressed to restrain the crowd of women and other relatives following their menfolk to the railway station."[38] With the rural population on the verge of starvation, the destruction of railways to keep trains packed with grain bound for Cairo from leaving became an appealing option for many small farmers in the countryside.[39] As On Barak has shown, telephone and telegraph infrastructure had long been associated with the imperial state, and the fact that telephone, telegraph, and railway stations were often co-located in many towns and villages meant that acts of sabotage were relatively easy to carry out.[40]

One of the earliest examples of railway sabotage took place in the Delta town of Tanta on March 12, 1919, when a crowd of thousands surrounded the station and destroyed the single-track railroad between Tanta and Talkha.[41] Similar incidents took place on a smaller scale throughout the countryside, with lines sabotaged in Barak al-Sab'a, Dessuq, Rashid, Zifta, Kafr al-Shaykh, Qalyubiyya, Sharqiyya, Zaqazig, Wasta, Asyut, and Qina.[42] On March 22 the head of the ESR sent a memo to the British Residency, noting, "A considerable amount of damage has been done to the Railways and Telegraphs during the recent disturbances . . . full details of all the damage are not available as rail and telegraph communication are cut South of Cairo in many places, but a certain amount of information has been received by river or aeroplane and there is no doubt that it will be a long time before the Railway will be able to deal with its former volume of traffic from Upper Egypt."[43]

Widespread infrastructural sabotage worked at cross-purposes with both British imperial officials and the *wafd*. Railways and telegraph lines normally provided the primary means of communication between Cairo and the provinces, and the increasing inability to use them made coordination difficult. British authorities were able to fall back on water transport up and down the Nile along with the surveillance capabilities of the Royal Air Force, but nationalist activists did not have these options. Acts of infrastructural sabotage make the most sense if we understand them as attempts by the local communities to close themselves off from the encroachments of *al-sulṭa*—the combined force of local Egyptian officials and British administrators responsible for recruiting the ELC, which was discussed in chapter 2. ELC workers and their home communities recognized this force, and they sang songs about it in their renditions of "Ya 'Aziz 'Ayni."[44]

With many of the railroads and telegraph lines connecting the villages to the central state having been sabotaged, imperial officials used air- and water-borne transport to deploy forces to pacify the countryside. In Asyut, the existing garrison of British soldiers protected the foreign residents of the town and took a defensive position in the city near the local secondary school.[45] On March 24, 1919, two planes of the RAF were deployed to bomb the assembled crowds of demonstrators, killing three people.[46] Meanwhile, state officials outfitted a Nile steamer with armor and machine guns and sent it down the river. Despite encountering some resistance along the way, the steamer arrived in Asyut the next day, and the troops on board surrounded the town. When demonstrators capitulated, four hundred were arrested and thrown in jail.[47]

Guarding state infrastructures also became a top priority. On March 13, 1919, the commander-in-chief of British forces in Egypt issued an order promising to punish all demonstrators involved in the sabotage of railways or cutting of telegraph or telephone wire. On March 23 the Royal Navy sent HMS *Vervena* to Port Sudan to guard the wireless telegraph station.[48] A March 20, 1919, memo from the Air Ministry to the Foreign Office summarizes the activities of the RAF during the unrest:

> Considerable Air Forces are being employed to maintain communications between coast towns and detached garrisons. During last two days aeroplanes have machine gunned with excellent effect crowds engaged in damaging railways and are now ordered to use bombs when targets offer. Have formed five squadrons from training squadrons and over 100 machines are now occupied.[49]

Airplanes were used for communication and reconnaissance purposes, as well as to deploy deadly force to punish and deter crowds engaged in damaging railways. During the 1919 Egyptian Revolution, British officials brought new technologies of violence from the war to bear on anticolonial demonstrators, breaking up crowds and safeguarding the logistical infrastructures that had become targets of rioters.

In addition to deploying military technologies developed during the war, British officials also resorted to collective punishment to pacify the demonstrations in the countryside.[50] It became standard policy to burn the village closest to the damaged railway tracks.[51] On March 25, in response to reports of railroad sabotage near the villages of ʻAziziyya and Badrashin in the province of Giza, a force of two hundred soldiers was dispatched and split in two to systematically search each village. According to Salah ʻAzzam, the soldiers started in the home of the *ʻumda*, where they searched everyone, including the women and children, and confiscated weapons. They finally searched the rest of the village, house by house. After all the homes had been evacuated, the village was burned to the ground.[52]

ASYUT AND MINYA

The important influence of ELC recruitment in structuring protest action seems especially apparent in the two northernmost provinces of Upper Egypt, Minya and Asyut. These provinces lie approximately 200 kilometers (125 miles) to 400 kilometers (250 miles) south of Cairo along the Nile. In the late nineteenth and early twentieth centuries, Asyut in particular emerged as an increasingly important city in this region; it was the first to get a railway station, and it hosted American president Ulysses S. Grant on his tour around the world.[53] Historical and anthropological research has demonstrated how Upper Egypt was long considered culturally different from the north—a fact best illustrated by its distinctive variety of Colloquial Arabic.[54] In the late nineteenth and early twentieth centuries, a popular culture industry centered in Cairo produced publications, recordings, theater productions, and jokes in Cairene Arabic that represented the Upper Egyptians of the south as uneducated, backward, and a kind of "internal Other."[55]

There is evidence that people in Asyut and Minya were uniquely aggrieved over the issue of ELC recruitment. Analyzing the reports of violent resistance from the summer of 1918 preserved in the British archives, it seems a disproportionate number of incidents took place in these two

Table 9.1. Violent resistance to Egyptian Labor Corps recruitment by province, summer 1918

Province	*Incidents*	*Deaths*	*Injuries*	*Arrests*
Aswan	1	2	0	0
Asyut	12	3	9	2
Bani Suwayf	1	3	1	0
Buhayra	1	1	1	0
Daqhiliyya	2	0	5	0
Gharbiyya	5	0	6	36
Girga	2	1	0	0
Manufiyya	3	0	14	47
Minya	4	8	14	0
Qina	4	5	4	0
Totals	*35*	*23*	*54*	*85*

Compiled by the author from British National Archives, Foreign Office 141/797/2.

provinces. Twelve of the thirty-five reports occurred in the single province of Asyut, more than four times the number that would be expected in an even distribution.[56] While the majority of these reports were individual acts, in four cases, laborers' family members got involved. Altogether, violence in Asyut during the summer of 1918 led to the deaths of two local guards and one villager, the wounding of nine local guards, and the arrest of two villagers. The neighboring province of Minya witnessed fewer incidents, but they were more violent and intense, including two of the seven mass uprisings. Altogether, incidents in Minya ended with eight dead villagers and eleven wounded, along with three wounded local guards. Moreover, this violence apparently continued after the summer of 1918 and into 1919. A memo from the British adviser to the Ministry of Interior in January 1919 complained about "scores of cases in two provinces, Asyut and Girga [both in Upper Egypt], where ghaffirs have suffered injuries bringing recruits in." The memo also noted, "in other Mudiriyyas there seems little or no trouble in this connection."[57] Violent incidents directed toward recruiting officials, it seems, were especially intense in this region in the months leading up to the revolution.

When the revolution came in March and April of 1919, ELC recruiting officials were again targeted in this region. The first and most famous incident was the so-called Dayrut Train Massacre. On the night of March 17, 1919, a train departed Luxor heading for Cairo with British officers on board, including four who had been commanding companies of the ELC in Palestine. When the train reached Nag' Hammadi, a crowd surrounded it and threatened the soldiers. Demonstrators entered the train and asked if there were Englishmen on board, but the officers were able to hide themselves in the first-class cabin. The train then departed and arrived at Asyut after midnight, where Alexander Pope, an inspector in the Prisons Department of the Ministry of Interior, got on board. The train departed Asyut the following morning and encountered threatening, stone-throwing crowds at the next three stations.[58]

According to the British report, when the train reached the next station at Dayrut, "A large number of rioters armed with nabuts (said to be to be fellahine, and not Bedouins or Sheikhs, though all sorts were in the crowd, including boys and women) attacked the train."[59] The demonstrators again forced their way on board, beating Pope and two of the soldiers to death. The train managed to start again and escape the crowd, but when it reached Dayr Muwas, another large crowd of demonstrators broke the windows and killed the rest of the British soldiers. All told, the bodies of seven soldiers were found, including four officers of the ELC.[60]

In a separate incident just days later and in the nearby town of Shalsh in the Dayrut district, Lieutenant Colonel William Hazel was murdered by a crowd of people.[61] Hazel was the British recruiting inspector with responsibility for Upper Egypt and, as such, he would have been the British face of military labor recruiting in the region.[62] It is hard to ascertain the motives of these protesters, but both attacks constitute circumstantial evidence that ELC officers were targeted in this region, likely because of the unpopularity of recruiting.

We can get a further sense of how the revolution developed in Asyut—or, at least, one small part of it—in *Mudhakkirat Qarya* (*Memoirs of a Village*, 1996) by 'Ismat Sayf al-Dawla. The narrator begins by lamenting how difficult it is to recount the life of an entire village. Every time he asks someone, they "substitute their own personal recollections for the recollections of the village as a whole."[63] He receives a reply from the wise old *shaykh* who once served as the chief of the local guards (*shaykh li-l-khufarā'*), explaining that any story from one individual presented as that of the collective will inevitably cause problems because "the people of Hamamiyya, like all people, differ amongst themselves."[64] The only time when people come together, according to the *shaykh*, was in the face of disaster.[65] "What kind of disaster?" the narrator asks. "Ask them about the days of *al-sulṭa* . . . or about the rape of their land in the *gazīra*," the *shaykh* replies.[66]

In the following pages, Sayf al-Dawla constructs a conversation between the narrator and a character by the name of Yunis ʿAbdallah who gets recruited into the ELC along with twenty-four others from the village. He is sent to serve in Calais, where he participates in one of the large mutinies against British officers there. When the *shaykh* uses the term *sulṭa*, then, he is referring to the force wielded by British and Egyptian officials responsible for recruiting the ELC. The ELC is considered a "disaster" (*kāritha*) that unites the village and makes it possible to narrate its history as a collective subject. We have already seen ELC laborers use the term *sulṭa*, in the popular song "Ya ʿAziz ʿAyni" that laments how "the authorities (*al-sulṭa*) have taken my son."

Mudhakkirat Qarya goes on to recount how the recruitment of young men into the ELC contributed to the conditions for revolutionary action in Hamamiyya. The coming of the revolution to the village unfolds through a dialogue between the narrator and the character Fikri ʿAbd al-Nabi. Fikri explains how the impact of the war was felt:

> It's not that the war made us poorer; we were already poor. But it increased our feeling of poverty, and when its economic effects exceed the limits of the basic material needs [of the people], it disturbed previously stable social relationships. . . . In truth, [the people] have the financial resources to return to stability, and they look to the *gazīra* as if it came from their dreams.[67]

The real problem with the war was not that it made the villagers marginally less wealthy—they had no wealth to speak of—but that it infringed on their basic ability to live. The combined effects of food deprivation, epidemic and pandemic disease, and the forced exodus of young men from the countryside had made production of life's basic necessities impossible. Fikri frames the war as a violation of what James Scott has termed "peasant moral economy"—the unspoken agreement between rural farmers and local elites that, at the very least, everyone will have enough food to eat.[68] But the natural environment *had* provided them with the means to restore equilibrium to the moral economy: the rich deposit of silt that had built up over generations of riverine floods referred to as the *gazīra*. This plot of land could be used to plant extra crops and meet the subsistence needs of the village, but it was owned by an absentee landlord.

Fikri tells the story of how he was on the train during the infamous Dayrut massacre, which he claims began when one of the British officers shot the train's driver for refusing to continue ahead.[69] After he returns home, Fikri agrees to join the revolution, but only on his own terms: "After the revolution, we will not give back our weapons, but we will get back our *gazīra* by the grace of God if they haven't returned it to us by then."[70] Fikri's main goal, then, was not necessarily the same as the *wafd*; he wanted to seize the *gazīra*, which appeared as an island just across from the village. In the years before the war, this *gazīra* had been commoditized as private property, but the revolution provided an opportunity to seize it back, by violent force if necessary. *Mudhakkirat Qarya* provides a plausible story of how the 1919 revolution could have been assimilated into local politics. The revolution came to Hamamiyya in the midst of an already difficult situation made worse by the recruitment of young men like Yunis ʿAbdallah for the ELC. While Fikri gladly took up arms to join the revolution, he was still fundamentally driven by local concerns, such as seizing the *gazīra*, and the nationalist revolution of the *wafd* was only a secondary goal.[71]

In analyzing popular protest during the revolution that took place throughout Minya and Asyut, there is evidence that events evolved in a way somewhat at odds with the *wafd*-ist project. According to al-Rafiʿi, on March 15, 1919, students and lawyers launched a protest movement in Asyut similar to the coordinated protests elsewhere, but soon events accelerated beyond the control of local nationalist activists.[72] Protesters lit fire to a huge barn stacked with hay requisitioned by the military authorities. The compressed hay was fuel for the fire, which burned for days.[73] Local officials left the city, and local lawyers and other notables formed "committees" (*lagān*; sing., *lagna*). According to al-Rafiʿi—the nationalist historian par excellence—these *lagān* began "patrolling the streets to secure people's lives and money (*amwāl*), and to prevent the efforts by some of the ruffians (*al-ashrār*) to go to the city for non-nationalist goals (*li-aghrāḍ ghayr waṭaniyya*)."[74] Reading against the grain, it seems that not all protesters saw themselves as nationalists. Those who protested for other reasons were referred to as "ruffians" (*ashrār*). ʿAbd al-ʿAzim Ramadan describes a similar incident in Asyut in March 1919: "Some of the revolutionaries surrounded the house of Muhammad Mahmud Pasha Sulayman, one of the men arrested with Saʿd Zaghlul, and they sacked it and lit it on fire. When some of the people asked those who burned it why they did so, they replied: 'has Muhammad Mahmud Pasha Sulayman ever given a loaf of bread to the hungry? We need food.'"[75] This report provides the most direct evidence of blatantly anti-*wafd* sentiment in revolutionary demonstrations.

The memoirs of Huda Shaʿrawi—the Egyptian feminist leader, nationalist activist, and wife of the *wafd* leader 'Ali Sha'rawi—provide more insight into the nuanced class dynamics at play in Minya. Her father was Muhammad Sultan, also known as the "King of Upper Egypt."[76] Sultan was appointed provincial governor of Minya and was the president of the Chamber of Delegates established by Khedive Ismail in 1866.[77] By 1882 he was the largest landowner in Minya, with holdings of over thirteen thousand feddans.[78] His daughter Huda was born to a white slave from the Caucasus region, and she was raised by a Black household slave from Sudan. As Eve Troutt-Powell puts it, "Sha'rawī's memoirs reveal her struggle against the constraints of her childhood and upbringing and her unique way of questioning the premises upon which Egyptian upper-class households were both structured and idealized in the late nineteenth century."[79]

Sha'rawi's critical approach to the upper-class milieu of her childhood in Minya becomes clear when she recounts the story of one of the protests she saw there during the revolution:

> Some of the people (*al-ahāli*) intensified in their revolutionary fervor, and they tried to attack the homes of the British employees [of the colonial state]. However, some of the *'ayān* blocked their way and prevented them from doing so . . . [one of them] exposed himself to the anger of the citizens and their attacks . . . [another one] stood in front of the door [to the house] of one of the British employees . . . and he puffed out his chest in front of the people, saying, "You won't kill him unless you kill me first![80]

She describes the common people of the town of Minya (*al-ahāli*) attacking the homes of white British officials who resided there. The local elites (*'ayān*) interfered with them and blocked their way, even risking their own lives to protect the lives of the English. According to this story, the common people and local elites could easily act at cross-purposes with one another. The occasion for such difference was the bodily safety of the few white residents in the town.

There is evidence, then, that repertoires of contentious politics, including the use of violent force, had been forged in response to ELC recruitment and local inequality in Asyut and Minya starting in the summer of 1918.[81] These protests picked up steam again in the late autumn of 1918 and the winter of 1919 and continued throughout the spring, running in parallel to the *wafd*-ist project. Protesters in this region consistently targeted ELC recruiting officials, including in the Dayrut Train Massacre and the murder of William Hazel. Protest action in this region sometimes buttressed nationalist efforts, but at other times popular anger worked at cross-purposes with the *wafd*. To reduce popular protest action in this region to nationalism misses important parts of this story.

LOYAL LABORERS

While others carried out a revolution partially in their name, the extent to which the ELC rank and file remained loyal to their British officers stands out in the sources. Venables moved from Qantara to Alexandria on March 12, 1919. He was aware of the revolutionary violence gripping the country, but his diaries indicate little direct experience of it.[82] Upon his arrival in Alexandria, he noted the "subdued demeanor of the natives."[83] A few weeks later, in early April, Alexandria experienced massive strikes, and Venables' diaries preserve his disdainful attitude toward them with the note: "disgust at triumphant attitude of Egyptian."[84] However, in contrast to the crowds of nationalist demonstrators, Venables' entry on April 8, 1919, notes, "ELC men working quietly and happily."[85]

In his unpublished manuscript, he provides more detail on the mood of his men during the revolution, writing that ELC laborers could be heard "retorting mockingly to the appeals of passing demonstrators, calling them town scum and the like."[86] Given his predilection to distrust the revolution, Venables' characterization should certainly be taken with a grain of salt. But if his report is true, it may give some insight into why Egyptian laborers, especially those encamped outside of Alexandria, did not join in the demonstrations—as migrant laborers of rural origin, they did not feel a sense of community and collective identity with the primarily urban demonstrators.

Whether or not Venables' depiction is true, it is clear that Egyptians remained employed with the ELC for the duration of the revolution and well after its conclusion. In late March and early April 1919, British authorities discussed the need to redeploy ELC laborers to Palestine and Syria to work on railroads in the OETA.[87] A British inspector in the Ministry of Interior in July 1919 claimed to have interviewed ninety-four recruits who were just leaving for tours of duty in the ELC. According to the inspector's report, "a few were going for the first time, most were going for the third, fourth, or fifth time."[88] The whole run of the *ELC News* was published *after* the war, between January and July 1919, showing the continued activity of this organization.[89] The ELC was in existence as late as January 1921, employed by the Mandatory authorities in Palestine during the early days of their administration.[90]

In one notable case, ELC laborers filled in for workers in Port Sa'id who were on strike in solidarity with nationalist aims. As the main port city at the northern entrance of the Suez Canal, Port Sa'id had long been the site of coalers' strikes that occurred mostly in response to their specific working conditions.[91] On May 13, 1919, another strike was planned at the Suez Canal Company, but this one spread and turned into a general strike across the city.[92] The director of the company felt that the strike was "of a political character . . . aimed with a definite motive at a vulnerable spot—a center of wealth and activity largely accruing through the British occupation of Egypt," and therefore more in accord with the 1919 revolution.[93] According to a telegram sent on May 17, 1919, the rear admiral of the Royal Navy assumed control of the coal supply at Port Sa'id and was "indenting upon ELC for labour up to government requirements."[94] The navy then called upon nearby ELC workers to fill in for laborers striking in solidarity with the nationalist cause. The men of the ELC seem to have fulfilled these duties without protest.

It was not only under the auspices of British military authority that ELC workers organized themselves at cross-purposes with the nationalist movement. There is one document that indicates the existence of an official political party formed by the men of the ELC that differed from the mainstream of the *wafd* during its negotiations with the British. After the revolution, at the beginning of negotiations that would ultimately stall, the colonial government was inundated with petitions and telegrams from different groups in the country. By the summer of 1921 the Egyptian government was on its fourth prime minister in three years—at that time 'Adli Yakin Pasha—who was traveling to London in an effort to negotiate face-to-face with British authorities.

In September of 1921 a petition was received from a group referring to itself as the "Egyptian Labour Corps Party," giving its take on the actions of the new government. The author was a certain "Mohamed Zaki Ibrahim Efendi," and he gave a Cairo address for his organization. The petition was sealed with what seems to be the party's official stamp, which contained a bilingual inscription that read "Egyptian Labour Corps Party" in English and *ḥizb al-'ummāl al-mutaṭu'aiyyin*, or "The Party of Volunteer Workers," in Arabic. The very existence of this party shows that some continued to identify with the ELC in the years after the revolution. The Arabic inscription on its seal is especially significant because its insistence on referring to *voluntary* laborers contrasts with representations of ELC recruitment as "kidnapping" (*khaṭaf*) or "slavery" (*'ibudiyya*) in *wafd*-ist discourse. More like the proud, thrifty laborers represented in Sayyid Dar-

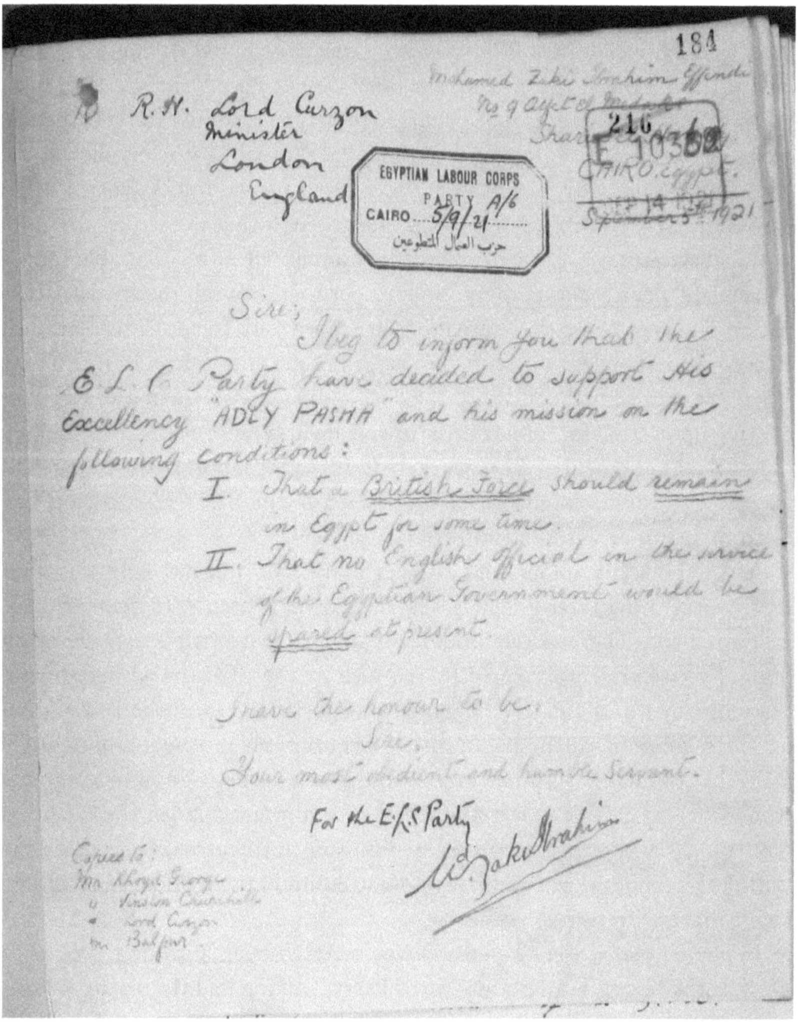

184

Mohamed Zaki Ibrahim Effendi

CAIRO, Egypt.

September 5 1921

To R.H. Lord Curzon
Minister
London
England

EGYPTIAN LABOUR CORPS
PARTY A/6
CAIRO 5/9/21
حزب العمال المتطوعين

Sir;

I beg to inform you that the E.L.C. Party have decided to support His Excellency "ADLY PASHA" and his mission on the following conditions:

I. That a British Force should remain in Egypt for some time.

II. That no English official in the service of the Egyptian Government would be spared at present.

I have the honour to be,
Sir,
Your most obedient and humble Servant.

For the E.L.C. Party
M. Zaki Ibrahim

Copies to:
Mr Lloyd George
" Winston Churchill
" Lord Curzon
Mr Balfour

FIGURE 9.1. Petition from the Egyptian Labour Corps Party to the British Residency. British National Archives, Foreign Office 371/6304.

wish's classic tune "Salma ya Salama," the notion of a political party of laborers who had "volunteered" to serve in the war centers on the agency of workers instead of the coercion of the British. This interpretation may have appealed to men who had just spent months if not years during the war fashioning an identity for themselves in the masculine, competitive culture of the ELC.

The petition from the "E.L.C. Party" is also notable because it differed from the official nationalist agenda at the time. The party supported 'Adli's mission, but only on the condition that a "British force should *remain* in Egypt for some time," and that "no English officials in the service of the Egyptian government would be *spared* at present (emphasis in original)."[95] These desires ran counter to the demands of 'Adli's government. As documents in the British archives make clear, 'Adli pushed for the withdrawal of occupation to the Canal Zone only, to secure "imperial communications," with no other British troops in the country.[96] In contrast to this, the official position of the ELC party was for British troops to remain in the country. One can only speculate that the prospect of losing their primary source of income was fearful to some of the men of the ELC, but for nationalist leaders who looked at the violence associated with ELC recruitment and saw "kidnapping" (*khaṭaf*) or "slavery" (*'ibudiyya*) (see chapter 8), the demands of this ELC party must have amounted to Stockholm Syndrome.

Men of the ELC and their families would go on to clash with the postrevolutionary government over the issue of receiving pensions and disability benefits. On January 29, 1921, the Egyptian government issued an official decree that any man who had been wounded and completely or partially disabled in their service during the First World War could receive a pension to provide for the "necessities of life" over and above the salary that was provided to them.[97] According to Egyptian historian Latifa Salim, the files of pension permissions for government workers (*milaffāt adhunāt m'āsh*) contain requests from workers seeking just compensation under this decree, some dating from as late as 1933.[98] Examples include the camel driver Mansur Shihata, who lost his eye during a battle in Palestine, and a certain Muhammad Ibrahim, a worker for the ELC who was wounded. Salim's research in the files of the Cairo city police force uncovers similar complaints from a father requesting compensation for his son who had died during his service.[99] Thus ELC laborers struggled to get material recognition from the postrevolutionary government in Egypt for over a decade. While the January 29, 1921, decree seemed to indicate that the government would repay these laborers for their loyal service, securing these payments was much more difficult in practice, and the largely rural population that was subject to Labor Corps recruitment was once again compelled to struggle in order to close the gap between rhetoric and reality.

There is a good deal of evidence, then, to indicate that actual ELC workers sometimes behaved and thought in ways that ran counter to the revolution and the postrevolutionary national project. Certainly, it is clear that the ELC continued to work during and after the revolution, while others—like the striking coalers of Port Sa'id—decided to protest in solidarity with nationalist goals. If Venables is credible, then at least some ELC men vocally expressed their alienation from the broader nationalist movement and their genuine desire to continue their employment. The most striking document is the petition from the "Egyptian Labour Corps Party," which is significant not only as evidence of the existence of the organization and its Arabic name—"The Party of Voluntary Workers," which openly refuted the *wafd*'s association of the ELC with "kidnapping" and "slavery"—but also because it indicates that organized groups of laborers articulated their political interests as different and at odds with the mainstream nationalist project. While the Egyptian delegation that traveled to London pushed for the withdrawal of British troops to the Suez Canal zone, the petition from the ELC Party called for troops to *remain* in the country. Differences between the men of the ELC and the government continued for more than a decade, with some making appeals to pay back pensions as late as 1933. It seems fair to say that the interests of actual laborers who served in the war were often not at the heart of the revolutionary project. If the war was not theirs, then the revolution was not necessarily theirs, either.

CONCLUSION

If we analyze popular culture and popular protest actions that spread throughout the country during the 1919 revolution, the unitary political subject that underwrote Egyptian racial nationalism at the time begins to fall apart. For one thing, while many have told the story of the 1919 revolution as a movement that originated with the formation of the *wafd* and only spread to the rural provinces *after* the arrest and exile of Sa'd Zaghlul, an extensive protest movement had begun in the summer of 1918, months *before* the *wafd* was founded. This movement reemerged after the war, as expectations of demobilization went unfulfilled. Instead of peace, Egyptians continued for years to be recruited by the hundreds of thousands to meet demand for logistical labor in occupied territory. When the revolution broke out in March 1919, these repertoires of violent resistance to recruitment were reactivated, and solidarity with ELC laborers again animated protests throughout the country. Especially in the two northernmost provinces of Egypt's culturally distinct southern region, violence directed against ELC officials was a significant aspect of revolutionary protest. Focusing on the ELC helps us to appreciate the impact of rural Egyptians in kick-starting and maintaining protest throughout the 1919 revolution.

While popular protest at home and activist rhetoric abroad claimed to carry out a revolution in the name of workers who had been "kidnapped" and condemned to "slavery," laborers themselves remained loyal to their British officers throughout the revolution. Officers' accounts attest to this loyalty, and ELC workers were even used to fill in for others striking in solidarity with the nationalist movement. The British archives preserve a petition from the "Egyptian Labor Corps Party," or *ḥizb al-ʿummāl al-muṭatawuʿaiyyin* ("The Voluntary Worker's Party"), which indicates ELC laborers organized to represent their collective interest on the political stage that emerged after the 1919 revolution, and did so in ways that ran counter to the goals of the *wafd*. While British officials had a strong incentive to represent Egyptians as "volunteers"—and we should therefore look toward any evidence substantiating this notion preserved in the British archives with a skeptical eye—the document seems to be a genuine artifact. If it is, then it points to the maintenance of social and organizational ties between laborers who had served together in the war years after the armistice and revolution.[100] On a more ad hoc basis, individual laborers worked until 1933 to advance claims against the postrevolutionary government for pensions they had been denied, suggesting that the impact of the ELC was being felt in Egypt long after the war was over.

The story of the ELC adds depth and nuance to historians' understandings of the 1919 revolution in Egypt. It complicates urban-centric, unitary, and quasi-racial conceptions of the Egyptian political subject during the revolution by showing how rural migrant laborers inspired alternative political solidarities that could not always be reduced to nationalism. Some of this evidence is circumstantial and confined to select populations. Nevertheless, it clashes with the received historical narrative and helps us to understand the diversity of political imaginaries that existed in different regions of the country as the 1919 revolution unfolded.

CONCLUSION

IN 2014, while Ashraf Sabry was on Egyptian television representing the men of the ELC as soldiers from the army, a team of researchers, artists, and activists told the mens' stories in a different way. Directed by Laila Soliman, *Hawa' al-Huriyya* (*Winds of Freedom*, 2014) was a unique theatrical experience combining archival research, musical theater, and academic lecturing. Soliman is a pioneer of this unique style of documentary theater, and for this production she teamed up with historian Alia Mossallam and ethnomusicologist Mustafa Said. For months, the team worked in Cairo and London gathering archival sources on Egypt's history during the period from 1914 to 1919.[1] They cast two actresses to play the main roles: Zainab as the academic lecturer who easily switches between Egyptian Colloquial Arabic and refined English, and Nanda as the Syrian immigrant with a beautiful singing voice.[2] Throughout the show, Zainab lectures about documents from the British archives and Egyptian press sources, while Nanda embodies the great performers of early twentieth-century Egyptian pop culture like Na'ima al-Misriyya and Sayyid Darwish.

The revolution that Soliman and her team had recently lived through themselves, known popularly as the "Arab Spring," hangs like a specter over the performance. In one scene, Nanda and Zainab trace the origins of ousted former president Hosni Mubarak's infamous "emergency laws" back to British martial law during the First World War. Later, a copy of the Egyptian magazine *Al-Lata'if al-Musawwira* is projected on stage, featuring two large pictures of the ELC. The headline reads, "A Quarter of a Million Strong Egyptians Gathered as Friends of the Allies."[3] Standing in front of the image, Zainab offers a critical interpretation: "Despite what you see in an article like this, the conscription of workers into the army happened by force (*al-tagnīd al-'ummāla fi-l-gaysh 'āmila bi-l-*

sulṭa).” She continues, “That was one of the reasons for the huge uprisings [in 1918] in the Delta and in some cities in Upper Egypt,” referring to the wave of violence in response to ELC recruitment that this book has documented in chapters 2 and 9. Ruminating on this forgotten spate of violent uprisings, Zainab says, “With time, I feel that comparing 1917 and 1919 bears a resemblance to comparisons between 2011 and 2013.” Suddenly, Nanda interrupts her: “Comparisons confine the imagination and oversimplify matters!” Nanda’s interruption throws the lecture off course, the scene shifts, and the image of the ELC disappears.

THE ELC AND THE FIRST WORLD WAR IN EGYPT

Like the team of scholars and activists behind *Hawa’ al-Huriyya*, this book has tried to tell the story of the ELC in order to interrupt oversimplified narratives of history, whether propagated by British imperial or Egyptian national authorities. The men of the ELC worked in a number of roles associated with military logistics, and a major goal of this book has been to document their forgotten contributions to the First World War. Most histories of the war focus on European instead of Middle Eastern theaters of battle, and tell the story of soldiers on the front lines instead of logistical laborers on the lines of supply and communication. But the ELC complicates our understanding of the war on both fronts. Although tens of thousands of Egyptians served in France, this was dwarfed by the hundreds of thousands who served in the battles against the Ottoman Empire in Gallipoli, Iraq, and, especially, in the little-known yet consequential invasion through the Sinai Peninsula and into Palestine. The ELC laid hundreds of miles of railway and water pipeline in a “bridge across the desert,” which transformed the possibilities for movement between Cairo and Jerusalem and provided the foundations for a new British Empire in the Middle East.

Close proximity to and awareness of vital logistical infrastructures gave the men of the ELC a unique ability to strike a blow at the heart of the British war machine, and the ELC protested every step of the way in their long journey from home to the front. They resisted recruiting officials and local authorities—sometimes violently, and with support from their communities. When they reached the district (*markaz*) lockups, they staged sit-ins and got the people of the surrounding town involved. Especially in France and Italy, the men of the ELC were some of the unruliest members of the military labor force. British authorities responded to these protests with changes in policy, reinstituting the *corvée*, surrounding supply depots with barbwire, and redeploying the ELC out of France before the winter hit in 1917. This illustrates how logistical laborers can leverage their position in networks of circulation to create "impassable chokepoints that have ripple effects through entire systems of production and distribution."[4]

Ultimately, the men of the ELC lived what Deborah Cowen has called "the deadly life of logistics." According to Cowen, the important role played by logistical laborers in networks of circulation makes them targets of increasingly intrusive and violent techniques of state control.[5] ELC recruitment was carried out with violence from the very beginning, with local authorities like the *'umad* simply grabbing men off their fields or from their homes and marching them to the nearest town lockup. If they resisted, they were beaten or even killed, and if resistance got out of hand, the nearest district or provincial town center could always send its police force to overwhelm the opposition. The condemned men moved from home to the front and back again, being poked and prodded by British sanitary inspectors, medical officers, and public health officials along the way. When they arrived at their worksite, they found themselves at the mercy of their British officers. Officers created a hierarchy within their companies, inspected the men morning and night, and enforced military discipline with courts-martial. When mass protests against these conditions took place in France, Italy, and Gallipoli, officers called in surrounding troops and put them down violently, killing dozens of ELC men in the process. Disrupting logistical flows was nonnegotiable, which may go some way in explaining why the British Empire held on to the Suez Canal long after the 1919 revolution in Egypt.

But the violence to which ELC men were exposed cannot be explained solely with reference to their role as logistical laborers. While logistical infrastructures brought people together, the logic of colonial racism worked to keep them apart. Chapter 5 showed how the men of the ELC were kept in segregated camps in France, with their movements closely monitored. When they went out in the surrounding towns, they were subjected to Jim Crow–like laws that prevented them from fraternizing with the local white population. In Egypt and Palestine, they had segregated hospital systems and were monitored by their white officers, who justified the use of whips to enforce discipline in ways that were clearly linked to the "peculiar racial characteristics" of Egyptians in their minds.

In this sense, the war was the clearest manifestation of what W. E. B. Du Bois called the "global color line." The ELC was just one part of the "coloured" or "native" labor corps. Through a series of colonial wars in the long nineteenth century, which were outlined in chapter 1, the British and French had built up specifically racial ideas about who was appropriate to perform certain kinds of military labor. As the global First World War imposed unprecedented logistical challenges, the Allies went back to these ready-made solutions and recruited racialized laborers from all corners of the globe for the war effort.

VIOLENCE AND VOLUNTARISM IN THE BRITISH EMPIRE

British imperial officials tried to justify their policies in Egypt by asserting that they had received some form of consent to them.[6] This was why they always insisted that ELC workers were "volunteers." As Aaron Jakes has argued, one way the British Empire attempted to manufacture consent in Egypt was through a discourse he calls "colonial economism."[7] Colonial economism was an elaboration of Egyptian racial identity that posited Egyptians as uniquely sensitive to petty economic motivations and unable to see the greater good sufficiently to exercise political rights. Jakes documents on how the British occupation from 1882 to 1914 instituted policies from the burgeoning discipline of political economy to turn Egypt into a massive machine for producing national wealth. If they could succeed at this task, British officials believed that Egyptians—as a race of people uniquely influenced by financial motivations—would come to consent to incorporation into the empire.

Colonial economism clearly influenced perceptions of the ELC in the British archives. The sources include many attempts by officials to adduce evidence that ELC workers were indeed volunteers, and pro-British propaganda reports in the Egyptian press concentrated on the competitive wages and material benefits gained by enlisted men. The colonial origins of this source material notwithstanding, there is significant evidence—both in Arabic and English—that some approached the authorities and signed up for terms of service in the ELC of their own volition. Perhaps the Egyptian press, which was under heavy British censorship at the time, provided questionable accounts of events, but the only firsthand narrative written by an ELC worker that I have been able to find tells the story of a young man who apparently found the work agreeable enough to enroll on multiple tours of duty. 'Abd al-Hamid Muhammad Husayn portrays himself as upwardly mobile in the ELC, and his story is recounted in the Egyptian magazine *Ruz al-Yusuf* in 1968 as a transnational parable linking Egypt and Palestine in the recent past, not an indictment of British abuses.

Despite the presence or absence of volunteers in the ELC, it is important to understand that the years of British occupation had so significantly transformed the natural and social environment in Egypt that millions of workers had become dependent on wage labor to survive. Husayn himself acknowledges the financial compulsion that underwrote his enlistment into the ELC. He writes, "Poverty governed over everything in [my] humble neighborhood . . . and poverty gives birth to certain values and laws (*wa-m'a al-faqr tawlida al-muthul wa-l-quwānīn*)."[8] He draws a metaphor here from the realm of jurisprudence; whereas Divine Law, with its origins in the Qur'an and prophetic tradition, was represented by the Arabic term *sharī'a*, *qānūn* (pl. *quwānīn*) rested on the authority of the state, and was established by violent conquest. Husayn's creative use of the term indicates that a third type of violence had emerged by the end of the occupation. Just as the British attempted to build a political relationship with Egyptians on the basis of the production of national wealth, they exerted a new type of force that enacted violence through poverty (*faqr*). As chapter 2 explored in more detail, the extension of perennial irrigation and the reorientation of agriculture toward cotton for export had fundamentally transformed the lives of the *fallāḥīn*. They had gone from planting crops like wheat—which could always be eaten in times of financial hardship or market failure—to harvesting cotton on large plantations financed by global commodity exchanges.

But the effectiveness of new technologies in increasing or erasing the national wealth of Egypt should not occlude historians' understandings of the broader dynamics at play in the British Empire. Imperialism in the late nineteenth and early twentieth centuries was a competition between European nation-states, and many statesmen feared it might squander their own national wealth just as easily as increase it.[9] Once the nation-states of Europe adopted the logic of continuous accumulation as an organizing principle of the polity, and not merely of political economy, they had created an entirely new form of government. The relative peace and stability that prevailed within Europe after the Franco-Prussian War allowed for a degree of pan-European solidarity to emerge that was expressed in the collective identity of *whiteness*. This was reinforced through decades of expansionist colonial wars across the globe, which set the precedent for complex schemes to transport racialized laborers across vast distances, including those examined in chapter 1. Whereas Lenin famously analyzed imperialism as the final stage in the development of capitalism, Hannah Arendt understands it as the first stage in the emergence of a new type of polity that is continuously managing the incorporation of racial difference.[10]

But Arendt's commitment to a flawed categorical schema keeps her from properly identifying antiracist violence as "political."[11] In her essay "On Violence," Arendt objects to Frantz Fanon's seminal work *The Wretched of the Earth*. While she acknowledges that the enactment of violence depicted by Fanon can cement collective identities like "suicide squads and revolutionary brotherhoods," Arendt writes, "no body politic I know of was ever founded on equality before death and its actualization in violence."[12] Arendt's essay was a response to the violent tactics of the Black Power movement in her adopted home of the United States, which looked to Fanon's work as a kind of prophecy.[13]

However, a thorough reading of *The Wretched of the Earth* shows that the sense of teleological certainty Arendt critiques does not actually exist in Fanon's text. For Fanon, the "first encounter" between colonizer and colonized was "marked by violence," and their existence together "was carried on by dint of a great array of bayonets and cannons."[14] In the face of the colonial war machine, Fanon argues that anticolonial politics must utilize "all means to turn the scale, including, of course, that of violence," which "will be claimed and taken over by the native at the moment when, deciding to embody history in his own person, he surges . . . to wreck the colonial world."[15]

But as Fanon continues, the teleological certainty that seems to underwrite his earlier rhetoric about "embodying history" breaks down. He describes the fading away of anticolonial certainty in one remarkable passage:

> This spectacular voluntarism which was to lead the colonized people in a single move to absolute sovereignty, the certainty one had that all the pieces of the nation could be gathered up in one fell swoop and from the same, shared perspective . . . proved in the light of experience to be a very great weakness. As long as he imagined he could switch straight from colonized subject to sovereign citizen of an independent nation, as long as he believed in the *mirage* sustained by his unmediated physical strength, the colonized achieved no real progress along the road to knowledge. His consciousness remained rudimentary.[16] (Emphasis mine)

Here, Fanon switches from the subjective to the objective modes of analysis, seeking to understand not why the colonized resort to violence, but what the effects of their actions proved to be in the light of history. Rather than making the colonized into a new kind of human, the promise of violence appears as a "mirage in which the dispossessed see their reflections but from which they cannot slake their thirst."[17] While Arendt sees a glorification of violence in Fanon that is fundamentally antipolitical, Homi Bhabha says of Fanonian violence: "It does not offer a clear choice between life and death or slavery and freedom, because it confronts the colonial condition of life-in-death."[18] In this sense, violence on behalf of the voiceless is analytically distinct from violence exercised by those who hold power in order to impose their will. Reading Fanon against Arendt helps us understand the political dimensions of antiracist violence, which is a last-ditch effort on the part of people who have been deprived of their voice in the public realm to make themselves heard.

During the 1919 revolution, violent protests in the countryside were put down with overwhelming force as the EEF made its way down the Nile by steamship with air support from above. But British officials knew that the spectacle of violence during the revolution had undermined any hope they had of claiming "consent" to their occupation of Egypt. So, they released Zaghlụl and his colleagues from prison, allowed them to travel to Paris, and began negotiations with the *wafd* that would end in a degree of national sovereignty granted to Egyptians.

RACE, SPACE, AND THE POSTCOLONIAL NATION-STATE

How can we conceive of a space that brings rural and urban Egyptians into community with one another? For nationalists organizing political action against the British occupation in 1919, the answer lay within the borders of the territorial nation-state itself. The space within these lines would become the space of Egyptian sovereignty. Operating from the empty, a priori conception of space criticized by Lefebvre (see chapter 3), as well as the racialized view of the world that had gained prominence by the end of the nineteenth century, nationalists in Egypt saw imperialism as a confrontation between different nations/races (*umam*) on the space of the world stage, and looked to national sovereignty as a legal mechanism to undo it. What the urban, educated lawyers of the *wafd* struggled to grasp, but the *fallāḥīn* of the countryside were in a position to understand intuitively, was that *imperialism was a spatial process that produced racial imaginaries, not a confrontation between objectively existing races in empty space.* This is why the *fallāḥīn* focused their energies on sabotaging railways, telegraphs, and telephone lines during the revolution; they saw the oppression to which they were exposed as a consequence of spatial change, and they knew that logistical infrastructures traced the outlines of the spaces in which they were most intimately enmeshed. It was these actions—not the desire of the *wafd* to travel to Paris during the Peace Conference—that must have threatened the British Empire the most, for while they relented their pressure on Zaghlul and his colleagues, they clamped down on the rural saboteurs (see chapter 9).

Instead of ending at the arbitrary borders of the province or nation-state, logistical infrastructures and the migrant laborers who built and maintained them cut across borders and facilitated flows that animated war and commerce alike. Following the men of the ELC as they made their way from their home villages to the front and back again forces us to draw new boundaries around these networks of circulation. This recasts the history of Egypt "from the inside out," aligning it with geographies besides empire and nation.[19]

In the wake of the First World War, nationalists across the globe hoped that if they could just draw the right lines on the map so that the territorial space of the nation-state was congruent with the borders of the racial/national political subject, then they could solve the problems created by imperialism. But the space of politics and collective identity is a mental space just as much as it is a territorial one. If we see the emergence of modern nationalism as the product of a small group of educated, urban intellectuals imposing their will rather than as collective political action, we risk confusing the mental space of the *polis* with the territorial space of the nation-state. As Fanon warned, this can lead to a loss of the sense of voluntarism that underwrote mass participation in initial waves of anticolonial nationalism.

The theoretical musings of intellectuals like Fanon are important insofar as they give us insight into the conceptual worldviews of our sources and the potential pitfalls associated with them. But it was the actions of the men of the ELC and their home communities that provided the occasion for such observations to be written in the first place. Workers like these men built the very environment in which the sources bequeathed to us were written. As they traveled from their home villages to the major cities and towns of Egypt and on to serve in the war, they interacted with some of the major figures of Egyptian history. Yet while we know the stories of men like Allenby and Cromer, Sa'd Zaghlul and Salama Musa, and even a few important women like Huda Sha'rawi, the men of the ELC have been largely forgotten. The men and women who do the hidden work of production, reproduction, and distribution have enabled so many others to live a life of the mind. Historians have an ethical imperative to seek out analytical categories that can bring their stories to light.

NOTES

INTRODUCTION

1. The Seventy-Second, Seventy-Fifth, and Seventy-Sixth Companies of the ELC arrived at Dunkirk, twenty kilometers to the west of Adinkerke, between March and May 1917. Calais, which is sixty kilometers to the west of Adinkerke, is the next closest city in which ELC laborers were employed on French docks. ELC Companies Eighty-One, Eighty-Two, Eighty-Three, and Eighty-Four were assigned to the Fourth Army Area, which was involved in launching an amphibious assault against the Germans on the Belgian coastline twenty kilometers to the east of Adinkerke during the Third Battle of Ypres. The National Archives, London, War Office (hereafter cited as TNA, WO) 137/37: "Report on British Labour," November 14, 1919.

2. Entries for the British soldiers buried at Adinkerke typically include information on their company, battalion, cause of death, closest relatives, and place of birth. See "Index No. B 172, Adinkerke Military Cemetery," *Grave Registration Reports*, Imperial War Graves Commission, from Commonwealth War Graves Commission, accessed August 14, 2018, https://www.cwgc.org/find-war-dead/casualty/164133/sabit-harun-mohamed,-/.

3. Longworth, *Unending Vigil*, 33.

4. Barret, "Subalterns at War," 156–176.

5. Laqueur, "Memory and Naming," 150–167.

6. Fuchs, "Sites of Memory."

7. Barret, "Subalterns at War," 158.

8. Fuchs, "Sites of Memory," 8.

9. Ruiz, "Manly Spectacles."

10. Xu, *Strangers*; Starling and Lee, *No Labour, No Battle*; Stovall, "Color Line."

11. Douglass, "The Color Line."

12. Murphy, *Shadowing*, 13. See Du Bois, *Souls of Black Folk*, 359 for the first appearance in print of the term "the global color line."

13. For the 1915 Singapore Mutiny, see Harper, "Singapore, 1915." For the 1916 Easter Rebellion in Ireland, see McGarry, *The Rising*. For the Amritsar Massacre of 1919 and other uprisings in British India during and following the war, see Lloyd, *Amritsar Massacre*.

14. According to a recent anthology on the subject, "a near-consensus is apparent . . . on the popular association of Africans' color and origin—here, perceived 'blackness' and sub-Saharan origin—with servile status. This, obviously was a consequence of the large proportion of slaves who were trans-Saharan Africans." Cuno and Walz, *Race and Slavery*, 8. In Cairo, most Black slaves were women; see Walz, "Black Slavery." In rural Egypt there were three scenarios in which enslaved Black men were used in agriculture: on the privileged estates of 'Ali's royal family and the people to whom they granted land, manning the water pumps in the Upper Egyptian town of Isna, and in the villages and cotton plantations of the Nile Delta. See Cuno, "African Slaves."

15. Troutt-Powell, *A Different Shade*.

16. Gasper, *Power of Representation.*

17. The population of Egypt in the 1917 census was approximately 12.7 million; see Khalifa, *Population*, 3.

18. "Behind the Lines," *Sydney Morning Herald*, November 2, 1916, 6.

19. The British Broadcasting Corporation (BBC) has been active in commemorating the colonial troops who served in the First World War, but the ELC has barely been mentioned in any of their programs. See *The World's War*, *Soldiers of Empire*, and *The War That Changed.* Al-Jazeera also ignored the ELC in its three-part documentary series *World War One through Arab Eyes.*

20. Ulrichsen, *Logistics and Politics*; Starling and Lee, *No Labour, No Battle.*

21. Ruiz, "Photography."

22. Mossallam, "Strikes, Riots, and Laughter,"; Mossallam, "Ya Aziz 'Aini,"; Mossallam, "al-Wajh al-Akhir."

23. Owen, *Cotton and the Egyptian Economy*; 'Abbas and El-Dessouky, *The Large Landowning Class*; Barakat, *Tatawwur al-Mulkiyya*; Mitchell, *Colonising Egypt*; Mitchell, *Rule of Experts*; Derr, *The Lived Nile.*

24. Beinin and Lockman, *Workers on the Nile.*

25. Cowen, *Deadly Life of Logistics.*

26. An example is Robert Tignor, whose two-volume history of British influence in Egypt leaves out the period 1914–1918 entirely; see Tignor, *Modernization*, and Tignor, *State.* Beinin and Lockman skip from chapter 5, "Labor Activism, 1899–1914," to chapter 6, "1919: Labor Upsurge and National Revolution," treating the period of the First World War in a couple of pages and mentioning the ELC in only one sentence; see Beinin and Lockman, *Workers on the Nile.*

27. Al-Rafi'i, *Thawrat 1919*, 17.

28. Salim writes of the ELC, "the return journey was more difficult for those who wrote of it than leaving, filled with torture, hardship, yearning, and longing for the homeland (*li-arḍ al-waṭan*) after a long period of deprivation and difficult feelings of being in a strange land, which was reflected in the words they repeated overflowing with desire and love of Egypt." Salim, *Misr fi-l-Harb*, 264. Earlier, she writes of their recruitment, "there were no patriotic feelings (*sha'ūr waṭani*) that attracted [the Egyptian peasant] (*al-fallāḥ al-miṣri*) to serving in the army." Salim, *Misr fi-l-Harb*, 248.

29. Chatterjee writes, "The point . . . is no longer one of . . . break[ing] down the totalizing claims of a nationalist historiography. Now the task is to trace in their mutually conditioned historicities the specific forms that have appeared, on the one hand, in the domain defined by the hegemonic project of nationalist modernity, and on the other, in the numerous fragmented resistances to that normalizing project." Chatterjee, *The Nation*, 13.

30. 'Izz al-Din, "Awwal Dirasa."

31. Sayf al-Dawla, *Mashayikh Jabal al-Badari*; 'Izz al-Din, *Al-Faylaq.*

32. K. Fahmy, "The Great Theft."

33. "Sabah ON," YouTube, accessed May 18, 2016, https://www.youtube.com/watch?v=QIZRaB-Swwo.

34. Some troops from the Egyptian army did participate in British-led campaigns against the Ottoman attack on the Suez Canal in 1915 and in Sudan against the forces of 'Ali ibn Dinār, the Sultan of Darfur, from 1916 to 1918. For more on the *tirailleurs algériens*, see Koller, "Recruitment of Colonial Troops."

35. K. Fahmy, "The Great Theft"; "'Arba' bi-Jaysh Misr al-Watani," al-'Araby.tv, accessed May 20, 2016, http://www.alaraby.tv/Article/2042.

36. K. Fahmy, "The Great Theft."

37. See Wendell, *Evolution*; Reid, *Whose Pharoahs*; Colla, *Conflicted Antiquities.*

38. Gershoni and Jankowski, *Egypt, Islam, and the Arabs.*

39. For example, in the wartime writings of Muhammad Husayn Haykal, Gershoni and Jankowski read statements trumpeting the "unity of the Nile Valley" as an expression of "Egyptian territorial nationalist theory." See Gershoni and Jankowski, *Egypt, Islam, and the Arabs*, 36. However, as Eve Troutt-Powell has shown, this ignores how the phrase had been used to advance a conception of Egyptian racial superiority and fitness to rule over the Black Sudanese and Ethiopian populations that lived upriver; see Troutt-Powell, *A Different Shade*, chap. 4. Haykal's writing not only could be read to promote the hopeful expansion of collective identity beyond the parochial borders of sectarian affiliations and villages, but also had a connotation that posited Egyptians as racially superior to Black Africans. According to Gershoni and Jankowski, Haykal borrowed a concept of race (*la race*) from French naturalist Hippolyte Adolph Taine, which they say was "not purely or even primarily biological and should not be identified with later racialist theories"; see Gershoni and Jankowski, *Egypt, Islam, and the Arabs*, 35. But Haykal was writing over fifty years after the publication of Taine's work, and his thinking could not help but be influenced by interceding intellectual currents. An interpretation of Haykal's writings that is much more attuned to the dynamics of racism as an ideology in the late imperial age is offered by Omnia El Shakry, who lists Haykal alongside other thinkers who "went so far as to claim a biological or racial link between the ancient pharaohs and the modern Egyptians." See El Shakry, *Great Social Laboratory*, 62.

40. Anthony D. Smith, *Ethnic Origin of Nations.*

41. Gershoni and Jankowski, *Egypt, Islam, and the Arabs*, vii–viii.

42. Gershoni and Jankowski, *Egypt, Islam, and the Arabs*, vii–viii. Althusser famously describes the "epistemological break" between "a science and the theoretical ideology in which the object it gave the knowledge of was 'thought' before the foundation of the science"; see Louis Althusser, *For Marx* (New York: Penguin, 1969), 13. The break, then, is the moment when past superstition is replaced by science and people discover the true nature of the problematic they confront in reality.

In etymological dictionaries, the English words "race" and "nation" have a similar meaning, but different origins. Nation derives directly from the Latin verb *nasci*, which means "to be born." For the Romans, it is connected to notions of tribe, breed, and stock. This moved into Old French as *nacion* and adopted an added sense of country or homeland. The older Latin meaning informs the application of the term "native" to the indigenous inhabitants of North America in English from the fifteenth century, while the newer sense of nation was preserved to refer to more geographically proximate political communities. A more charitable reading of Gershoni and Jankowski in this selection, then—and one that I happen to agree with—would be to say that Egyptians were trying to transform themselves from being treated like "natives" into becoming members of a fully fledged "nation." But this would require acknowledging ideas of race as shifting intellectual constructs in conversation with ideas of nation, not as "raw materials" existing "outside of human consciousness."

43. Morrison, *Playing in the Dark*; Vitalis, *America's Kingdom*, 16.

44. Miles, *Racism*, 75.

45. Weindling and Turda, *Blood and Homeland.*

46. Brennan, "Realizing Civilization."

47. According to Elshakry, the process of translating Darwin into Arabic "disarmed the racialized readings of Le Bon's discussion of 'the evolution of races' and transformed it into a debate about the perfection of peoples (*umam*)." Elshakry, *Reading Darwin*, 12. See also Burton, *Genetic Crossroads*, 14–15.

48. The English word "race" comes from Middle French *race*, which means "a class of persons, animals, or plants." It is attested from the sixteenth century along with cognates like *razza* in Italian, or *raza* in Spanish and Portuguese. While Hoad asserts it is of "unknown origin," Ernest Klein suggests it probably derives from the Arabic word *rā's*, which means "head," as well as "beginning" or "origin." See Hoad, *Concise Oxford Dictionary*; Klein, *Klein's Comprehensive*, 613. If Klein's suggestion holds weight, then this further emphasizes the deep roots of the race concept in the Arabic tradition, which I explore further in chapter 8.

49. Hannaford, *Race*, 227.

50. Said, *Orientalism*, 2.

51. Hannaford, *Race*, 187.

52. El Shakry, *Great Social Laboratory*, 30.

53. Hannaford, *Race*; Elshakry, *Reading Darwin.*

54. Mantena, *Alibis*, 5.

55. Sartori, *Bengal.*

56. Cuno, *Modernizing Marriage*, 26.

57. Troutt-Powell, *Different Shade*, 31.

58. Toledano, *As if Silent*, 12.

59. K. Fahmy, *All the Pasha's Men*, 86.

60. Cuno and Walz, *Race and Slavery.*

61. Helal, "Ali's First Army."

62. Aydin, *Idea of the Muslim World.*

63. Makdisi, *Culture of Sectarianism.*

64. Makdisi, *Age of Coexistence.*

65. Aydin, *Idea of the Muslim World.*

66. Aydin, *Idea of the Muslim World*, 62. For more on the antiracist dimensions of Pan-Islamism, see Aydin, *Politics of Anti-Westernism.*

67. Aydin, *Idea of the Muslim World.*

68. Troutt-Powell, *A Different Shade.*

69. Loring, *Confederate Soldier.*

70. Troutt-Powell, *Different Shade.*

71. El Shakry, *Great Social Laboratory*, 29. According to El Shakry, "throughout [the late nineteenth and early twentieth century up until the war], the numerous terms used to designate what we would now refer to as 'race' included *al-ajnas al-bashariyya* (human varieties), *al-sulalat al-bashariyya* (human stock), *al-ansaf al-bashariyya* (human types), *al-anwa' al-bashariyya* (human species), *al-'anasir al-bashariyya* (human elements), *tabaqat al-umam* (national groups), and even *shu'ub* (people)—all of which indicate the ambiguity if not malleability of notions of human difference" (p. 60). The shifting semantics of race in Egypt, which were complicated by the process of translating European ideas into Arabic, are explored in depth in chapters 2 and 8.

72. El Shakry, *Great Social Laboratory*, 42–45. For more on how rural Egyptians were associated with "Egyptian-ness" (*miṣriyya*) in the prewar press, see Gasper, *Power of Representation*.

73. Soja, *Thirdspace*, 46.

74. Aoki, "Space Invaders"; Aoki, "Race, Space, and Place."

75. Hayden, *Power of Place*.

76. Wimmer, "Elementary Strategies."

77. Spivak, *Critique of Postcolonial Reason*.

78. Scott, *Weapons of the Weak*.

79. Stoler, *Along the Archival Grain*.

80. Armbrust, *Mass Culture*; Z. Fahmy, *Ordinary Egyptians*.

81. Clément, "À La Recherche"; Clément, "Rethinking 'Peasant Consciousness.'"

CHAPTER 1. A BROKEN PROMISE

1. The National Archives, London, Foreign Office (hereafter cited as TNA, FO) 371/1964/0001: Mallet (February 2, 1914).

2. For more on Ottoman spiritual sovereignty, see Can, *Spiritual Subjects*.

3. Kiernan, *The Lords of Human Kind*.

4. TNA, FO 371/1635 No. 395: Kitchener (December 29, 1912).

5. Blyden, "Mohammedanism and the Negro Race." Visiting Egypt in 1887—the same year that Blyden's tract was published—Douglass wrote, "I do not know of what color and features the ancient Egyptians were, but the great mass of the people I have yet seen would in America be classified as mulattoes and negroes. This would not be a scientific description, but an American description. I can easily see why the Mohomidan religion commends itself to these people, for it does not make color the criterion of fellowship as some of our so called Christian nations do." Douglass, *Frederick Douglass Diary Tour of Europe and Africa*, September 15, 1886. The manuscript/mixed material can be found on the Library of Congress website, https://www.loc.gov/item/mfd.01001/.

6. Kamil, *Al-Shams al-Mushriqa*, 3–4.

7. TNA, FO 371/1964/0001: Mallet (February 2, 1914).

8. Elgood, *Egypt and the Army*, 84.

9. TNA, FO 471/1970: Cheetham (November 5, 1914).

10. For more on the discourse of "subject races" in late imperial Britain and its connection to military labor in the First World War, see Griffin, "Use of Chinese Labour."

11. Lord Cromer said of the rebellion: "The full and immediate policy of 'Egypt for the Egyptians' . . . was, and still is, impossible . . . it may be doubted whether any instance can be quoted of a sudden transfer of power in any civilized or semi-civilized community to a class so ignorant as the pure Egyptians. . . . these latter have, for centuries past, been a subject race. . . . The special aptitude shown by Englishmen in the government of Oriental races pointed to England as the most effective and beneficent instrument for the gradual introduction of European civilization into Egypt." Cromer, *Modern Egypt*, 353.

12. TNA, "Report on the Battle of Tel-el-Kebir," accessed September 17, 2015, http://www.nationalarchives.gov.uk/battles/egypt/popup/telel4.htm.

13. Quoted in Arendt, *Origins of Totalitarianism*, 213.

14. Tignor, *Modernization*; Cookson-hills, "Historical Perspectives," 66.

15. Welch Jr., *No Country for a Gentleman*, 3.

16. Summer, *The Indian Army.*

17. Starling and Lee, *No Labour, No Battle*, 19.

18. For example, in 1904, 121 Indian Pioneers constructed the thirteen-mile-long Matheran Light railroad. See Starling and Lee, *No Labour, No Battle.*

19. Gaylor, *Sons of John Company.*

20. Barua, "Inventing Race."

21. Roy, "Race and Recruitment."

22. Buckley, "British Army's African Recruitment Policy."

23. Ellis, *History of the First West India Regiment.*

24. Ukpabi, "West Indian Troops and the Defence of British West Africa in the Nineteenth Century."

25. McClendon, *White Chief, Black Lords*; Du Bois, "Towards a New Labour Dispensation," 13.

26. Pakenham, *The Boer War*, xxi.

27. Brown, "The Anglo-Boer War."

28. Cookson-hills, "Historical Perspectives," 67; Troutt-Powell, *A Different Shade.*

29. Jackson, *Our Caughnawagas in Egypt.*

30. Starling and Lee, *No Labour, No Battle*, 19.

31. TNA, FO 371/1637 No. 9546: Grey to Kitchener (February 28, 1913).

32. TNA, FO 371/1637 No. 9546: Kitchener to Grey (March 22, 1913).

33. TNA, FO 371/1640 No. 51569: "Course of Instruction with Camel Corps" (November 13, 1913); TNA, FO 371/1965 No. 3144: Kitchener (January 22, 1914); TNA, FO 371/1965 No. 3494: Kitchener (January 14, 1914).

34. Riddick, *The History of British India*, 97.

35. Summer, *The Indian Army*, 5.

36. Starling and Lee, *No Labour, No Battle*, 164.

37. Indian cavalry did continue to serve on the Western Front; see Rashid, "Colonial Labour Migration."

38. See Starling and Lee, *No Labour, No Battle*, 77.

39. Starling and Lee, *No Labour, No Battle*, 78.

40. The British army in France increased from 270,000 men at the end of 1914 to 464,000 by April 1, 1915. Starling and Lee, *No Labour, No Battle*, 81–82.

41. Koller, "Recruitment of Colonial Troops"; Fogarty, *Race and War.*

42. Xu, *Strangers on the Western Front*, 17.

43. Xu, *Strangers on the Western Front*, 17.

44. Starling and Lee, *No Labour, No Battle*, 95.

45. TNA, FO 141/797/2 No. 2689: MacMahon (March 24, 1916).

46. TNA, FO 141/797/2: FO to HC (April 11, 1916); the National Archives, London, Cabinet Files (hereafter cited as TNA, CAB) 37/145/28: "Proceedings of a Meeting of the War Committee" (April 11, 1916).

47. Starling and Lee, *No Labour, No Battle*, 275.

48. Starling and Lee, *No Labour, No Battle*, 275.

49. Starling and Lee, *No Labour, No Battle*, 275.

50. The question of the exact number of men who served in the ELC in France is a complex one. One official report puts the number at 10,024; see TNA, WO 107/37:

"Controller of Labour Report" (November 14, 1919). Secondary studies in Arabic and English suggest that the number is closer to 15,000; see 'Izz Al-Din, "Awwal Dirasa," and Starling and Lee, *No Labour, No Battle*. Christian Koller seems to be the statistical outlier, citing 82,000 Egyptians in Europe, and is likely confusing the total number of Egyptians serving in the war at a certain time with the number of Egyptians serving in France throughout the entire war; see Koller, "Recruitment of Colonial Troops."

51. Consideration was given to raising another two companies of the ELC for work in Marseilles in June, but this was prevented by demand on other fronts. See Starling and Lee, *No Labour, No Battle*, 276.

52. TNA, CAB 27/14.

53. TNA, WO 95/4255: "War Diaries: Taranto."

54. TNA, WO 107/37: "Controller of Labor Report" (November 14, 1919).

55. Starling and Lee, *No Labour, No Battle*, 187–188.

56. Starling and Lee, *No Labour, No Battle*, 187–188.

57. Elgood, *Egypt and the Army*, 77–78. See also "Al-Miyah fi Sina'," *Al-Ahram*, February 15, 1915, which describes how "soldiers carry machine guns and carts because the horses get their hooves stuck in the sand, unable to free themselves."

58. Badcock, *History of the Transport Services*, 20–22.

59. Badcock, *History of the Transport Services*, 25.

60. Germans were some of the biggest proponents of Pan-Islamism and hoped to take advantage of its supposed ability to generate solidarity among Muslims worldwide during the war. See Avci, "Pan-Islamism and the Jihad Discourse."

61. Evans-Pritchard, *Sanusi*, 121.

62. Falls and MacMunn, *Military Operations*, 104–105.

63. Egyptians received medals for their participation, including Cpt. Muḥammad Afandi 'Azmi, Lt. Ḥana Wasif, 2nd Lt. 'Ali Afandi al-Sabihi, and 2nd Lt. Ziad Afandi al-Amin. See "Mukafa'at al-Dubat," *Al-Waṭan*, November 2, 1918.

64. "Firqat Al-'Ummal," *Al-Muqattam*, September 17, 1917.

65. "150 men would unload up to 100 tons of supplies from transports in one day on the campaign." "Firqat al-'Ummal," *Al-Muqattam*, September 17, 1917.

66. Salim, *Misr fi-l-Harb*, 239.

67. "Firqat al-'Ummal," *Al-Muqattam*, September 17, 1917.

68. See 'Izzat, "Safahat min Mudhakkirat," *Ruz al-Yusuf*, June 17, 1968, for an example of an ELC laborer who served in Darfur. Salim, *Misr fi-l-Harb*, 238, provides details of the advance. TNA, FO 141/797/2 No. 2689/17: "Extract from telegram from Murray" (May 24, 1917) mentions "15,000 voluntary men of the Egyptian Army" in service in Darfur.

69. Elgood, *Egypt and the Army*, 222.

70. Starling and Lee, *No Labour, No Battle*, 107; 'Izz Al-Din, "Awwal Dirasa."

71. Starling and Lee, *No Labour, No Battle*.

72. Starling and Lee, *No Labour, No Battle*, 210.

73. "Firqat al-'Ummal," *Al-Muqattam*, September 17, 1917.

74. Starling and Lee, *No Labour, No Battle*, 170.

75. Starling and Lee, *No Labour, No Battle*, 172.

76. Starling and Lee, *No Labour, No Battle*, 173.

77. Barker, *The Bastard War*, 271–272.

78. Starling and Lee, *No Labour, No Battle*, 175.

79. Starling and Lee, *No Labour, No Battle*, 174, 209.

80. Starling and Lee, *No Labour, No Battle*, 174.

81. Western sources (e.g., Sir Charles Preston Lucas, cited in Starling and Lee, *No Labour, No Battle*, 278) agree with Arabic figures (e.g., 'Izz al-Din, "Awwal Dirasa," and Salim, *Misr fi-l-Harb*, 245), which put the number in Mesopotamia at 8,500. TNA, FO 141/797/2 No. 2689/10: Murray to Wingate (March 24, 1917) puts the number serving in "France, Mesopotamia, etc." in Spring 1917 at 23,000.

82. Starling and Lee, *No Labour, No Battle*, 210.

83. Lawrence, *Seven Pillars*, 521–524.

84. Elgood, *Egypt and the Army*, 222–226.

85. Badcock, *History of the Transport Corps*, 21.

86. Salim, *Misr fi-l-Harb*, 245.

87. See Badcock, *History of the Transport Corps*, 22, for company figures, and Salim, *Misr fi-l-Harb*, 266, for figures on total number of camels.

88. Elgood, *Egypt and the Army*, 233, 237.

89. Elgood, *Egypt and the Army*, 233, 237.

90. Falls and MacMunn, *Military Operations*, 160.

91. Bou, *Light Horse*, 157.

92. Egyptians could enroll multiple times, so this does not necessarily translate in 327,000 men having served in the EEF in this period.

93. TNA, FO 141/797/2 No. 2689/142: Wingate to Balfour (September 15, 1918).

CHAPTER 2. THE NEW *CORVÉE*

1. Anis, *Tatawwur al-Mujtama'*.

2. Beckert, *Empire of Cotton*, 131.

3. According to Mikail, the construction of a canal between the Nile and Alexandria in 1820 was made possible by the "forced labor of more than three hundred thousand peasants . . . and the death of a third of those workers." Mikhail, *Nature and Empire*, 3.

4. Cuno, "African Slaves," 81.

5. Anis, *Tatawwur al-Mujtama'*, 12; Brown, "Who Abolished Corvee Labor?"

6. Baer, "The Village Shaykh," 50–51.

7. Hourani, "Ottoman Reform"; P. Khoury, "Urban Notables"; Gelvin, "The Politics of Notables."

8. Baring, *Modern Egypt*, 416.

9. Brown, "Who Abolished Corvee Labor?"

10. For labor contractors and public works projects, see Derr, *The Lived Nile*. For labor contractors and private industry, see Chalcraft, *Striking Cabbies*.

11. As Baring puts it, "It has not as yet been found possible to abolish completely this description of corvée, but the number of men employed every year is small, and is steadily diminishing." Baring, *Modern Egypt*, 419.

12. See Burke III, "Changing Patterns."

13. TNA, FO 141.797/2 No. 2689: General Staff Army HQ (July 23, 1915).

14. Elgood, *Egypt and the Army*, 239–240.

15. TNA, FO 141.797/2 No. 2689: General Staff Army HQ (July 23, 1915).

16. TNA, FO 141/797/2 No. 2689: McMahon (April 1, 1916).

17. TNA, FO 141/797/2 No. 2689: McMahon (April 1, 1916).

18. Derr, *The Lived Nile.*

19. TNA, FO 371/3713 No. 20835: "War Service" (September 6, 1919).

20. One memo suggests "asking Alexandrini to raise gangs on six months indentures"; see TNA, FO 141/797/2 No. 2689: MacMahon (March 24, 1916). Another mentions "General Altham's arrangements with yourself and Alexandrini for the recruitment of labor"; see TNA, FO 141/797/2 No 2689: Graham (March 26, 1916). A third refers to "preliminary contracts . . . drawn up with Alessandrini and Belleni, and between contractors and workmen"; see TNA, FO 141/797/2 No. 2689: MacMahon (March 31, 1916).

21. Brown, *Peasant Politics*, 190.

22. TNA, FO 141/797/2 No. 2689/13: Chief London (May 21, 1917).

23. TNA, FO 141/797/2 No. 2689/17: Extract of Telegram from Murray (May 24, 1917).

24. The total desired strength of the ELC was to be 100,000. Murray put the number of active ELC workers at that time at approximately 98,000, including 15,000 casual laborers. See TNA, FO 141/797/2 No. 2689/16: telegram no. 685 (July 6, 1917).

25. TNA, FO 141/797/2 No. 2869/12: Minutes of Meeting (May 28, 1917).

26. TNA, FO 141/797/2 No. 2689/17: FO (June 18, 1917).

27. TNA, FO 141/797/2 No. 2689/19: Graham (August 23, 1917).

28. TNA, FO 141/797/2 No. 2689/21: Wingate (August 23, 1917).

29. TNA, FO 141/797/2 No. 2689/21: Wingate (August 23, 1917).

30. TNA, FO 141/797/2 No. 2689/31: "Traduction de deus circulaires" (August 28, 1917).

31. TNA, FO 141/797/2 No. 2869/42: Ministry of War (October 19, 1917).

32. "Firqat al-'Ummal," *Al-Afkar*, October 22, 1917.

33. TNA, FO 141/797/2 No. 2689/7: Herbert to Haines (May 3, 1917).

34. TNA, FO 141/797/2 No. 2689/8: Haines to Herbert (May 13, 1917).

35. TNA, FO 141/797/2 No. 2689/8: Hazel to Haines (May 12, 1917).

36. TNA, FO 141/797/2 No. 2689/64: Allenby to Wingate (February 13, 1918).

37. There were also five *muḥāfiẓāt* (governorates) directed by a *muḥāfiẓ*, including the governorates of Cairo, Alexandria, Suez, the Canal Zone, and Damietta.

38. Jakes, *Egypt's Occupation.*

39. For example, according to Charles Smith, Muhammad Husayn Haykal's family "seems to have gained the position of village *'umda* early in the nineteenth century . . . they retained the position, passing it to the next eldest male, brother to brother, rather than father to son. The family acquired land and became wealthy in comparison to the ordinary *fallāḥīn* of the village." See Smith, *Islam and the Search*, 33.

40. TNA, FO 141/797/2 No. 2689/44: Rushdi (October 21, 1917).

41. TNA, FO 141/797/2 No. 2689/22: Rushdi (August 24, 1917).

42. "Wajibat al-'Umad," *Al-Ahram*, March 23, 1915.

43. "Al-'Ummal al-Mutatu'un," *Al-Muqattam*, April 21, 1917.

44. Elshakry, *Reading Darwin*, 80.

45. Elshakry, *Reading Darwin*, 9.

46. Hofstadter, *Social Darwinism*, chap. 2. W. E. B. Du Bois mentions the vogue of Spencer and the impact of "survival of the fittest" ideology in his third autobiography; see Du Bois, "Dusk of Dawn," 590, 625.

47. Elshakry, *Reading Darwin*, 12. Elshakry does not use the term "social Darwinism," but I deploy it here to acknowledge the important role that a certain reading of Darwin via thinkers like Herbert Spencer, Gustave Le Bon, and Edmund Demolins had on the global circulation of the race concept in the late nineteenth century. See Hannaford, *Race*.

48. Wendell, *Evolution*.

49. The trope became a prominent part of colonial racism; see Anghie, "Francisco de Vitoria."

50. Ryzova, *Age*.

51. Goldschmidt, *Biographical Dictionary*, 233; Ryzova, *Age*, 106n58.

52. The Arabic reads "*ḥasaba al-ṭabaqāt al-nāzila inna zuwāl al-ṭabaqāt al-ʿāliyya min al-umma bi-muthābat zuwāl al-rūḥ min al-jism*"; see A. Zaghlul, *Sirr Taqaddum*, 26.

53. A. Zaghlul, *Sirr Taqaddum*, 24.

54. Wendell mentions only one European work that impacted Lutfi al-Sayyid during his years at the Khedieval Secondary School, Shibli al-Shumayyil's translation of Darwin's *Descent of Man*. See Wendell, *Evolution*, 208.

55. Lutfi wrote, "it seems that Fathi Pasha is especially enamored with the ideas of Dr. Gustave Le Bon in matters of sociology. And rightly so, since the ideas of this great writer on society represent the high point of traditional sociological knowledge as well as the last word on modern observation." See Lutfi al-Sayyid, *Taʿammulat*, 82.

56. Lutfi al-Sayyid, *Taʿammulat*, 128.

57. See Kazziha, "Jaridah-Ummah Group."

58. TNA, FO 141/797/2 No. 2689/1: Whittingham (May 1, 1916).

59. Badcock, *History of the Transport Services*, 31.

60. TNA, FO 141/797/2 No. 2689/60a: Haines (February 5, 1918).

61. TNA, FO 141/797/2 No. 2689/134: Haines (August 6, 1918).

62. Musa, *Tarbiyyat*, 113.

63. Elgood, *Egypt and the Army*, 318.

64. TNA, FO 141/667/1 No. 2689/171: Claghin, "Synopsis of voluntary recruiting circulars" (July 5, 1920).

65. Salim, *Misr fi-l-Harb*, 266.

66. "ʿUmdat Asyut," *Al-Afkar*, October 10, 1917.

67. TNA, FO 141/797/2 No. 2689/31: Rushdi (August 28, 1917).

68. Z. Fahmy, *Ordinary Egyptians*, 124.

69. Z. Fahmy, *Ordinary Egyptians*, 123.

70. Salim, *Misr fi-l-Harb*, 229; Anus, *Shakhsiyat al-ʿUmda*, 29.

71. *Ma 'ultalak ya Abu Kuliyya? / imshī matitʿugish!*
li-ḥusn al-ʿumda / mabiyaḥibaksh
ramāk shaykh khafar fi yāfā / wa ma hiyya walla taqabḍish!
See ʿIzz al-Din, "Awwal Dirasa," 76.

72. Yousef, *Composing Egypt*.

73. Salim, *Misr fi-l-Harb*, 408.

74. Quoted in ʿIzz al-Din, "Awwal Dirasa."

75. TNA, FO 141/797/2 No. 2689/64: Allenby (February 13, 1918).

76. Salim puts the average wage rate for a migrant laborer during the war at three piastres per day. Salim, *Misr fi-l-Harb*, 188. Clément's close study of one of the daily

workers on the archaeological excavation site at Karnak provides a more nuanced breakdown: "For the backbreaking task of participating in the clearing of a canal, he earned 4.5 piasters a day—or perhaps a little more if the job was completed well and in a timely manner—during a period which generally did not exceed a week. While working on the excavation site, Ahmad received 2 piastres per day." Clément, "Rethinking 'Peasant Consciousness,'" 83–84. She also writes of "the children who from dawn to dusk carry away the heavy baskets full of mud for 1.5 piaster a day" (p. 93).

77. TNA, FO 141/797/2 No. 2689/64: Allenby (February 13, 1918).

78. 'Izzat, "Safahat min Mudhakkirat."

79. 'Izzat, "Safahat min Mudhakkirat."

80. 'Izzat, "Safahat min Mudhakkirat," 24–25.

81. Elgood, *Egypt and the Army*, 51.

82. Salim, *Misr fi-l-Harb*, 104–105.

83. Salim, *Misr fi-l-Harb*, 175.

84. But the "vast majority" of laborers received no bonus for reenrollment; see TNA, FO 141/797/2 No. 2689/38: Wingate (September 20, 1917).

85. TNA, FO 141/797/2 No. 2689/63: Ministry of Finance (February 9, 1918).

86. TNA, FO 141/797/2 No. 2689: Haines (June 30, 1918).

87. Imperial War Museum, London, Earnest Kendrick Venables Papers (hereafter cited as IWM, EKV) 3/11: Ephraim (September 19, 1918), 128.

88. TNA, FO 141/797/2 No. 2689/31: Rushdi (August 28, 1917).

89. This policy still persists in the mandatory conscription of young men for the Egyptian Armed Forces today.

90. "Al-Dafa'a 'an Misr," *Al-Muqattam*, January 30, 1915.

91. "Al-Dafa'a 'an Misr," *Al-Muqattam*, January 30, 1915.

92. TNA, FO 141/667/1 No. 2689/171: Claghin (July 5, 1920).

93. TNA, FO 141/667/1 No. 2689/171: Claghin (July 5, 1920).

94. TNA, FO 141/797/2 No. 2689/52a: "Note on El Afkar's Article" (December 20, 1917).

95. Brown, *Peasant Politics*, 174.

96. Chalcraft, "Engaging the State," 304.

97. TNA, FO 142/797/2: "Raising the Egyptian Labour Corps."

98. For example, see TNA, FO 141/797/2 No. 2689/110: Ministry of Interior (June 19, 1918) for a report from the Delta province of Gharbiyya about an act of individual resistance in which villagers used a kitchen knife and a "nabut," or a wooden stick used in a popular combat game, to resist.

99. TNA, FO 141/797/2 No. 2689/123: Residency Telegram (July 13, 1918).

100. TNA, FO 141/797/2 No. 2689/103: Haines (June 13, 1918).

101. The Egyptian newspaper *Al-Ahali* criticized "women of the village shouting because of the demand for conscription" of the army reservists. See *Al-Ahali*, "Da'wa al-Radif," January 22, 1916.

102. 'Izz al-Din, "Awwal Dirasa."

103. TNA, FO 141/797/2 No. 2689/119: Ministry of Interior (July 3, 1918).

104. Abul-Magd, *Imagined Empires*, 143.

105. TNA, FO 141/797/2 No. 2689/86: Haines (May 23, 1918).

106. TNA, FO 141/667/1 No. 2689/167: "Compulsory Recruitment" (May 14, 1919).

107. TNA, FO 141/797/2 No. 2689/88: Haines (May 25, 1918).
108. TNA, FO 141/797/2 No. 2689/88: Haines' Report (May 26, 1918).
109. Jakes, *Egypt's Occupation.*
110. TNA, FO 141/797/2 No. 2689/60a: Haines (February 5, 1918).
111. TNA, FO 141/797/2 No. 2689/75: Meeting at the Residency (May 6, 1918).
112. TNA, FO 141/797/2 No. 2689: Haines (May 26, 1918). See also TNA, FO 141/798: "Circulaire Concernent l'Enrôlement Volontarie."
113. TNA, FO 141/797/2 No. 2689/66: MacDonald (March 2, 1918).
114. TNA, FO 141/797/2 No. 2689/129: Wingate (July 25, 1918).
115. TNA, FO 141/797/2 No. 2689/96: Rushdi circular No. 10 (May 26, 1918).
116. TNA, FO 141/797/2 No. 2689/78: Copy of Letter from Rushdi (May 8, 1918).
117. TNA, FO 141/797/2 No. 2689/89: Haines (May 26, 1918) and No. 2689/87b: Keon-Boyd (May 26, 1918).
118. TNA, FO 141/797/2 No. 2689/96: Rushdi circular No. 10 (May 26, 1918).
119. TNA, FO 141/797/2 No. 2689/96: Rushdi (May 30, 1918).
120. TNA, FO 141/797/2 No. 2689/134: Haines (August 6, 1918).
121. TNA, FO 141/797/2 No. 2689/85: Keon Boyd (May 30, 1918).
122. TNA, FO 141/797/2 No. 2689/134: Haines (August 6, 1918).
123. Mitchell, *Colonising Egypt.*

CHAPTER 3. FROM HOME TO THE FRONT

1. "Qism al-Ashghal al-Misri," *Al-Muqattam*, April 13, 1917.
2. Stoler, *Along the Archival Grain.*
3. Lefebvre, *Production of Space*, 38.
4. Lefebvre, *La Droit*; Lefebvre, *Writings on Cities.* In Egypt, scholars focus on Cairo and Alexandria. For Cairo, see J. Abu-Lughod, "Tale of Two Cities"; Raymond, *Artisans et Commerçants*; Reynolds, *City Consumed.* For Alexandria, see Reimer, "Colonial Bridgehead"; Carminati, "Alexandria, 1898."
5. Cowen, *Deadly Life.*
6. Virilio, *Speed and Politics*, 31.
7. Cited in Cowen, *Deadly Life*, 163.
8. Lane, Lexicon, vol. 2, 2777, http://ejtaal.net/aa/#HW=489,LL=4_283,LS=2,HA=380.
9. Virilio, *Speed and Politics*, 31.
10. Russell, *Egyptian Service*, 27–28.
11. Russell, *Egyptian Service*, 48.
12. IWM, EKV/2: *They Also Served.*
13. IWM, EKV/2: *They Also Served*, 49.
14. TNA, FO 141/667/1 No. 2689/171: Ministry of Interior (July 5, 1920).
15. TNA, FO 141/667/1 No. 2689/171: Ministry of Interior (July 5, 1920).
16. Charles Coles, "Prison Problems in Egypt," The Near East 14, no. 348 (January 4, 1918): 12.
17. TNA, FO 848/6: Rev. W. W. Cash (1920).
18. TNA, FO 141/667/1: Synopsis (August 1918).
19. TNA, FO 141/667/1: Synopsis (August 1918).
20. TNA, FO 141/667/1: Synopsis (September 14, 1918).

21. TNA, FO 141/667/1: Synopsis (December 1918).
22. RAMC, *With the RAMC in Egypt*, 296–297.
23. RAMC, *With the RAMC in Egypt*, 296–297.
24. TNA, FO 141/797/2 No. 2689/86: Ministry of Interior (May 20, 1918).
25. TNA, FO 141/797/2 No. 2689/86: Ministry of Interior (May 20, 1918).
26. TNA, FO 141/797/2 No. 2689/86: Ministry of Interior (May 20, 1918).
27. TNA, FO 141/797/2689/64: Allenby (February 13, 1918).
28. TNA, FO 141/797, 167.
29. TNA, FO 141/797, 167.
30. Salim, *Misr fi-l-Harb*, 252.
31. Cowen, *Deadly Life*.
32. Ulrichsen, *Logistics and Politics*, 21.
33. TNA, FO 141/469/1 No. 1615/6: "Egypt and the War" (July 7, 1917).
34. TNA, FO 141/469/1 No. A.M. 1953: Extract (May 24, 1917).
35. Murray, *Murray's Despatches*, 219.
36. Murray, *Murray's Despatches*, 206.
37. Murray, *Murray's Despatches*, 207.
38. Murray, *Murray's Despatches*, 207.
39. Murray, *Murray's Despatches*, 206.
40. Murray, *Murray's Despatches*, 207–208.
41. Murray, *Murray's Despatches*, 207–208.
42. TNA, FO 141/797/2 No. 2689/64: Allenby (February 13, 1918).
43. RAMC, *With the RAMC*, 297.
44. RAMC, *With the RAMC*, 297.
45. RAMC, *With the RAMC*, 298.
46. IWM, EKV/2: *They Also Served*, 5.
47. TNA, WO 107/37: "Report on British Labor in France" (November 14, 1919).
48. TNA, FO 141/797/2 No. 2869/12: Minutes (May 28, 1917).
49. TNA, FO 141/797/2 No. 2689/64: Allenby (February 13, 1918).
50. Badcock, *A History*, 26; IWM, EKV 3/1: Sinai (September 3, 1917), 6.
51. Badcock, *A History*, 26.
52. TNA, WO 107/37: "Report on British Labour" (November 14, 1919).
53. Badcock, *A History*, 26.
54. IWM, EKV 3/1: Sinai (September 3, 1917), 3–4.
55. Badcock, *A History*, 28.
56. IWM, EKV/2: *They Also Served*, 12.
57. Carman and McPherson, *Bimbashi McPherson*, 155.
58. TNA, FO 141/797/2 No. 2689: General Staff (July 23, 1915).
59. TNA, FO 141/797/2 No. 2869/12: Minutes (May 28, 1917).
60. TNA, FO 141/797/2 No. 2869/12: Minutes (May 28, 1917).
61. As protests were breaking out against recruitment elsewhere in the violent summer of 1918, Allenby said of Suhag, "no disturbances have occurred, and it has not been found necessary to augment the normal small staffs of the camps." See TNA, FO 141/797/2 No. 2689/98: Allenby (June 1, 1918).
62. RAMC, *With the RAMC*, 89.
63. Murray, *Murray's Despatches*, 9.
64. Murray, *Murray's Despatches*, 9.

65. Murray, *Murray's Despatches*, 9.
66. Elgood, *Egypt and the Army*, 234.
67. Murray, *Murray's Despatches*, 193.
68. Murray, *Murray's Despatches*, 193.
69. Murray, *Murray's Despatches*, 188.
70. Murray, *Murray's Despatches*, 188; Elgood, *Egypt and the Army*, 236.
71. Murray, *Murray's Despatches*, 189.
72. Murray, *Murray's Despatches*, 199.
73. Murray, *Murray's Despatches*, 189.
74. Barak, *On Time.*
75. "Iron Track," *ELC News*, January 15, 1919.
76. IWM, EKV/2: *They Also Served*, 8. See also *ELC News*, January 15, 1919.
77. RAMC, *With the RAMC in Egypt*, 126.
78. Murray, *Murray's Despatches*, viii.
79. *ELC News*, January 15, 1919.
80. *ELC News*, January 15, 1919. For more on the "overland route," see Barak, *On Time.*
81. IWM, EKV 3/2: Deir el-Belah (September 12, 1917), 10–11.
82. RAMC, *With the RAMC*, 277–278.
83. TNA, FO 141/797/2 No. 2689: Foreign Office (March 24, 1916).
84. RAMC, *With the RAMC*, 90.
85. The National Archives, London, Ministry of Transport (hereafter cited as TNA, MT) 23/761: Memorandum for the Imperial Conference (n.d.).
86. TNA, MT 23/761: Telegram (February 2, 1917).
87. TNA, FO 141/797/2 No. 2689: GHQ (July 23, 1915).
88. "Fa'al Firqat Jamal al-Naql," *Al-Muqattam*, August 1, 1917.
89. 'Izzat, "Safahat min Mudhakkirat," *Ruz al-Yusuf*, March 1968.
90. Koerver, *German Submarine Warfare*, xxxi.
91. "Fa'al Firqat Jamal al-Naql," *Al-Muqattam*, August 1, 1917.
92. "ELC at Collision Quarters," *ELC News*, March 1, 1919.
93. Cowen, *Deadly Life*, 5.

CHAPTER 4. "IF THIS IS THE HOLY LAND, WHAT MUST HELL BE LIKE?"

1. Bennett, "Anglo-Egyptian Sudanese Influence."
2. Korda, *Hero: The Life and Legend of Lawrence of Arabia*, 353.
3. Lalonde, *Determining Boundaries*, 94.
4. Bennett, "Anglo-Egyptian Sudanese Influence," 15.
5. The Arab Bureau, established in the department of the British colonial government in Egypt responsible for military intelligence in Egypt and Sudan, is perhaps best known for fomenting the Sharifian revolt in Mecca during the war. With members like Gilbert Clayton going on to hold important positions in OETA, the Arab Bureau found itself with established assets in Egypt, Sudan, the Hijaz (i.e., T. E. Lawrence and the Hashemites), and Syria/Palestine. See Bennett, "Anglo-Egyptian Sudanese Influence."
6. IWM, EKV 3/1: Sinai (September 3, 1917), 7.
7. IWM, EKV 3/2: Deir-el-Belah, Palestine (September 12, 1917), 14–15.
8. IWM, EKV 3/2: Deir-el-Belah (September 12, 1917), 14.

9. IWM, EKV 3/2: Deir-el-Belah (September 12, 1917), 18.
10. IWM, EKV 3/2: Deir-el-Belah (September 12, 1917), 20–21.
11. IWM, EKV 3/3: St. James Park (September 30, 1917), 22.
12. RAMC, *With the RAMC in Egypt*, 93–94.
13. RAMC, *With the RAMC in Egypt*, 281.
14. IWM, EKV 3/4: Wadi Gaza (October 20, 1917), 38.
15. IWM, EKV/2: *They Also Served*, 24. See also Starling and Lee, *No Labour, No Battle*, 274.
16. IWM, EKV 3/6: Judaea (December 5, 1917), 50.
17. Falls and Becke, *Military Operations*, 66.
18. IWM, EKV 3/6: Judaea (December 5, 1917), 50–51.
19. Murray, *Murray's Despatches*, 215.
20. TNA, WO 107/37: "Report on British Labour" (November 14, 1919).
21. TNA, WO 107/37: "Report on British Labour" (November 14, 1919).
22. IWM, EKV 3/3: St. James Park (September 30, 1917), 26.
23. IWM, EKV/2: *They Also Served*, 21.
24. IWM, EKV/2: *They Also Served*, 21.
25. IWM, EKV 3/3: St. James Park (September 30, 1917), 29.
26. IWM, EKV 3/3: St. James Park (September 30, 1917), 29.
27. IWM, EKV/2: *They Also Served*, 9.
28. IWM, EKV/2: *They Also Served*, 101.
29. IWM, EKV 3/9: K22 (April 24, 1918), 93.
30. RAMC, *With the RAMC in Egypt*, 82.
31. RAMC, *With the RAMC in Egypt*, 127.
32. "Firqat al-'Ummal," *Al-Muqattam*, July 3, 1917.
33. IWM, EKV 3/7: Near Ramleh (February 13, 1918).
34. IWM, EKV 3/7: Near Ramleh (February 13, 1918).
35. IWM, EKV 3/7: Near Ramleh (February 13, 1918).
36. IWM, EKV 3/7: Near Ramleh (February 13, 1918).
37. IWM, EKV 3/7: Near Ramleh (February 13, 1918).
38. IWM, EKV 3/7: Near Ramleh (February 13, 1918).
39. IWM, EKV 3/7: Near Ramleh (February 13, 1918).
40. IWM, EKV 3/7: Near Ramleh (February 13, 1918).
41. IWM, EKV 3/7: Near Ramleh (February 13, 1918).
42. See White and White, *Sounds of Slavery*, xi.
43. IWM, EKV 3/7: Near Ramleh (February 13, 1918), 81.
44. IWM, EKV 3/7: Near Ramleh (February 13, 1918), 81.
45. Starling and Lee, *No Labour, No Battle*, 165.
46. Bean, *Story of Anzac*, 835.
47. RAMC, *With the RAMC in Egypt*, 278.
48. Starling and Lee, *No Labour, No Battle*, 189.
49. TNA, WO 107/37: "Report on British Labour" (November 14, 1919), Appendix I.
50. TNA, FO 848/6: R. Wellesley (1920).
51. IWM, EKV 3/9: K22 (April 24, 1918), 97.
52. Falls and Becke, *Military Operations*, 272.
53. Murray, *Murray's Despatches*, 215.

54. Murray, *Murray's Despatches*, 218.

55. Murray, *Murray's Despatches*, 214.

56. Massey, *How Jerusalem Was Won*, Appendix XI.

57. *ELC News*, July 15, 1919.

58. TNA, WO 107/37: "Report on British Labour" (November 14, 1919).

59. TNA, WO 107/37: "Report on British Labour" (November 14, 1919), Appendix I.

60. TNA, WO 107/37: "Report on British Labour" (November 14, 1919), Appendix I.

61. TNA, WO 107/37: "Report on British Labour" (November 14, 1919), Appendix I.

62. TNA, WO 107/37: "Report on British Labour" (November 14, 1919), Appendix I.

63. "Fa'al Firqat Jamal al-Naql," *Al-Muqattam*, August 1, 1917.

64. "Fa'al Firqat Jamal al-Naql," *Al-Muqattam*, August 1, 1917.

65. "Firqat al-'Ummal," *Al-Ahram*, April 13, 1917.

66. "Mukafa'at al-Buwasil," *Al-Muqattam*, October 5–6, 1917. The men were listed as follows: Adam Muhammad, no. 306, L co., CTC; Hasan Abdallah, no. 1730, A co., CTC; Sulayman Hasan, no. 285, D co., CTC; Musa 'Abd al-Rahim Muhammad, no. 2313, M co., CTC; Shihata 'Abd al-Murli, no. 1281, B co., CTC; Husayn Ahmad Tayyib, no. 705, B co., CTC; Amr Muhammad Amr, no. 3581, D co., CTC; Husayn Muhammad Abu Zayd, no. 3420, D co., CTC; Muhammad 'Ali Muhammad, no. 3427, D co., CTC; 'Abdin Husayn Ahmad, no. 11933, K co., CTC; 'Abd al-Malik Muhammad, no. 11922, K co., CTC; Ahmad Husayn Muhammad, no. 10869, K co., CTC; Muhammad 'Ali Salam, no. 1220, G co., CTC; Ibrahim Farghali Muhammad, no. 993, G co., CTC; Hamid Iman, no. 1834, G co., CTC; 'Abbas Sayyid Muhammad, no. 7157, B co., CTC; Muhi Zidan, no. 4926, B co., CTC; 'Abduh Muhammad 'Ali, no. 5626, B co., CTC; Harun Muhammad Sayyid, no. 314, M co., CTC; Paul Kibsis, no. 4381, ELC; Hifni 'Abd al-Rahman, no. 114231, ELC; Muhammad Ibrahim Sulayman, no. 123690, ELC.

67. "Mukafa'at al-Dubat," *Al-Watan*, November 2, 1918.

68. Murray, *Murray's Despatches*, 218.

69. IWM, EKV 3/4: Wadi Gaza (October 20, 1917), 40.

70. IWM, EKV 3/9 K22 (April 24, 1918), 93.

71. IWM, EKV 3/9 K22 (April 24, 1918), 93.

72. IWM, EKV/2: *They Also Served*, 24.

73. IWM, 86/51/1: Thomas Brookes Minshall, 3.

74. IWM, 86/51/1: Thomas Brookes Minshall, 7–8.

75. IWM, 86/51/1: Thomas Brookes Minshall, 8.

76. TNA, WO 107/37: "Report on British Labour" (November 14, 1919), Appendix I.

77. TNA, FO 141/797/2 No. 2689/64: Allenby (February 13, 1918).

78. TNA, WO 107/37: "Report on British Labour" (November 14, 1919), Appendix I.

79. TNA, FO 141/797/2 No. 2689/38: Wingate (September 20, 1917).

80. TNA, FO 141/797/2 No. 2689/64: Allenby (February 13, 1918).

81. IWM, EKV 3/10: Ephraim (June 2, 1918), 107–108.

82. TNA, WO 107/37: "Report on British Labour" (November 14, 1919), Appendix I.

83. TNA, WO 107/37: "Report on British Labour" (November 14, 1919), Appendix I.

84. Salim, *Misr fi-l-Harb*, 262–264.

CHAPTER 5. RACE AND SPACE IN ELC CAMPS

1. 'Izzat, "Safahat min Mudhakkirat."

2. IWM, EKV/1: EK Venables.

3. Tignor, *Modernization*; Jakes, *Egypt's Occupation*. For a recent work that breaks down the usual distinction between literacy and illiteracy in Egypt, see Yousef, *Composing Egypt*.

4. Aoki, "Space Invaders."

5. TNA, WO 107/37: "Report on British Labour" (November 14, 1919), 24–25.

6. Griffin, "Use of Chinese Labour," 13.

7. Griffin, "Use of Chinese Labour," 13.

8. Griffin, "Use of Chinese Labour," 13.

9. IWM, EVK 3/1: Sinai (September 3, 1917), 7.

10. IWM, EKV 3/2: Deir el-Belah (September 12, 1917), 16.

11. IWM, EKV 3/7: Near Ramleh (February 13, 1918), 76.

12. "Editor's Section," *ELC News*, March 1, 1919.

13. "Egyptian Labour Corps," *Times of London*, August 17, 1918, 5.

14. Fuchs, "Sites of Memory."

15. Fuchs, "Sites of Memory," 38.

16. El Shakry, *Great Social Laboratory*, 31.

17. IWM, EKV/2: *They Also Served*, 8–9.

18. For more on Egypt's "civilizing mission" in Sudan, see Troutt-Powell, *A Different Shade*.

19. "Da'wa al-Radif al-Misri," *Al-Ahali*, February 18, 1916.

20. "Fa'al Firqat Jamal al-Naql," *Al-Muqattam*, August 1, 1917.

21. His personal diaries from March 1916 contain a lengthy section titled "Natural History Notes," describing birds and camels in rich biological detail; see IWM, EKV 1/2: Venables Diaries (March 28, 1916).

22. IWM EKV/2: *They Also Served*, 2.

23. Burton, *Genetic Crossroads*, 32-34.

24. Burton, *Genetic Crossroads*, 36-37.

25. RAMC, *With the RAMC in Egypt*, 293–295.

26. Said, *Orientalism*, 2.

27. "Fred Garrett's War Diary," Grant's Militaria, accessed September 2017, http://www.grantsmilitaria.com/garrett/html/aug1915.htm.

28. IWM, EKV 3/2: Deir-el-Belah (September 12, 1917), 15.

29. IWM, EKV 3/2: Deir-el-Belah (September 12, 1917), 15.

30. IWM, EKV 3/2: Deir-el-Belah (September 12, 1917), 16–17.

31. "Army of Labour," *Times of London*, December 27, 1917.

32. Stovall, "Color Line."

33. Archives Nationales, Pierrefitte-sur-Seine Guerre de 1914-1918 14/11331: Installation du camp.

34. Bayor, *Race*, 58.

35. Stovall, "Color Line," 744.

36. Horne, "Immigrant Workers," 7.

37. Stovall, "Color Line," 744.

38. The South African Native Labor Corps was regimented by "tribe." See TNA, WO 107/37: "Report on British Labour" (November 14, 1919).

39. TNA, WO 107/37: "Report on British Labour" (November 14, 1919), 31.

40. Imperial War Museum, London, William Bret St. Leger Papers (hereafter cited as IWM, WSL) 1/6.

41. Stovall, "Color Line," 745.

42. TNA, WO 107/37: "Report on British Labour" (November 14, 1919), Appendix I.

43. TNA, WO 107/37: "Report on British Labour" (November 14, 1919), Appendix I.

44. TNA, WO 107/37: "Report on British Labour" (November 14, 1919), Appendix I.

45. TNA, WO 107/37: "Report on British Labour" (November 14, 1919), Appendix I.

46. TNA, WO 107/37: "Report on British Labour" (November 14, 1919), 28.

47. IWM, EKV 3/6: Judaea (December 5, 1917), 60.

48. RAMC, *With the RAMC in Egypt.*

49. "Port Said," *ELC News*, January 30, 1919.

50. Ruiz, "Photography."

51. IWM, EKV/2: *They Also Served*, 5.

52. TNA, WO 95/5279: War Diary: ELC in Mesopotamia.

53. TNA, WO 107/37: "Report on British Labour" (November 14, 1919), Appendix I.

54. TNA, WO 107/37: "Report on British Labour" (November 14, 1919), Appendix I.

55. TNA, WO 107/37: "Report on British Labour" (November 14, 1919), Appendix I.

56. TNA, WO 107/37: "Report on British Labour" (November 14, 1919), Appendix I.

57. The lone man who died under Venables' command in Palestine was given a funeral that contained a hybrid of British military and popular Muslim traditions to consecrate the body. See IWM, EKV 3/7: Near Ramleh (February 13, 1918), 7980.

58. TNA, WO 107/37: "Report on British Labour" (November 14, 1919), Appendix I.

59. "Editor's Section," *ELC News*, March 1, 1919.

60. IWM, EKV 3/10: Ephraim (June 2, 1918), 102–103.

61. IWM, EKV 3/10: Ephraim (September 10, 1918), 124.

62. Stoler, *Along the Archival Grain.*

63. Foucault, *Discipline and Punish*, 177.

64. IWM, EKV 3/10: Ephraim (June 2, 1918), 104.

65. IWM, EKV 3/10: Ephraim (June 2, 1918), 104.

66. IWM, EKV 3/10: Ephraim (June 2, 1918), 102–103.

67. Wood, *Natural History*, 88.

68. IWM, EKV 3/10: Ephraim (June 2, 1918), 103.

69. IWM, EKV 3/5: Wadi Gaza (October 21, 1917), 45.
70. IWM, EKV 3/4: Wadi Gaza (October 20, 1917), 37.
71. IWM, WSL/1/6: W. B. St. Leger (November 6, 1917).
72. Imperial War Museum, London, William Knott Papers (hereafter cited as IWM, WK) 1/2: W. Knott Diary (April 2, 1918).
73. IWM, WK 1/2: W. Knott Diary (October 31, 1917).
74. IWM, WK 1/2: W. Knott Diary (April 2, 1918).
75. Fuchs, "Sites of Memory," 651–652.
76. Paternek, "Norms and Normalization."

CHAPTER 6. LISTENING IN ON THE ELC

1. IWM, EKV/2: *They Also Served*, 9.
2. IWM, EKV 3/10: Ephraim (June 2, 1918), 112–113.
3. For more on white alienation, see White and White, *Sounds of Slavery*, 8.
4. Clément, "À La Recherche."
5. Corbin, *Village Bells*, 7.
6. Ong, *Orality and Literacy.*
7. IWM, EKV/2: *They Also Served*, 9.
8. IWM, EKV 3/5: Wadi Gaza (October 21, 1917), 55.
9. IWM, EKV 3/11: Ephraim (September 10, 1918), 130.
10. Gullett, *Australian Imperial Force*, 678.
11. "The Egyptian Labour Corps," *Times of London*, August 17, 1918, 5.
12. RAMC, *With the RAMC in Egypt*, 289.
13. IWM, EKV 3/10: Ephraim (June 2, 1918), 112.
14. RAMC, *With the RAMC in Egypt*, 289.
15. IWM, EKV 3/7: Near Ramleh (February 13, 1918), 72–73.
16. "In the Orderly Room," *ELC News*, January 30, 1919.
17. IWM, EKV 3/2: Deir-el-Belah (September 12, 1917), 19.
18. Fred Garrett's War Diary, October 13, 1915, accessed February 22, 2017, http://www.grantsmilitaria.com/garrett/html/oct1915.htm.
19. IWM, EKV 3/4: Wadi Gaza (October 20, 1917), 31–34.
20. IWM, EKV 3/12: Nablus (October 10, 1918), 147.
21. "Egyptian Labour Corps," *Times of London*, August 17, 1918, 5.
22. "Behind the Lines," *Sydney Morning Herald*, November 2, 1916.
23. IWM, EKV 3/10: Ephraim (June 2, 1918), 112.
24. IWM, EKV 3/2: Deir-el-Belah, Palestine (September 12, 1917), 17.
25. "Firqat al-'Ummal," *Al-Muqattam*, July 3, 1917.
26. "Firqat al-'Ummal," *Al-Muqqattam*, September 17, 1917.
27. RAMC, *With the RAMC in Egypt*, 291.
28. "Three Men and a Joke," *ELC News*, January 30, 1919.
29. "Reflections," *ELC News*, January 15, 1919.
30. "Truth at Last!" *ELC News*, January 15, 1919.
31. IWM, EKV 3/3: St. James Park (September 30, 1917), 26.
32. IWM, EKV 3/6: Judaea (December 5, 1917), 51.
33. IWM, EKV 3/10: Ephraim (June 2, 1918), 112–113.

34. IWM, EKV 3/7: Near Ramleh (February 13, 1918), 78–79.

35. RAMC, *With the RAMC in Egypt*, 291.

36. "Egyptian Labour Corps," *Times of London*, August 17, 1918.

37. Tuma, *Music*, 38.

38. Racy, "Improvisation."

39. Clément, "Rethinking 'Peasant Consciousness,'" 86.

40. Mughazy, "Pragmatics," 3. For more on belief in the "evil eye" among rural Egyptians in the early twentieth century, see Blackman, *Fellahin*, 218.

41. IWM, EKV/2: *They Also Served*, 13–14.

42. Clément, "Rethinking 'Peasant Consciousness,'" 92. Chalcraft has discovered a similar dynamic in the petitions *fallāḥīn* sent to the Egyptian Khedieve; see Chalcraft, "Engaging the State."

43. *ELC News*, March 15, 1919.

44. IWM, EKV 3/10: Ephraim (June 2, 1918), 112.

45. White and White, *Sounds of Slavery*, 22.

46. Interview with Alia Mossallam, September 9, 2015; Interview with Laila Soliman, January 20, 2016.

47.

Yā 'azīz 'ayni / ana biddi arawwaḥ baladi
baladi yā baladi / wa al-sulṭa khadit waladi
yā 'azīz 'ayni / ana biddi arawwaḥ baladi
yā ḥakimbāshi / t'ala akshaf 'ala waladi
gibt al-ṭabīb wa-l-ḥakīm / yakshifu 'ala 'lbi
'al al-ṭabīb wa-l-ḥakīm / ma-laksh duwwa' 'andi
'ashr 'zāyiz ward / wara' 'ayn min al-'ṭīfa
li-l-maḥbūb bitsalīni / min al-gamāl bitkifīni.

Arabic and English versions provided in interviews with Alia Mossallam (September 9, 2015) and Laila Soliman (January 20, 2016).

48. "Ya 'Aziz 'Ayni," Youtube.com, accessed December 9, 2020, https://www.youtube.com/watch?v=dwSIvKcVEbI.

49. IWM, EKV/2: *They Also Served*, 12.

50. IWM, EKV 3/7: Near Ramleh (February 13, 1918), 79–80.

51. IWM, EKV/2: *They Also Served*, 12.

52. At-Tirmidhi, *Jami' At-Tirmidhi*, 356.

53. Chittick, "On the Cosmology," 49.

54. Hourani, "Rashid Rida," 232.

55. Amin, *Ra'id al-Fikr*, chap. 4.

56. Hourani, "Rashid Rida," 235.

57. Hourani, "Rashid Rida," 236.

58. Rida was a member of the Naqshbandi order, characterized by its silent and solitary *dhikr* and strict emphasis on obedience to *sharia*. Hourani, "Rashid Rida," 235.

59. IWM, EKV 3/10: Ephraim (June 2, 1918), 112–113.

60. IWM, EKV/2: *They Also Served*, 12.

61. TNA, WO 107/37: "Report on British Labour" (November 14, 1919), Appendix I.

62. IWM, EKV/2: *They Also Served*, 12.

63. IWM, EKV/2: *They Also Served*, 12.

64. TNA, WO 107/37: "Report on British Labour" (November 14, 1919), Appendix I.

65. IWM, EKV 3/10: Ephraim (June 2, 1918), 113–114.

66. IWM, EKV 3/10: Ephraim (June 2, 1918), 113–114.

67. Bakhtin, *Rabelais*, 15.

68. Bakhtin, *Problems*, 128.

69. Z. Fahmy, *Ordinary Egyptians*, 70.

70. Z. Fahmy, *Ordinary Egyptians*, 128.

71. IWM, EKV/2: *They Also Served*, 13.

72. IWM, EKV 3/10: Ephraim (June 2, 1918), 115–116.

73. Blackman, *Fellahin*.

74. IWM, EKV 3/10: Ephraim (June 2, 1918), 115–116.

75. IWM, EKV 3/10: Ephraim (June 2, 1918), 115–116.

76. IWM, EKV 3/10: Ephraim (June 2, 1918), 107.

77. IWM, EKV/2: *They Also Served*, 43.

78. "Temporary Crusaders," *Bookman* 57, no. 337: 45.

79. TNA, FO 141/797/2 No. 2689/100: Curtis (June 1, 1918).

80. Hirschkind, *Ethical Soundscape*.

CHAPTER 7. THE MEN OF THE ELC TAKE ACTION

1. Arendt, *Human Condition*, 214.
2. Arendt, *Human Condition*, 212.
3. Arendt, *Human Condition*, 215.
4. 'Izzat, "Safahat min Mudhakkirat," *Ruz Al-Yusuf*, March 1968.
5. TNA, WO 107/37: "Report on British Labour" (November 14, 1919), 31.
6. IWM, EKV 3/1: Sinai (September 3, 1917), 4.
7. TNA, FO 141/797/2 No. 2689: General Staff Army HQ (July 23, 1915).
8. IWM, EKV/2: *They Also Served*, 42.
9. IWM, EKV/2: *They Also Served*, 40.
10. Clément, "À La Recherche."
11. "Our Little Say," *ELC News*, January 30, 1919.
12. IWM, EKV 3/2: Deir-el-Belah (September 12, 1917), 20.
13. IWM EKV 3/10: Ephraim (June 2, 1918), 101.
14. IWM, EKV/2: *They Also Served*, 8.
15. "Port Said," *ELC News*, January 30, 1919.
16. "Port Said," *ELC News*, January 30, 1919.
17. Jacob, *Working Out Egypt*.
18. "Fa'al Firqat Jamal," *Al-Muqattam*, August 1, 1917.
19. RAMC, *With the RAMC*, 141.
20. RAMC, *With the RAMC*, 141.
21. RAMC, *With the RAMC*, 280.
22. Murray, *Murray's Despatches*, 210.

23. "Firqat al-'Ummal," *Al-Muqattam*, September 17, 1917.
24. IWM, EKV 3/6: Judaea (December 5, 1917), 60–61.
25. IWM, EKV 3/9: K22 (April 24, 1918), 94.
26. *ELC News*, January 15, 1919.
27. TNA, FO 141/797/2 No. 2689/142: Wingate (September 15, 1918).
28. IWM, EKV 3/6: Judaea (December 5, 1917), 60–61.
29. IWM, EKV 3/6: Judaea (December 5, 1917), 60–61.
30. IWM, EKV/2: *They Also Served*, 49.
31. IWM EKV/2: *They Also Served*, 49.
32. "Editor's Section," *ELC News*, March 1, 1919.
33. Scott, *Weapons of the Weak*, 29.
34. Scott, *Weapons of the Weak*, 29.
35. IWM, EKV 3/1: Sinai (September 3, 1917), 7.
36. IWM, EKV 3/2: Deir-el-Belah (September 12, 1917), 15.
37. Venables' impromptu courts defaulted to punishing slackers with "the natural penalty of extra work, with perhaps a pack-drill added." See IWM, EKV 3/10: Ephraim (June 2, 1918), 117.
38. IWM, EKV 3/8: K22 (April 3, 1918).
39. IWM, EKV 3/8: K22 (April 3, 1918).
40. IWM, EKV 3/8: K22 (April 3, 1918).
41. IWM, EKV 3/8: K22 (April 3, 1918), 87.
42. IWM, EKV 3/5: Wadi Gaza (October 21, 1917), 42–48.
43. IWM, EKV 3/5: Wadi Gaza (October 21, 1917), 42–48.
44. Scott, *Weapons of the Weak*, 30.
45. IWM, EKV 3/8: K22 (April 3, 1918).
46. IWM, EKV 3/8: K22 (April 3, 1918).
47. *ELC News*, March 1, 1919.
48. "Love Letters," *ELC News*, March 15, 1919.
49. 'Izzat, "Safahat min Mudhakkirat," *Ruz al-Yusuf*, March 1968, 24.
50. 'Izzat, "Safahat min Mudhakkirat," *Ruz al-Yusuf*, March 1968, 24.
51. "Fred Garrett's War Diary," Grant's Militaria, published August 23, 1915, accessed February 28, 2017, http://www.grantsmilitaria.com/garrett/html/aug1915.htm.
52. Starling and Lee, *No Labour, No Battle*, 275.
53. TNA, WO 107/37: "Report on British Labour" (November 14, 1919), 31.
54. Starling and Lee, *No Labour, No Battle*, 275.
55. TNA, WO 107/37: "Report on British Labour" (November 14, 1919).
56. IWM, WSL/1/6: WB St. Leger (November 6, 1917).
57. TNA, FO 371/2945 no. 204955: Taranto (1917).
58. TNA, FO 371/2945 no. 204955: Taranto (1917).
59. Starling and Lee, *No Labour, No Battle*, 275.
60. Starling and Lee, *No Labour, No Battle*, 275.
61. TNA, WO 71/600: Court Martial.
62. TNA, WO 71/600: Court Martial.
63. TNA, WO 71/600: Court Martial.
64. TNA, WO 71/600: Court Martial.
65. TNA, WO 71/600: Court Martial.
66. TNA, WO 107/37: "Report on British Labour" (November 14, 1919).

67. TNA, WO 107/37: "Report on British Labour" (November 14, 1919).
68. TNA, FO 371/2945 No. 204955: Taranto (1917).
69. TNA, FO 371/2945 No. 204955: Taranto (1917).
70. TNA, WO 71/690: "Husein Mohamed el Arabi, Mohamed Abdalla Hassan."

CHAPTER 8. "I WILL NOT ACCEPT SLAVERY!"

1. S. Zaghlul, *Mudhakkirat*, vol. 1, 52.
2. Lutfi al-Sayyid, *Qissat Hayati*, 15.
3. Goldschmidt, *Biographical Dictionary*, 234.
4. Schülze, "Colonization and Resistance"; E. Goldberg, "Peasants in Revolt."
5. Al-Rafi'i, *Thawrat 1919*, chap. 6.
6. Heshmat, *Egypt 1919*.
7. For more on racial nationalism, see Wiendling and Turda, *Blood and Homeland*; Brennan, "Realizing Civilization"; Brennan, *Taifa*; Sautman, "Racial Nationalism and China."
8. D. Goldberg, "Semantics of Race," 557.
9. Anderson, *Imagined Communities*.
10. D. Goldberg, "Semantics of Race."
11. Bucur, "Fallen Women," 337; Yeomans, "Of 'Yugoslav Barbarians,'" 87.
12. Burton, *Genetic Crossroads*, 14.
13. Schine, "The Racialized Other."
14. Burton, *Genetic Crossroads*, 15.
15. Quoted in Wendell, *Evolution*, 24.
16. Zafer, *Ecumenical Community*.
17. Aydin, *Idea of the Muslim World*.
18. Elshakry, *Reading Darwin*, 119.
19. Al-Afghani and 'Abduh, *Al-'Urwa al-Wuthqa*, 41.
20. Al-Afghani and 'Abduh, *Al-'Urwa al-Wuthqa*, 41.
21. Al-Afghani and 'Abduh, *Al-'Urwa al-Wuthqa*, 64.
22. Khaldun, *The Muqaddimah*.
23. Wendell, *Evolution*, 173.
24. Rida, *Tarikh Al-Ustadh*, vol. 1, 82.
25. Lutfi was a close companion of 'Abduh during his stay in Geneva, Switzerland; see Lutfi al-Sayyid, *Qissat Hayati*, 18–19.
26. Landau, *Parliaments and Parties*, 139.
27. Lutfi al-Sayyid, *Qissat Hayati*, 41.
28. Lutfi al-Sayyid, *Al-Muntakhabat*, vol. 1, 308–309.
29. Lutfi al-Sayyid, *Ta'ammulat*, 61.
30. Lutfi al-Sayyid, *Qissat Hayati*, 7.
31. For more on the link between the *fallāḥīn* and "Egyptianness" (*miṣriyya*), see Gasper, *Power of Representation*.
32. Wendell, *Evolution*, 247.
33. Lutfi al-Sayyid, *Al-Muntakhabat*, vol. 1, 170.
34. Wendell, *Evolution*, 13–14.
35. Lutfi al-Sayyid, *Safahat Mutwiyya*, 43–44.
36. Jakes and Shokr, "Finding Value," 108.

37. Jakes and Shokr, "Finding Value"; Jakes, *Egypt's Occupation*, 222.
38. Troutt-Powell, *A Different Shade.*
39. Wendell, *Evolution*, 261–262.
40. Wendell, *Evolution*, 261–263.
41. Wendell, *Evolution*, 262.
42. Al-Afghani and 'Abduh, *Al-'Urwa al-Wuthqa*, 255.
43. Wendell, *Evolution*, 264.
44. Talhami, "The Zanj Rebellion."
45. S. Zaghlul, *Mudhakkirat*, vol. 7, 36.
46. Salim, *Misr fi-l-Harb*, 252.
47. Shafiq, *Hawliyyat Misr*, 91–92.
48. Salim, *Misr fi-l-Harb*, 253.
49. Salim, *Misr fi-l-Harb*, 252.
50. Al-Rafi'i, *Thawrat 1919*, 70.
51. Musa, *Tarbiyyat*, 112.
52. 'Izz Al-Din, "Awwal Dirasa."
53. Salim, *Misr fi-l-Harb*, 253.
54. E. Goldberg, "Peasants in Revolt," 263.
55. El Shakry, *Great Social Laboratory*, 62; Egger, "A Fabian in Egypt," 123–126.
56. Elshakry, *Reading Darwin*, 246.
57. Musa, *Tarbiyyat*, 72.
58. Musa, *Tarbiyyat*, 112.
59. Musa, *Tarbiyyat*, 246–247.
60. Musa, *Misr*, 9.
61. Musa, *Misr*, 9.
62. Musa, *Misr*, 17–21.
63. Musa, *Misr*, 10.
64. El Shakry, *Great Social Laboratory*, 61.
65. Goldschmidt, *Biographical Dictionary*, 172.
66. Sabry, *La Révolution*, 12.
67. Sabry, *La Révolution*, 18.
68. Sabry, *La Révolution*, 21–22.
69. Sabry, *La Révolution*, 22.
70. Sabry, *La Révolution*, 24.
71. Sabry, *La Révolution*, 23.
72. Halls, "'Not Worthy of Belief.'"
73. Archives Diplomatiques, Ministère des Affairs Étrangères, La Courneuve (hereafter cited as MAE) K/56/1/12: "Africa, Consular" (April 21, 1919).
74. Gershoni and Jankowski, *Egypt, Islam, and the Arabs*, 164–190.
75. Gershoni and Jankowski, *Egypt, Islam, and the Arabs*, 50.
76. Coury, "Politics of the Funereal," 191.
77. Coury, "Politics of the Funereal," 191.
78. 'Abd al-Karim, *Khamsun 'Aman*, 135.
79. Fahmi, *Mudhakkirat*, 51–52.
80. For details on household slavery in Sha'rawi's social milieu, see Baron, *Egypt as a Woman*, chap. 1; for the persistence of slavery in Black Africans after its official abolition, well into the 1890s, see Troutt-Powell, *A Different Shade.*

81. Cuno and Walz, *Race and Slavery*, 10.
82. Zagloul, *White Book*, 12–13.
83. Zagloul, *White Book*, 27.
84. Murray, *Murray's Despatches*, 123.
85. Zagloul, *White Book*, 42.
86. A. Zaghlul, *Sirr Taqaddum*, 15.
87. Selim, *The Novel*.
88. Zagloul, *White Book*, 42.
89. Rottenberg, "Passing."
90. For example, Ginsberg, "Politics of Passing," 2.
91. Williams, "Race-ing and Being Raced," 62.
92. Al-'Aqqad, *Sa'd Zaghlul*, 157.
93. Sabry, *La Révolution*, 28.
94. Sayf Al-Dawla, *Mashayikh Jabal al-Badari*, 2.
95. Sayf Al-Dawla, *Mashayikh Jabal al-Badari*, 168.
96. Goldschmidt, *Biographical Dictionary*, 167.

CHAPTER 9. THE ELC AND THE 1919 REVOLUTION

1. Al-Rafi'i, *Thawrat 1919*, 17.
2. Safran, *Egypt in Search*, 101.
3. Gershoni and Jankowski, *Egypt, Islam, and the Arabs*, 40.
4. Zaghlul, *Mudhakkirat*, vol. 7, 36.
5. See E. Goldberg, "Peasants in Revolt"; Schülze, "Colonization and Resistance."
6. Golberg, "Peasants in Revolt," 272.
7. "Al-'Ummal al-Mutatu'un," *Al-Muqattam*, April 21, 1917.
8. 'Izz al-Din, "Awwal Dirasa."
9. TNA, FO 141/797/2 No. 2689/75: Meeting at Residency (May 6, 1918).
10. Z. Fahmy, *Ordinary Egyptians*, 115.
11. Z. Fahmy, *Ordinary Egyptians*, 115.
12. Ryzova, *Age of the Efendiyya*.
13. The text goes as follows:

'āyyishīn fi wadi al-nīl nashrub / min 'adādāt 'ala mululi wa-sinti
Min ghāz li-malḥ wa-min al-sukr / wa tramwāyāt li-khawāga triyānti
Rabbina mayuwurīksh dūkhatina / al-gīb naḍīf ama al-bayt anḍf
Wa-l-hadūma di illi 'ala gatitna / maḥgūz 'alayha di 'ayīsha t'araf.
(We live in the Nile Valley, yet our drinking water / is rationed by water meters
From gas, salt and sugar / to the tramways of *khawaga* Kiryaniti
May you never experience our desperation / our pockets are clean [empty] and our houses even cleaner
Even the clothes we are wearing are already pawned / what a ghastly life.)

Arabic and English versions provided in personal interview with Laila Soliman, January 20, 2016.

14. Ryzova, *Age of the Efendiyya*, 116, n90.

15.

Sālma yā salāma / ah yā sālma yā salāma
ṣafar yā wabūr wa 'urbat 'andak / nazilni fi-l-balad-di
ba-la amrika ba-la uruba / ma-fīsh aḥsan min baladi
di al-markab illi bitgīb / aḥsan min illi bitwadi
yā usta bishandi
sālma yā salāma / ah yā sālma ya salama
sulṭa ma sulṭa kullaha maksab / ḥawishna malu wa gayna
shufna al-ḥarb wa shufna al-ḍarb / wa shufna al-dīnāmīt bi-'aynayna
rabak wāhid umrak wāhid / adiha ruḥna wa gayna
ya khūsh 'alayna
sālma yā salāma / ah yā sālma ya salāma.

Arabic and English versions provided in personal interview with Laila Soliman, January 20, 2016. See also Z. Fahmy, *Ordinary Egyptians*, 116n89.

16. IWM, EKV 3/10: Ephraim (June 2, 1918), 112; "Love Letters," *ELC News*, March 15, 1919.

17. TNA, FO 141/797/2 No. 2689/135: "Confidential: Complaints" (August 10, 1918).

18. TNA, FO 141/797/2.

19. For example, "Ba'd al-Salih," *Al-Watan*, November 4, 1918.

20. TNA, FO 141/667 No. 2689/163: Haines (January 11, 1919).

21. TNA, FO 141/797/2 No. 2689/152: Rushdi (November 9, 1918).

22. TNA, FO 141/667/1 No. 2689/154: Allenby (November 17, 1918).

23. RAMC, *With the RAMC in Egypt*, 291–292.

24. Fawaz, *Land of Aching Hearts*, 202.

25. TNA, FO 141/797/2 No. 2689/57a: Brunyate (February 3, 1918).

26. Rose, "Famine, Disease, and Death."

27. Rose, "Famine, Disease, and Death."

28. Johnson and Mueller, "Updating the Accounts."

29. TNA, FO 371/3713/20835: "Egypt and the War" (February 6, 1919), 7–8.

30. E. Goldberg, "Peasants in Revolt."

31. E. Goldberg, "Peasants in Revolt," 264.

32. Real reductions may have been much larger, as aggregate consumption of foodstuffs also declined steadily throughout the war, so that a small marginal decrease in 1918 consumption levels actually represents a significant decrease from prewar levels. E. Goldberg, "Peasants in Revolt," 267.

33. TNA, FO 141/667/1 No. 2689/158: Haines (December 26, 1918); TNA, FO 141/667/1 No. 2689/162: Haines (January 9, 1919).

34. TNA, FO 141/667 No. 2689/163: Haines (January 11, 1919).

35. TNA, FO 371/3714/50207: "Egyptian Unrest" (April 1, 1919).

36. TNA, FO 371/3714/50207: "Egyptian Unrest" (April 11, 1919).

37. TNA, FO 371/3714/49561: "Situation in Egypt" (March 22, 1919).

38. IWM, EKV/2: *They Also Served*, 5.

39. E. Goldberg, "Peasants in Revolt."

40. Barak, *On Time.*

41. Al-Rafi'i, *Thawrat 1919*, 243.

42. Al-Rafi'i, *Thawrat 1919*, chap. 6.

43. TNA, FO 371/3715/56539: "Damage Done" (March 22, 1919).

44. Mossallam, "Ya Aziz 'Aini"; Mossallam, "Strikes, Riots, and Laughter."

45. According to Al-Rafi'i, there were 146 foreigners who had taken refuge in the school, including 70 women and children. See Al-Rāfi'i, *Thawrat 1919*, 260.

46. Al-Rāfi'i, *Thawrat 1919*, 260.

47. Al-Rāfi'i, *Thawrat 1919*, 260.

48. TNA, FO 371/3714/45823: Royal Admiralty (March 23, 1919).

49. TNA, FO 371/3714/45524: Air Ministry (March 20, 1919).

50. Al-Rafi'i, *Thawrat 1919*, 218.

51. Z. Fahmy, *Ordinary Egyptians*, 139.

52. 'Azzam, "Maris 1919," chap. 2.

53. Hopkins and Saad, "Region."

54. Gran, "Upper Egypt"; Abul-Magd, *Imagined Empires*; Hopkins and Saad, "Region."

55. Z. Fahmy, *Ordinary Egyptians*; Gasper, *Power of Representation.*

56. At the time, there were fourteen rural provinces (*mudiriyyat*) and five urban governorates (*muhafizat*). Given that Labor Corps recruitment was concentrated in rural areas, this assumes an even distribution over the provinces.

57. TNA, FO 141/667 No. 2689/163: Haines (January 11, 1919).

58. TNA, FO 141/753: "Luxor Train Murders," 2.

59. TNA, FO 141/753: "Luxor Train Murders," 2.

60. TNA, FO 141/753: "Luxor Train Murders," 2.

61. Al-Rafi'i, *Thawrat 1919*, 260.

62. TNA, FO 141/797/2: "Raising."

63. Sayf al-Dawla, *Mashayikh Jabal al-Badari*, 9.

64. Sayf al-Dawla, *Mashayikh Jabal al-Badari*, 10.

65. "Ask the people of the village about the disasters that have passed through here, and you will hear from them collectively . . . every one of them will not differ in their recollections." Sayf al-Dawla, *Mashayikh Jabal al-Badari*, 10.

66. Sayf al-Dawla, *Mashayikh Jabal al-Badari*, 10.

67. Sayf al-Dawla, *Mashayikh Jabal al-Badari*, 154–155.

68. Scott, *Moral Economy.*

69. Sayf al-Dawla, *Mashayikh Jabal al-Badari*, 166.

70. Sayf al-Dawla, *Mashayikh Jabal al-Badari*, 169.

71. The conflict between the '*umda* of Brimsha and the villagers of Manshiyyat Halfa recounted in chapter 2 has already shown how ELC recruitment could inflect local politics with a volatile dynamic.

72. Al-Rafi'i, *Thawrat 1919*, 258.

73. Al-Rafi'i, *Thawrat 1919*, 258.

74. Al-Rafi'i, *Thawrat 1919*, 258.

75. Ramadan, *Tatawwur al-Harika*, 131.

76. Baron, *Egypt as a Woman*, 20.

77. Baron, *Egypt as a Woman*, 20.

78. One feddan is equal to approximately one acre.

79. Troutt-Powell, *A Different Shade*, 181.

80. Sha'rawi, *Mudhakkirat Huda Sha'rawi*, 171–172.

81. For more on the concept of repertoires of contentions politics, see Shorter and Tilly, *Strikes in France*.

82. IWM, EKV 1/4: Diary of EK Venables, 1919 (March 12, 1919).

83. IWM, EKV 1/4: Diary of EK Venables, 1919 (March 12, 1919).

84. IWM, EKV 1/4: Diary of EK Venables, 1919 (April 7, 1919).

85. IWM, EKV 1/4: Diary of EK Venables, 1919 (April 8, 1919).

86. IWM, EKV/2: *They Also Served*.

87. See TNA, FO 141/667 No. 2689/164: Tweedy (March 20, 1919), and TNA, FO 141/667 No. 2689/165: MacCauley (April 7, 1919).

88. TNA, FO 141/667 No. 2689/168: Davidson (July 19, 1919).

89. British National Library, *ELC News*.

90. The records of the British War Office contain a FGCM execution sentence handed down to a certain "Husein Mohamed el Arabi" in January 1921 in connection with an incident in Qantara that had taken place the previous autumn. See TNA, WO 71/690: "Husein Mohamed el Arabi."

91. Chalcraft, "Coal Heavers."

92. TNA, FO 371/3717/75612: Strike at Port Said (May 19, 1919).

93. TNA, FO 371/3717/75612: Strike at Port Said (May 19, 1919).

94. TNA, FO 371/3717/75612: Strike at Port Said (May 19, 1919).

95. TNA, FO 371/6304/10360: Egyptian Negotiations (September 5, 1921).

96. TNA, FO 371/6304/9814: Egyptian Negotiations (August 30, 1921).

97. Salim, *Misr fi-l-Harb*, 262–264.

98. Salim, *Misr fi-l-Harb*, 262–264.

99. Salim, *Misr fi-l-Harb*, 262–264.

100. Nefertiti Takla has uncovered evidence of the maintenance of ties between ELC laborers in postwar Alexandria. See Takla, "Murderous Economies."

CONCLUSION

1. Personal interview with Laila Soliman (January 20, 2016); personal interview with Alia Mossallam (October 29, 2015).

2. Personal interview with Zainab Magdy (October 28, 2015).

3. "Ruba'a Miliyun," *Al-Lata'if al-Musawwira*, September 24, 1917.

4. Cowen, *Deadly Life*, 94.

5. Cowen, *Deadly Life*, 4.

6. According to Harold Nicolson, "The justification of our presence in Egypt remains based, not upon the defensible right of conquest, or on force, but upon our own belief in the element of consent." Nicolson, Curzon, 166.

7. Jakes, *Egypt's Occupation*, 3.

8. 'Izzat, "Safahat min Mudhakkirat," *Ruz al-Yusuf*, June 17, 1968.

9. Hobson, *Imperialism*.

10. Arendt, Origins of Totalitarianism, 148; Lenin, "Imperialism."

11. Gines, *Hannah Arendt and the Negro Question*.

12. Arendt, *On Violence*, 68–69.

13. Bhabha, "Framing Fanon," xxi, xxviii–xxxi.

14. Fanon, *Wretched of the Earth*, 36.
15. Fanon, *Wretched of the Earth*, 40.
16. Fanon, *Wretched of the Earth*, 88.
17. Bhabha, “Framing Fanon,” xl.
18. Bhabha, “Framing Fanon,” xxxvi.
19. Harper, “Singapore, 1915.”

REFERENCES

ARCHIVAL AND UNPUBLISHED SOURCES

London, United Kingdom, The British National Archives (TNA), Kew Gardens
- Cabinet Files (CAB)
- Foreign Office Files (FO) 141—Embassy and Consular Archives, Egypt, Correspondence
- FO 371—General Correspondence, Political
- FO 848—Evidence Presented to the Milner Commission
- War Office Files (WO) 71—Field General Court Martials
- WO 95—War Diaries
- WO 107—Controller of Labor
- Ministry of Transport Files (MT) 23—Military Transport in World War I

London, United Kingdom, Imperial War Museum (IWM)
- E. K. Venables Papers
- World War I Diaries of W. B. St. Leger
- Notes on Palestine by Thomas Brookes Minshall
- W. Knott Papers

London, United Kingdom, British National Library
- Humanities Reading Room—Periodicals
  - *ELC News*

Cairo, Egypt, Dar Al-Kutub Al-Misriyya (Egyptian National Library)
- Periodicals
  - *Al-Muqattam*
  - *Al-Afkar*
  - *Al-Watan*
  - *Al-Ahali*
- Books
  - Ashraf Sabry, Rihlat al-Israr: Misr Sabab al-Nasr fi-l-Harb al-'Alimiyya al-Ula. Unpublished manuscript, Cairo, 2012.

Cairo, Egypt, American University in Cairo, Rare Books and Manuscripts
- Periodicals
  - *Al-Ahram*
  - *Ruz al-Yusuf*
  - *Al-Musawwir*

Paris, France, Archives Nationales, Pierrefitte-sur-Seine
- F/14—Guerre de 1914–1918

Paris, France, Archives Diplomatiques, La Courneuve
- K—Consular Archives, Africa

Minneapolis, Minnesota, USA, Kautz Family YMCA Archives, University of Minnesota
- Y.USA.9-2-22—Egypt
- Y.USA.4-1—Armed Services: World War I
- Biographical Records—William Mort and Louise Jessop

PUBLISHED PRIMARY AND SECONDARY SOURCES

'Abbas, Raouf [Ra'uf 'Abbas], and Assem El-Dessouky. *The Large Landowning Class and the Peasantry in Egypt, 1837–1952*. Syracuse, NY: Syracuse University Press, 2011.

'Abbas, Ra'uf. *Al-Nizam al-Ijitima'i fi Misr fi Zill al-Mulkiyat al-Zira'iyah al-Kabira*. Cairo: Dar al-Fikr al-Hadith li-l-Taba'a wa-l-Nashr, 1973.

'Abd al-Karim, Ahmad 'Izzat. *Khamsun 'Aman 'Ala Thawrat 1919*. Cairo: Markaz al-Watha'iq wa-l-Buhuth al-Tarikhiyya li-Misr al-M'uasr, 1969.

Abu-Lughod, Janet. "Tale of Two Cities: The Origins of Modern Cairo." *Comparative Studies in Society and History* 7, no. 4 (1965): 429–457.

Abu-Lughod, Lila. *Remaking Women: Feminism and Modernity in the Middle East*. Princeton, NJ: Princeton University Press, 1998.

Abul-Magd, Zeinab. *Imagined Empires: A History of Revolt in Egypt*. Berkeley: University of California Press, 2013.

Al-Afghani, Jamal al-Din, and Muhammad 'Abduh. *Al-'Urwa al-Wuthqa*. Cairo: Mu'assasat Hindawi li-l-Ta'lim wa-l-Thiqafa, 2012.

Al-'Aqqad, 'Abbas Mahmud. *Sa'd Zaghlul Za'im al-Thawra*. Cairo: Mu'assasat Hindawi li-l-Ta'lim wa-l-Thiqafa, 2013.

Al-Rafi'i, 'Abd al-Rahman. *Thawrat 1919: Tarikh Misr al-Qawmi min 1914 illa 1921*. Cairo: Dar al-Ma'arif, 1947.

Amin, 'Uthman. *Ra'id al-Fikr al-Misri: Al-Imam Muhammad 'Abduh*. Cairo: Al-Hay'a al-'Ama l-Shu'un al-Matba'a al-Amiriyya, 1996.

Anderson, Benedict. *Imagined Communities: Reflections on the Origin and Spread of Nationalism*. Rev. ed. London and New York: Verso, 2006.

Anghie, Anthony. "Francisco de Vitoria and the Colonial Origins of International Law." In *Laws of the Postcolonial*, edited by Eve Darian-Smith and Peter Fitzpatrick, 89–108. Ann Arbor: University of Michigan Press, 1999.

Anis, Muhammad. *Tatuwwur al-Mujtama' al-Misri min al-Iqta' illa Thawrat 23 Yuliyyu 1952*. Cairo: Matba'a al-Jablawi, 1977.

Anus, Najwa Ibrahim. *Shakhsiyat al-'Umda fi-l-Masrah al-Misri: min al-Harb al-'Alimiyya al-Ula illa Thawrat 1952*. Cairo: Dar al-Thiqafa al-Jadida, 1989.

Aoki, Keith. "Race, Space, and Place: The Relation between Architectural Modernism, Post-Modernism, Urban Planning, and Gentrification." *Fordham Urban Law Journal* 20, no. 4 (1992): 699–829.

———. "Space Invaders: Critical Geography, the 'Third World' in International Law, and Critical Race Theory." *Villanova Law Review* 45, no. 5 (2000): 913–957.

Arendt, Hannah. *The Human Condition*. 2nd ed. Chicago: University of Chicago Press, 1998.

———. *On Violence*. New York: Harcourt Brace & Co., 1970.

———. *The Origins of Totalitarianism*. New York: Harcourt Brace & Co., 1968.

Armbrust, Walter. *Mass Culture and Modernism in Egypt*. Cambridge, UK: Cambridge University Press, 1996.

At-Tirmidhi. *Jami' At-Tirmidhi*. Vol. 4. Translated by Abu Khaliyl. Darussalam, Tanzania: Maktaba Dar-us-Salam, 2007.

Avci, Remzi. "Pan-Islamism and the Jihad Discourse of the German Orientalists in the First World War." *Jurnal al-Tamaddun* 2, no. 3 (2019): 25–35.

Aydın, Cemil. *The Idea of the Muslim World: A Global Intellectual History.* Cambridge, MA: Harvard University Press, 2017.

———. *The Politics of Anti-Westernism in Asia: Visions of World Order in Pan-Islamic and Pan-Asian Thought.* New York: Columbia University Press, 2007.

'Azzam, Salah. "Maris 1919 al-Dammi wa-l-Fallahun." *Ikhtarna li-l-Fallah* 2, no. 5 (1967).

Badcock, G. E. *A History of the Transport Services of the Egyptian Expeditionary Force 1916–1918.* London: Hugh Rees, Ltd., 1925.

Baer, Gabriel. "The Village Shaykh, 1800–1950." In *Studies in the Social History of Modern Egypt.* Chicago: University of Chicago Press, 1969: 30–61.

Bakhtin, Mikhail. *Problems of Dostoevsky's Poetics.* Edited by Caryl Emerson. Minneapolis: University of Minnesota Press, 1984.

———. *Rabelais and His World.* Bloomington: Indiana University Press, 1984.

Barak, On. *On Time: Technology and Temporality in Modern Egypt.* Berkeley: University of California Press, 2011.

Barakat, 'Ali. *Tatawwur al-Mulkiyya al-Zira'aiya fi Misr wa-Athruhu 'Ala al-Harikah al-Siyasiyya, 1813–1914.* Cairo: Dar al-Thaqafa al-Jadida, 1977.

Barker, A. J. *The Bastard War: The Mesopotamia Campaign of 1914-1918.* New York: Dial Press, 1967.

Baron, Beth. *Egypt as a Woman: Nationalism, Gender, and Politics.* Berkeley: University of California Press, 2005.

Barret, Michèle. "Subalterns at War: First World War Colonial Forces and the Politics of the Imperial War Graves Commission." In *Can the Subaltern Speak? Reflections on the History of an Idea*, edited by Rosalind C. Morris, 156–176. New York: Columbia University Press, 2010.

Barua, Pradeep. "Inventing Race: The British and India's Martial Races." *The Historian* 58, no. 1 (Autumn 1995): 107–116.

Bayor, Ronald H. *Race and the Shaping of Twentieth-Century Atlanta.* Chapel Hill: University of North Carolina Press, 2000.

Bean, C. E. W. *The Story of Anzac: From 4 May 1915 to the Evacuation.* Vol. 2 of *The Official History of Australia in the War of 1914–1918.* 11th ed. Sydney: Angus & Robertson Ltd., 1924.

Beckert, Sven. *Empire of Cotton: A Global History.* London: Penguin Books, 2014.

Beinin, Joel, and Zachary Lockman. *Workers on the Nile: Nationalism, Communism, Islam, and the Egyptian Working Class, 1882–1954.* Princeton, NJ: Princeton University Press, 1987.

Bennett, Richard Allen. "The Anglo-Egyptian Sudanese Influence in the Occupied Enemy Territory Administration, South, 1917–1920." PhD diss., Florida State University, 1992.

Bernes, Jasper. "Logistics, Counterlogistics, and the Communist Prospect." *Endnotes* no. 3 (2013).

Bhabha, Homi. "Foreword: Framing Fanon." In Frantz Fanon, *The Wretched of the Earth.* New York: Grove Press, 2004.

Blackman, Winifred. *The Fellahin of Upper Egypt.* London: Frank Cass & Co., 1963 [1927].

Blyden, Edward W. "Mohammedanism and the Negro Race." In Edward W. Blyden,

Christianity, Islam, and the Negro Race, 2nd ed., 1–79. Baltimore: Black Classic Press, 1994 [1887].

Bou, Jean. *Light Horse: A History of Australia's Mounted Arm*. Port Melbourne, Australia: Cambridge University Press, 2009.

Brennan, James R. "Realizing Civilization through Patrilineal Descent: The Intellectual Making of an African Racial Nationalism in Tanzania, 1920–1950." *Social Identities* 12, no. 4 (July 2006): 405–423.

———. *Taifa: Making Nation and Race in Urban Tanzania*. Athens: Ohio University Press, 2012.

A Brief Record of the Advance of the Egyptian Expeditionary Force under the Command of General Sir Edmund H. H. Allenby. London: His Majesty's Stationery Office, 1919.

Brown, Judith M. "The Anglo-Boer War: An Indian Perspective." *Kunapipi* 21, no. 3 (1999): 24–35.

Brown, Nathan J. *Peasant Politics in Modern Egypt: The Struggle Against the State*. New Haven, CT: Yale University Press, 1990.

———. "Who Abolished Corvee Labor in Egypt and Why?" *Past & Present* 144, no. 1 (August 1994): 116–137.

Buckley, Roger N. "The British Army's African Recruitment Policy, 1790–1807." *Contributions to Black Studies: A Journal of African and Afro-American Studies* 5 (2008): 1–12.

Bucur, Maria. "Fallen Women and Necessary Evils: Eugenic Representations of Prostitution in Interwar Romania." In *"Blood and Homeland": Eugenics and Racial Nationalism in Central and Southeast Europe, 1900–1940*, edited by Paul Weindling and Marius Turda, 335–352. Budapest and New York: Central European Press, 2007.

Burke, Edmund, III. "Changing Patterns of Peasant Protest, 1750–1950." In *Peasants and Politics in the Modern Middle East*, edited by Farhad Kazemi and John Waterbury, 24–37. Miami: Florida International University Press, 1991.

Burton, Elise K. *Genetic Crossroads: The Middle East and the Science of Human Heredity*. Stanford, CA: Stanford University Press, 2021.

Can, Lale. *Spiritual Subjects: Central Asian Pilgrims and the Ottoman Hajj at the End of Empire*. Stanford, CA: Stanford University Press, 2020.

Carman, Barry, and John McPherson, eds. *Bimbashi McPherson: A Life in Egypt*. London: British Broadcasting Corporation, 1983.

Carminati, Lucia. "Alexandria, 1898: Nodes, Networks, and Scales in Nineteenth-Century Egypt and the Mediterranean." *Comparative Studies in Society and History* 59, no. 1 (2017): 127–153.

Chalcraft, John. "The Coal Heavers of Port Sa'id: State-Making and Worker Protest, 1869–1914." *International Labor and Working-Class History* 60 (October 2001): 104–124.

———. "Engaging the State: Peasants and Petitions in Egypt on the Eve of Colonial Rule." *International Journal of Middle East Studies* 37, no. 3 (August 2005): 303–325.

———. *The Striking Cabbies of Cairo and Other Stories: Crafts and Guilds in Egypt, 1863–1914*. Albany, NY: SUNY Press, 2005.

Chatterjee, Partha. *The Nation and Its Fragments: Colonial and Postcolonial Histories*. Princeton, NJ: Princeton University Press, 1993.

Chittick, William C. "On the Cosmology of Dhikr." In *Paths to the Heart: Sufism and the Christian East*, edited by James S. Cutsinger, 48–63. Bloomington, IN: World Wisdom, 2002.

Clément, Anne. "À La Recherche Des Voix Des Fallahīn Dans un Dossier d'archives Judiciaries Égyptiennes." *Ateliers d'anthropologie* 26 (2012): 1–16.

———. "Rethinking 'Peasant Consciousness' in Colonial Egypt: An Exploration of the Performance of Folksongs by Upper Egyptian Agricultural Workers on the Archaeological Excavation Sites of Karnak and Dendera at the Turn of the Twentieth Century (1885–1914)." *History and Anthropology* 21, no. 2 (2010): 73–100.

Colla, Elliott. "How *Zaynab* Became the First Arabic Novel." *History Compass* 7, no. 1 (2009): 214–225.

Cookson-hills, Claire. "Historical Perspectives on Whole-of-Government Approaches: The 1882 British Occupation of Egypt." *Canadian Army Journal* 15, no. 1 (2013): 65–71.

Corbin, Alain. *Village Bells: Sound and Meaning in the Nineteenth-Century French Countryside*. New York: Columbia University Press, 1998.

Coury, Ralph M. "The Politics of the Funereal: The Tomb of Saad Zaghlul." *Journal of the American Research Center in Egypt* 29 (1992): 191–200.

Cowen, Deborah. *The Deadly Life of Logistics: Mapping Violence in Global Trade*. Minneapolis: University of Minnesota Press, 2014.

Cromer, Evelyn Baring. *Modern Egypt*. London: Macmillan, 1908.

Cuno, Kenneth. "African Slaves in Nineteenth Century Rural Egypt: A Preliminary Assessment." In *Race and Slavery in the Middle East: Histories of Trans-Saharan Africans in Nineteenth-Century Egypt, Sudan, and the Ottoman Mediterranean*, edited by Kenneth Cuno and Terrance Walz, 77–98. Cairo: American University in Cairo Press, 2010.

———. *Modernizing Marriage: Family, Ideology, and Law in Nineteenth- and Early Twentieth-Century Egypt*. Syracuse, NY: Syracuse University Press, 2015.

Cuno, Kenneth, and Terrance Walz. *Race and Slavery in the Middle East: Histories of Trans-Saharan Africans in Nineteenth-Century Egypt, Sudan, and the Ottoman Mediterranean*. Cairo: American University in Cairo Press, 2010.

Davis, Muriam Haleh. "Colonial Capitalism and Imperial Myth in French North Africa." In *A Critical Political Economy of the Middle East and North Africa*, edited by Joel Beinin, Bassam Haddad, and Sherene Seikaly, 161–178. Stanford, CA: Stanford University Press, 2020.

Derr, Jennifer. *The Lived Nile: Environment, Disease, and Material Colonial Economy in Egypt*. Stanford, CA: Stanford University Press, 2019.

Di-Capua, Yoav. *Gatekeepers of the Arab Past: Historians and History Writing in Twentieth-Century Egypt*. Berkeley: University of California Press.

Douglass, Frederick. "The Color Line." *North American Review* 132, no. 295 (June 1881): 567–577.

Doumani, Beshara. *Rediscovering Palestine: Merchants and Peasants in Jabal Nablus, 1790–1900*. Berkeley: University of California Press, 1995.

Du Bois, Duncan. "Towards a New Labour Dispensation: Background to the Arrival of Indians in Natal in 1860." *Natalia* 40 (December 2010): 12–19.

Du Bois, W. E. B. "Dusk of Dawn: An Essay Toward an Autobiography of a Race Concept." In *Du Bois Writings*, edited by Nathan Higgins, 549–802. New York: Library of America, 1986 [1940].

———. "The Souls of Black Folk." In *Du Bois Writings*, edited by Nathan Higgins, 357–548. New York: Library of America, 1986 [1903].

Egger, Vernon. *A Fabian in Egypt: Salamah Musa and the Rise of Professional Classes in Egypt, 1909–1939*. Lanham, MD: University Press of America, 1986.

Elgood, P. G. *Egypt and the Army*. Oxford, UK: Oxford University Press, 1924.

Ellis, A. B. *The History of the First West India Regiment*. Project Gutenberg Ebook #29984. http://www.gutenberg.org/ebooks/29984?msg=welcome_stranger.

Elshakry, Marwa. *Reading Darwin in Arabic, 1860–1950*. Chicago: University of Chicago Press, 2013.

El Shakry, Omina. *The Great Social Laboratory: Subjects of Knowledge in Colonial and Postcolonial Egypt*. Stanford, CA: Stanford University Press, 2007.

Evans-Pritchard, Edward. *The Sanusi of Cyrenaica*. Oxford, UK: Clarendon Press, 1949.

Fahmi, 'Abd Al-Rahman. *Mudhakkirat 'Abd al-Rahman Fahmi: Yawmiyyat Misr al-Siyasiyya, Vol. 1*. Cairo: Al-Hay'a al-Misriyya al-'Amma li-l-Kitab, 1988.

Fahmy, Khaled. *All the Pasha's Men: Mehmed Ali, His Army and the Making of Modern Egypt*. 2nd ed. Cairo: American University in Cairo Press, 1997.

———. "The Great Theft of History: World War I and the Prelude to Revolution." Paper presented at the Egyptian Revolution of 1919 Conference. London, 2019.

Fahmy, Ziad. *Ordinary Egyptians: Creating the Modern Nation through Popular Culture*. Stanford, CA: Stanford University Press, 2011.

Falls, Cyril, and A. F. Becke. *Military Operations Egypt and Palestine from June 1917 to the End of the War, Part 1*. London: His Majesty's Stationery Office, 1930.

Falls, Cyril, and George MacMunn. *Military Operations in Egypt and Palestine: From the Outbreak of War with Germany to June 1917*. London: His Majesty's Stationery Office, 1930.

Fanon, Frantz. *The Wretched of the Earth*. New York: Grove Press, 1963.

Fawaz, Leila Tarazi. *A Land of Aching Hearts: The Middle East in the Great War*. Cambridge, MA: Harvard University Press, 2014.

Fogarty, Richard S. *Race and War in France: Colonial Subjects in the French Army, 1914-1918*. Baltimore: Johns Hopkins University Press, 2008.

Foucault, Michel. *Discipline and Punish: The Birth of the Prison*. New York: Vintage Books, 1995.

Fuchs, Ron. "Sites of Memory in the Holy Land: The Design of the British War Cemeteries in Mandate Palestine." *Journal of Historical Geography* 30, no. 4 (October 2004): 643–664.

Gasper, Michael Ezekiel. *The Power of Representation: Publics, Peasants, and Islam in Egypt*. Stanford, CA: Stanford University Press, 2009.

Gaylor, John. *Sons of John Company: The Indian and Pakistan Armies, 1903–1991*. London: Spellmount, 1992.

Gelvin, James L. "The 'Politics of Notables' Forty Years After." *Middle East Studies Association Bulletin* 40, no. 1 (June 2006): 19–29.

Gershoni, Israel, and James P. Jankowski. *Egypt, Islam, and the Arabs: The Search for Egyptian Nationhood*. Oxford, UK: Oxford University Press, 1986.

Gines (Belle), Kathryn T. *Hannah Arendt and the Negro Question*. Bloomington: Indiana University Press, 2014.

Ginsberg, Elaine K. "Introduction: The Politics of Passing." In *Passing and the Fic-*

tions of Identity, edited by Elaine K. Ginsburg, 1–16. Durham, NC: Duke University Press, 1996.

Goldberg, David Theo. "The Semantics of Race." *Ethnic and Racial Studies* 14, no. 4 (1992): 543–569.

Goldberg, Ellis. "Peasants in Revolt—Egypt 1919." *International Journal of Middle East Studies* 24, no. 2 (1992): 261–280.

Goldschmidt, Arthur. *Biographical Dictionary of Modern Egypt.* Cairo: American University in Cairo Press, 2000.

Gran, Peter. "Upper Egypt in Modern History: A Southern Question?" In *Upper Egypt: Identity and Change*, edited by Nicholas Hopkins and Reem Saad, 79–96. Cairo: American University in Cairo Press, 2004.

Griffin, Nicholas. "The Use of Chinese Labour by the British Army, 1916–1920." PhD diss., University of Oklahoma, 1973.

Gullett, H. S. *Australian Imperial Force in Sinai and Palestine.* Sydney: Angus & Robertson Ltd., 1923.

Halls, Katharine. "'Not Worthy of Belief': Testimonies of Rape in Egypt, 1919." Paper presented at Interwar Revolutions in the Middle East/North Africa Conference. London, 2019.

Hammad, Hanan. *Industrial Sexuality: Gender, Urbanization, and Social Transformation in Egypt.* Austin: University of Texas Press, 2016.

Hannaford, Ivan. *Race: The History of an Idea in the West.* Baltimore: Johns Hopkins University Press, 1996.

Harper, Tim. "Singapore, 1915, and the Birth of the Asian Underground." *Modern Asian Studies* 47, no. 6 (November 2013): 1782–1811.

Hayden, Dolores. *The Power of Place: Urban Landscapes as Public History.* Cambridge, MA: MIT Press, 1995.

Helal, Emad Ahmed. "Muhammad Ali's First Army: The Experiment in Building an Entirely Slave Army." In *Race and Slavery in the Middle East: Histories of Trans-Saharan Africans in Nineteenth-Century Egypt, Sudan, and the Ottoman Mediterranean*, edited by Kenneth Cuno and Terrance Walz, 17–42. Cairo: American University in Cairo Press, 2010.

Heshmat, Dina. *Egypt 1919: The Revolution in Literature and Film.* Edinburgh: Edinburgh University Press, 2019.

Hirschkind, Charles. *The Ethical Soundscape: Cassette Sermons and Islamic Counterpublics.* New York: Columbia University Press, 2006.

Hoad, T. F. *The Concise Oxford Dictionary of English Etymology.* Oxford, UK: Oxford University Press, 1996.

Hobson, J. A. *Imperialism: A Study of the History, Politics, and Economics of the Colonial Powers in Europe and America.* Monee, IL: Adansonia Press, 2018 [1902].

Hofstadter, Richard. *Social Darwinism in American Thought.* Boston: Beacon Press, 1944.

Hopkins, Nicholas, and Reem Saad. "The Region of Upper Egypt: Identity and Change." In Nicholas Hopkins and Reem Said, eds., *Upper Egypt: Identity and Change*, 1–24. Cairo: American University in Cairo Press, 2004.

Horne, John. "Immigrant Workers in France during World War I." *French Historical Studies* 24, no. 1 (1985): 57–88.

Hourani, Albert. "Ottoman Reform and the Politics of Notables." In Albert Hourani,

The Emergence of the Modern Middle East, 36–66. Berkeley: University of California Press, 1981.

———. "Rashid Rida and the Sufi Orders: A Footnote to Laoust." *Bulletin d'Études Orientales* T. 29 (1977): 231–241.

Ibn Khaldun. *The Muqaddimah: An Introduction to History*. Translated and introduced by Franz Rosenthal, abridged and edited by N. J. Dawood, with a new Introduction by Bruce B. Lawrence. Princeton, NJ: Princeton University Press, 2005.

'Izz Al-Din, Amin. "Awwal Dirasa 'an Sabab Ham Min Asbab bi-Thawrat 1919: Al-Shughul Fi-l-Sulta: Qissat Faylaq al-'Ummal al-Misri wa Faylaq al-Jamal." *Al-Musawwir*, March 1969.

———. *Al-Faylaq*. Cairo: Markaz al-Fustat li-l-Dirasat, 1999.

'Izzat, Samir. "Safahat min Mudhakkirat Shaykh Majhul: Khamsa wa Saba'iyyin 'Aman Bayn Qibbat al-Masajid wa Jaysh al-Injliz, wa Sajun Isra'il." *Ruz al-Yusuf*, June 17, 1968.

Jackson, Louis. *Our Caughnawagas in Egypt*. Montreal: W. M. Drysdale & Co., 1895.

Jacob, Wilson Chacko. *Working Out Egypt: Effendi Masculinity and Subject Formation in Colonial Modernity, 1870–1940*. Durham, NC: Duke University Press, 2011.

Jakes, Aaron. *Egypt's Occupation: Colonial Economism and the Crises of Capitalism*. Stanford, CA: Stanford University Press, 2020.

Jakes, Aaron, and Ahmad Shokr. "Finding Value in Empire of Cotton." *Critical Historical Studies* (Spring 2017): 107–136.

Johnson, Niall, and Juergen Mueller. "Updating the Accounts: Global Mortality of the 1918–1920 'Spanish' Influenza Pandemic." *Bulletin of the History of Medicine* 76, no. 1 (Spring 2002): 105–115.

Kamil, Mustafa. *Al-Shams al-Mushriqa*. Cairo: Huquq Al-Taba'a wa-l-Tarjama Mahfuza, 1904.

Kazziha, Walid. "The Jaridah-Ummah Group and Egyptian Politics." *Middle Eastern Studies* 13, no. 3 (1977): 373–385.

Khalifa, Atef M. *The Population of the Arab Republic of Egypt*. Cairo: Institute of Statistical Studies and Research, 1973.

Khoury, Philip S. "The Urban Notables Paradigm Revisited." *Revue Du Monde Musulman et de La Méditeranée* 55, no. 1 (1990): 215–230.

Kiernan, V. G. *The Lords of Human Kind: Black Man, Yellow Man, and White Man in an Age of Empire*. New York: Columbia University Press, 1972.

Klein, Ernest. *Klein's Comprehensive Etymological Dictionary of the English Language*. Amsterdam: Elsevier B.V., 1971.

Koerver, Hans Joachim. *German Submarine Warfare 1914–1918 in the Eyes of British Intelligence: Selected Sources from the British National Archives, Kew*. Berlin: Schaltungsdienst Lange o.H.G., 2010.

Koller, Christian. "The Recruitment of Colonial Troops in Africa and Asia and Their Deployment in Europe during the First World War." *Immigrants and Minorities: Historical Studies in Ethnicity, Migration, and Diaspora* 26, no. 1–2 (2008): 111–133.

Korda, Michael. *Hero: The Life and Legend of Lawrence of Arabia*. New York: HarperCollins, 2010.

Lalonde, Suzanne. *Determining Boundaries in a Conflicted World: The Role of Uti Possidetis*. Montreal: McGill-Queen's University Press, 2002.

Landau, Jacob M. *Parliaments and Parties in Egypt.* New York: Taylor and Francis, 2015 [1953].

Laqueur, Thomas. "Memory and Naming in the Great War." In *Commemorations: The Politics of National Identity*, edited by John R. Gillis, 150–167. Princeton, NJ: Princeton University Press, 1994.

Lawrence, T. E. *Seven Pillars of Wisdom.* Oxford, UK: Alden Press, 1935.

Lefebvre, Henri. *La Droit À La Ville.* Paris: Anthopos, 1968.

———. *The Production of Space.* Vol. 9. Translated by Donald Nicholson-Smith. Cambridge, MA: Blackwell, 1991.

———. *Writings on Cities.* Selected and translated by Eleonore Kofman and Elizabeth Lebas. Cambridge, MA: Blackwell, 1996.

Lenin, V. I. "Imperialism, the Highest Stage of Capitalism." In *Lenin's Selected Works*, 667–766. Moscow: Progress Publishers, 1963.

Lloyd, Nick. *The Amritsar Massacre: The Untold Story of One Fateful Day.* London: I. B. Tauris, 2011.

Longworth, Philip. *The Unending Vigil: A History of the Commonwealth War Graves Commission, 1917–1984.* London: Leo Cooper, 1985.

Loring, William Wing. *A Confederate Soldier in Egypt.* New York: Dodd, Mead & Co., 1884.

Lutfi al-Sayyid, Ahmad. *Al-Muntakhabat.* Vol. 1. Edited by Isma'il Mazhar. Cairo: Dar al-Nashr al-Hadtih, 1937.

———. *Qissat Hayati.* Cairo: Mu'ssasat Hindawi li-l-Ta'lim wa-l-Thiqafa, 2013.

———. *Safahat Matwiyya: Min Tarikh al-Harika al-Istiqlaliyya fi Misr.* Edited by Isma'il Mazhar. Cairo: Maktabat al-Nahda al-Misriyya, 1936.

———. *Ta'ammulat fi-l-Falsafa wa-l-Adab wa-l-Siyasa wa-l-Ijtima'.* Cairo: Dar al-Ma'arif li-l-Taba'a wa-l-Nashr bi-Misr, 1946.

Makdisi, Ussama. *Age of Coexistence: The Ecumenical Frame and the Making of the Modern Arab World.* Berkeley: University of California Press, 2019.

———. *The Culture of Sectarianism: Community, History, and Violence in Nineteenth-Century Ottoman Lebanon.* Berkeley: University of California Press, 2000.

Mantena, Karuna. *Alibis of Empire: Henry Maine and the Ends of Liberal Imperialism.* Princeton, NJ: Princeton University Press, 2010.

Massey, W. T. *How Jerusalem Was Won: Being the Record of Allenby's Campaign in Palestine.* New York: Scribner, 1920.

McClendon, Thomas V. *White Chief, Black Lords: Shepstone and the Colonial State in Natal, South Africa, 1845–1878.* Rochester, NY: University of Rochester Press, 2010.

McGarry, Fearghal. *The Rising: Ireland, Easter 1916.* Oxford, UK: Oxford University Press, 2006.

Mikhail, Alan. *Nature and Empire in Ottoman Egypt: An Environmental History.* Cambridge, UK: Cambridge University Press, 2011.

Miles, Robert. *Racism.* London: Routledge, 1989.

Mitchell, Timothy. *Colonising Egypt.* Berkeley: University of California Press, 1988.

———. *Rule of Experts: Egypt, Techno-Politics, Modernity.* Berkeley: University of California Press, 2002.

Morrison, Toni. *Playing in the Dark: Whiteness and the Literary Imagination.* New York: Random House, 1993.

Mossallam, Alia. "Al-Wajh al-Akhir li-Thawrat 1919 al-Misriyya: Thawrat Fallahi al-Hamamiyya." *Bidayat* 23, no. 24 (2019): https://bidayatmag.com/node/1052.

———. "Strikes, Riots, and Laughter: Al-Himamiyya Village's Experience of Egypt's 1918 Peasant Insurrection." *Social Movements and Popular Mobilisation in the MENA* 40 (September 2020).

———. "'Ya Aziz 'Aini Ana Bidi Arawah Baladi': Voyages of an Egyptian Tune from Estrangement at Home to Longing on the Fronts of WWI." In *Cultural Entanglement in the Pre-Independence Arab World: Arts, Thought and Literature*, edited by Anthony Gorman and Sarah Irving. London: I. B. Tauris, 2020.

Mughazy, Mustafa A. "Pragmatics of the Evil Eye in Egyptian Arabic." PhD diss., Georgia State University, 1999.

Murphy, Gretchen. *Shadowing the White Man's Burden: U.S. Imperialism and the Problem of the Color Line.* New York: New York University Press, 2010.

Murray, Archibald. *Sir Archibald Murray's Despatches: June 1916–June 1917.* London: J. M. Dent & Sons Ltd., 1920.

Musa, Salama. *Misr Asl al-Hadara.* Cairo: Mu'assast Hindawi li-l-Ta'lim wa-l-Thiqafa, 2011.

———. *Tarbiyyat Salama Musa.* 4th ed. Cairo: Al-Hay'a al-Misriyya al-'Amma li-l-Kitab, 2012.

Nicholas, I. C. "British Supply Operations during the Palestine Campaign, with Particular Reference to Operations Following the Capture of Gaza." Unpublished thesis, Command and General Staff School, Fort Leavenworth, Kansas, 1931–1932.

Nicolson, Harold. *Curzon: The Last Phase 1919–1925.* London: Constable and Co., Ltd., 1934.

Ong, Walter. *Orality and Literacy: The Technologizing of the Word.* New York: Methuen, 1982.

Owen, Roger. *Cotton and the Egyptian Economy, 1820–1914: A Study in Trade and Development.* Oxford, UK: Oxford University Press, 1969.

Pakenham, Thomas. *The Boer War.* New York: Random House, 1979.

Paternek, Margaret A. "Norms and Normalization: Michel Foucault's Overextended Panoptic Machine." *Human Studies* 10, no. 1 (March 1987): 97–121.

Racy, Ali Jihad. "Improvisation, Ecstasy, and Performance Dynamics in Arabic Music." In *In the Course of Performance: Studies in the World of Musical Improvisation*, edited by Bruno Nettl and Melinda Russell, 95–112. Chicago: University of Chicago Press, 1998.

Ramadan, 'Abd al-'Azim. *Tatawwur al-Harika al-Wataniyya Fi Misr, 1918–1936.* Cairo: Dar al-Kutub al-'Arabi, 1968.

RAMC, Sejeant-Major. *With the RAMC in Egypt.* London: Cassell and Company, Ltd., 1918.

Rashid, Syeda Rozana. "Colonial Labour Migration from India during the First World War: Present Implications." Paper presented at War and Colonies: 1914–1918 Conference. Dhaka, 2014.

Raymond, Andre. *Artisans et Commerçants Du Caire Au XVIIIe Siècle.* Damascus: Presses de l'Ifpo, 1973.

Reid, Donald Malcolm. *Whose Pharaohs? Archaeology, Museums, and Egyptian National Identity from Napoleon to World War I.* Berkeley: University of California Press, 2002.

Reimer, Michael J. "Colonial Bridgehead: Social and Spatial Change in Alexandria, 1850–1882." *International Journal of Middle East Studies* 20, no. 4 (1988): 531–553.

Reynolds, Nancy Y. *A City Consumed: Urban Commerce, the Cairo Fire, and the Politics of Decolonization in Egypt*. Stanford, CA: Stanford University Press, 2012.

Rida, Muhammad Rashid. *Tarikh al-Ustadh al-Imam al-Shaykh Muhammad 'Abduh*. Vol. 1. Cairo: Matba'at al-Manar, 1931.

Riddick, John F. *The History of British India: A Chronology*. London: Greenwood Publishing Group, 2006.

Rose, Christopher S. "Famine, Disease, and Death in Egypt: 1914–1919." Paper presented at Egypt and the Great War Conference. Oxford, 2018.

Rottenberg, Catherine. "Passing: Race, Identification, and Desire." *Criticism* 45, no. 4 (Fall 2003): 435–452.

Roy, Kaushik. "Race and Recruitment in the Indian Army: 1880–1918." *Modern Asian Studies* 47, no. 4 (2013): 1310–1347.

Ruiz, Mario M. "Manly Spectacles and Imperial Soldiers in Wartime Egypt, 1914–19." *Middle Eastern Studies* 45, no. 3 (2009): 351–371.

———. "Photography and the Egyptian Labor Corps in Wartime Palestine, 1917–1918." *Jerusalem Quarterly* 56–57 (Winter/Spring 2014): 52–66.

Russell, Thomas. *Egyptian Service, 1902–1946*. London: John Murray, 1949.

Ryzova, Lucie. *The Age of the Efendiyya: Passages to Modernity in National Colonial Egypt*. Oxford, UK: Oxford University Press, 2018.

Sabry, Mohammed. *La Révolution Égyptienne: D'Après des Documents Authentiques et des Photographiers Prises au cours de la Révolution*. Paris: Librairie J. Vrin, 1919.

Safran, Nadav. *Egypt in Search of Political Community: An Analysis of the Intellectual and Political Evolution of Egypt, 1804-1952*. Cambridge, MA: Harvard University Press, 1961.

Said, Edward W. *Orientalism*. New York: Pantheon Books, 1978.

Salim, Latifa. *Misr fi-l-Harb al-'Alimiyya al-Ula*. Alexandria: Al-Hay'a al-'Ama li-Maktabat al-Iskandariyya, 1984.

Sartori, Andrew. *Bengal in Global Concept History: Culturalism in the Age of Capital*. Chicago: University of Chicago Press, 2008.

Sautman, Barry. "Racial Nationalism and China's External Behavior." *World Affairs* 160, no. 2 (Fall 1997): 78–95.

Sayf Al-Dawla, 'Ismat. *Mashayikh Jabal al-Badari: Al-Juz' al-Thani Min Mudhakkirat Qarya*. Cairo: Dar al-Hilal, 1996.

Schine, Rachel. "The Racialized Other in Early Arabic Literature: Literature as an Institution of Community." In *Routledge Handbook of Islam and Race*, edited by Zain Abdullah. New York: Routledge, forthcoming.

Schülze, Reinhard. "Colonization and Resistance: The Egyptian Peasant Rebellion in 1919." In *Peasants and Politics in the Modern Middle East*, edited by Farhad Kazemi and John Waterbury, 171–202. Miami: Florida International University Press, 1991.

Scott, James C. *The Moral Economy of the Peasant: Rebellion and Subsistence in Southeast Asia*. New Haven, CT: Yale University Press, 1979.

———. *Weapons of the Weak: Everyday Forms of Peasant Resistance*. New Haven, CT: Yale University Press, 1985.

Selim, Samah. *The Novel and the Rural Imaginary in Egypt, 1880–1985*. New York: Routledge, 2004.

Shafiq, Ahmad. *Hawliyyat Misr al-Siyasiyya*. Cairo: Matba'a Shafiq Basha bi-Shar'a Sami Raqm 28, 1926.

Sha'rawi, Huda. *Mudhakkirat Huda Sha'rawi: Ra'ada al-Mar'a al-'Arabiyya al-Haditha*. Cairo: Dar al-Hilal, 1981.

Shorter, Edward, and Charles Tilly. *Strikes in France, 1830–1968*. London: Cambridge University Press, 1974.

Smith, Charles D. *Islam and the Search for Social Order in Modern Egypt: A Biography of Muhammad Husayn Haykal*. Albany, NY: SUNY Press, 1983.

Soja, Edward. *Thirdspace: Journeys to Los Angeles and Other Real-and-Imagined Places*. Cambridge, MA: Blackwell, 1996.

Spivak, Gayatri. *A Critique of Postcolonial Reason: Toward a History of the Vanishing Present*. Cambridge, MA: Harvard University Press, 1999.

Starling, John, and Ivor Lee. *No Labour, No Battle: Military Labour during the First World War*. London: History Press, 2009.

Stoler, Ann. *Along the Archival Grain: Epistemic Anxieties and Colonial Common Sense*. Princeton, NJ: Princeton University Press, 2009.

Stovall, Tyler. "The Color Line behind the Lines: Racial Violence in France during the Great War." *American Historical Review* 103, no. 3 (June 1998): 737–769.

Summer, Ian. *The Indian Army 1914–1917*. Oxford, UK: Osprey, 2001.

Takla, Nefertiti. "Murderous Economies: Sex Trafficking and Political Economic Change in Alexandria, Egypt: 1941–1921." *Égypte/Monde Arabe* 17 (2018): 23–48.

Talhami, Ghada Hashem. "The Zanj Rebellion Reconsidered." *International Journal of African Historical Studies* 10, no. 3 (1977): 443–461.

"Temporary Crusaders." *Bookman* 57, no. 337 (1919): 45.

Tignor, Robert. *Modernization and British Colonial Rule in Egypt, 1882–1914*. Princeton, NJ: Princeton University Press, 1966.

———. *State, Private Enterprise, and Economic Change in Egypt, 1918–1952*. Princeton, NJ: Princeton University Press, 1984.

Toledano, Ehud. *As if Silent and Absent: Bonds of Enslavement in the Islamic Middle East*. New Haven, CT: Yale University Press, 2007.

Troutt-Powell, Eve. *A Different Shade of Colonialism: Egypt, Great Britain, and the Mastery of the Sudan*. Berkeley: University of California Press, 2003.

Tuma, Habib. *The Music of the Arabs*. Translated by Laurie Schwartz. Berlin: Amadeus Press, 1996.

Turda, Marius, and Paul J. Weindling, eds. *"Blood and Homeland": Eugenics and Racial Nationalism in Central and Southeast Europe, 1900–1940*. Budapest and New York: Central European Press, 2006.

Ukpabi, S. C. "West Indian Troops and the Defence of British West Africa in the Nineteenth Century." *African Studies Review* 17, no. 1 (April 1974): 133–150.

Ulrichsen, Kristian Coates. *The Logistics and Politics of the British Campaigns in the Middle East, 1914–22*. London: Palgrave Macmillan, 2011.

Virilio, Paul. *Speed and Politics*. Los Angeles: Semiotext(e), 1977.

Vitalis, Robert. *America's Kingdom: Mythmaking on the Saudi Oil Frontier*. Stanford, CA: Stanford University Press, 2006.

———. *White World Order, Black Power Politics: The Birth of American International Relations*. Ithaca, NY: Cornell University Press, 2015.

Walz, Terrance. "Black Slavery in Egypt during the Nineteenth Century as Reflected in the Mahkama Archives of Cairo." In *Slaves and Slavery in Muslim Africa*, edited by John Ralph Willis, 137–160. London: Frank Cass and Co. Ltd., 1985.

Welch Jr., William M. *No Country for a Gentleman: British Rule in Egypt, 1883–1907*. New York: Greenwood Press, 1988.

Wendell, Charles. *The Evolution of the Egyptian National Image: From Its Origins to Ahmad Lutfi Al-Sayyid*. Berkeley: University of California Press, 1972.

White, Shane, and Graham White. *The Sounds of Slavery: Discovering African American History through Songs, Sermons, and Speech*. Boston: Beacon Press, 2005.

Williams, Teresa Kay. "Race-ing and Being Raced: The Critical Interrogation of 'Passing.'" *Amerasia Journal* 23, no. 1 (1997): 61–65.

Wimmer, Andreas. "Elementary Strategies of Ethnic Boundary Making." *Ethnic and Racial Studies* 31, no. 6 (August 2008): 1025–1055.

Wood, John G. *The Natural History of Man; Being an Account of the Manners and Customs of the Uncivilized Races of Men—Australia, New Zealand, Polynesia, America, Asia, and Ancient Europe*. London: George Routledge and Sons, 1870.

Xu Guoqi. *Strangers on the Western Front: Chinese Workers in the Great War*. Cambridge, MA: Harvard University Press, 2011.

Yeomans, Rory. "Of 'Yugoslav Barbarians' and Croatian Gentlemen Scholars: Nationalist Ideology and Racial Anthropology in Interwar Yugoslavia." In *"Blood and Homeland": Eugenics and Racial Nationalism in Central and Southeast Europe, 1900–1940*, edited by Paul Weindling and Marius Turda, 83–122. Budapest and New York: Central European University Press, 2006.

Yousef, Hoda A. *Composing Egypt: Reading, Writing, and the Emergence of a Modern Nation*. Stanford, CA: Stanford University Press, 2016.

Zafer, Hamza. *Ecumenical Community: Language and Politics of the Ummah in the Qur'an*. Boston: Brill, 2020.

Zaghlul, Ahmed Fathi. *Sirr Taqaddum al-Inkliz al-Saksuniyyin*. Cairo: Al-Mashru'a al-Qawmi li-l-Tarjama, n.d.

Zaghlul, Sa'd. *Mudhakkirat Sa'd Zaghlul*. Vol. 1. Cairo: Al-Hay'a al-Misriyya al-'Amma lil-Kitab, 1988.

———. *Mudhakkirat Sa'd Zaghlul*. Vol. 7. Cairo: Al-Hay'a al-Misriyya al-'Amma lil-Kitab, 1996.

Zagloul, Saad [Sa'd Zaghlul]. *The White Book: Collection of Official Correspondence from November 11, 1918, to July 14, 1919*. Paris: The Delegation, 1919.

INDEX

Page numbers in italics refer to figures and tables.

www.ingramcontent.com/pod-product-compliance
Lightning Source LLC
LaVergne TN
LVHW100024310826
846742LV00012B/31